DISNEYWORLD WITH KIDS

ABOUT THE AUTHOR

Jay Fenster, a resident of Virginia since 1995, first traveled to Orlando in 1987. Since then he has written nonfiction, fiction, and drama, and is also a Washington, DC club DJ. Jay is a graduate of the University of Virginia's McIntire School of Commerce. We welcome your comments on this book. You can reach the author directly via email at *OpenRoadOrlando@mail.com*.

BE A TRAVELER, NOT A TOURIST - WITH OPEN ROAD TRAVEL GUIDES!

Open Road Publishing has guide books to exciting, fun destinations on four continents. As veteran travelers, our goal is to bring you the best travel guides available anywhere!

No small task, but here's what we offer:

•All Open Road travel guides are written by authors with a distinct, opinionated point of view – not some sterile committee or team of writers. Our authors are experts in the areas covered and are polished writers.

• Our guides are geared to people who want to make their own travel choices. We'll show you how to discover the real destination – not just see some place from a tour bus window.

• We're strong on the basics, but we also provide terrific choices for those looking to get off the beaten path and experience the country or city – not just see it or pass through it.

• We give you the best, but we also tell you about the worst and what to avoid. Nobody should waste their time and money on their hard-earned vacation because of bad or inadequate travel advice.

• Our guides assume nothing. We tell you everything you need to know to have the trip of a lifetime – presented in a fun, literate, no-nonsense style.

• And, above all, we welcome your input, ideas, and suggestions to help us put out the best travel guides possible.

OPEN ROAD PUBLISHING

We offer travel guides to American and foreign locales. Our books tell it like it is, often with an opinionated edge, and our experienced authors always give you all the information you need to have the trip of a lifetime. Write for your free catalog of all our titles, including our golf and restaurant guides.

Catalog Department, Open Road Publishing
P.O. Box 284, Cold Spring Harbor, NY 11724

E-mail:
Jopenroad@aol.com

4th Edition

Library of Congress Catalog Card No. 99-85824
ISBN 1-892975-30-0

TABLE OF CONTENTS

SIDEBARS

1. INTRODUCTION

It used to be so much simpler.

The first time I visited Orlando, which was not so many years ago, the options on how to spend a vacation in and around the Vacation Kingdom were relatively limited. You had the Magic Kingdom and you had Epcot, which you could polish off in three days, four days in the busy seasons. For the remainder of the week, you could choose from River Country and Discovery Island, two of Disney's slower-paced attractions, which would eat up a day, tops.

Outside Walt Disney World, Sea World pretty much rounded out the A-list of Orlando attractions. Sure, there were a couple of water parks such as Wet'N'Wild and Water Mania, but for the most part, you could see all there was to see in Orlando and still have a day or two to lay out by the pool or head out of town to Busch Gardens in Tampa, the Kennedy Space Center, or the beaches on either side of Florida.

Ahh, the difference a decade (give or take) makes.

In 1989 the Disney-MGM Studios opened, and the Universal Studios followed suit the following year. Since then, Disney has added the Animal Kingdom, Typhoon Lagoon, Blizzard Beach, Pleasure Island, the Downtown Disney and Boardwalk complexes, plus a handful of golf clubs and recreational facilities. Universal has added Islands of Adventure and Citywalk. Sea World opens its Discovery Cove park in summer 2000. New entertainment and shopping complexes are opening every day, it seems, ever adding to the dizzying array of things to see and do while in Orlando.

This book strives to be the most complete collection of information on Disney, Universal, Sea World, and the rest of Orlando's attractions, plus area hotels, restaurants, and shops, presenting you with all the options you need to plan out your Orlando vacation in style. For those of you on a budget, we've included dozens of hints on how to stretch your vacation dollar farther. If you're looking to add a little seasonal snap to your Orlando vacation, we've also listed dozens of special events that take place in and around the area throughout the year. We have also included dozens of links to area businesses and sources of tourist information who will always have the most up-to-date information on Orlando area attractions.

Have a great trip!

2. OVERVIEW

An Orlando vacation's possibilities are bounded only by your budget and your wildest imagination. But with so much to do, where do you begin? In this chapter, I'll give you a quick preview of all that Disney World, Universal, Sea World, and all the other fantastic theme parks and attractions have in store so you can best plan your stay in Orlando.

When I first visited Walt Disney World and Orlando, I made all sorts of tourist mistakes and wasted a lot of time and money. My goal here is to prevent you from doing the same.

The object of this book is to make it easier to tour Orlando and its major attractions with the least possible cost and aggravation and the greatest amount of fun.

We believe this to be the most comprehensive Orlando guide available, offering detailed descriptions of everything you'll find inside the Magic Kingdom, EPCOT, Disney-MGM Studios, Animal Kingdom, Universal Studios Florida, Islands of Adventure, Sea World, along with reports from Busch Gardens, Cypress Gardens, Wet'n'Wild, and dozens of other attractions, shopping centers, and eateries in and around Orlando.

Keep this book with you throughout your vacation, from the planning stages to the park touring to the return home. So return your seats to the full upright position, buckle up, and get ready to party!

ORLANDO AREA CODE

Unless otherwise noted, the area code for any Orlando and any other place listed in this book is 407.

An Orlando vacation's possibilities are bounded only by your budget and your wildest imagination. But with so much to do, where do you begin? In this chapter I'll give you a quick preview of all that Disney World,

Sea World, and all the other fantastic theme parks and attractions have in store so you can best plan your stay in Orlando.

Remember – prices are constantly in flux. Don't be surprised if the prices given here have gone up somewhat by the time you visit.

DISNEY'S MAGIC KINGDOM

There are three major theme parks and five minor theme parks in Walt Disney World. The first and foremost is the **Magic Kingdom**, sister attraction to Disneyland in Anaheim, California. Here you'll find a great variety of attractions, ranging from kiddie classics like Peter Pan's Flight and the famous It's A Small World to intricate, detailed thrill rides.

When most people think of Walt Disney World, they envision Cinderella's Castle – the icon that stands at the center of the **Magic Kingdom**, sister attraction to the original Disneyland in Anaheim, California. Here you'll find a wide variety of attractions, ranging from kiddie classics to thrill rides.

There are seven themed lands in the Magic Kingdom. The point of entry places guests on **Main Street USA**, a living time capsule of the turn of the last century. **Adventureland** includes the jolly Pirates of the Caribbean, the campy Jungle Cruise, and the fascinating Swiss Family Treehouse. **Frontierland** sets the clock back to 1850 in the Old West, as the Big Thunder Mountain Railroad carves its way through tall red rocks. **Liberty Square** evokes the patriotic feel of colonial America, nowhere more than at the rousing Hall of Presidents.

Fantasyland draws its inspiration from fairy tales and animated Disney classics, creating a world of wonder sure to enchant younger children. **Mickey's Starland** is the home of the world's most beloved mouse, alongside the hangouts of pals Minnie, Donald, and Pluto. **Tomorrowland** is the future-perfect vision of Jules Verne brought to life in attractions such as the ExtraTERRORestrial Alien Encounter and the Timekeeper.

EPCOT

In 1981, this attraction opened up as a sort of permanent World's Fair. The park is twice as big as the Magic Kingdom and is made up of two sections.

Future World provides impressive views of the role that technology has played in our lives, in the form of everything from communication devices to medical advances. The attractions here are often as enlightening as they are entertaining. New this year is the Test Track attraction, which puts you through the paces of automobile R&D tests.

World Showcase shines the spotlight on eleven different nations, with pavilions featuring authentic food, merchandise, and entertainment. Breathtaking films and authentic décor showcase the natural beauty and native architecture of the countries. New for '99 is Millenium Village, a collection of exhibits from over 20 countries never before seen in World Showcase.

DISNEY-MGM STUDIOS THEME PARK

This park pays tribute to the past, present and future of the celluloid arts, from Steamboat Willie to Buzz Lightyear, from Judy Garland to C-3P0, offering studio tours alongside thrill rides and amazing multimedia presentations. The Rock'n'Roller Coaster is Disney's newest white-knuckled addition to the park, while Fantasmic! wows them in the lagoons surrounding the Studios at night.

DISNEY'S ANIMAL KINGDOM

Disney's newest theme park juggernaut, the Animal Kingdom takes guests across the continents and the centuries in a wild 500-acre array of thrill rides, films, shops, and themed restaurants, to tell the story of all animals, real and imagined. Guests find themselves surrounded by hundreds of free-roaming animals, in addition to the Audio-Animatronic variety found in Disney's other parks.

SEA WORLD OF FLORIDA

The other Central Florida "world," this is often described as an aquarium, which really doesn't do justice to this beautiful marine theme park, home to Shamu and his friends. New this year are the Journey to Atlantis, a themed water thrill ride, a new nighttime pyrotechnics extravaganza, and several new shows.

Additionally, in 2000, Discovery Cove will open its doors to visitors, offering them a chance to swim with dolphins and otherwise engage in one-on-one interaction and activities with the creatures that live here.

UNIVERSAL STUDIOS FLORIDA

Orlando's largest theme park, Universal Studios contains several of the premier theme park attractions in the world – from the visually stunning Terminator 2 – 3D to the wild Back to the Future... The Ride and the surprisingly frightening Twister, and contans several themed neighborhoods that will absolutely blow you away with their realism and atmosphere.

UNIVERSAL ISLANDS OF ADVENTURE

The second awe-inspiring jewel in Universal's crown, the brand new (May 1999) theme park sets a new standard for theme park attractions in six themed lands. The **Port of Entry** lights the way for adventure, setting the mood that will be carried through the other lands. **Marvel Superhero Island** is the home to the Amazing Adventures of Spiderman, a technological triumph that's possibly the best theme park ride *anywhere,* and the Incredible Hulk Coaster, a coaster bound to wind up on many top ten lists. **Toon Lagoon** hosts wild and wet rides based on Dudley Do-Right and Popeye cartoons in a neighborhood straight out of the Sunday comics.

Jurassic Park needs no introduction, but you will come close enough to a triceratops and a T-rex to shake their hands... if you were so inclined. **The Lost Continent** is a nod to flights of fantasy from the medieval era to the Greece of legend. Finally, **Seuss Landing** provides a little something for the little someones.

OTHER ATTRACTIONS

You could spend a fun-filled week in Orlando and never go to any of the top-tier theme parks. Disney World contains several minor parks including the wild **Blizzard Beach** waterpark and the **Downtown Disney** entertainment complex as well as the **Wide World of Sports.**

Off WDW grounds, there's the **Kennedy Space Center, Busch Gardens Tampa** and **Cypress Gardens,** all within an hour's drive of Orlando. Closer by are interactive wonderlands such as **WonderWorks** and **Ripley's Believe It or Not! Museum,** water parks such as **Water Mania** and **Wet'N'Wild.**

ACCOMMODATIONS

In Orlando and its surroundings, there are more than 200 resorts, hotels, motels, and inns. Nearly 30 of these are inside Walt Disney World itself. We've included information on all the Disney hotels plus a cross-section of hotels in the surrounding areas.

SHOPPING

There are a number of malls in the area where you can satisfy all your shopping cravings. The **Downtown Disney Marketplace** and **West Side** offer a great variety of unique shopping and entertainment options. The **Mercado** on International Drive is a specialty mall tucked away in a Spanish fortress. **Pointe Orlando** offers upscale shopping, entertainment, and restaurants.

Bargain hunters will drool at the options available to them in Central Florida. From the 200-shop **Belz Factory Outlet Mall** to smaller strip malls of outlet shops in Kissimmee, Lake Buena Vista, and elsewhere in Orlando, there's something for every taste and budget.

DINING

Orlando really is a dichotomy when it comes to food. On the one hand, it caters to tourists who need their grub on the quick and on the cheap with fast food, buffets, and family style restaurants. While the food at these establishments may disappoint more sophisticated palates, they're a good bet for families and budget travelers. That, however, doesn't mean that there isn't good food to be had in Orlando.

Dux in the Peabody Hotel is one of the city's best choices for continental cuisine, as is **Victoria and Albert's** in Disney's Grand Floridian Hotel. Additionally, great seafood restaurants abound, as do steakhouses and a cornucopia of ethnic eats, including a pile of them in EPCOT's World Showcase, the most notable being **Akershus**, serving the best Norwegian food you'll find south of the 60th parallel, and **Marrakesh** for authentic Moroccan feasts.

We'll also list all the dining options in all the theme parks, with pricing information, as well as alternatives to the options in the parks.

NIGHTLIFE

With the addition of Universal's **CityWalk** and the **Pointe Orlando** complexes, the area's nightlife scene has gotten a lot wilder. The former has options like Jimmy Buffett's Margaritaville, Pat O'Brien's, and the groove, an underground dance club which draws world class talent, while the latter focuses more on bars like Hooters, Adobe Gila's, and the NFL Players' Grill.

Other options include standbys **Church Street Station** and **Pleasure Island**, as well as several other clubs downtown and elsewhere. If you're more in the mood for a dinner show, there's a variety of those in the area as well, including the legendary **Medieval Times** and the charming equestrian extravaganza **Arabian Nights**.

OFF THE BEATEN PATH

Try walking though the **Audubon Nature Preserve** on the grounds of the Grand Cypress Resort. You can pack a picnic and stroll around, seeing a taste of the real Florida.

Like art? The **Orlando Museum of Art** and the **Morse Museum of American Art** offer a fine variety. Like mini-golf? **Pirate's Cove Adventure Golf** and **Disney's Fantasia Gardens** give you miniature golf in an unforgettable setting. Or check out **Skull Kingdom**, **Wonderworks**, or **Mystery Fun House** for rainy-day fun.

SPORTS & RECREATION

Disney World is not generally thought of as a destination for a sports vacation. However, there are nearly 40 tennis courts, 99 holes of golf, dozens of pools, lakes for boat rentals, bike/jogging/exercise trails, water skiing, and more.

3. PLANNING YOUR TRIP

All right - you've decided to spend your vacation in Central Florida playing at Disney World and Orlando's other exciting theme parks and attractions. The first thing you'ßll want to do is some trip planning.

Let's start with the obvious question: when to go.

WHEN SHOULD I GO?

This question is one of the first asked by Orlando vacationers-to-be, and probably the most vital. This last statement will seem somewhat paradoxical when I tell you that there is no real answer to the question.

There are, however, four factors on which your decision should be based. These are:

- Crowds
- Operating Hours
- Weather
- Special Events

AVERAGE ATTENDANCE PER DAY, PER PARK

January and February (excl. President's Week)	20,000
President's Week	45,000
March	25,000
Easter/Spring Break	55,000
April and May	35,000
Memorial Day Weekend	40,000
June through August	55,000
September through Thanksgiving Week	30,000
Thanksgiving Week	55,000
Thanksgiving Week/Christmas Week	15,000
Christmas Week through New Year's Day	75,000 & up

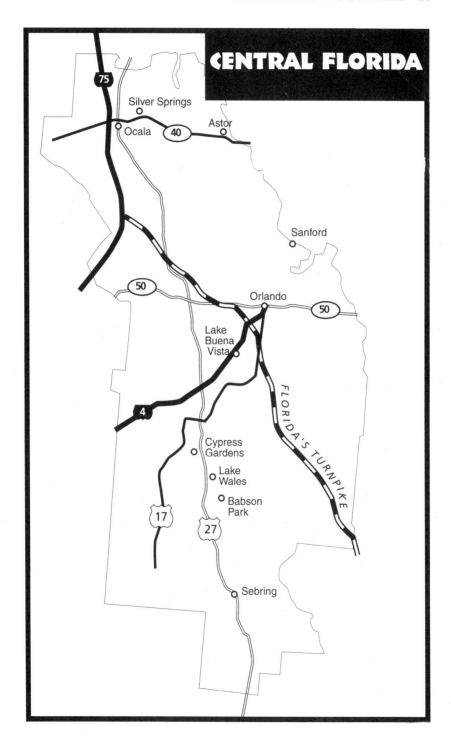

On days when under 25,000 people visit each park, you'll pretty much have the place to yourself. Lines will be short or non-existent at most attractions.

At 25,000-30,000 people, the park seems less exclusive, but you've still got a good chance to experience most of the what the parks have to offer. The parks will still be relatively comfortable and waits for popular rides should not exceed a few minutes.

The parks are fairy thronged if you are surrounded by 30,000-45,000 other visitors. Lines will start to get tricky, so be prepared for a good bit of waiting in lines. At 45,000-60,000 visitors – a typical summer day – chances of a successful touring day become minute. Crowds queue at all attractions by the gross. More than 60,000 come during the Christmas season (and a few other times during the rest of the year). These conditions can make first-time touring a living nightmare. Any rookie visitor who considers coming at this time and intends to see all the attractions is really living in Fantasyland.

THEME PARK HOURS

SEASONS OF LOW ATTENDANCE

Magic Kingdom	9am-5pm
EPCOT	9am-9pm
Disney-MGM	9am-730pm
Animal Kingdom	8am-6pm
Universal Studios	9am-6pm
Islands of Adventure	9am-7pm
Sea World	9am-7pm

SEASONS OF HIGH ATTENDANCE

Magic Kingdom	9am-11pm
EPCOT	9am-930pm
Disney-MGM	9am-9pm
Animal Kingdom	7am-7pm
Universal Studios	9am-10pm
Islands of Adventure	9am-9pm
Sea World	9am-10pm

HINT: If your primary concern as far as scheduling goes is avoiding the crowds, the ideal times to visit are September, October, and November; February, March, the second half of April, and May.

Low Attendance seasons are generally January-Easter, excluding President's Weekend and Thanksgiving week until Christmas week; Moderate Attendance seasons are President's Week, April, and May (excluding Easter and Memorial Day weeks) and September until Thanksgiving week; and High Attendance seasons are Easter week, June-August, Thanksgiving week, and Christmas week. This is only intended as a rough guide of operating hours, call the specific parks for exact hours.

During seasons when the parks close early, certain shows do not function, namely the Fantasy in the Sky Fireworks and Main Street Electrical Parade at the Magic Kingdom. Others, such as Illuminations at EPCOT and Fantasmic! at the Disney-MGM Studios are performed to close out the day at the respective parks.

Although the parks "officially" open at 9am (the exception being the Animal Kingdom), the reality is somewhat different. The Disney parks sometimes open anywhere from 15 minutes to an hour before published opening times. How much earlier depends on attendance, but as a general rule of thumb, it's a good idea to arrive at the parks 15 to 30 minutes early in the off-season and 30 to 45 minutes early during peak seasons. If nothing else, you can grab a bite to eat and do a bit of shopping at the establishments in the points-of-entry "lands" (i.e., Hollywood Boulevard in Disney-MGM, the Front Lot at Universal, Main Street USA at the MK, etc.) at the theme parks.

The exception to this is on the days when Disney offers early admission to its resort guests – on these days you can expect the gates to open at the posted time. See the chapters on the individual parks for more information on the early entry program. At Universal Studios and Islands of Adventure, getting to the gates before the posted time is futile, as they reserve early admission to their resort guests as well.

WEATHER

Central Florida weather is unpredictable at best. In an attempt at predicting the erratic, here are some guidelines of what to say the guidebook told you to expect when Mother Nature throws my research out the window.

From June to September, precipitation usually manifests itself in the form of thunderstorms and short-lasting deluges that occur during the afternoon. In the event that it does rain on days when you plan to visit the parks, don't worry about it. The rain will serve to drive away some of the crowds as well as cool off the air. Besides, almost all of the attractions are indoors or under shelter, and the same can be said for most of the lines. And few and far between is the Florida thunderstorm that lasts more than a few minutes.

The weather most favorable to park touring occurs in February, March, April, October, and November.

ORLANDO WEATHER CHART

	Highs (f)	Lows (f)	Precip. (inches)
January	70	50	2.28
February	72	51	2.95
March	76	56	3.40
April	82	62	2.72
May	87	67	2.94
June	89	71	7.11
July	90	73	8.29
August	90	73	6.73
September	88	72	7.20
October	82	66	4.07
November	76	57	1.55
December	71	51	1.90

SPECIAL EVENTS

There are happenings throughout the year that may influence your decision about when to visit the area. For up-to-the-minute information about events in the area, contact the Orlando/Orange County Convention and Visitors' Bureau, *Tel. 407/363-5872 or 800/551-0181*, or on the web at *http://www.go2orlando.com*.

January

COMPUSA FLORIDA CITRUS BOWL: Pitting the SEC's second-ranked team against the Big Ten Champions, this match-up takes place at Orlando Stadium on New Year's Day. Tickets for the 2000 edition were $60. For more information, call *407/423-2476* or visit the official Citrus Bowl website at *http://www.fcsports.com*.

SCOTTISH HIGHLAND GAMES: Music, athletic events, demonstrations of skills and crafts, caber tossing, highland dancing, and more are on the bill at this cultural celebration. Surf to *http://www.flascot.com or call 407/426-7268*.

WALT DISNEY WORLD INDY 200: Cars from the Indy circuit run a 160-lap race at the Walt Disney World Speedway, near the Magic Kingdom. For information, *call 407/363-6600*.

WALT DISNEY WORLD MARATHON: It's not just the cars that are racing at WDW this month. Witness this 26-mile endurance test at Disney's Wide World of Sports Complex.

February

BACH FESTIVAL: Held at Rollins College's Knowles Memorial Chapter since 1935, this has become one of the area's most anticipated cultural events, featuring over 100 singers and musicians. *Call 407/646-2182.*

BLACK HISTORY MONTH FESTIVAL: Celebrations of African-American culture and history abound across the region, including a kickoff reception, a multicultural festival, ethnic merchandise, entertainment, and theatre. *Admission varies by event, call 407/290-0193 for details.*

CENTRAL FLORIDA FAIR: Held annually at the Central Florida Fairgrounds on Colonial Drive in Orlando, this 11-day event features over 50 rides, a petting zoo, and entertainment for the whole family. *For more info, call 800-555-4361 or check out http://www.centralfloridafair.com.*

DAYTONA 500/DAYTONA SPEED WEEK: NASCAR's big names are in the hunt for the checkered flag at this Winston Cup event, which is the culmination of a whole week of racing. *For information, call 904/254-2700 or surf to http://www.daytona500.com.*

GASPARILLA PIRATE FEST: Every February for the last 100 years or so, "pirates" representing Ye Mystic Krewe of Gasparilla invade the city of Tampa, with 400,000 spectators coming out to witness the fun. The weekend includes a parade, street festival, midway, jazz and blues, and arts and crafts for sale. *Click on http://www.thcva.com/events/annual_swgasparilla.html or call 888/224-1733 for more information.*

GRANT SEAFOOD FESTIVAL: On the third weekend in February, this small town on the east coast serves up fresh Indian River seafood. A very big deal to locals. *Information: Seafood Festival, Box 44, Grant, FL 32949. Call 407/723-8687.*

March

BAY HILL INVITATIONAL, PRESENTED BY OFFICE DEPOT: Arnold Palmer's Bay Hill Club in the suburb of Windermere, about ten minutes from WDW, hosts this major PGA event every year. *Information: Tournament Office: Bay Hill Club, 9000 Bay Hill Blvd., Orlando, FL 32819, Tel. 407/876-2888.*

FLORIDA IRISH FESTIVAL: On the weekend of St. Patrick's Day, Orlando residents celebrate their Irish heritage with celebrations including Irish musicians and comedians, food, Gaelic football, shopping, and dancing at the Seminole Greyhound Park and Fairplex. Admission is $10 a day. *Call 407/872-7695.*

KISSIMMEE BLUEGRASS FESTIVAL: This four-day celebration features bluegrass, creole, and Texas swing music at the Silver Spurs Rodeo. A four-day pass is $53.50, three days for $46, one-day passes vary. *Call 800/473-7773 for more info.*

ST. PATRICK'S DAY FESTIVITIES: There's all kinds of cultural activities and parties going on to celebrate this holiday. Most notably are the parties at Disney's Pleasure Island *(Tel. 407/824-4321)*, Church Street Station *(Tel. 407/422-2434)*, and the parade in Winter Park *(Tel. 407/644-8281)*.

WINTER PARK SIDEWALK ART FESTIVAL: Held every year on the third weekend of March in a scenic little park full of moss-covered trees, this show of crafts, pottery, etchings, sculpture, paintings, and other art draws locals to the trendy community of Winter Park. *Information: Box 597, Winter Park, FL 32790, Tel. 407/644-8281 and website http://www.wpsaf.org.*

EASTER IN ORLANDO

EASTER SUNRISE SERVICE: Presented at the Atlantis Theater in Sea World. Information: Sea World, 7007 Sea World Drive, Orlando, FL 32821. Tel. 407/351-3600.

WALT DISNEY WORLD EASTER PARADE: Festive floats are captured on national television as they wind their way down Main Street. The parks are open late this time of year, but it is very, very crowded.

April

EPCOT INTERNATIONAL FLOWER & GARDEN FESTIVAL: Running from mid-April to mid-May, Disney's biggest horticultural festival features flower and garden displays representing the international themes of Epcot's World Showcase and includes tours of the gardens, a concert series, brunch, demonstrations, and a lecture series. *For more information call 407/824-4321.*

JAZZFEST KISSIMMEE: This festive two-day event, held at Kissimmee Lakefront Park, features professionals and local amateurs, art exhibits, a food court, and wine/beer garden. *For info call 407/846-6257.*

ORLANDO-UCF SHAKESPEARE FESTIVAL: Since 1989, a troupe of professional actors have performed the works of the Bard at the Walt Disney World Amphitheatre at Lake Eola Park in downtown Orlando. Tickets range from $6 to $35. *Call 407/245-0985 for more information.*

May

ZELLWOOD SWEET CORN FESTIVAL: Over 30,000 people descend upon Zellwood, approximately 25 miles northwest of Orlando, to eat corn. 200,000 ears of corn. The festival features corn-eating contests, carnival rides, live country music, games, arts and crafts. *For info, check out http://www.zellwoodsweetcornfest.org or call 407/886-0014.*

June

FLORIDA FILM FESTIVAL: Over 100 films, documentaries, and shorts from around the world are showcased. The festival also includes seminars, tributes, and a gala. *Admission varies. Call 407/629-1088 or go to http://www.floridafilmfestival.com.*

July

FOURTH OF JULY FIREWORKS: Extra oomph is added to the fireworks displays at the Magic Kingdom with an added display over Seven Seas Lagoon. Additionally, there are pyrotechnics displays to culminate day-long celebrations at Lake Eola Park downtown *(call 407/246-2827)*, and along the Kissimmee lakefront *(call 407/932-4050)*.

SILVER SPURS RODEO: Same as in October. Held on Fourth of July Weekend.

October

BOAT SHOW: At the Downtown Disney Marketplace, boats are displayed not only on the grounds of the Marketplace but also in Buena Vista Lagoon. This is one of the area's largest boat shows, with over 200 boats from manufacturers across the country.

EPCOT INTERNATIONAL FOOD AND WINE FESTIVAL: Over 30 regions are represented along the shores of World Showcase Lagoon, each with samplings of regional foods and wine – reasonably priced, usually under the $5 mark. Wine tastings, culinary demonstrations, and speakers are also highlights of this event. *For more info, call 407/824-4321.*

FLORIDA STATE AIR FAIR: A two-day agenda of airborne activities including a show of old military planes (on the ground), aeronautical displays, and demonstrations of acrobatics in the sky. *Information: Rotary Club of Kissimmee, Box 422185, Kissimmee, FL 34742-2185. Tel. 407/896-3654.*

HALLOWEEN HORROR NIGHTS AT UNIVERSAL STUDIOS FLORIDA: Universal Studios transforms its backlot into a creepy haunted area, with special entertainment, mazes to wander through, and all kinds of monsters wandering the park. This is hugely popular with locals, as is the raucous cos"tomb" party held at Citywalk the weekend of Halloween. Separate admission is required. *Call 407/363-8000 for details.*

HALLOWEEN PARTY AT DOWNTOWN DISNEY MARKET-PLACE: Local youngsters dress up for a costume contest, and the atmosphere is spiced up by "halloween-ifying" the Captain's Tower with cobwebs, Halloween merchandise, and the presence of villains from Disney flicks.

SILVER SPURS RODEO: A Kissimmee tradition since 1944, this biannual competition draws cowboys from all across the country to vie for thousands of dollars. The rodeo lasts four days. *Information: Kissimmee St. Cloud Convention and Visitor's Bureau, Box 422007, Kissimmee, FL 34742-2007 or call 407/677-6336.*

NATIONAL CAR RENTAL GOLF CLASSIC AT WALT DISNEY WORLD: This stop on the PGA tour draws pros and amateurs alike. Most of the Tour's top players enter. Admission is free. However, if you plan on golfing at one of the Disney courses during your vacation, a*void going this week.* Getting a start time during the tournament becomes impossible unless you are a member of the Classic Club. *Information: 800/582-1908 or 828-2255.*

November

FESTIVAL OF THE MASTERS: Celebrating its 25th anniversary in 2000, this popular festival features the works of over 150 artists who compete for over $30,000 in prizes. Food and music will be featured at various locations throughout the Downtown Disney Marketplace, with tastings that include Fulton's Crab House, Portobello Yacht Club, Missing Link, Rainforest Café, and Wildhorse Saloon among others. The festival runs from 9:30am to 5:30pm for three consecutive days. *For more information call 407/397-6476.*

December

ANNUAL HALF-MARATHON: A thirteen-mile race that departs from Lake Eola Park in the downtown area. *For info, call 407/898-1313.*

FIRST BAPTIST CHURCH SINGING CHRISTMAS TREES: Okay. Stay with me here for a minute. The 45-foot trees themselves don't sing, but 204 "ornaments" do, to the accompaniment of a full orchestra and a 118-rank Schantz pipe organ. Over 300,000 people have witnessed this spectacle since 1980. Admission is $7 and tickets must be purchased in advance. *Call 407/425-2555.*

HOLIDAY POPS: The Florida Symphony Orchestra kicks off the holiday season with their annual Holiday Pops concert in the Carr Centre in downtown Orlando. Tickets cost $18 to $34 and can be purchased through Ticketmaster. *Call 407/839-3900.*

MACY'S NEW YORK CHRISTMAS: The 6-story tall balloons made famous in the Macy's Day Parade come to their winter home on the New York Street on the backlot of the Disney-MGM Studios Theme Park. On display throughout December.

NUTCRACKER BALLET: For 100 years now, each winter has seen the tale of Drosselmeyer and Clara in the Christmas world of make-believe. The classical piece is performed at the Bob Carr Performing Arts Centre downtown. Tickets are $26 for adults, $18 for kids 6 to 12, and $5 for kids under 6. *Call Ticketmaster at 407/839-3900.*

CHRISTMAS FUN

In a town dedicated to family fun, you can bet that there's a whole array of things to do to celebrate Christmastime. From eye-popping parades to dignified processionals, this is an especially exciting time of year to visit Orlando. Unfortunately, it's also THE single most crowded time of year, with over 75,000 people streaming through the turnstiles at each park on the average day. Fortunately, many of the Christmas celebrations run the entire month of December, the beginning portion of which is considerably less crowded.

IN THE MAGIC KINGDOM: The park is transformed into a holiday postcard, with a 65-foot Christmas tree erected in Town Square the week before Thanksgiving. Additionally, Mickey's Very Merry Christmas Parade runs the last two weeks or so of the month, culminating with a live broadcast Christmas morning. Mickey's Very Merry Christmas Party allows you to take an after-hours (8pm-1am) rampage through the Magic Kingdom ($29.95 for adults and $19.95 for kids in advance, an extra $5 per person at the gate). Call 407/824-4321 for details. The normal show at the Country Bear Jamboree is pre-empted by a holiday edition, tree lighting ceremonies, and special shows featuring Mickey, Minnie, and the gang.

IN EPCOT: World Showcase is the home to Holidays Around the World, a celebration of stories and traditions that bring the world closer together. Additionally, the Candlelight Processional features a joyous retelling of the Christmas story by a celebrity narrator (the 1999 narrators include Angela Bassett, Brian Dennehy, and Andy Garcia), along with a live massed choir and orchestra. Vacation packages including priority seating are available.

AT THE DISNEY-MGM STUDIOS: The Residential Street on the backlot features the Osborne Family Lights, transplanted five million strong (!!!) from Little Rock.

AT DOWNTOWN DISNEY: Christmas in the City is the theme here, as the Marketplace, Pleasure Island, and the West Side are all decked out for the occasion, including visits from Santa, a skating rink, and nightly tree-lighting ceremonies.

AT UNIVERSAL STUDIOS FLORIDA: The Old-Fashioned Christmas Party features a Winter Carnival over two weekends in December. Strolling singers, chestnut vendors, a fifty-foot Christmas tree, hot cocoa, an outdoor ice show, a Yuletide Yacht Parade, and other festivities make this a special time here. And if the concept of snow in Orlando isn't bizarre enough, the Blues Brothers are singing Christmas carols.

AT CYPRESS GARDENS: The Poinsetta Festival and Garden of Lights provides a more laid-back but still high-voltage (400,000 lights) way to celebrate the holiday.

THE KISSIMMEE HOLIDAY FESTIVAL features live entertainment, 20 tons of snow, strolling performers, and a fireworks display at Kissimmee Lakefront Park. Call 407/932-4050 for details.

GATHERING INFORMATION

As I stated earlier, the key to a successful WDW vacation is planning. Here are some sources to go to to acquire the information you'll need.

The **Florida Department of Commerce's Tourism Division**, Visitor Inquiry Section will send you a free publication, the **Florida Vacation Guide.** *Just contact them at 126 Van Buren Street, Tallahassee, FL, 32339-2000 or call them at 904/487-1462,* tell them where you want to go and what you want to do and they'll try to oblige you.

Orlando's **Official Visitor Center**, which enjoys its spacious new digs at 8723 International Drive (at the corner of Austrian Row and International Drive, between Pointe Orlando and Mercado), is the public face of the Orlando/Orange County Convention/Visitors Bureau *(http://www.go2orlando.com, Tel. 407/363-5872 or 800/551-0181),* and should be your first stop once you arrive in Orlando, as you can pick up magazines filled with coupons and information, as well as brochures from just about all the attractions, hotels, and restaurants discussed in this book and more. You can also make hotel reservations here. The Visitor Center is open 8am to 7pm every day of the year except Christmas. You should call them up as soon as you decide you want to visit, and request copies of their Official Accommodations Guide and Official Visitors Guide as well as the latest brochure of Magicard discounts, the latter of which can save you hundreds of dollars over the course of a vacation.

The **Kissimmee-St. Cloud Visitors Guide** is another worthwhile acquisition *(http://www.floridakiss.com, 800/327-9159 or 407/847-5000),* featuring much of the same information but concentrated more on the establishments along U.S. 192 as opposed to the surrounding areas.

If you are driving to Orlando, another publication that belongs at the top of your wish list is the **Traveler Discount Guide** published by Exit Information Guides *(http://www.exitinformationguide.com or 800/222-3948).* This magazine publishes hundreds of coupons featuring discounts of up to 50% at hotels along all the main tourist drags and is available at selected businesses along major highways throughout the Eastern Seaboard. You can order them online (expect to pay $3 shipping for the first guide, $1 for each additional), check out the listings of sites where the guides are available, and even search, download, and print the coupons available in the print editions.

Several other coupon-filled magazines offer coupons and information and are definitely worth a look, since they can save you anywhere up to 50% or more on hotels, attractions, meals, shopping, and other

NEW YEAR'S EVE

There's no shortage of places to ring in the New Year either. The theme parks are open late if you want to watch the calendar change from there, or you can check out other options. Note that if you're spending the last night of the year in a Disney theme park, dinner reservations are often booked solid months in advance. Call 407/WDW-DINE after September 2nd to make yours.

PLEASURE ISLAND celebrates New Year's Eve every night as it is, so you can imagine the blowout they throw when it actually is December 31. The 1999 NYE celebration featured musical performances from Hootie and the Blowfish and the B-52's, and tickets went for $250 per person. Note that this is a 21 and up celebration. Call 407/939-7715 for details.

CIRQUE DU SOLEIL's party is as unique and innovative as the troupe that performs here. It starts off with a jazz buffet, and then a performance of the breathtaking La Nouba show. Following the show, the performers and audience mingle on the waterfront for desserts and a champagne toast, with a stellar view of the Pleasure Island fireworks. Call 407/939-7713 for details or reservations. Tickets are $210 per person.

The ATLANTIC DANCE CLUB at Disney's Boardwalk hosts a NYE party that includes a five-course plated dinner, four band sets, three performer sets, fireworks, open bar, and more for $300 per person.

CHURCH STREET STATION is the original party destination in Orlando, and you'd better believe that this is the place to be for NYE, with a party that gets rocking at 5pm and rages on through the free champagne toast when the ball drops at midnight, with a wide variety of music and entertainment in the clubs and on the street. This event sells out every year, so get your tickets in advance by calling 407/422-2434.

UNIVERSAL STUDIOS ESCAPE has its own cork-popping celebrations, complete with champagne, fireworks, parades, and other special events throughout the parks. At the Studios, the traditional street parade is augmented with stretch limos, celebrity impersonators, a DJ at the end of Hollywood Boulevard, and a huge pyro display that kicks off when a speedboat flies through a 40-foot high wall of fire in the lagoon. Islands of Adventure hosts a parade featuring the characters from the park, plus its own DJ and Merlin the Magician serving as emcee for the fireworks display. There are other options as well – The Party Zone ($75/person) entitles guests to hors d'oeuvres and open bar in a special fireworks viewing area. Deluxe dinner packages at theme park restaurants are also available ($90-$125/person). Citywalk's street party features live performances across the spectrum of live music ($150/person). The Hard Rock Live also features a party with world-class DJs such as house legend Peter Rauhofer of Club 69 ($100/person in advance, $135/person day of event).

necessities. A lot of these publications come and go, but there's a few mainstays who you can depend on for reliable information, generous discounts, and accurate free maps.

Bear in mind, though, that most of the articles in the magazines are re-chewed press releases from the companies mentioned, so objectivity isn't something you're going to find in most of these.

Best Read Guide Orlando: Over 100 pages of articles, ads, and coupons for area attractions, restaurants, and shops. By mail, single copies are $3 and annual 12-issue subscriptions are $20. The online edition *(http://www.bestread.com)* features some of the articles found in the print version but not the coupons. You can also order issues on-line.

Enjoy Florida: A 50-page publication with press-release articles, lots of coupons, and big fold out maps. *Check out http://www.informationflorida.com for details.* The magazine can be ordered along with two sister publications for $5 on the website.

Golf Orlando: This guide offers information on golf and lodging packages, as well as local golf course info with course ratings, greens fees, and more information. *Call 888/GOLF-FLORIDA or check out http://www.teetimesusa.com.* Online you can make tee time reservations, order free brochures, or create your own package deal, not only for local golf courses, but for those all over the state.

International Drive Resort Area Magazine/Inside Orlando: Approximately 50 pages in length, this publication is almost entirely ads – however, the resort area maps are pretty comprehensive. Published quarterly, a subscription is $12, *Tel. 407/351-1573.*

Orlando Magazine: This monthly magazine caters more to locals than tourists – which means it's just the thing to give you an insider perspective on what's going on. Annual subscriptions are $17.97 and can be purchased online at *http://www.orlandomag.com.* Their ConciergeOrlando section is particularly informative for visitors, with guides to dining, attractions, shopping, and more.

Orlando Weekly: O-town's alternative newspaper (think Village Voice or Washington CityPaper) offers a way to put your ear to the ground to find out about musical and cultural events plus offbeat offerings, plus restaurant reviews, movie times, and more. *Check them out at http://www.orlandoweekly.com or call 407/645-5888.*

See Orlando: With over 200 pages of informative articles – not just the promotional fluff, complete maps of the area including all of their advertisers' locations, and scores of coupons, this is, along with Best Read Guide, your best option. At their website *(http://www.see-florida.com)*, you can check out online listings in a limited selection of categories. *Call 800/683-1000 for more information.*

WHAT TO PACK

This is another item of vital importance which can keep a good vacation from being great, regardless of where you go. In the parks, the rule of thumb is to dress comfortably. T-shirts and shorts are the norm most of the year. However, as it grows colder, clothes grow thicker and longer. But above all, wear comfortable sneakers. As you will be doing a lot of walking at any of the theme parks, this cannot be stressed enough. If you forget your sneakers, purchase a pair. Otherwise, your feet'll be screaming bloody murder by your second day of touring.

As for restaurants, only a few in the Orlando area require a shirt and tie or a dress. Otherwise, dress is casual.

A bathing suit is a given necessity regardless of the time of your visit. On winter nights, temperatures can dip into the 40s, so a sweater or jacket is a good idea. It's even a good idea to bring a light jacket in the 100-degree heat of July because most Florida hotels have arctic air conditioning. Other items that you may want to bring include: cameras or camcorders, film (often forgotten), and sporting equipment.

PACKAGE DEALS

The vast diversity of central Florida packages makes this an option well worth exploring. You can stay anywhere from low-budget chains to one-of-a-kind luxury hotels. There are bus packages, air packages, drive packages all options are covered.

If you decide that you want a package, you can get all the appropriate literature from your local travel agency. Shop around. Different chain agencies will sometimes offer their own packages. When you are deciding on your package, it is crucial that you find out exactly what is included in it. Some packages include airfare and hotel only, others come with transfers or rental cars, admissions, meals, tips, taxes, and entertainment. Bear in mind that although things like nightly cocktails or coffee and juice in the morning sound nice, but you're probably paying for it.

Also, beware of packages that offer as selling points options available to all Disney guests, i.e., use of transportation in WDW.

Walt Disney Travel Company

The Walt Disney Travel Company offers a wide array of tour and package options for all budgets and all personalities. You can select from the 20 Disney-owned and operated hotels and all variations of packages, from romantic getaways to honeymoons to golf packages to all inclusive resort rampages. For specifics including availability and prices, surf to *http://travel.disney.go.com*. Note that none of the Disney plans include admission to off-site attractions such as Universal or Sea World.

Universal Studios Vacations

As Universal Escape comes into its own as a vacation destination on a par with Disney, their vacation packages rise to the challenge as well. They offer a variety of packages that include admission to not only Universal Studios Florida and Islands of Adventure, but also to Wet 'n Wild, Sea World, and even Busch Gardens Tampa. The selection of hotels available with these plans is impressive, ranging from Universal's own Portofino Bay Hotel and the AAA five-diamond Hyatt Regency Grand Cypress to moderate resorts up and down the International Drive corridor. Note that Universal packages do not include admission to Disney. *You can find out more by calling 800/711-0080 or by surfing to http://www.usevacations.com.*

SURFING SAFARI - FINDING YOUR PERFECT VACATION ON THE INTERNET

In addition to vacation packages administered by the attractions themselves, there are dozens if not hundreds of tour companies offering vacation packages of all shapes, sizes, and colors online. It can be daunting to wade through all the different websites, trying to figure out which companies are legitimate and which are a bit on the sketchy side. The best bet is to surf around the megasites, since while they don't actually coordinate and arrange the packages themselves, they sort out the chaff from the wheat and present you with the widest variety of options in one place.

In addition to the companies listed below, many individual hotels, chains, airlines, and other transportation providers offer their own metaphorical baskets o' goodies, so contact them for more information. You can find contact information for these companies in the chapters that follow.

American Express

American Express, while no longer offering its own dedicated travel department, works hand in hand with several airlines to provide packages featuring a variety of hotels aross the metropolitan area, featuring admission to all the major parks plus additional perks, at *http://www.americanexpress.com/travel*. Note that Delta's packages offer accommodations at Walt Disney World resorts, while Continental's feature Orlando, Lake Buena Vista, and Kissimmee area hotels.

Vacation Packager

The site that Go2Orlando.com links to for its package referrals *(http://www.vacationpackager.com)*, this is your one-stop shop for tours provided by TWA Getaway Vacations, Players' Choice golf and tennis vacations,

GoGo Worldwide Vacations, Kingdom Vacations, Friendly Holidays, Delta Vacations, and more.

Expedia

Microsoft's travel ubersite, Expedia has a colossal search engine for vacation packages from the likes of American Airlines, Hyatt, Travelscape.com, and more. *Check out http://www.expedia.com.*

Travelocity

Travelocity is another one-stop-shop for car, hotel, and air reservations as well as a reseller of packages from American, Delta, Continental, OnlineVacationMall.com, and VacationSpot.com. *Check them out at http://www.travelocity.com.*

4. DISCOUNTS, DEALS, & BARGAINS

74 GREAT MONEY-SAVING TIPS

Even with the best of intentions, you can spend a lot more money in Orlando than you need to. If you follow these 74 tips and suggestions listed in this chapter, you'll find some great ways to stretch your hard-earned dollars!

BEFORE YOU GO

1. If you can swing it, plan your vacation for an "off-season" period, i.e. anytime except summer and holidays.

2. Order an Orlando Magicard from the Orlando/Orange County CVB *(http://www.go2orlando.com, Tel. 800/551-0181 or 407/363-5872)*.

3. Order the Kissimmee-St. Cloud CVB's coupon-filled Visitors' Guide *(http://www.floridakiss.com, Tel. 800/327-9159 or 407/327-9159)*

4. Contact your local travel agent or the Internet sites listed in Chapter 3 for information on package deals.

5. Contact Exit Information Guides *(Tel. 904/371-3948 or http://www.exitinformationguides.com)* for a copy of their Traveler Discount Guide for Florida (free, $3/first guide, $1/additional for shipping) and any other states you will be driving through and in need of accommodations. This book, published quarterly, has over 100 pages of coupons for hotels and restaurants within easy reach of major highways.

6. Remember videotape, film, your preference for relieving stomach-aches and headaches, sunscreen, and other sundries. They are vastly overpriced in Orlando.

7. Join the Magic Kingdom Club. Many companies (with 500 employees or more) offer this as a fringe benefit to employees. Check with your employer, you may be eligible and not even know it. MKC members receive special vacation packages as well as discounts on admission media,

hotels, dining, shopping, and golf in Disney World, plus discounts at Disneyland parks in California, Paris, and Tokyo, Disney Store locations nationwide, National Rent-a-Car, and many more. If your employer doesn't offer the club membership, you can purchase a two-year Gold Card for $65.

ACCOMMODATIONS

8. Magic Kingdom Club members receive discounts of 10% to 20% on selected rooms in Disney hotels during certain periods of the year.

9. There are websites that allow you to name your price on hotel accommodations and airfare. The best choice for this is Priceline *(http://www.priceline.com)*, which additionally offers name-your-price options for new cars, home financing, and even groceries. But you can just stick to the travel services for now.

10. Disney runs an information booth on I-75 in Ocala, and a percentage of rooms are sold from here at discounts up to and above 40%. However, this is a very risky way to go about getting accommodations. *You can inquire about room availability by calling 352/854-7040.*

11. AAA members receive discounts of up to 25% at chain hotels including Days Inn, Holiday Inn, and more.

12. When calling hotels, when you ask initially for the room rate, you will generally be quoted the "rack rate," which has no discounts applied to it. Sometimes, following up that question with a request for the "best rate" can yield a more favorable response.

13. Many frequent-flyer plans have tie-ins with hotel chains. This may entitle you to earn miles or spend the miles for free nights, room upgrades, etc.

14. Non-profit associations often sell thick Entertainment books as fundraisers. The back of these books contain listings of villa accommodations and hotels offering Entertainment cardholders 50% discounts.

15. For large families that would otherwise be forced to rent multiple rooms, villas offer a cost-effective alternative, and as an added bonus, many have kitchens.

16. Conde Nast Traveler did a study of chain hotel rates quoted by the central reservations office and the individual hotels themselves, and they found some discrepancies. If you are thinking about staying at a chain, call both numbers.

17. You pay for proximity. If you don't mind a longer drive, you can save a few bucks by staying in more remote areas of Central Florida. However, it's a trade-off between this and the extra aggravation of a longer drive.

18. If you're staying on Disney property and aren't planning on visiting any non-Disney attractions, renting a car is unnecessary.

19. You can save a couple of bucks by staying at a hotel that includes a daily continental breakfast or breakfast buffet. These are mainly all-suite or budget establishments.

20. Many hotels have no extra charge for children under 18 in the same room as their parents. Check the cut-off age.

21. If possible, choose a hotel that includes free local calls in the price of a room. If you can't swing this, bring your calling card or buy a pre-paid one, as the service fees for local calls at most hotels is ridiculous.

22. Ask about corporate rates and how to qualify for them.

AIRFARE

23. Be flexible about when you fly. If you can swing your schedule a few hours in each direction, you may be able to fly for substantially less.

24. Check into benefits of frequent flyer plans you are a member of. If you are not a member, join one of the plans. Some offer discounts on hotels and car rentals.

25. Many airlines offer deep discounts on last minute flights, some through periodical e-mail lists delivered right to your inbox.

26. Look into bucket shops, agencies that resell tickets at deeply discounted prices.

27. Entertainment books offer coupons for discounts on airline tickets.

28. Fly when fewer people choose to, on Tuesday, Wednesday, and Saturday when possible. Note that you will not be eligible for many low rates without a Saturday stayover.

29. Some travel agencies subscribe to a service that tracks airfares and automatically seeks out the lowest one. *You can search yourself at http://www.travelocity.com or http://www.lowestfare.com.*

30. Buy your tickets at least 14 and preferably 21 days in advance. This way you can be eligible for advance purchase discounts. If you're traveling during peak seasons, you may need to make yours even earlier than that.

31. Be flexible about your airport of departure if you have more than one to choose from. Flying into and out of less busy airports can save you a few bucks.

DRIVING TO & AROUND ORLANDO

32. Follow up your initial rate inquiry on a rental car with a "best rate" inquiry, just like with hotels.

33. AAA, AARP, and other clubs often are offered car rental discounts as well.

34. If you pay for a rental car with certain credit cards, a collision damage waiver (CDW) may not be neccesary, as any damage would be insured by the card.

35. Instead of stopping at a roadside fast-food joint while en route, pack homemade sandwiches or snacks in a cooler.

36. The closer to WDW you are, the more gas will cost you.

37. Magic Kingdom Club members receive a discount on cars from National InterRent, up to 30% off.

38. Frequent flyer? Chances are your air carrier has deals that can get you discounts with car rental companies.

39. Consider renting from an agency located outside the airport, as their rates are often considerably lower than on-site agencies, and the inconvenience is minimal.

40. If you've chosen airport transfers in lieu of a rental car, consider limousines rather than shuttles if you have a big family. If there's four people or more in your party, a limo might be a cost-effective option. And oh, the style.

41. Some hotels offer complimentary shuttles to the theme parks. If you're not planning on renting a car, this can save you some serious cash.

DINING

42. Make your main meal of the day lunch, instead of dinner. The same meals are often much cheaper then.

43. Instead of eating a fast food lunch in the parks, you might consider leaving for one of the better-quality chain or buffet restaurants on U.S. 192 or S.R. 535, depending on how tight your schedule is.

44. Avoid eating expensive, run-of-the-mill burgers and dogs in the parks by bringing your own food and just eating when the mood suits you. This is against the rules of the parks, but unless you walk around the Magic Kingdom carrying a pizza box, nobody's going to question you.

45. Guests at hotels with kitchens or kitchenettes can save a substantial amount of money by cooking their own meals.

46. If you don't have a kitchen, you can save time and money by purchasing breakfast the night before. Bottled juices and baked goods are a good choice.

47. Buffet restaurants in the tourist strips offer hearty eaters the chance to fill their tanks for one low price.

48. Magic Kingdom Club members get a 10% discount on selected theme park restaurants.

49. Use your American Express card at selected restaurants and receive a 10% discount.

50. In the theme parks, you can save time and money by getting lunch from one of the carts roaming the park. Turkey legs are now sold for about $4 in most of the parks, a filling alternative to the traditional hot dog.

51. In visiting Disney's water parks, pack a picnic lunch. They allow it, besides, it's cheaper and better than the stuff you can get there.

52. Some hotels have promotions that allow kids to eat free in the hotel's restaurant.

53. Snacking has become a lot healthier and a lot cheaper since produce stands were brought into the parks. The prices are higher than what you'd pay at a local supermarket, but they're still a good option.

SHOPPING

54. Allot a certain amount of time and money for souvenirs, and stick to the limit.

55. Comparison-shopping inside Walt Disney World is useless. The same items have the same prices in all shops.

56. However, Magic Kingdom Club members should concentrate their purchases in the Downtown Disney Marketplace, West Side, and Pleasure Island shops, as they can reap a 10% discount at them.

57. Orlando, Kissimmee, and Lake Buena Vista are home to hundreds of factory outlet shops, all of them a good bet for finding brand-name merchandise at deep discounts.

58. Visitor information centers often have vouchers for coupons at area malls like the Mercado, Old Town, and Belz Factory Outlet World.

59. Everywhere you look in Orlando are gift shops offering huge selections of Disney, Orlando, and Florida merchandise. Many of them advertise 99-cent mugs, $1.99 t-shirts, and the like, but bear in mind that if you want something that's not entirely tacky you'll probably have to pay more normal prices. Regardless, souvenirs here are often cheaper than at the theme parks, and many of them offer Disney character merchandise not available in the parks.

60. Hotel gift shops are the most expensive places for sundry purchases such as film and aspirin. Supermarkets and convenience stores are cheaper.

ATTRACTIONS

61. If you'll be staying at a Walt Disney World resort and looking to experience everything that WDW has to offer (not just the four major parks), you may want to look into an Unlimited Magic Pass, which provides unlimited admission to all the major and minor theme parks on Disney property for the length of your stay.

62. Many off-site hotels have guest services counters where discounted tickets can be purchased without any lines. The only problem with purchasing tickets from these brokers is that they can be pushy. If you say you need tickets, they immediately ring them up. Be assertive and don't be talked into buying tickets if you can get a better deal elsewhere.

63. If you are not staying on-site, and looking to experience the minor Disney attractions as well as the major ones, the Five-Day Park Hopper Plus pass is your most cost-effective bet.

64. Magic Kingdom Club members recieve small discounts on admission media to WDW.

65. Coupons to many area attractions can be found in magazines like Best Read Guide, Enjoy Florida, and SEE Orlando. These magazines are available from visitors' bureaus and area businesses.

66. AAA, AARP, and other groups often are offered discounts. Veterans, seniors, and Florida residents have been offered discounts at WDW in special annual programs.

67. Many water parks offer discounted admission after a certain time in the afternoon, usually between 3 and 6 PM, dependent upon the season.

68. Disney usually increases their ticket prices by 5% annually, in the spring (the last increase prior to publication happened in May 1999). Since the passports never expire, you can purchase your admission media early in the year, paying last year's rate for this year's vacation.

69. If you're planning on making a Disney trip a perennial event, here's a way to save significant money the second time around. Purchase an annual passport rather than a multi-day pass. That's good for unlimited admission for one year from the date of purchase. So go have your fun this year, and when next year rolls around and it's time to plan your next Disney vacation, plan it for one or two weeks earlier in the year, so your annual passports will still be valid and you don't need to purchase tickets at all for your second visit.

70. If your focus is more on the other attractions in Orlando, such as Sea World and Universal, an Orlando FlexTicket may be your best bet. These allow unlimited admission to Universal Studios, Islands of Adventure, Sea World, and Wet 'n Wild for one price.

SPORTS & RECREATION

71. Inside WDW, golf is cheaper at the Lake Buena Vista, Palm, and Magnolia courses than at the new Eagle Pines and Osprey Ridge courses.

72. The Oak Trail course at Shades of Green is a par-36 executive golf course, with 9 holes measuring 2,913 yards from the back tees. The cost of 18 holes here is $48, significantly lower than that of the other courses.

73. Resort golf is generally more expensive than public or municipal courses.

74. Many golf clubs offer twilight rates for those willing to pick up late-afternoon tee times.

5. BASIC INFORMATION

Convenience stores: There are Circle K, Cumberland Farms, and 7-Eleven stores around every corner in Orlando and its environs. In addition, many gas stations in the area have small stores where convenience items can be purchased.

Drinking Laws: You must be 21 or over to be served alcohol. However, many bars and clubs will admit 18-and-ups.

Driving Laws: Add: Also, to avoid a ticket, heed the lane restrictions on I-4. During rush hour, access to the left lanes is restricted to HOV's, high occupancy vehicles with at least 2 occupants. The restrictions are westbound from 7-930AM and eastbound from 4-630.

Emergencies: Dial 911 for police, fire, or ambulance. The police department's non-emergency number is *407/246-2414.*

Hunting and Fishing: For information on the necessary permits, contact the Florida Game and Freshwater Fish Commission, *Tel. 888/HUNT-FLORIDA or 888/FISH-FLORIDA.* Ten-day non-resident hunting licenses are $26.50 and seven-day non-resident fishing licenses are $16.50. Comprehensive information is available at their website, *http://www.state.fl.us/fwc.*

Newspapers: The primary newspaper in Orlando is the Orlando Sentinel, *Tel. 420-5000, http://www.orlandosentinel.com.* The daily, founded in 1876, is now the nation's 33rd largest paper. On Fridays, there's the Calendar insert, giving information on local eateries, nightlife, festivals, concerts, and other entertainment. It's an extremely comprehensive way of finding out what's up. Many hotels and convenience stores also offer national and out-of-town papers.

Sundries: Bring them with you from home if you can, as they're more expensive down here.

Supermarkets: Gooding's supermarkets are located at the Crossroads of Lake Buena Vista shopping center on SR 535, 7840 US 192 in Kissimmee, and 8255 International Drive.

Taxes: Florida sales tax is 6% or 7% on most items, depending on the county. There's an additional resort tax of 2% to 5% (depending on county) for hotel rooms.

Telephone: Note that the entire central Florida area uses ten digit calling for all calls, even local. You must always dial the area code before the seven digit number. The primary area code for central Florida is 407, and new numbers issued since January 1, 2000 are in the 321 overlay area code.

Television: NBC is on channel 2, CBS is 6, ABC is 9, FOX is 35, WB is 18, UPN is 65, and PBS is 24.

Time: All of central Florida lies inside the Eastern Time Zone. For current time and temperature, *call 407/646-3131.*

Tropical Storms: Landlocked Orlando doesn't get hit very often by the hurricanes that often descend upon the coast of Florida. However, the more powerful hurricanes can dump significant amounts of rain on Orlando. Most attractions stay open unless there's a full blown hurricane bearing down on them. Stay tuned to news broadcasts and weather forecasts for updates.

Weather: *Call 407/851-7510.*

6. ARRIVALS & DEPARTURES

GETTING THERE & GETTING BACK

There are nearly as many ways to get to WDW as there are to skin a cat. You can come by plane, bus, car, ship, or train. In addition, there is the matter of getting around the town once you arrive in Orlando. WDW itself has an intricate system of internal transportation, including buses, boats, monorails, and 123 miles of roads. Orlando has a mass-transit system also, but the most popular option is car rental. All of this will be discussed in the next chapter, *Getting Around Orlando*.

BY CAR

For many a family living in the Eastern Seaboard or deep South, driving to Orlando is by no means an unreasonable or inconvenient choice, and for some families it can save over a thousand dollars. The major routes leading into Orlando are I-4 leading from Tampa to Daytona Beach and the Florida's Turnpike from Ocala to Miami.

Listed are some routes from major cities around the east:

- Atlanta, Chicago, Cincinnati, Dallas, Indianapolis, Louisville, Minneapolis, Ocala: Take I-75 to U.S. 27, U.S. 27 to U.S. 192.
- Baltimore, Boston, Buffalo, Cleveland, Jacksonville, Montreal, New York, Philadelphia, Pittsburgh, Richmond, Toronto, and Washington D.C.: Take I-95 south to I-4 west.
- Miami and points southeast: Florida's Turnpike or I-95 north to I-4 west (Exit 259 from the turnpike).
- Daytona Beach, St. Petersburg, Tampa: Use I-4.

It is wise to join AAA, the American Automobile Association, before going anywhere. If nothing else, join for their Triptik service, which plans out a map for you to follow to your destination. Another advantage of joining is the special (and sometimes sizeable) room discounts at chain hotels across the country.

AAA estimates that the average cost of a day of driving for two adults and two children is $173 for lodging and meals, and $8.40 in car expenses every hundred miles. Your costs may be higher or lower, depending on variables.

Welcome stations, filled with helpful workers and informative brochures, can be found on all major highways as you enter the state. They're located on I-95 in Yulee, on I-75 in Jennings, I-10 in Pensacola, US 1-301 in Hillyard, and US 231 in Campbellton.

One important thing to remember if you've got a long drive ahead of you: hunger pangs are not synchronizedwith freeway exits. So it's wise to pack a few snacks or stop for them at gas stations when you go for gas and a bathroom stop. Also, it is much easier to retain your sanity if you bring books, magazines, or tapes for use in the car (unless you're driving).

From the airport you can take the Beeline Expressway (SR 528) to I-4, Sea World, Universal, and the International Drive area, or the Central Florida Greenway (SR 417) south to Walt Disney World and Kissimmee.

BY AIR

Orlando International Airport is clearly not a Mickey Mouse facility, although he can be found all around the spot.

If you haven't been to the airport recently, you would have a hard time recognizing it. Recently completed overhauls have modernized and expanded it with more renovations than you would expect anyone to pour into a ten-year old building.

The main facility is composed of three levels. On the lower level, you'll find rental car counters and access to buses as well as transportation to rental car lots and offsite agencies, plus hotel reservation phones and tunnels to the nearby parking garage. Level two has baggage claim areas, currency exchange, taxis and van shuttles and off-airport car rental phones. Level three has ticketing facilities, shops and newsstands, restaurants and lounges, a bank, USO, duty free shop, lockers, information, and currency exchange. The shuttles to the gates can also be boarded here. Maps of the facility as well as walkthroughs and general information can be found at the airport's website, *http://fcn.state.fl.us/goaa*.

At press time there were over 60 large and small, domestic and international airlines serving Orlando International Airport, offering direct service to over 100 US destinations and many others worldwide.

Booking Your Flight

On-line travel services have made the process of finding the perfect flight for you much easier than it had been. Finding the best rate has never been easier, as you can search one site and find flights from a half dozen different carriers, allowing you to pick at a glance which one best suits your budget and schedule. In addition to the individual airlines' websites, which offer on-line reservations in many cases, you can make them through sites like Expedia *(www.expedia.com)*, Travelocity *(www.travelocity.com)*, and Preview Travel *(www.previewtravel.com)*. Of course, telephone reservations are also accepted for the less technologically inclined.

DOMESTIC AIRLINES SERVING ORLANDO

AirTran	Tel. 800/247-8726	www.airtran.com
America West	Tel. 800/235-9292	www.americawest.com
American	Tel. 800/433-7300	www.aa.com
Continental	Tel. 800/525-0280	www.flycontinental.com
Delta	Tel. 800/221-1212	www.delta-air.com
Eastwind	Tel. 888/327-8946	www.eastwindairlines.com
Kiwi Int'l	Tel. 800/538-5494	www.jetkiwi.com
Midway	Tel. 800/446-4392	www.midwayair.com
Northwest	Tel. 800/225-2525	www.nwa.com
Southwest	Tel. 800/435-9792	www.iflyswa.com
TWA	Tel. 800/893-5436	www.twa.com
United	Tel. 800/241-6522	www.ual.com
US Airways	Tel. 800/428-4322	www.usairways.com

BY BUS

Bus travel is one of the cheapest, but most time-consuming ways to get from Point A to Point B, and is only recommended for those for whom money is a primary consideration and time is not.

The nation's biggest bus line, **Greyhound** *(Tel. 877/GO-BY-BUS or www.greyhound.com)* can get you there from most of the continental United States, but it'll be a long ride. Figure 10 hours from Atlanta, 16 hours from Washington, DC, and 24 hours from New York City. Not much of an option, but an option nonetheless.

BY TRAIN

This is another of the less popular ways to get to WDW, but it's a good way to see America and it saves you the hassle of air travel or driving. **Amtrak's Silver Meteor** and **Silver Star** trains travel southward from New York's Penn Station daily.

The Silver Star leaves New York at 11:30 AM daily, arriving at Orlando roughly 24 hours later. The Silver Meteor leaves New York at 7 PM and arrives at 4 PM the next day. The trains' stops include: Newark (NJ),

Trenton, Philadelphia, Wilmington, Baltimore, Washington, Richmond, Raleigh, Charlotte, Columbia (SC), Savannah, and Jacksonville. Amtrak also offers service to points west, but the routes down the Eastern seaboard are the most popular. Like many airlines, Amtrak offers discounts to many different groups, including seniors, students, children, disabled passengers, and more.

Or check out Amtrak's website, *www.amtrak.com*, for reservations, timetables, fares, and Rail Sales, special Net-only deals, often on last-minute seats, at discounts up to 90% off regular coach fares.

One of Amtrak's most popular services is the **Auto Train,** which transports your car along with your family from Lorton, Virginia, just south of DC, to Sanford, Orlando, 20 minutes north of Orlando. You simply drive your car onto one of the car carriers at the end of the train and settle into your seat in one of the bi-level Superliner cars. The train leaves at 430 pm and arrive at 9am the next day.

Train travel isn't generally the most popular way to visit Orlando, because chances are, it'll take you as long as if you drove yourself, and cost you as much as if you flew.

BY CRUISE SHIP

The **Disney Cruise Line** combines three- or four-day cruises with Walt Disney World vacations that fill up the rest of the week. The brand-spanking-new Disney Wonder and Disney Magic ships leave Port Canaveral and stop at Nassau and Disney's private Castaway Cay Island. Three day cruises leave on Thursdays and Fridays, while four day cruises leave on Sundays and Mondays. The vacation packages offered include accommodations at Walt Disney World resorts, unlimited admission to the theme parks, water parks, Pleasure Island, and Wide World of Sports, and transportation between WDW and Port Canaveral. *Call Tel. 800/951-3532 or surf to www.disneycruise.com to request a brochure or other information.*

Several other cruise lines offer land/sea packages including Disney or Orlando attraction tickets, hotels, and other goodies.

Premier Cruise Lines first came into prominence with their official cruise line status, which allowed them to offer cruise-and-Disney-week packages. Their collaboration with Disney has expired with the advent of the Disney Cruise Line, but they still offer Orlando packages to accompany their three- and four-day cruises. Their Disney packages include Park Hopper passes, a rental car, admission to either Wet 'n Wild or the Kennedy Space Center and accommodations at the Hilton Walt Disney World Resort, Doubletree Guest Suites Resort, Best Western Plaza International, Howard Johnson Inn Maingate East or other area hotels. They also offer packages that include 2-day Universal Escape passes and

Sea World tickets or 4-Park Orlando Flex Tickets in lieu of the Disney passes. *Check them out online at www.premiercruise.com or call 800/990-7770.*

Carnival Cruise Lines and Universal Studios combine to offer cruise and vacation packages for five, six, or seven days, with two to four of those days available on land. Plans include Universal admission or Flex Tickets, rental car, accommodations, and more. *These vacations are offered through Universal's vacation website, www.usevacations.com, or you can call 800/711-0080.*

Celebrity Cruise Lines offers two- and three-night add-on packages that include accommodations plus rental car or airfare and transfers. *Visit www.celebrity-cruises.com or call Tel. 800/437-3111 for information.*

7. GETTING AROUND ORLANDO

BY BUS

LYNX, the Central Florida Regional Transportation Authority, offers inexpensive, efficient travel across the entire metropolitan area, including the tourist corridor. Single ride fares are $1, with transfers costing a dime. Weekly passes are $10, and tickets are available exclusively at Cumberland Farms stores. For the location of the nearest one, call *407/841-8240*. Also check them out online at *www.golynx.com* or call their general info line, *Tel. 407/841-2279*.

BY CAR

Renting a Car

When you plan your trip to WDW, you need to decide whether or not you will rent a car once you get there. You may ask, "Well, do I need to rent a car?" The answer is absolutely, positively, definitely, "sort of."

It is by no means necessary to rent a car when you are in central Florida. If you are staying at a WDW hotel, transportation throughout the property is complimentary and convenient. If you are staying off-property, shuttles are usually available. However, with no car, there is no way other than taxi to get to attractions or restaurants outside of WDW and off the beaten path. Even if you intend to stay inside the Vacation Kingdom for your entire vacation, a car will save you some time. If you are staying in one of the Village Area Resorts, a car will save you as much as a thirty minute wait on both ends of your commute.

A pleasant surprise: rates for car rental in Orlando are among the lowest in the country, possibly due to the destination's popularity. Competition is rampant, and the winner is always the consumer.

Remember that in a worst-case scenario, a collision damage waiver (CDW) can insure against trouble, expense, and hassle later. However, if you pay with a credit card, you already may be insured for it.

If you are renting a car, proceed to the second level of airport's the main passenger facility. Each of the firms listed below either has an office in the airport or close to it in which case, a direct line to the airport will alert them to your arrival and they will pick you up.

MAJOR RENTAL CAR AGENCIES

Alamo	Tel. 800/327-0400 or 407/857-8200, www.goalamo.com
Avis	Tel. 800/331-1212 or 407/825-3754, www.avis.com
Budget	Tel. 800/527-0700 or 407/850-6700, www.budgetrentacar.com
Dollar	Tel. 800/ 800-4000 or 407/583-8000, www.dollarcar.com
Enterprise	Tel. 800/736-8222 or 407/281-3555, www.enterprise.com
Hertz	Tel. 800/654-3131 or 407/859-8400, www.nationalcar.com
Interamerican	Tel. 800/327-1278 or 407/859-0414, www.interamerican.com
National	Tel. 800/227-7368 or 407/855-4170, www.nationalcar.com
Preferred	Tel. 800/526-5499 or 407/855-1330, www.bnm.com/preferred.htm
Rent A Wreck	Tel. 800/841-5371 or 407/438-0300, www.rent-a-wreck.com
Thrifty	Tel. 800/367-2277 or 407/269-1084, www.thrifty.com

Parking

Travelers who have visited New York or Washington often grumble about the city's parking (or lack thereof). If you are visiting Orlando, though, there's only one place where you may have any trouble finding a parking spot, that area being downtown.

All four WDW theme parks have colossal parking lots, which at press time cost $6 to use, free for WDW resort guests. Sea World and Universal also have huge lots, with parking for $6. If you forget where you've parked at any of these lots, speak to a security guard, as they can help point you in the right direction if you remember what time you arrived in the morning.

If you are planning to leave the parks and return later, get your hand stamped before you leave the parks and hang on to your parking pass, so you can return without having to pay again. Also, write down the section in which your car is parked, or you'll have a hell of a time trying to find it. The last thing you want to do at the end of a long, tiring day is to have to wait for all the other cars to pull away before you find yours.

Typhoon Lagoon, Blizzard Beach, and Downtown Disney all have their own large, free parking lots. However, Fort Wilderness and River Country guests must shell out $6, as must CityWalk visitors.

Main Roads

If you are planning to drive around central Florida, it helps to have a general idea of the main traffic arteries on which you'll be travelling. The

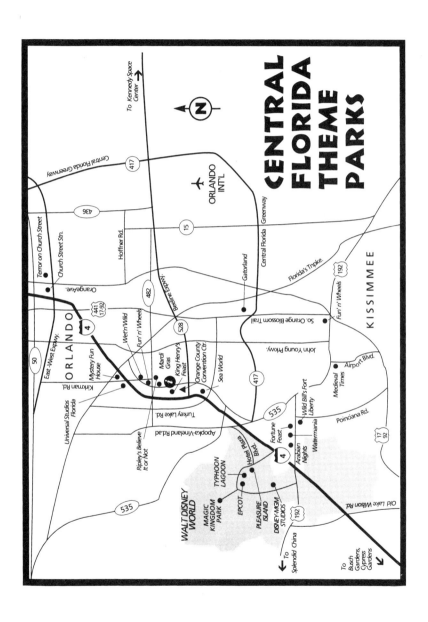

foremost highway in central Florida is Interstate 4. It runs from I-95 at Daytona Beach in the east to Tampa on the west coast. Coming east from Tampa, here are the major exits of tourist interest.

Exit 23 puts you on US 27, by Cypress Gardens and Bok Tower Gardens.

Exit 24C/D will put you in Kissimmee, and in close proximity to the Magic Kingdom and Disney-MGM Studios.

Exit 24E provides access to Kissimmee, Celebration, and the Airport via the Central Florida Greeneway (SR 417).

Exit 25A puts you on US 192 eastbound, towards Kissimmee and Old Town, Medieval Times, Arabian Nights, and Water Mania.

Exit 25B puts you on US 192 westbound, towards the WDW main gate as well as Splendid China.

Exit 26A puts you on SR 536 eastbound, towards Kissimmee, the southernmost tip of International Drive, and the Greeneway.

Exit 26B is your exit for EPCOT Center, Downtown Disney, and Typhoon Lagoon.

Exit 27 lets out onto SR 535, right outside Downtown Disney, close to the Hotel Plaza and the Crossroads of Lake Buena Vista and Vista Center shopping/dining/entertainment complexes.

Exit 27A (exit eastbound only, re-enter westbound only) puts you on Westwood Blvd., close to Sea World and the south end of International Drive, as well as the Central Florida Parkway.

Exit 28 will lead you to the airport and Cape Canaveral via SR 528, the Beeline Expressway. This is also the exit for Sea World, the Convention Center, Mercado, WonderWorks, Pointe Orlando, and the south end of International Drive.

Exit 29 puts you on Sand Lake Drive, between that road's intersections with International Drive and Turkey Lake Road. This exit is convenient to Universal Studios, Islands of Adventure, Citywalk, Wet'n'Wild, Mercado, Florida Mall, and the Official Visitor Center.

Exit 30A puts you right at the northern end of International Drive, right net to the Belz Factory Outlet Mall and Wet'n'Wild.

Exit 30B provides direct access to the Universal complex.

Exit 31 is an interchange with Florida's Turnpike, a toll road stretching from Miami to Ocala.

Exit 33 is the South Orange Blossom Trail, home to Gatorland Zoo, Florida Mall, the easiest route from downtown to the airport, and the home of a huge selection of strip bars and adult bookstores.

Exit 38 is near Church Street Station and other downtown attractions.

Note: the entire tourist corridor on I-4 contains HOV lanes. Access to the left lane in each direction is restricted to vehicles with two or more occupants (during morning rush westbound and afternoon rush east-bound). Chances are that unless you're doing Disney alone, your car will be eligible to ride in the HOV lanes, but just be aware of that restriction. Other main routes include **US 192**, aka W. Irlo Bronson Memorial Highway, the main drag in Kissimmee, connecting hundreds of hotels, inexpensive restaurants, gift shops, and right smack in the middle, the main entrance to Walt Disney World. **International Drive** is another main drag, stretching from Belz Factory Outlet World and Universal Studios at its north end, past Wet'n'Wild, the Convention Center, several shopping/dining/entertainment complexes, and Sea World. Eventually construction on the road will be completed, extending it all the way to US 192 in Kissimmee. At press time the road ended at the intersection of World Center Drive, aka SR 536 (which runs straight into the heart of Disney) and SR 417. Running parallel to I-Drive from the Convention Center to Universal is **Universal Blvd.,** formerly Republic Drive.

SR 535, Apopka-Vineland Road, connects Sand Lake Drive and Lake Buena Vista, with plenty of hotels and traveler services along the way.

Two toll roads offer access to the airport, SR 528, the venerable **Bee Line Expressway**, so named for the straight shot it cuts from I-4 to Daytona Beach, and SR 417, the **Central Florida Greeneway,** which connects Kissimmee, Celebration, and Walt Disney World more directly.

DRIVING DIRECTIONS

Getting from point A to point B has never been easier thanks to online map and direction services such as Mapquest *(www.mapquest.com)* and Yahoo Maps *(maps.yahoo.com)*. Just punch in your starting address (your hotel) and your ending address and customized turn-by-turn directions that are usually spot on accurate.

BY SHUTTLE & LIMO

For those of you choosing not to rent a car, several shuttle limousine services are available from the airport and major hotels every half hour, every hour to less popular destinations. One of the most popular and prominent carriers is **Mears Motor Shuttle**, whose large yellow vans and buses can often be seen crisscrossing the tourist corridor. They operate 24 hours a day, and generally charge $20 to $25 for one-way transportation from the airport to major tourist areas, slightly less for children 12 and under or for round trips. *You can reach Mears at Tel. 800/759-5219 or 407/422-4561, or on the web at www.mears-net.com.*

Limos are another viable option, as they only cost slightly more than taxis ($50-80 per hour), and if you have a large family or group traveling with you it may actually be cheaper than riding a 50-person motor coach. Most take major credit cards and offer toll-free reservation lines.

LIMOUSINES, VANS, & TOWN CARS

A Accell	Tel. 800/482-2694 or 407/298-9677, www.aceluxury.com
A Advantage	Tel. 800/438-4114 or 407/438-8888, www.advantagelimo.com
A-Belais	Tel. 800/350-0228 or 407/354-0228
A-Rainbow	Tel. 800/350-1989 or 407/944-9003
A Selective	Tel. 800/730-0211 or 941-420-1025, www.selectivelimo.com
De Elegance	Tel. 800/258-5466 or 407/522-5466
Orlando Limo	Tel. 888/788-5466 or 407/788-0355, www.orlandolimo.com
Showtime	Tel. 800/329-5466 or 407/329-5466, www.showtimelimo.com

Once you've arrived at your hotel, you still need to arrange transportation to the theme parks. Ask your guest services desk for details, as many hotels are serviced by shuttles on a regular basis, either on a complimentary or paid basis. I strongly recommend that if you're not renting a car, you seek out a hotel with complimentary shuttle service, as it will save you up to $20 a day for a family of four.

Additionally, if you're on International Drive, there's another option open to you. You can use the **I-Ride** trolley system, which stops at over 50 points from Sea World north to Belz Factory Outlet World. The trolleys operate every day from 7am to midnight, every 15 minutes. Single fares are 75 cents, 25 cents for seniors over 65, and free for kids under 12. One, three-, five-, and seven-day passes are available for $2, $3, $5, and $7 respectively and can be purchased from the I-Ride sales office or at dozens of locations along the route, including quite possibly your hotel's guest services desk. *For more information, surf to www.iridetrolley.com or call 407/ 248-9590.*

BY TAXI

Taxis are plentiful in Orlando, if not necessarily cheap. There are only a few companies licensed to pick up passengers at the airport, you can locate them outside the baggage claim areas on Level 2 on the A and B sides of the terminal. Expect to pay $26 to get to International Drive, $32 for Lake Buena Vista, and $40 for Kissimmee and Walt Disney World.

There's lots of companies offering taxi service elsewhere in the Orlando metropolitan area. **Yellow, City,** and **Checker Cab** *(Tel. 407/699-9999, 407/870-0000 in Kissimmee)* make up the Mears Transportation Group, the oldest and largest cab company in the area. Expect prices to run approximately $2.50 for the first mile and $1.50 each additional.

DISNEY TRANSPORTATION

If you're staying in a Walt Disney World resort and aren't planning on leaving WDW, you don't have to worry about getting around, as Disney provides ample transportation between all points of the resort. Their system of buses, elevated monorails, and watercraft is more comprehensive than the mass transit systems of many cities, and is quite easy to use in most cases. Transportation between the theme parks and resorts is generally straightforward, but if you're headed to Downtown Disney or the water parks, transfers may be necessary. It's a good idea to stop by the guest services desk at any of the theme parks or the Ticket and Transportation Center and request a property map, which delineates *exactly* how to get from point A to point B.

Monorail

Disney's monorail is one of the largest systems of its kind in the world, transporting up to 20,000 passengers per hour in each direction, approximately the equivalent of a 22-lane freeway.

There are three monorail lines, each arriving every 15 minutes from 7:30 AM to 11 PM or one hour after the parks close, whichever is later. The **Express** monorail runs between the Ticket and Transportation Center and the Magic Kingdom. The **Local** monorail connects the TTC and Magic Kingdom to the Polynesian, Contemporary, and Grand Floridian resorts. The **Epcot** line connects that theme park to the TTC.

Watercraft

Walt Disney World has one of the largest private fleets in the world, with over 750 ships in tow. The best-known ships in the "navy" are the ferryboats that cross Seven Seas Lagoon between the TTC and Magic Kingdom. The trip takes about five minutes and runs every twelve. If there's a line to board the monorail, the ferry will be quicker.

Additionally, the Magic Kingdom is connected via boat launch to the Polynesian, Contemporary, Grand Floridian, Fort Wilderness, and Wilderness Lodge resorts. The Epcot resorts (Swan, Dolphin, Yacht & Beach Club, Boardwalk) are connected to Epcot and the Disney-MGM Studios by boat as well.

Buses

Clean, convenient, and safe, Disney's buses connect all of the major and minor resort areas, mostly by direct connections. Consult the property map for details on transfers.

8. WHERE TO STAY

Since Disney's arrival on the Orlando scene in October 1971, the number of hotel rooms in the city has soared from 5,900 to over 90,000 today. A good number of these are in WDW itself, several thousand in plain sight of one of the theme parks.

Outside Walt Disney World, there are several main concentrations of hotels and motels. They are found primarily in Kissimmee on and around US 192, in Lake Buena Vista on and around SR 535, and in Orlando on and around International Drive. Of course, many hotels are located elsewhere, but these locations are the most convenient and popular ones for tourists.

WALT DISNEY WORLD RESORTS

There are currently 27 hotels in the land of the Mouse, and between them they pepper the Vacation Kingdom with over 25,000 rooms, suites, villas, and campsites. WDW owned resorts and hotels are more expensive than similar lodgings offsite, and while the All-Star resorts offer a budget alternative, it's still more expensive than its equivalents elsewhere. However, there are advantages to staying in WDW that justify the extra cost to many.

First of all, your kids will get a kick out of actually staying IN Disney World. It might even make your grown-up heart tingle and whet your appetite for what lies inside the admission gates. Second, there's a not-insignificant perk of being able to charge purchases at shops and sit-down restaurants throughout WDW, including the theme parks, and room delivery for your theme park purchases.

Additionally, you gain early entrance to the theme parks every day of the week. WDW Resort guests get into theme parks an hour early on selected mornings. Call *407/824-4321* or check out *www.disneyworld.com* to find out which days are early admission days at which parks. If you're

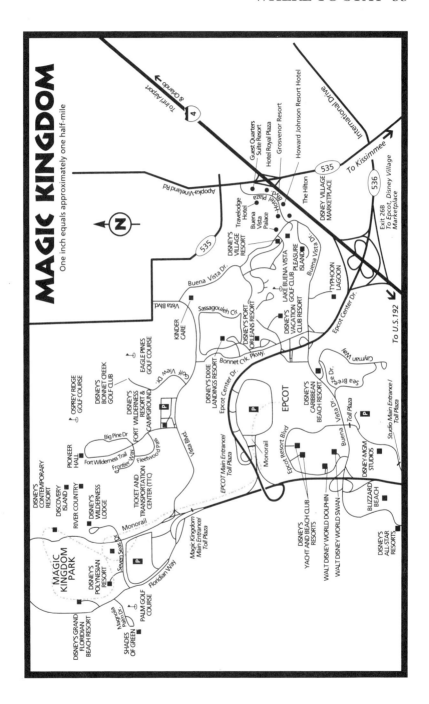

MAGIC KINGDOM

One inch equals approximately one half-mile

staying off-site, it's a good idea to get this information too, as it's best to avoid the theme park that opens early, because it'll be thronged with WDW resort guests all day long. Other advantages of staying onsite include:

- Guaranteed admission to the theme parks even when they're full.
- Access to Unlimited Magic passes and E-Ride Nights tickets, admission media not available to off-site guests. These include unlimited admission to all the Disney theme parks, water parks, Pleasure Island, Disney Quest, and the Wide World of Sports (see below).
- Resort guests can make priority reservations at WDW golf courses up to 60 days in advance.
- Free parking at the theme parks.
- Resort guests can board their pets overnight at the Disney theme park kennels.
- Free wheelchair rental for the length of your stay.

Rooms can accommodate five in most of the resorts. The exceptions are WDW Dolphin, Swan, Caribbean Beach, Port Orleans, Dixie Landings, and All-Star Resorts. Check in is at 3pm and checkout is for 11am for all WDW hotels, except for Old Key West, All-Star Resorts, Boardwalk, and Disney Institute, where it's 4pm. An 11am early check in is available, where you will be able to get all the paperwork out of the way, even if your room is not ready.

RESERVATIONS

It's a good idea to make your reservations as soon as you have your dates selected, as Disney hotels fill quickly. If possible, you should reserve your rooms six months to a year in advance for peak seasons and three to six months early for off-peak seasons. Reservations can be made:

- Online, at Disney's website: *wdw.reservations.disney.go.com*
- By calling the Central Reservations Office at *407/W-DISNEY*. The CRO is open from 7am to 10pm weekdays and 7am to 8pm on weekends.
- Online, at the travel sites mentioned earlier, such as Expedia, Preview Travel, or Travelocity.
- Through your travel agent.
- By mail: *Box 10100, Lake Buena Vista, FL, 32380.*
- At Disney's **Ocala Information Center** on I-75. They offer steep discounts on accommodations, but it's a crapshoot, as you can only make them in person, and the room you want may not be available. *Call 352-854-0770 for details.*

Note that you can not make reservations by calling the hotels themselves, unless it's for that same night.

After you make your reservations, Disney requires a one-night deposit placed within 14 days. Your deposit is refundable if you cancel five or more days before your reservation. *For more information, call 407/W-DISNEY or check out www.disneyworld.com.*

UNLIMITED MAGIC PASS

*The **Unlimited Magic Pass** is a form of Disney admission media available exclusively to WDW Resort guests. It includes unlimited admission to the Magic Kingdom, Epcot, Disney-MGM Studios, Animal Kingdom, Typhoon Lagoon, Blizzard Beach, River Country, Pleasure Island, Disney Quest, and Wide World of Sports for the length of your stay. Prices are as follows:*

Nights/Days	Adult	Child 3-9
1 Night/2 Days	$109	$87
2 Nights/3 Days	$149	$119
3 Nights/4 Days	$193	$154
4 Nights/5 Days	$229	$183
5 Nights/6 Days	$259	$207
6 Nights/7 Days	$289	$231
7 Nights/8 Days	$319	$255

DISNEY'S ALL STAR MOVIES RESORT
DISNEY'S ALL STAR MUSIC RESORT
DISNEY'S ALL STAR SPORTS RESORT

Phone: 407/939-7000 for Movies, 407/939-6000 for Music, 407/939-5000 for Sports. Rates: $74-$104. At a Glance: Three inexpensive, massive, and unfortunately cookie-cutter Disney resorts complexes paying tribute to sports, musical genres, and Disney movies, located near the Animal Kingdom.

As a concept, Disney's All-Star Resorts were intriguing. Resorts that would pay homage to different sports, movie, and music legends. But somewhere between the drawing board and reality, Disney managed to do something I would have thought unthinkable of them: they have created an utterly ordinary product.

The complexes are simply garish. They're neon-colored and adorned with gigantic icons of music, movies, and sports relating to the specific hotel buildings. For example, there are 38-foot surfboards along the side of "Surf's Up," a size 270 cowboy boot on the side of the "Country Fair," and a 35-foot Buzz Lightyear on the "Toy Story" building. Other themes include baseball, basketball, football, and tennis at Sports, calypso,

Broadway, rock, and jazz at Music, and 101 Dalmatians, Mighty Ducks, Herbie the Love Bug, and Fantasia at Movies.

What's really disappointing is not so much that Disney lowered their own standards for excellence in the name of cost-effectiveness, but they did it *three times*. The floor plans and facilities are identical at all three resorts, only with a different coat of paint and different knick-knacks.

These hotels are obviously geared towards budget-conscious families with small children. If you don't fit the demographic, you may want to look elsewhere.

Rooms

There are 1,920 rooms at each of the three resorts, divided into ten buildings each. Each pair of buildings boasts a kitschy themed title and the props to go along with it. As for the rooms, they're the smallest of the Disney empire. They're decorated like children's bedrooms and sleep four in two double beds.

Eat

There are identical food courts at each resort, boasting bakery, grill, pizza and pasta, market, and barbecue stands as well as poolside bars. The food courts are called Intermission (Music), End Zone (Sports), and World Premiere (Movies).

Drink

Each resort has a poolside bar serving beer, wine, and mixed drinks. They are Singing Spirits (Music), Team Spirits (Sports), and Silver Screen Spirits (Movies).

Be Merry

Each resort has two themed swimming pools, shaped like a guitar, piano, surfboard, baseball diamond, the Mighty Ducks' hockey rink, or Sorcerer Mickey, as well as an arcade in each lobby building and a playground. There's also a gift shop at each hotel.

DISNEY'S ANIMAL KINGDOM LODGE

(Coming Spring 2001)

"Maybe the dingo ate your baby." When Disney's newest resort opens next year, you may think this to yourself if you lose sight of your young'uns. But never fear, there are no predators lurking around this 1,307-room safari lodge. However, you will be able to look out of your hotel room and see three savannahs that are home to over 200 species of birds and grazing animals such as zebras, giraffes, and antelopes. The five-story lodge will be themed after an African village, complete with thatched roofs, reed walls, and tribal décor. Amenities will include three restaurants, a swimming pool, arcade, and gift shop. Rates start at $185 for a standard room.

DISNEY'S BOARDWALK INN & VILLAS

Phone: 407/939-5100. Rates: $254 to $580 for rooms, $254 to $1540 for villas. At a Glance: Standard Disney luxury in large rooms and villas in a seaside atmosphere. Some of Disney's most memorable lodgings, conveniently located between Epcot and Disney-MGM.

The newest Disney resort, part of their BoardWalk entertainment complex, harkens back to the days= of boardwalks and cotton candy, evoking images of Asbury Park, New Jersey in its heyday. The atmosphere is comfortable, charming, and relaxed, creating a synergy with the shops, restaurants, and entertainment of the rest of the complex.

Rooms

The 378 rooms of the Inn proper feature two queen-sized or one king-sized bed, ceiling fan, double vanities, and marble bathrooms. Villas include studios with refrigerator, wet bar, and microwave; and one- to three-bedroom villas with full kitchens, private balconies, washer and dryer, and a whirlpool tub.

Eat

There are several restaurants in the Boardwalk complex, including Spoodle's, featuring Mediterranean dishes, the Flying Fish Cafe, serving seafood with an attitude, and the Big River Grille and Brewing Works, WDW's only brew pub.

Drink

The Bellevue Room is a lounge offering butler service in the main lobby of the Inn. An outdoor balcony overlooks Crescent Lake. The re is also a pool bar, Leaping Horse Libations.

Be Merry

There are two pools here in addition to the Muscles and Bustles Health Club, featuring Cybex weightlifting equipment, dumbbells, cardiovascular equipment, and massage services.

DISNEY'S CARIBBEAN BEACH RESORT

Phone: 407/934-3400. Rates: $119 to $164. At a Glance: The original moderately-priced Disney resort, this complex recalls the carefree life of the islands.

This was Disney's first venture into the moderately priced hotel pool, and it's become one of Disney's best-loved resorts. It spans 200 acres, centered around a 42-acre lake. Called Barefoot Bay, it's the focal point for the five villages that make up the guest areas.

The main guest facilities are located at Old Port Royale and the Custom House. The former features stone walls, pirate flags, cannons, tropical birds and flowers and houses the resort's restaurants and shops. The latter is the reception building. Both public buildings are decorated in Caribbean fashion.

One problem with the resort us that it is too big for its own good. Let me explain. The hotel's food court, located at Old Port Royale, can seat a maximum of 500 people at any given time. The hotel has 2,112 rooms. Four people a room, if 10% of the hotel's guests (during peak season) visit at the same time, visitors will have to endure sizable waits for a meal. Another disadvantage of this hotel: rooms can only accommodate four people each. If you have more than that in your family, the least expensive Disney lodgings with room for five or more would be the Village Resort's Club Lake Suites or the trailer homes at Fort Wilderness.

Rooms

The 2,112 rooms here are located in five villages surrounding the lake, each named after a Caribbean island Martinique, Barbados, Trinidad, Aruba, and Jamaica. Each village contains several two-story buildings containing the rooms, laundry facilities, a pool, and a section of beach on the lake. The buildings housing the rooms are soft pastels, the roofs brighter colors crimsons and jade greens. Deeply painted towers look over each village. Each village is designed slightly differently, to give them a slight feel of their namesake islands.

All of the rooms are the same in terms of size and amenities. The only thing differentiating the different-priced rooms is the view. The units here are about 400 square feet, smaller than the rooms at other Disney hotels. The rooms are decorated in soft, light pastels. The beds are covered in pinks and blues, the furniture is oak. Bathrooms here are large and comfortable. Each room has a portable coffee-maker.

Eat

The Captain's Tavern is the only full-service restaurant on the property. The menu includes snow crab legs, prime rib, and marinated chicken. Dinner is the only meal served here.

Diners at all six counter-service restaurants eat in the 500-seat commons of Old Port Royale. Each stand offers children's and health-conscious meals. Reggae music plays in the background and there's a lake view. The Bridgetown Broiler serves chicken fajitas, rotisserie-grilled chicken, and taco salad. For the sweet tooth, the Cinnamon Bay Bakery sells continental breakfasts, fresh croissants, rolls, and other pastries. Cookies and ice cream are also served here.

The Kingston Pasta Shop features a breakfast "buffeteria" and traditional Italian favorites the rest of the day. Soups, salads, and deli sandwiches are sold at Montego's Deli. The menu at Old Port Royale Hamburger Shop features hot dogs, chicken, burgers, hot sandwiches, and soft drinks. The Royale Pizza Shop offers pizza by the slice or the pie plus a medley of specialty pizzas. Fresh fruit is available at the Straw Market Fruit Cart.

Drink

Next to the pool at Old Port Royale is Banana Cabana, a pool bar where drinks and snacks are served. The largest lounge in the resort is the Captain's Tavern, a 200-seat bistro in Old Port Royale. Beer, wine, mixed drinks, and tropical cocktails are purveyed there.

Be Merry

Bicycles and the usual array of Water Sprites, sailboats, and pedalboats can be rented at the Barefoot Bay Bike Works and Boat Yard. Trails for biking or walking meander across the property and around the lake.

A gameroom, Goombay Games, is located at Old Port Royale. For those who prefer their activity more active, there is about a mile and a half of jogging to be had in the form of a promenade circumnavigating the lake. Nature walks are held on Parrot Cay Island, in the middle of Barefoot Bay. There are six swimming pools: one at each of the five villages and another at Old Port Royale.

The pool at Old Port Royale is a work of art: concrete bridges transverse the waters and cannons loom over the water. Also worked into what seems like a recreation of a pirate stronghold are several waterslides. Swimming is also available in Barefoot Bay, as each village sits on a stretch of white sand there.

Shopping

Items sold at Calypso Straw Market include island-themed gifts and Caribbean Beach logo items. The Calypso Trading Post stocks a good variety of sundries as well as character merchandise and souvenirs.

DISNEY'S CONTEMPORARY RESORT

Phone: 407/824-1000. Rates: $214 to $410. At a Glance: A 15-story complex with an a-frame building and two extensions, with a huge concourse of shops, restaurants, and lounges.

This resort gets a decidedly split rating from those who spend their vacations here. There are a few visitors who don't care for the place at all because of future shock. Another major turn-off is that some people think of the white, concrete structure as bleak and sterile. However, this is the favorite of many because it has the most hustle and bustle, which, ironically, is another turn-off to some.

Artist Mary Blair created the towering, 90-foot mural on one of the walls at the Grand Canyon Concourse. The floor-to-ceiling mosaic is composed of over 18,000 hand-painted tiles. The designs, including Indian families, flowers, trees, and a five-legged goat, are inspired by native American art of the Southwest. It is one of the World's more intriguing pieces of art, so you might want to check it out, if you happen to find yourself here.

Rooms

The fifteen-story Tower, the most recognized part of the Contemporary, holds about half of its 1,052 rooms. This is the more expensive section of the hotel, these rooms at a premium because they have the best views. The higher up the structure you go, the finer the view, the bigger the bill. Those on the west side of the Tower overlook the Magic Kingdom, and make a great vantage point for the fireworks, whereas the windows of the more easterly rooms make great panoramas of Bay Lake with Discovery Island and Fort Wilderness as a backdrop.

The downside to staying in the Tower is the speed of the elevators, or more accurately, the lack thereof. The North and South Garden Wings, formerly known as the Bayfront Wings, do not boast such striking views and thus, do not boast such striking tabs. However, those rooms in the Garden Wings farthest from the Tower have stunning views of a white-sand beach and Bay Lake. These vistas rival those from any room in the Tower. Garden View rooms have more of an away-from-it-all and relaxed feeling than those in the Tower.

Rooms in both the Tower and Garden Wings share some common features. The rooms in both sections are fairly large and can accommodate five. All the rooms have a day bed plus either a king or two queen beds. Most have a small terrace or balcony. The bathrooms are large too, and nicely laid out. They each contain double sinks, a bathtub with a shower head, or a bathtub with a separate shower stall.

Note that the Garden Wing rooms listed as offering a "Magic Kingdom view" do look towards the Magic Kingdom, but across the vast parking lot of the hotel.

Eat

The centerpiece of the Contemporary's dining facilities is the spectacular California Grill. Located on the 15th floor of the resort, it boasts a stellar view of the Magic Kingdom and features ever-changing menus including wood-fired meats, sushi, and other California delicacies.

On the fourth floor is the Concourse Steakhouse. All three meals are served. Fare includes such staples as eggs and pancakes for breakfast, soups, salads, burgers, and sandwiches for lunch, and fish, steak, chicken, and ribs for dinner. Reservations are suggested for dinner, though not required. Chef Mickey's Buffet, also on the fourth-floor Concourse, features an all-you-can-eat character buffet for dinner and a daily character breakfast buffet and is considered one of the best buys in the World.

If you get the munchies at 3:48 am or any other desolate (or not-so-desolate) hour of the day, head on over to the Food and Fun Center on the first floor.

Drink

On the Grand Canyon Concourse is the Outer Rim Cocktail Lounge. This appealing bistro serves sandwiches, seafood, and specialty drinks. Next to the marina, the Sand Bar serves mixed drinks, while the Food 'n Fun Center Snack Bar offers beer and wine. Cocktails are also available at the California Grill.

Be Merry

Boat rentals are available at the marina next to the beach. Water Sprites, sailboats, float boats, and pedal boats are available.

Kids go into fits of ecstasy when they see the Food and Fun Center, and even grown-ups tend to sneak down there. More than just a game room, this entertainment complex boasts not only standbys such as pinball and air hockey, but new arcade favorites like Mortal Kombat and VR systems. The rule here is variety. You can find pretty much any game you want to play here. Also, for those without the penchant for video games, this complex offers a movie theater and a snack bar. The facility is open 24 hours a day, and is jumping for a sizable portion of them. All kids staying here will insist a trip here, and most consider it well worth the trip. If you're in the mood for seeing movies, there is a theatre in the Fiesta Fun Center showing Disney flicks three times nightly. A great place to get off your feet for a while.

Those who prefer their entertainment more vigorous can head to the Olympiad Health Club on the third floor of the Tower. This facility is complete with Nautilus gym equipment, saunas, personal whirlpools, and everything else necessary for a decent workout. The club is open to both resort and day guests, and its hours are 9 AM to 6 PM Monday through Saturday. Call 824-3410 for more information.

There is a playground Located near the North Garden Wing and the wading pool.

Swimming opportunities prevail at the Contemporary. There are two swimming pools. One, a 20' by 25' rectangular pool, one of the best-suited WDW pools for lap swimming. The other is a smaller, round pool, deep in the center and shallow in the fringes. There is also a wading pool near the North Garden Wing. On Bay Lake is a small, pleasant white-sand beach. Swimming is allowed in the roped-off areas only and when a lifeguard is on duty.

Just north of the Tower are the Contemporary's six tennis courts. This is the World's major tennis facility, boasting in addition to the courts, three backboards, an automatic ball machine, and a tennis clinic program. The cost for use of the courts is free for WDW resort guests and $12 an hour for day guests. *Reservations can be made 24 hours in advance by calling 824-3578.* There are also volleyball nets set up on the beach. For the adventurous, water skiing and parasailing can be done here. Rentals include boat, driver, and equipment.

Shopping

Bay 'n Beach is a character merchandise outlet. Bay View Gifts has a misleading name. From the title, you would think that this is one of the hundreds of Disney-themed merchandise outlets found in and around Walt Disney World. Not so. This shop features Southwestern and Native American-themed objects, including silk flowers and pottery. The bright, airy, atmosphere and skylights make this a pleasant place to browse.

If you don't want to head to one of the lounges but you still want a drink or a snack, visit the Concourse Sundries and Spirits shop on the Concourse, next to Fantasia. They sell newspapers, magazines, snacks, and liquors, as well as soft drinks. Here, you can get all you need for a cocktail party or a quick nibble. Two adjoining shops on the other side of the Concourse are Contemporary Man and Contemporary Woman. These two shops have no clear boundary, and with today's fashions, that line is even more blurred. The men's store sells casual and beachwear, and rents tuxedos. The women's store sells upbeat fashions and swimsuits.

Fantasia is one of Disney's best-loved films and also the largest shop in this futuristic lodging. This is one in a genre of shops that Disney people refer to as "character shops" shops that sell Disney merchandise and

WDW souvenirs, and has probably the best selection of the merchandise outside the parks and shopping village. Of particular interest is the fiberoptic display on the back wall of the store, depicting the WDW logo, Mickey Mouse, and fireworks. As far as the wares are concerned, t-shirts, postcards, stuffed animals, figurines, and other Disney memorabilia are available.

Kingdom Jewels, Ltd. is across from Concourse Spirits and Sundries and next to Contemporary Man. Here, baubles of precious stones and things that glitter tantalize both men and women. The Racquet Club sells character merchandise, sports apparel, and specialty items.

The Contemporary Hair Styling Salon is located on the third floor of the Tower. Here, among the list of available services are manicures, shampoos, setting, coloring, and waving.

Services

A business center with personal computers, telefax machines, copiers, and secretarial service is located on the first floor. Delta Airlines has a counter in the lobby. The Travel and Tour Desk offers information on public transit, airline reservations, auto rental, and tours to other area attractions. A Western Union desk is also located here.

DISNEY'S CORONADO SPRINGS RESORT

Phone: 407/939-1000. Rates: $119 to $164. At a Glance: A moderately priced resort themed after the travels of the conquistadors.

Disney's most recent resort addition, in late 1997, is the Coronado Springs Resort, themed after Francisco de Coronado's travels from Northern Mexico to the American southwest. The 1,967 moderately priced rooms are flanked by colorful plazas, palm-shaded courtyards, and a rocky shoreline surrounded by pyramids. A Mayan pyramid towers over the themed pool area. There's also 95,000 square feet of meeting space.

Rooms

The rooms are furnished with two double beds or one king sized bed, and the average room measures about 314 square feet.

Eat

The Maya Grill offers Mayan cuisine and breakfast daily. The Pepper Market Food Court features American cuisine, Tex-Mex, and baked goods.

Drink

Siesta's is the Coronado Springs pool bar. Francisco's is a 200-seat lounge offering hors d'oeuvres, snacks, and regional specialties.

Be Merry

The Jumping Bean Arcade in the main building and the Iguana Arcade by the pool provide a contemporary selection of video, pinball, driving, and air hockey games. The "Dig Site" feature pool area includes a pyramid, a playground, a water slide, a kiddie pool, and a 22-person jacuzzi. Three quiet pools are also available. There's also a health club, a walking/jogging trail, the Esplanade, surrounding Lago Dorado, and rental boats and beach volleyball.

DISNEY'S DIXIE LANDINGS RESORT

Phone: 407/934-6000. Rates: $119 to $164. At a Glance: A large, moderately priced resort featuring over 2,000 Plantation- and Bayou-style rooms in the Downtown Disney area.

The resort is composed of 2,048 rooms (bigger than all the WDW resorts but the Caribbean) built in two distinct architectural styles, Bayou and Plantation. The Plantation rooms, closer to the entrance, are dignified and stately, while Bayou rooms have a decidedly rugged feel to them.

The main pubic facilities are located in the Colonel's Cotton Mill, a building designed as a steam ship. Among the facilities here are the registration, restaurant, food court, and gift shop. The centerpiece of the recreational facilities is Ol' Man Island, a 3 1/2 acre amusement island with a pool, playground, and fishing hole.

Rooms

The rooms are all the same in terms of size and comfort, only the architecture and decor differ. Rooms at both types of structure share common features in terms of amenities but everything from the carpeting to the beds to the ceiling fans has its own specific flavor.

Antebellum-style Magnolia Bend Plantation rooms are found in elegant estate homes with cream-colored siding and pale grey-shingled roofs. Brick chimneys and hanging flowers accentuate the Southern feel. Balconies with elaborate railings and porches with wooden benches give an impression of lazy satisfaction.

The Alligator Bayou buildings are rugged and scruffy in their appearance, their tin roofs and weathered wood siding a sharp foil to the elegance of the Plantation. Furnishings here carry a distinct bayou flavor, the walls a simple ivory with wood trim, wood and tin armoires, and tin lamps. The bedposts are textured and colored like logs. The bathrooms have ample space, and the double pedestal sinks are a nice touch.

Eat

The hotel's full-service eatery, Boatwright's Dining Hall, was fashioned after a boatmaking warehouse. The table-service restaurant features Cajun specialties and Southern dishes. If you'll notice, the carpeting was custom-made to look like wood chips.

The main dining facility, however, is a 480-seat food court, the Captain's Cotton Mill. The first of the restaurants here is Acadian Pizza 'n' Pasta, offering fresh pizza with an assortment of toppings. Pasta dishes are also sold here. If you wish, pizza is available for delivery. Bleu Bayou Burgers and Chicken sells a variety of burgers as well as fried and grilled chicken. The Cajun Broiler serves Cajun dishes and broiled chicken. The Riverside Market and Deli serves deli fare and snack food. Pastries, fresh breads, and sticky buns are available at Southern Trace Bakery.

Drink

The Cotton Co-op is modeled after a cotton exchange and serves specialty drinks and hors d'oeuvres. Next to the pool at Ol' Man Island is Muddy Rivers, a poolside lounge serving snacks and drinks. Open during pool hours.

Be Merry

There are five swimming pools scattered between the parishes, as well as Ol' Man Island, which consists of a themed pool, a spa, and a wading pool. On the island as well are a playground and a fishing hole, stocked with catfish.

You can bike along the footpaths connecting the parishes. Bike and boat rentals are available at Dixie Levee. A gameroom, the Medicine Show Arcade, is located at the Colonel's Cotton Mill, offering a small selection of electronic Games. The footpaths between the parishes are perfect for jogging.

Shopping

Located in the Colonel's Cotton Mill, Fulton's General Store offers character merchandise, sundries, and souvenirs.

DISNEY'S FORT WILDERNESS RESORT & CAMPGROUND

Phone: 407/824-2900. Rates: $35 to $74 for campsites, $179 to $275 for Wilderness homes and cabins. At a Glance: Disney's 780-acre campground and resort, complete with a lakeside beach, horses, bike trails, and organized recreational activities. All this and a 5 minute boat ride from the Magic Kingdom

This 780-acre tract is only a stone's throw from the Magic Kingdom, but it seems a million miles away. Many visitors to WDW are either are unaware of its existence or believe it to be associated with Frontierland in the Magic Kingdom.

The resort is set amid cypress and pine, its campsites and trailers nestled along placid canals or on the fringes of majestic forest. And while camping out can have a negative connotation to some, "roughing it" here can be completely pleasant, given the wealth of recreational facilities available at Fort Wilderness. Or, for those of you who would rather not be such a close partner with the Great Outdoors, trailer homes with accomodations not unlike those at the Village Resort are available for about the same price as Club Suites at the Village.

Campsites

The 21 camping loops at Fort Wilderness contain 827 Campsites. The size of the sites ranges from 25 to 65 feet in length. The sites are rented to either tenters or RV users. Each site has a 110/220-volt electrical outlet, barbecue, and a picnic table. The majority of the sites have hookups for sanitary-disposal units. But each of the loops has a comfort station with restrooms, showers, phones, ice machines, and laundry facilities. Each site can accommodate up to 10 people for a single fee.

The loops are indicated by number: 100 to 500 are closest to the beach, Settlement Trading Post, and Pioneer Hall. Loops 1700 to 2100 are in the deeper concentrations of forest and have much more privacy.

Fleetwood Trailers

Non-campers are accommodated at Fort Wilderness just as easily as the outdoorsmen. For those who would like all the advantages of a hotel plus the serenity of a campground, Disney offers 407 rental Fleetwood Trailer Homes. Not what you would expect, these are very similar in size and furnishings to a villa at Disney Village Resort.

There are two varieties of trailers: the first can hold four people in a double bed in the bedroom and a sofa bed in the living area. The other trailers can accommodate four adults and two children in a double bed, a bunk bed, and a pulldown. The trailers all have a good-sized living room and a bathroom laid out like at the villas.

A major advantage is the presence of kitchens in every trailer, complete with dishes, cookware, and other equipment – plus color TV and daily maid service. The kitchens here offer the option of being able to cook your own meals. This saves time and money, and you can usually have somewhat better food than at the parks. Because of their size and reasonable price, these make good choices for families who want something more than the typical-sized hotel room.

Eat

Most of the Fort Wilderness patrons choose to cook their own food, especially those staying in the trailers. However, if you don't want to cook, there are several places you can visit for edibles. Fort Wilderness's foremost eatery is the Trail's End Buffet, also inside the confines of Pioneer Hall. It serves large breakfasts, including such Western staples as grits and biscuits and gravy, as well as country fare, pot pies, and fish the other two meals. Pizza is served here nightly starting from 9 until 11. They host a Southern buffet on Fridays and an Italian buffet Saturday nights.

Crockett's Tavern is the other full-service restaurant in Pioneer Hall. It serves steaks, ribs, chicken, and appetizers in a rustic atmosphere filled from wall to wall and floor to ceiling with Davy Crockett memorabilia.

The Hoop-Dee-Doo Revue is one of Disney's best-loved dinner shows. There are three shows daily, at 5, 7:30, and 10. The food is unlimited ribs, chicken, corn on the cob, and strawberry shortcake. The entertainment is top-notch, a dazzling production full of humor, song, and dance. The Beach Shack, located on the Bay Lake coastline, sells chips, sandwiches, ice cream, and other snack fare. In the Meadow Recreational Complex is the Meadow Snack Bar, a seasonal establishment serving the usual array of snack fare.

Drink

There is a full-service lounge at Crockett's Tavern.

Be Merry

There are a few baseball/softball diamonds near the bike barn. These are open to WDW resort guests only. Equipment is not provided, you must bring your own. Basketball courts are scattered throughout the camping loops. These are available at no cost and solely to WDW resort guests. Bikes are available for rental: tandems, dirt bikes, and others. Visit the Bike Barn to charter one.

On Bay Lake at the north end of the campground is situated a large marina, offering boat rentals, specifically Water Sprites, pontoon boats, float boats, pedal boats, and sailboats. Near the Meadow Trading Post, a nightly campfire program complete with Disney movies, cartoons, sing-alongs, and an appearance of Chip and Dale. Free, available to WDW resort guests only.

Canoes can be rented for use rowing down the serene Fort Wilderness canals at the Bike Barn.

The large beach on Bay Lake is a great spot to view the Electrical Water Pageant. It passes around 9:45 PM nightly. Guided excursions into Bay Lake for fishing are available. The trips are two hours long and include gear, refreshments, boat, and guide. Note that fishing on your own is not allowed in Bay Lake. However, it is permitted in the canals of Fort Wilderness without a guide. Largemouth bass are the catch in both places. Those with a yen to fish in the canals but no equipment can purchase it at the Trading Posts or rent the poles and lures at the Bike Barn. No license is required.

Fort Wilderness boasts a fitness and jogging trail, 2.3 miles long. There are exercise stations situated at a rate of about one every quarter mile. This is a draw for guests at all the Magic Kingdom resorts. HINT: The best time to use the facilities is early in the morning or around dusk. Fort Wilderness possesses two gamerooms named after the two greatest frontiersmen of all time. Daniel Boone has his arcade in Pioneer Hall, while Davy Crockett's can be found at the Meadow Trading Post.

If you're one of those deprived souls who hasn't been on a hayride recently, here's your chance. The wagon departs from Pioneer Hall and heads to Bay Lake before returning. The trip takes about an hour; tickets are available from the host. Allergy sufferers are exempt. Ever been told to take a hike? This is among the best places in the World to do so, on the Wilderness Swamp Trail, a mile-and-a-half-long path that offers picturesque views of Bay Lake and a huge forest of cypress. The trail is located near Marshmallow Marsh, at the northern end of the campground.

Horseback enthusiasts also get what they want here. Organized trips through the campground leave from the center of the campground four times in the morning and early afternoon hours of each day. The rides are slow-paced (sorry, no galloping) and offer great vistas of the Florida wilderness. Riding knowledge is not required. Facilities for a round of horseshoes are scattered throughout the property.

One of the nightly events at the Fort Wilderness Resort (only during the summer, though) is the Marshmallow Marsh Excursion, an event including a marshmallow roast, a canoe trip down one of the canals, and a hike to the beach, where the Electrical Water Pageant can be seen. Mosquito repellant is a must.

Near Pioneer Hall sits a small petting farm, which houses animals such as goats, a miniature bull, rabbits, sheep, and chickens. If you arrive at the Hoop-Dee-Doo Revue early, you might want to pass a little time here.

Swimming options are plentiful here. There are two swimming pools for starters, plus a beach on Bay Lake 175 feet wide and longer than a football field. Swimming is allowed in the roped-off areas only. Fort Wilderness also plays host to River Country, WDW's older, smaller, but more aesthetic swimming park. This, however, requires a separate admission fee.

Recently, two tennis courts were added to the list of amenities of Fort Wilderness. They are lit at night, and are located at the Meadow Recreation Complex, behind the Meadow Trading Post. Tetherball and volleyball courts are scattered throughout the resort.

Water skiing can be done out of the Fort Wilderness marina but you must call the Contemporary's marina and make reservations 2 to 3 days in advance.

In addition to the "real" amenities, Fort Wilderness has a few unique sights worth finding. One of them is the blacksmith shop where the horses of Walt Disney World get their footwear. The blacksmith is usually on hand for a time every day to answer questions and speak about this profession. Occasionally, you will be able to watch him shoe the animals' hooves.

The canals of Fort Wilderness hold a particular beauty to them, a very different kind of beauty than what Disney dishes up in the parks.

Then there's something called the Lawn Mower Tree: A tree that managed to somehow tangle itself up in the workings of, well, a lawn mower. Or possibly the other way around... In any case, it has kept on growing (the tree, not the lawn mower) since then and is one of Fort Wilderness's oddities. You can see it as you walk towards the marina. A poem sits by the tree. It reads: Too long did Billy Bowlegs/Park his reel slow mower/Alas, one warm and sunny day/Aside a real fast grower. Strange. Very strange.

The horses who pull trolleys up Main Street in the Magic Kingdom are kept at the Tri Circle D Ranch here on their days off. You might happen to see a horse with its colts if you're lucky.

Shopping

Sundries, souvenirs, character merchandise, specialty items, snacks, deli sandwiches, and groceries can be purchased at the Meadow and Settlement Trading Posts.

DISNEY'S GRAND FLORIDIAN BEACH RESORT

Phone: 407/824-3000. Rates: $299 to $645. At a Glance: Disney's premier lodging experience, this is a Victorian hotel evoking thoughts of the turn of the century luxury hotels of Palm Beach. This hotel is located on the monorail line.

Walt Disney's father came to Florida around the turn of the century and opened up a hotel in Daytona Beach. That Victorian failed. Walt Disney's company came back and in 1988, opened up a grand hotel on Seven Seas Lagoon. This Victorian will not meet the same fate.

The Grand Floridian was the first part of the intense expansion of WDW's guest areas, opening its doors in August 1988. The facilities offer all the pleasant little quirks of the hotels of Florida's heyday, such as wide verandahs, wicker chairs, ceiling fans, latticework, red-gabled roofs, brick chimneys, turrets, and towers. A white-sand beach is touched on the east by the Seven Seas Lagoon.

But Disney is not living in the past. That's obviously demonstrated by the presence of a monorail station. This hotel also plays host to restaurants, lounges, a health club, and other modern amenities. In the main building is the Grand Lobby, a 15,000 square-foot area, five stories high. This structure houses stained-glass domes, an aviary, potted palms, and sparkling crystal chandeliers. A vintage open-cage elevator links the main level with the shops and eateries on the second floor.

Rooms

The 901 rooms reflect the fact that this is the Vacation Kingdom's most costly resort. They are decked out lavishly, with light oak armoires and furnishings, Victorian woodwork, ceiling fans, and marble-topped sinks. The walls are painted in delicate green and salmon.

The main building embodies 61 concierge rooms and 34 suites. Five lodge buildings surround it. Each is four or five stories high, and all told, they contain 624 standard-sized rooms and 176 smaller "attic" rooms. The standard rooms measure about 400 square feet, about the size of a two-car garage. Each of the rooms has a pair of queen beds and a sofa bed, and most of them have terraces. Each room also has a private pantry with sundries available for a nominal fee.

All of the suites and concierge rooms are located on the third, fourth, and fifth floors of the main wing. Access to the third story and up is limited solely to those staying on those floors. The suites have a parlor and one to three bedrooms. Located in the turrets of the third through fifth floors are honeymoon suites, each of which boasts views out five windows.

The third through fifth floors are the concierge levels. Among the amenities exclusively available to those staying on these levels are wet bars in each room; a concierge desk offering services such as rapid check-in and check-out, information, and reservations; access to the private fourth floor sitting area, serving daily continental breakfast; and the private lounges on the fourth and fifth floor.

Eat

The finest food in Walt Disney World can be savored at the Grand Floridian at Victoria and Albert's. This dining room has won its share of awards, including being named to the list of Florida's Top 100 Restaurants, one of three WDW establishments to achieve that distinction. This restaurant has a prix fixe policy, a tab of $100 per person. Another idiosyncrasy of Victoria and Albert's is the lack of printed menus. The specialties change daily, and usually include entrees of veal, red meat, fish, lamb, and fowl. The dinner includes choice of soups, salads, and desserts, all of the latter sinfully delicious, including souffles of chocolate or berries. There is a lengthy wine list. Only dinner is served, reservations and jackets are necessary.

The hotel's largest restaurant, Flagler's, offers food with splashes of French and Italian influence. All meals are kicked off by a complimentary appetizer. The restaurant overlooks the marina and serves elegant seafood and beef dishes. If you're lucky, you'll be here when the waiters and waitresses break into song, which has been known to happen on occasion.

Narcoosee's is an interesting restaurant, to say the least. The place is octagonal and located right on the fringe of the sugar-sand beach. The kitchen is open and airy, and the fare focuses on seafood, but also includes steak, lamb chops, veal chops, and grilled chicken. There is nightly entertainment.

The biggest attraction of 1900 Park Fare is not the food but the surroundings in which patrons dine. The centerpiece is Big Bertha, a century-old band organ. Mary Poppins and her friends preside over the character breakfast, and at dinner, Chip and Dale's Rescue Rangers entertain. The food is utterly American – seafood, salads, vegetables, breads, pork, lamb, and sirloin. The menu changes weekly.

Next to the pool is the Gasparilla Grill and Games, a take-out, self-service snack bar. Continental breakfast is served here in the morning, hot dogs, burgers, and chicken the rest of the day. Open 24 hours. The Grand Floridian Cafe also serves a character breakfast with Mary Poppins. The fare here is pure South. Lunch and dinner choices include catfish fillet with bell pepper relish, Cajun burgers, and honey-dipped fried chicken.

Drink

Overlooking the garden and pool is the Garden View Lounge, a pleasant little place serving specialty drinks and afternoon tea. Mizner's Lounge pays homage to the father of Palm Beach architecture. Quiet and friendly. Narcoosee's (see above) serves beer in mugs, half-yards, and yards (as in three feet!). The name of this peculiar form of drink service is Yards of Beer. The Summerhouse is the Floridian's pool bar.

Be Merry

An arcade makes up the latter part of Gasparilla Grill and Games. The Floridian's marina, the Captain's Shipyard, offers all sorts of boats for rent. Near Gasparilla Grill and Games sits a playground.

The hotel's health club, St. John's offers an exercise room complete with the latest equipment, steam rooms, lockers, and massages. There is a nicely landscaped, 275,000 gallon swimming pool here, as well as a powder-sand beach on Seven Seas Lagoon. Water skiing can be done here as well. Also, the Floridian has two clay tennis courts.

Shopping

On the second floor, Commander Porter's sells menswear. Also on the second level is M. Mouse Mercantile, a character shop. And you can guess what the "M" stands for. Sandy Cove, located on the first floor, is a good place to pick up sundries and souvenirs. Women can purchase articles of clothing and jewelry at Summer Lace.

The Ivy Trellis Barber and Beauty Shop is a full-service salon offering services from haircuts and coloring perms to pedicures.

Services

A business center with PCs, typing service, fax machine, and copier is located on the first floor of the convention center.

DISNEY'S OLD KEY WEST RESORT

Phone: 407/934-5000. Rates: $229 to $1050. At a Glance: Capturing the ambiance of a quaint turn-of-the-century retreat, this resort features spacious studios and villas.

Disney's Old Key West resort features some of the most spacious accommodations on the property, from studios to three-bedroom grand villas. This resort is located at the Downtown Disney area and offers transportation there via pleasant pontoon boats.

When these units are not being used as timeshare properties, they will be rented out as hotel rooms. *For more information on membership, call 800/ 800-9100.*

Rooms

The exteriors of the buildings are done in grays and pastel greens, with tin roofs, back porches, gazebos, gingerbread, and latticework abounding. Its architecture is somewhat reminiscent of the Yacht Club Resort.

The one, two, and three-bedroom vacation homes are all decorated in a whimsical Key West motif, pinks and light greens dominating the color schemes here, the furniture bleached wood. amenities of the units include ceiling fans, full kitchens (including microwave oven, china, flatware, and cookware), TVs with VCR, hardwood floors, whirlpool tubs in the master suite, and full-sized washers and driers. Windows are large and take advantage of the environment: each room has a view of either the forest, water, or golf course.

Eat

Olivia's Cafe features dining indoors and outdoors on a terrace and offers Key West specialties like conch fritters, homemade French fries, and Key Lime white chocolate mousse. The cuisine here is seasoned with spices straight from the restaurant's herb garden.

The poolside snack bar Good's Food to Go offers the usual lineup of fast food, but the house specialty is conch fritters.

Drink

The Turtle Shack offers pina coladas, daquiris, sandwiches, salads, and hot dogs. Overlooking the island-themed swimming area is The Gurgling Suitcase, an open-air bar serving a variety of mixed drinks, beer, and wine.

Be Merry

An original feature of the Resort, the Clubhouse, is themed after a Key West retreat, with hardwood floors, historical photos, and Papa's

---

GETTING DISCOUNTS AT DISNEY HOTELS

With the addition of the tacky but inexpensive All-Star Resorts, the argument that Disney hostelries are too expensive is now moot. However, a myriad of discounts can still be had for the higher-end hotels, but only by those who know how to get them.

• Off-Peak Travel: Rates during off-peak seasons can be as much as $40 less than during peak seasons.

• AAA Discounts: Disney has periodically offered AAA members a 15% discount on Disney resort rates and 20% off package deals.

• Magic Kingdom Club: Many companies, credit unions, and organizations offer membership in the Magic Kingdom Club as a fringe benefit. Members get up to a 30% discount on hotels plus a small discount on admission media, so ask your employer if it is offered. If it is not, you can get a Magic Kingdom Club Gold Card, which entitles the holder to a 2-year subscription to the Disney News, savings at Disney hotels and attractions, and savings on various cruise lines, Delta Airlines, and National Car Rental. The Gold Card is available for $49, call 800/248-7833 or write Magic Kingdom Club Gold Card, P.O. Box 3850, Anaheim, CA, 92803-3850.

• Ocala Information Center: The Disney information center on I-75 offers discounts of up to 43% to visitors who don't already have hotel accommodations. The number of available units depends on season and hotel, but this is a risky way to get discounts during peak seasons, because rooms may not be available. Information: 904/854-7040.

• Travel Agents: Travel agents are a good source of information on money-saving deals and packages that may not be otherwise known.

Den: a comfortable reading room with bookshelves filled with the works of authors who once inhabited Key West.

Slappy Joe's is a health club complete with massage, free weights, exercise equipment, and sauna.

Bicycles, boats, balls, beach towels, and "anything that isn't nailed down" can be rented at Hank's Rent 'N Return.

An island-themed swimming pool is located here. Volleyball can be played at poolside. There are shuffleboard courts here as well. Two tennis courts are available for use.

The younger set seems to gravitate to the Electric Eel Gameroom.

Shopping

There is a well-stocked general store here.

DISNEY'S POLYNESIAN RESORT

Phone: 407/824-2000. Rates: $274 to $530. At a Glance: A South Seas-themed resort complex with restaurants, lounges, and general ambiance that carry out the Pacific theme. Unquestionably the best-loved of Disney resorts, it's located right on the monorail and a stone's throw from the Ticket and Transportation Center hub

This hotel's kitschy motto, "Aitea-Paitea," means "Tomorrow will be another day just like today." Few would take objection to that sentiment. This hotel has the greatest popularity among repeat visitors. That, combined with its convenience, elegance, and the contented atmosphere that pervades the hotel, makes this one of the first Disney hostelries to sell out. About 60% of the Polynesian's guests have stayed there before. This should tell you something about the hotel.

As is the case with Disney, lobbies here are not really lobbies. This one is known as the Great Ceremonial House. Most of the hotel's public areas are located here, and as you might expect, this is the focal point of the resort. Disney grabs your attention the minute you walk into any of their lobbies, and they certainly accomplish that here. Most of the Poly's lobby is covered by a vast, three-story garden. Amid 250 square feet of indoor rainforest are orchids, trees, ferns, and in the center, a fountain themed after a waterfall. Volcanic rocks and tropical plants rim the wellspring, and the climate of the lobby allows the lush vegetation to be in bloom, regardless of when you visit.

Situated on either side are the eleven two- and three-story "longhouses" where the hotel's rooms are located. The longhouses are identified by names of Polynesian islands.

Rooms

The 855 rooms are located in eleven longhouses, all of which lie alongside the Great Ceremonial House. Most of the rooms have either a patio or balcony, offering varying panoramas. The rooms are priced according to view, and the scale goes from longhouse view (least expensive), monorail, garden, and pool to marina view (most expensive). Features shared by all the guest rooms are two queen-sized beds and a sleep sofa, which accommodate five. The largest rooms are in the Oahu longhouse. Non-smoking and adjoining rooms are available.

On its new concierge level, the Polynesian Resort offers a program similar to the one at the Contemporary, called Royal Polynesian. The service includes free valet parking, special check-in and check-out privileges, juice and coffee in the morning, soft drinks and snacks in the afternoon, and a special concierge on duty to serve the concierge guests between 8am and 9pm. These are located in the Tonga, Moorea, and Samoa longhouses.

Eat

Ohana at Papeete Bay recently replaced the dated Papeete Bay Verandah. The centerpiece of the prix fixe, family-style Polynesian restaurant is a 16-foot-long open fire pit where guests can watch their meals being grilled.

Disney doesn't miss a trick. At the Luau Cove, they take advantage of the fancy-tickling atmosphere of the Polynesian and blend it with dancing, music, and those omnipresent Disney characters to create one of the World's most popular dinner shows, the Polynesian Revue (also called the Luau). The entertainers, many of whom have studied at the Polynesian Cultural Center in Hawaii, are top-notch and the food, although less than authentic, is tasty.

The Coral Isle Cafe is located around the corner from Papeete Bay Verandah on the second floor of the Great Ceremonial House. This is pretty much a customary coffee shop, serving good, unpretentious meals. One exception is their banana-stuffed French toast, which is nearly legendary among Disneyphiles. Snack Isle, a seasonal snack bar by the pool, offers sandwiches, pizza, and continental breakfast.

On the lobby level of the Great Ceremonial House is Captain Cook's Snack and Ice Cream Company. This small establishment serves continental breakfasts and burgers, hot dogs, snacks, and ice cream later on.

Drink

The Barefoot Bar, next to the pool, serves soda, beer, and mixed drinks. The newly remodeled Tambu Lounge is a cozy bistro adjoining

Ohana. Frozen fruit drinks, espresso, cappucino, appetizers, and wild mixed drinks are served here.

Be Merry

Boat rentals are available at the Polynesian's marina on Seven Seas Lagoon. Sailboats, Water Sprites, pedal boats, flote boats, and outrigger canoes can be rented. Next to the Tangaroa Snack Isle is the hotel's gameroom, Moana Mickey's Fun Hut. This facility is smaller than the Fiesta Fun Center, but is still a formidable diversion for the younger set. There is a large and well-planned playground by the Great Ceremonial House.

The Polynesian has one of the World's nicest swimming areas: the Swimming Pool Lagoon. This lushly landscaped, free-form pool is bordered by a set of boulders that join to form a waterslide. A pathway crossed by a waterfall leads to the top of the slide. Also, the East Pool, which is by the Oahu, Tonga, Hawaii, Bora Bora, and Maui longhouses; and the beach on Seven Seas Lagoon offer opportunities for those with water on their minds. Water skiing, boats, equipment, and drivers can be found here.

Shopping

Robinson Crusoe Esq. sells mens' and boys' swimwear and casuals. Guests can find a nice assortment of childrens' clothing and accessories at Kanaka Kids. Sundries and supplies are available at News from Civilization. Here, in addition to tobacco, film, newspapers, magazines, and gifts, you can buy a grass skirt or Florida conch shells.

Outrigger's Cove is the Polynesian equivalent of Bay View Gifts. Items with a South Seas flair are sold here, including gifts and souvenirs. For women, Polynesian Princess is the place to stop for bathing suits, resortwear, and accessories. Food, beer, wine, and spirits can be purchased at the Grog Hut. Trader Jack's is the place for Disney merchandise and gift items.

DISNEY'S PORT ORLEANS RESORT

Phone: 407/934-5000. Rates: $119 to $164. At a Glance: Another moderately-priced Disney resort, Port Orleans has all the charm and romance of New Orleans' French Quarter, a boat's ride away from Downtown Disney.

This 1,008-room resort teems with the taste of the Delta City, with its wrought-iron railings and ubiquitous plantings. The entrance driveway leads to the center of the resort, Port Orleans Square. Located here are the main building (the Mint), the food court (Sassagoula Floatworks and Food Factory), Bonfamilles Cafe, and a shop.

The Mint, whose architecture was actually based on that of a mint (circa 1900), has a vaulted ceiling under which all the check-in and check-out facilities are located. The desks are designed like antiquated bank teller windows. Visible behind the reception desk is a mural depicting a Mardi Gras street scene. The hotel has a more urban feel to it than the Dixie Landings, and the property is transversed by streets, complete with road signs, black street lanterns, and tightly packed garden areas and brick and wrought iron gates.

Rooms
Located in seven three-story buildings are the 1,008 rooms of the Port Orleans Resort. The structures housing the units are all different, their hues range from cream, pink, and yellow to purple and blue. The wrought iron railings surrounding each building vary in design. Two double beds in each room sleep up to four people. Some king-size beds are also available. The rooms are all the same in terms of space and comfort, the rate system is based on view.

Eat
The Bonfamilles Cafe, located near the Sassagoula Floatworks and Food Factory, serves steak, seafood, and Creole dishes in a relaxed, table-service atmosphere. The casual setting is achieved thanks in part to the presence of courtyards, paddle fans, brick, wood, tile, and colorful fabrics. Specialties of the house include a Creole skillet breakfast, a Mardi Gras combo, shrimp and crawfish remoulade, and barbecue oysters.

The food court here, the Sassagoula Floatworks and Food Factory, seats 300. Basin Street Burgers and Chicken sells a varied selection of burgers, plus deli items and batter-fried chicken. Jacques Beignet's Bakery, another food-court location, serves ice cream, pastries, and "N'awlins-style" beignets. One of the World's better selections of Creole fare, the King Creole Broiler serves spit-roasted chicken with jambalaya and other Cajun dishes. Pizza and pasta, as well as other Italian specialties, are available at the Preservation Pizza Company. Delivery is also available.

Drink
The Scat Cat's Club is a spirited bar serving drinks and hors d'oeuvres with entertainment several nights a week. Mardi Grogs is a poolside bar serving specialty drinks and popcorn, hot dogs, and pretzels.

Be Merry
The Port Orleans' themed swimming pool, Doubloon Lagoon, is a beguiling place. Scales, the sea serpent whose body pokes out of the ground in several places and whose tongue serves as a waterslide,

apparently has an infatuation with jazz music, and is entertained by his buddies, the alligator musicians performing on the clam shell in the center of a nearby fountain.

Boat rentals including pedal boats, rowboats, canopy boats, and flote boats are available at Port Orleans Landing. Located at Port Orleans Square is a gameroom, South Quarter Games.

Shopping

At Port Orleans Square is the resort's only shop, Jackson Square Gifts and Desires, which sells character merchandise, clothing, and sundries.

DISNEY'S WILDERNESS LODGE

Tel. 407/824-3200. Rates: $184 to $245. At a Glance: Turn-of-the-century National Park lodges are lovingly recreated in this 728-room masterpiecece.

Do not make the mistake of confusing the Wilderness Lodge, a full-service resort hotel, with Fort Wilderness, a campground facility. People who shy from this hotel because of the similarity in syntax are missing out on one of the premier lodging experiences on the East Coast.

Secluded from the hustle and bustle of the theme parks, it is even segregated from the ultra-modern, urban sight of the Contemporary Resort by a bank of thick vegetation. The grounds are strewn with pines and granite and punctuated by brooks, geysers, and color pools.

The centerpiece of the resort is Silver Creek, which runs from a fountain in the main lobby, down a waterfall, into the swimming pool, and down to the shore of Bay Lake. To keep from contaminating the water in the pool and the lake, there are actually three separate water systems, concealed by the magic of Disney.

The lobby is breathtakingly magnificent and homey at the same time, featuring a six-story atrium decorated with totem poles and strewn with porches and libraries for guests to discover. Your attention is immediately drawn to the 82-foot tall, three-sided fireplace in the center of the atrium. It represents 2 billion years of geology with fossilized animal and plant life throughout the colorful rock strata, re-created in the same proportions that occur in the Grand Canyon.Even the musical score that plays in the common areas evokes thoughts of the old West, drawing themes from Dances with Wolves, Silverado, How the West Was Won, and more classic westerns.

The idea for the Wilderness Lodge has been on the drawing board for over 30 years, according to resort tour guides ... in fact, they say that the idea was hatched by none other than Walt Disney himself. The Wilderness Lodge captures the romance and detail that made vacationing in National Park lodges such a memorable experience. As endearing and faithful to the subject as the Lodge is, it's easy to lose sight of the fact that first and foremost, it is a wonderful hotel. In fact, this is where Michael Eisner, chairman of the Walt Disney Company, stays when he visits the property.

Rooms

The 728 rooms are decorated in browns, greens, and beiges, with red accents on windowpanes that recall the architecture of Frank Lloyd Wright. Patchwork quilts, artwork depicting the mystery of the old West, and light-wood armoires with etchings of mountain scenes enhance the homey feel of the rooms. Most rooms have balconies that overlook waterfalls, geysers, courtyards, lodgepole pine forests, or Bay Lake.

Eat

Artist Point is the premier restaurant of the resort, and it is absolutely one-of-a-kind. The menu includes such delicacies as elk sausage, whiskey-marinated salmon, and other Northwestern specialties. The restaurant is decorated with two-story landscape paintings and looks out upon Bay Lake and Silver Creek Falls. The restaurant also offers a daily character breakfast.

The Whispering Canyon Cafe is another unique dining experience. Here, food is served skillet-style. All the food you can eat is laid out on a lazy-susan in the center of the table. Wood-roasted and oven-roasted meats are the specialties in the family-style cafe.

Roaring Fork Snacks & Arcade is the Wilderness Lodge snack bar. It's open 24 hours a day and serves breakfasts, snacks, salads, and sandwiches. Breakfast is available at Coffee Express, located adjacent to the library. Fare includes pastries, muffins, coffee, and tea.

Drink

The Territory Lounge features its own micro-brew, specialty drinks, wines, a lunch menu, and evening appetizers. The Trout Pass Pool Bar offers more of the same afternoons at poolside.

Be Merry

Silver Creek, the river which winds from the hotel's lobby to Bay Lake, becomes the pool area, seemingly carved out of the rockscape. Further down the creek, there is a white sand beach on Bay Lake.

There is a small selection of video games at Roaring Fork Arcade. Boats and bikes are available at Teton Boat & Bike Rental.

Shopping

Wilderness Lodge Mercantile is the only shop in the resort, and it offers everything from sundries to Western wear. Curios, hats, logowear, books, beer, wine, jerky, and assorted snacks make up the offerings.

DISNEY'S YACHT & BEACH CLUB RESORTS

Phone: 407/934-8000 for Beach Club, 407/934-7000 for Yacht Club.
Rates: $264 to $540. At a Glance: A dual resort evoking images of the coast of
New England around the turn of the century. Though connected, each hotel has
its own distinct flavor and personality.

These two hotels, designed by Robert A. M. Stern, sit next to each other just outside the new International Gateway entrance of EPCOT Center and a boat ride away from the Studios. These resorts are convenient choices for those who plan on spending a lot of time at the Studios or EPCOT.

The hotel complex, which totals 1,215 rooms (635 rooms at the Yacht Club, 580 at the Beach), features a central recreation and dining area where most of the resorts' public areas are located. Also, three restaurants and two lounges are located at each resort. The centerpieces of the resort are a 25-acre lake and a 3-acre swimming lagoon, called Stormalong Bay.

The Yacht Club's architecture is designed as a New England beach resort, circa 1880, with gray clapboard and flags poking up from the roof, five stories up. A pier and a lighthouse carry the nautical theme here, as do the rooms and restaurants. The Beach Club is decorated nicely, its blue and white stick house architecture blends amiably with its sister hotel, the Yacht Club. The staff here is decked out in period costumes that echo the beach theme found in all the hotel's areas.

Rooms

At the Yacht Club, the rooms are designed with a nautical flair. The rooms are bright and airy, the appointments are faithful to the motif, rose and cobalt blue linens and carpet. The furniture is painted a fresh white, as are the walls, which are accented by blue trim where they meet the ceiling. The bathrooms are large and feature double sinks and brass-trimmed mirrors. Rooms are also highlighted by color TVs, ceiling fans, a minibar, a table (that doubles as a checkerboard) and chairs, and chess and checkers sets. The rooms here are quite spacious.

The rooms at the Beach Club are laid out similarly to the ones at the Yacht Club, but reflect more of a beach attitude in their decor. These rooms are apparelled in coral and sea green, with a splash of robin's-egg-blue. Furniture here is in natural tones, and the rooms contain two double beds, ceiling fans, and other amenities similar to those in the Yacht Club's rooms.

Concierge rooms and suites sleeping five to ten persons are available at both resorts.

Eat

Ariel's is the signature restaurant of the Beach Club. Serving breakfast and dinner, this restaurant is a pleasant place to dine. A 2,500-gallon saltwater aquarium is situated at this eatery, but the seafood served at this establishment comes from sources other than that.

The Yacht Club Galley features a buffet at breakfast and dinner, and an a la carte menu at lunch. The dinner buffet features dishes that represent New England cuisine. Also located at the Yacht Club is the Yachtman's Steakhouse. Like the Cape May Cafe, diners can watch the chef as he chooses cuts of meat and then prepares them in an open kitchen. Steak, chicken, and seafood are the standards here.

A song in the Rodgers and Hammerstein classic Carousel proclaims "It was a real nice clambake, and we all had a real good time." Well, that statement rings true in the Cape May Cafe, one of the Beach Club's restaurants, where an indoor New England clambake is held each evening. Food is steamed in a cooking pit in full view of the patrons, making for an interesting atmosphere. A character breakfast buffet and a buffet lunch are also held here.

The Beaches and Cream Soda Shop, in the area shared by the two hotels, is a turn-of-the-century ice cream parlor, the menu is the epitome of American cuisine, featuring sundaes, floats, shakes, cones, ice cream sodas, and the Fenway Park Burger, which is available in four forms, (what else?) the single, double, triple, and grand slam.

Hurricane Hannah's Grill is another of the shared restaurants. The bill of fare here is light and features American favorites. Sandwiches, fries, and ice cream are served and there is a full bar. Near the smaller pool at the Beach Club is the Portside Snack Bar. Fast food such as sandwiches, salads, and hot dogs is served, along with beer, wine, and specialty drinks.

The Yacht Club's pool area boasts the Sip Ahoy Snack Bar, the counterpart of Portside at the Beach Club. Burgers, dogs, sandwiches, soft drinks, and liquor are served at both locations.

Drink

The Ale and Compass Lounge is located in the lobby of the Yacht Club. The lounge is open until 1 each night and serves specialty drinks, including ale and coffee. Next to the Yachtman's Steakhouse is the Crew Cup Lounge. This "pub" is a pleasant spot for a dinner aperitif.

Martha's Vineyard Lounge is situated at the Beach Club, right next to Ariel's. The lounge's drawing card is its extensive wine list, featuring domestic and European wines. The Riptide Lounge, the Beach Club's chic lobby bar, serves California wines, specialty drinks, and wine coolers. Open 'til 1am.

Be Merry

The 25-acre lake here is a prime location for boating, and watercraft can be rented at Bayside Marina. Boats available include Water Sprites, sailboats, flote boats, pedal boats, and row boats.

Ever wanted to play croquet? This is the place to do it. There is a grass court on the Beach Club side. But you don't have croquet equipment? It's not a problem. Disney provides the equipment at no cost.

The Ship Shape Health Club, offering exercise machines, aerobics classes, massage rooms, spa, steam room, and saunas, is located in the central area, as are about 40 video games and pinball machines at the twin resorts' shared gameroom, the Lafferty Place Arcade.

Swimming is a major attraction here. Both hotels have their own pool and a section of lakeside beach, plus the centerpiece of the resort: Stormalong Bay. This 3-acre swimming complex features a 750,000 gallon main pool, next to another pool with a pair of waterslides coming off a shipwreck, a snorkeling lagoon complete with aquatic life, an active lagoon with bubbling jets of water and whirlpools, and yet another lagoon for the sedentary. On the Beach Club side of the resort are two lit tennis courts. There is a volleyball court on the sand of the Beach Club. Equipment can be borrowed or rented at the Ship Shape Health Club.

Shopping

Atlantic Wear & Wardrobe Emporium at the Beach Club and Fitting & Fairings' Clothes & Notions at the Yacht Club sell similar merchandise: sundries, souvenirs, character merchandise, and items that follow the nautical and beach themes.

The Periwig Salon, in the hotels' common area, is a barber shop/beauty parlor for men and women. Open from 9 to 5 daily.

Services

A business center, complete with personal computers, fax machines, copiers, and secretarial service is available at the Convention Center.

THE WALT DISNEY WORLD DOLPHIN

Phone: 407/934-4000. Rates: $295 to $465. At a Glance: A 27-story tower rising off the 14-story main building, eccentric doesn't even begin to describe it.

This hotel (operated by Sheraton), an odd creation of Michael Graves, was recognized by Progressive Architecture magazine for "its striking post-modern design." The tallest hotel in WDW and one of the strangest, it can be recognized by the twin dolphin statues that stand guard atop either side of the 14-story main building. The 55-foot high statues overlook lush landscaping, grotto pools, and Crescent Lake, which connects the Studios and EPCOT. The exterior of the hotel is done in oranges, greens, and blues, while the public areas are an eccentric melange of all the colors of the spectrum. The hotel is a new genre of structure called "Entertainment Architecture," as is the Swan Hotel. By the entrance, a waterfall trickles down through a series of shell-shaped fountains propped up by dolphin statues. From here, trams depart to the new International Gateway entrance to EPCOT Center, to which it is very convenient. Keep your eyes open as you travel the Dolphin, or you may miss an intricate detail, like a dolphin carved into a bench, or a monkey hanging from a chandelier.

Rooms

The Dolphin's 1,369 rooms are just as outlandish as the hotel's brash exterior. As they reflect the tropical theme, the rooms are all decorated in soft, light pastels. Palm trees are etched on the furniture, while the bedcovers are striped in coral and blue. Common features here include clock-radios, mini-bars, cable TV, newspaper, and voice mail.

Eat

The Dolphin has its own 24-hour eatery, the Coral Café. Buffets are served here for breakfast and dinner, while those who prefer à la carte dining can do so during all three meals. Wednesdays and Sundays offer character breakfast buffets.

Opening in 2000, Shula's promises specialties such as New York sirloin, porterhouse steak, filet mignon, and Florida seafood. Juan and Only's Cantina features authentic Mexican food including sizzling fajitas and homemade pico de gallo, in addition to rare tequilas and beers from all over Mexico.

At poolside is the Cabana Bar & Grill, a snack bar serving burgers, chicken, sandwiches, yogurt, and fruit. The Dolphin Fountain, however, is the place for exotic flavors of ice cream .

Tubbi's Buffeteria is a cafeteria-service restaurant with an unusual checkerboard setting. This is a good bet for when you want a quick, hot meal.

Drink

Only's Bar and Jail serves tequilas and Mexican beers aplenty. Atmosphere? With a name like that, what can you really say? Any voyager has a story to tell. That includes "Harry" of Harry's Safari Bar here.

Copa Banana's tabletops are shaped like slices of fruit. The food and drink served here reflect the tropical theme of the hotel. Karaoke nightly. The Lobby Lounge is an affable place to sit with a cool drink and an appetizer and people-watch.

Be Merry

Near the pool is the hotel's health club, a branch of the chain Body by Jake, run by Jake Steinfeld. The equipment is top-rate, and available benefits include saunas, steam rooms, whirlpools, and personal trainers.

Swimming here is quite pleasurable, and just sitting back and watching is a enjoyable pastime. There is a rectangular pool, great for laps, and a grotto pool featuring waterfalls, a waterslide, bridges, and mountains. Also, swimmers can partake in the waters of Crescent Lake.

The Dolphin and her sister property, the Swan, share eight lit tennis courts. Note that the courts cost $12 an hour before 7 PM but are free after then. A selection of boats are available for rent at the Cabana Marina, near the grotto pool. Near the Camp Dolphin area is a gameroom.

Shopping

Brittany Jewels offers a good selection of Cartier gems. Daisy's Garden is this hotel's combination character and sundry outlet. If you're a chocoholic or just someone who appreciates an occasional sugar rush, Indulgences is the place for you.

Resortwear for both men and women can be purchased at Signatures of Fashion.

THE WALT DISNEY WORLD SWAN

Phone: 407/934-3000. Rates: $295 to $465. At a Glance: The Dolphin's smaller sister hotel, it's located right across Crescent Lake in the Epcot area.

The theme at the Swan (operated by Westin) is oceanic, as the turquoise and coral designs of the building suggest a tropical resort hotel. The Swan's namesakes are represented in the form of two 45-foot high, 14-ton statues on either end of the hotel. Facing the Dolphin, this hotel is just as convenient as her sister. Like the Dolphin, this is an example of "Entertainment Architecture." In fact, most of the Swan's features are shared by the sister property, the Dolphin.

The guestrooms are located in the 12-story main building and a pair of seven-story wings. The hallways are adorned in patterned carpeting, murals covering the walls. Chandeliers in the halls are shaped like seahorses. This is only slightly less weird than the Dolphin.

Rooms

The motif here is mainly the same as that of the Dolphin, the rooms in the same turquoise and coral as the exterior. The units have amusing little touches that help to enforce the waterfront semblance of the hotel, touches like pineapples painted on the headboards and parrot-shaped lamps. amenities of the rooms include safes, clock-radios, voice mail, cable TV, mini-bars, bathrobes, hair dryers, and newspaper delivery each morning. A variety of suites and concierge "Royal Beach Club" rooms is located on the eleventh and twelfth floors.

Eat

A nice Italian bistro, Palio, features stellar homemade pizza made in a wood-burning oven and six ambitious, homemade pasta dishes. Named after the town of Sienna's famed horse race, Palio's surroundings feature authentic banners representing the Italian counties who participated in the race. Guitarists promenade through the restaurant nightly. The restaurant calls itself casual, but the price tags seem to suggest otherwise.

The Garden Grove Cafe is a 24-hour spot where the "greenhouse effect" can be experienced. That's probably because of the location: inside a airy, high-ceilinged greenhouse. Fresh Florida seafood is the feature presentation here. The pastry kitchen is glassed in, so diners can watch as desserts advertised as "the most sinful pastries in town" are prepared. At the Splash Grill, light snack fare is served for breakfast and lunch. Snacks and drinks are also served.

Drink

Kimono's is a surprising lounge. There's a likable Japanese environment here, and drinks and sushi are served. There are sofas and chairs throughout the Lobby Court Lounge for visitors to sit with a drink in hand and watch life's parade passing by.

Be Merry

Swimming can be done in the hotel's large, rectangular pool or in Crescent Lake. Between the two hotels are eight lit tennis courts. Boat rentals are available at the marina between the Dolphin and Swan. The hotel possesses a small health club, featuring aerobics classes and exercise equipment. Near the pool is a small gameroom.

Shopping

Located in the lobby, Swan Disney Cabana sells sundries, souvenirs, and character merchandise. The Swan Fashion Cabana sells men's and women's resortwear plus jewelry.

THE VILLAS AT THE DISNEY INSTITUTE

Phone: 407/827-1100. Rates: $204 to $510 per night. At a Glance: The former Village Resort, this features lovely and spacious villa accommodations in a laid-back campus atmosphere.

Add one part luxury resort to one part university and what do you get? This innovative resort experience, which is unlike anything south of the

Mason-Dixon line, that's what. Inspired by the Chautauqua Institute in upstate New York, the DI offers guests a hands-on experience in a curriculum that they design according to their interests and hobbies. Disney Institute programs are available to Day Visitors and Villa guests do not need to enroll in the programs, but the two are designed for one another.

DI Accommodations

The Disney Institute houses guests in the accommodations formerly known as Disney's Village Resort. Bungalows sleep up to five and feature a wet bar with a small refrigerator and microwave oven. One- and two-bedroom townhouses sleep four and six, respectively, and include a fully equipped kitchen.

Eat

The Seasons Dining Room is the main restaurant at the DI, offering all three meals daily. Floridian cuisine is featured at dinner, including such exotic dishes as orange chili pepper shrimp and Florida rock lobster ravioli. Reflections is a coffeeshop on Willow Lake, offering pastries and lighter fare.

Drink

The Seasons Terrace and Bar offers alcoholic and non-alcoholic beverages as well as lunch items on the patio. The Seasons Lounge offers drinks indoors.

Be Merry

The DI includes the Sports and Fitness Center with an indoor exercise pool, CYBEX exercise equipment, and aerobics studios. Other recreational facilities include six outdoor swimming pools, bike paths, canals for canoeing, the 18-hole Lake Buena Vista golf course, clay tennis courts, a multi-purpose sports field, and a rock climbing wall.

The Spa at the Disney Institute offers a variety of spa treatments from licensed aestheticians and therapists. Treatments range from hydrotherapy and massage to body wraps, facials, and aromatherapy. The Spa also offers locker rooms, steam rooms, saunas, and indoor whirlpools.

The DI offers nightly entertainment ranging from guest speakers to movies to concerts and dramatic presentations. The DI facilities also include television and radio stations.

Shopping

Dabblers is the Disney Institute store, with a variety of sundries and souvenirs. There is also a golf pro shop.

Disney Institute Programs, Packages, and Pricing

The Disney Institute offers four-day programs in such curricula as gardening, culinary arts, animation, photography, and television, each offering a variety of specialized workshops that delve deeper into your chosen disciple. The classes are hands-on, participatory, and creative, with plenty of instructor attention, as the average class size is 15 students. Reservations can be made up to 6 months in advance for the four-day packages. For the kids, Camp Disney offers three programs for kids 7 to 10, and three more for those 10 to 15, exploring art, theatre, or nature.

Day visitors can make their program reservations 30 days in advance, and can choose half-day sessions with one program for $69 or a full two-program day for $99. Packages have a minimum stay of 3 nights and run $599 to $1099 per person, with additional nights costing $77 to $244, depending on the type of accommodation and season. Each package includes three or more nights accommodations, four programs, professional workshops and journals, unlimited use of the fitness center, breakfast daily, plus your choice of selected theme park, recreation, or dining activities. *For more information and reservations, call 800/282-9282 or surf to www.disneyinstitute.com.*

HOTEL PLAZA BOULEVARD
Official Hotels of Walt Disney World

The seven hotels on Hotel Plaza Boulevard, while neither owned nor operated by the Disney company, share many of the same amenities as the WDW-owned-and-operated establishments. Hotel Plaza guests have free use of the WDW bus system, access to priority reservations for dining, golf, and other recreational activities.As a general rule of thumb, expect slightly less pampering and significantly less cost for these hotels.

On the downside, they're less luxurious and not "themed" and have more of a typical hotel feel, more faceless than the WDW resorts. However, the location on Hotel Plaza Boulevard offers easy access to the multitude of dining, shopping, and entertainment options in the Downtown Disney area as well as Crossroads of Lake Buena Vista, Vista Centre, and other complexes outside WDW. Additionally, I-4 is only a half mile away from Hotel Plaza Blvd. *Check out all the hotels online at www.downtowndisneyhotels.com.*

BEST WESTERN LAKE BUENA VISTA RESORT HOTEL
2000 Hotel Plaza Blvd., Lake Buena Vista, FL 32830. Phone: 407/828-2424 or Tel. 800/348-3765. Rates: $89 to $129. At a Glance. Formerly the

Travelodge (and not the Grosvenor, which was associated with Best Western in the past), this 18-story hotel is one of Best Western's nicest properties in the world. This 325-room hotel is undoubtedly one of Best Western's finest properties. Rooms here are spacious and nicely decorated, while the public areas are aesthetically pleasing as well. The hotel is themed to resemble a Bahamas plantation house.

Rooms

The rooms here are quite spacious and geared towards families, with two queen-sized beds in each room. The walls, carpeting, and bedcovers are done in light pastels while the furniture is hued a light cream . Each room has a private balcony overlooking the Downtown Disney area or Lake Buena Vista, a stocked bar, in-room coffee, hair dryers, remote-control TV with the Disney Channel and pay movies, and morning newspaper.

Eat

The Parakeet Cafe is a coffeeshop in the lobby, serving homemade pizza, sandwiches, burgers, and salads. This is also the place for afternoon tea. The largest restaurant here is the Traders Restaurant, serving a la carte items plus buffets at breakfast and dinner. The menu is moderately priced and the atmosphere is casual. Diners can also eat on an outdoor terrace, weather permitting. Specialties include shrimp, chicken, steak, and ribs.

Drink

Calypso's Pool Bar serves a selection of tropical drinks including Caribbean coolers. The Flamingo Cove Lounge serves a variety of mixed drinks, beer, wine, and cocktails in a comfortable setting.

Be Merry

The Best Western's amenities include a heated outdoor pool, playground, and a game room.

COURTYARD BY MARRIOTT

1805 Hotel Plaza Blvd., Lake Buena Vista, FL 32830. Phone: 407/828-8888 or Tel. 800/223-9930. Rates: $114 to $140. At a Glance: One of the less interesting hotels on the strip, it's a good bet for business travelers. Website: www.courtyard.com.

This hotel, while one of the cheapest in Downtown Disney, has the least personality. Guestrooms are located in a 14-story tower centered around an uninspiring atrium, as well as a 6-story extension.

Rooms

The rooms here are decorated adequately (if unmemorably) in light pastel greens and pinks. The rooms in the main building open up onto an inner hallway that overlooks the lobby and each feature a balcony or patio. One advantage for families, rooms here are spacious.

Eat

Streamers Restaurant features festive American cuisine served in a casual setting, accompanied by regional wines and unique desserts. There's also Streamers Market offering food and snacks as well as gifts. The Tropical Pool Bar also offers some light fare.

Drink

Streamers Lounge offers nightly specials and cocktails inside Streamers Restaurant. Additionally, there's the pool bar for your tropical cocktail sipping needs.

Be Merry

The exercise room has Nautilus equipment. There is a small gameroom and a playground located here. Swimming can be done in two medium pools and a wading pool.

DOUBLETREE GUEST SUITES RESORT

2305 Hotel Plaza Blvd., Lake Buena Vista, FL 32830. Phone: 407/934-1000 or Tel. 800/222-TREE. Rates: $116 to $203. At a Glance: The only all-suite hotel on Disney turf. Website: www.doubletreeguestsuites.com.

The latest hospitality trend, the all-suite hotel, is popping up in every city. So, it's only fitting that a suite hotel has appeared on Hotel Plaza Boulevard. This is a stereotypical all-suite hotel, to a certain extent. Like many others, there's an impressive atrium, a lobby restaurant and lounge, and a free breakfast each morning. This hotel is located at the northeastern terminus of Hotel Plaza Boulevard. Located within two blocks of the hotel are two non-Disney shopping, dining, and entertainment complexes, Vista Centre and the Crossroads of Lake Buena Vista. I-4 is also very convenient from here.

Suites

The 229 suites here measure about 600 square feet, about 40% bigger than standard rooms in Disney-owned lodgings. Each suite can sleep six persons on two double beds in a bedroom and on a sleeper sofa in the living room. Two-bedroom suites are also available.

The suites' amenities include custom-designed furniture, televisions remote controlled ones in bedroom and living room plus a smaller one in the bathroom, in-room movies, custom-made furniture, full-length mirrors, vanities, stocked refrigerators, coffee-makers, wet bars, and built-in hair dryers. Microwaves are available in 100 suites.

Eat

Streamers Restaurant features festive American cuisine served in a casual setting, accompanied by regional wines and unique desserts. There's also Streamers Market offering food and snacks as well as gifts. The Tropical Pool Bar also offers some light fare.

Drink

Streamers Lounge offers nightly specials and cocktails inside Streamers Restaurant. Additionally, there's the pool bar for your tropical cocktail sipping needs.

Be Merry

There is a gameroom and a playground by the pool, an exercise room, a swimming pool plus a whirlpool and wading pool, and two tennis courts.

GROSVENOR RESORT AT WALT DISNEY WORLD VILLAGE

1850 Hotel Plaza Blvd., Lake Buena Vista, FL, 32830. Phone: 407/828-4444 or Tel. 800/223 5652 for reservations. Rates: $105 to $155. At a Glance: A pleasant hotel with a slight Bahamas feel and some interesting restaurants. Website: www.grosvenorresort.com.

The least expensive of the Hotel Plaza choices, the Grosvenor boasts some of the most interesting restaurants and lounges on the block. The cavernous lobby is decorated in a mix of faint teal and rose and a nice pub sits just behind it to welcome returning guests after a long day of park touring.

Rooms

The rooms, all of which have been recently redecorated, are nicely laid out. Each guestroom has two double beds or a king-sized sleeper, and rollaways are available. The rooms have a slight Bahamas air to their decor, a pleasant blend of pale greens, pinks, and peach. amenities of the rooms include VCRs, color cable television, large bathrooms, and a small stocked bar and refrigerator.

Eat

Baskerville's is a casual restaurant serving continental fare for breakfast, lunch, and dinner. But here, the food takes second billing to the atmosphere, namely, a Sherlock Holmes museum. In the center of the restaurant is a glassed-in model of the parlor of 221B Baker Street. The mock-up contains items such as Mr. Holmes's violin, his tobacco, his newspapers, and his correspondence pierced with a knife. Very interesting, a must for Holmes aficionados. Every Saturday night, this restaurant hosts Murderwatch Mystery Theatre, a murder mystery show featuring an unlimited prime rib dinner and a cast of professional actors. Sleuths who solve the puzzle win prizes.

In the lobby is Crumpets, a small cafe serving continental breakfasts and snack fare. Burgers, salads, and sandwiches are also served. Open 24 hours. The Barnacles poolside snack bar offers light fare and beverages.

Drink

Moriarty's Pub, an unpretentious bar next to the lobby, features darts (darts and beer — what a combination!) and live entertainment. The portrait hanging on the wall belongs to the eponymous Moriarty, Holmes' arch-enemy. The Crickets Sports Lounge serves drinks and light snack fare.

Be Merry

For recreation, you've got your choice of basketball courts; a small gameroom; handball courts; two tennis courts; volleyball; and horseshoes. A selection of movies is available at the guest services desk for use on the in-room VCRs.

A playground is located near the hotel. Racquetball can be played here on two courts. A shuffleboard court is located here, and there are two swimming pools and a hot tub.

Shopping

Grosvenor Disney sells an assortment of goods, including sundries and character merchandise.

HILTON IN THE WALT DISNEY WORLD RESORT

1751 Hotel Plaza Blvd., Lake Buena Vista, FL 32830. Phone: 407/827-4000 or Tel. 800/774-1500. Rates: $129 to $235. At a Glance: The second-largest of the Hotel Plaza establishments, this perennial favorite has quite a few interesting restaurants and lounges. Website: www.hilton.com.

This 814-room hotel occupies 23 acres at the southern end of Hotel Plaza Boulevard and is directly across the street from Downtown Disney Marketplace. Convenient, luxurious, and pleasant, this hotel includes nine restaurants and lounges and plenty of cool stuff to keep you occupied.

Rooms

These are some of the nicest hotel rooms you're likely to find anywhere, packed to the gills with amenities. In addition to the standard stuff, each hotel room offers two phone lines, Internet access, data ports, video games, and a trouser press and iron.

Eat

Finn's Grill serves dinner nightly along with specialty drinks in a Key West atmosphere, while Covington Mill will take you to New England for breakfast, lunch, and dinner. The Benihana Steakhouse offers Japanese specialties including shrimp, scallops, lobster tail, chicken, and of course, the steak that made Benihana famous. The Main Street Market delicatessen features Boar's Head meats and cheeses as well as Ben & Jerry's ice cream, novelties, and snacks. The Rum Largo Poolside Café also offers light fare.

Drink

John T's Sports Bar features athletic action and plenty o' libations in a plantation atmosphere. The Rum Largo Pool Bar offers mixed drinks and other goodies at the water's edge, while Mugs Coffee & Wine Bar features specialty coffees and elegant wines in a lounge accented by mahogany and hardwood.

Be Merry

The Hilton features a pool, fitness center, arcade, and pool table in addition to all the other options available at Downtown Disney right across the street.

HOTEL ROYAL PLAZA

1905 Hotel Plaza Blvd., Lake Buena Vista, FL 32830. Phone: 407/828-2828 or Tel. 800/248-7890. Rates: $99 to $240. At a Glance: A 17-story tower and two 7-story wings, the Royal Plaza is one of the more overlooked hotels on the strip. Website: www.royalplaza.com.

This hotel is one of the smaller properties at Hotel Plaza, with only 396 rooms in its tower and two extensions. The hotel has been freshly renovated, and seems to buzz with energy, making this a good choice for young adults and families with older children and teenagers.

Rooms

Each room is decorated harmoniously in contemporary hues, and each spacious room has a balcony or patio. amenities of the rooms include safe deposit boxes, color cable televisions, and clock radios.

If you are counting on getting a lot of uninterrupted sleep, request a room on one of the higher floors or in one of the wings.

Eat

The Plaza Diner serves all-American food in a nostalgic Art Deco atmosphere from morning until night. Fare includes daily Blue Plate Specials, pizza, and burgers. Take-out is available.

Drink

The Intermissions lounge offers drinks and light snacking. There's also a poolside bar.

Be Merry

There are men's and women's saunas here. Shuffleboard can be played at the hotel. A heated swimming pool and a hot tub are available here for use. Four lighted tennis courts are available for use. There is also a gameroom here.

Services

There is a beauty salon located here, as well as a barber shop. There is a one-day film development service on the premises. Video cameras can be rented at MagiCam, a kiosk at the hotel.

WYNDHAM PALACE RESORT

1900 Hotel Plaza Blvd, Lake Buena Vista, FL 32830. Phone: 407/827-2727 or Tel. 800/327-2990. Rates: $149 to $498. At a Glance: The largest and most luxurious hotel on the Plaza, the former Buena Vista Palace boasts among other things one of the area's finest dining establishments. Website: www.bvpalace.com.

This recently-remodeled hotel, formerly known as the Buena Vista Palace, is the focal point of the entire Hotel Plaza, and is also the most convenient hotel to Downtown Disney, just across the street from the Marketplace. The 27-story tower is the highest point in the entire Vacation Kingdom.

Rooms

The recently-renovated rooms are found in a 27-story tower and three smaller towers, while the 100 Palace Suites are located on the recreation island in two five-story structures connected by a seven-story atrium building. Every one of the 1,014 rooms in the Palace and the Palace Suites has its own balcony or patio, and all of the rooms are spacious. The decor consists of combinations of varying shades of tan, and the furniture has a slightly modernistic twang to it. The appointments of the rooms include king beds or two queens, remote controlled color cable TVs, ceiling fans, and two telephones; one in the bathroom and a Mickey Mouse phone in the bedroom.

Many rooms in the Palace's 27-story tower have sweeping views of either the Downtown Disney Marketplace, Pleasure Island, or EPCOT Center.

Eat

Arthur's 27 ranks right up there with Victoria and Albert's as one of the best restaurants in the World. Prix fixe or a la carte menus are available. The wine list ranges from the commonplace to the priceless. This restaurant is most popular on weekends, and there is only one seating nightly, so reservations are a must as soon as you book your room.

The Outback Restaurant is an Australian-themed eatery with pools, rock structures, and dull wood walls that make this interesting spot resemble a set from Crocodile Dundee. The food is hearty, mainly steak and seafood.

A pleasant 24-hour restaurant, the Watercress Cafe and Bake Shop, is located on the ground floor of the hotel, next to a picturesque lake. The theme here is casual Mediterranean, and the menu is priced and designed for families, and a character breakfast is held here each morning.

The Courtyard Pastries and Pizza Shop can satisfy munchies with simple meals and snacks. The Pool Snack Bar serves the usual selection of fast food and snack fare.

Drink

One of the Hotel Plaza's most active nightclubs is the Laughing Kookaburra "Good Time Bar", featuring dancing, 99 different brands of beer, a Happy Hour with free appetizers from 4 to 8, a dance floor, and a live band five nights a week.

On the 27th floor of the hotel is the Top of the Palace Lounge, where the live entertainment and the 800-bottle wine list take a backseat to the enchanting views of the Vacation Kingdom.

The Buena Vista Palace Lobby Lounge is a pleasant place to sit with your choice of mixed drinks, wines, specialty coffees and teas, and pastries, all to piano accompaniment. The Palace's Pool Bar serves cool beverages, tropical cocktails, and a Florida raw bar.

Be Merry

The Palace's amenities include four swimming pools, a 10,000 foot European-style spa, marina, comprehensive fitness center, three tennis courts, an arcade, steam rooms, and saunas.

ACCOMMODATIONS OUTSIDE DISNEY WORLD

Don't think for a second that staying at a Walt Disney World hotel is your only, or even necessarily your best option. If you'd like to check out the restaurants, shopping, and entertainment along International Drive, US 192, and elsewhere, staying in Disney puts those options a little farther out of your reach. Also, if your vacation focus is on the non-Disney theme parks, such as Universal and Sea World, staying on Disney property is completely unnecessary.

In the pages that follow, I'll offer you attractive lodging options in all price categories and locations as well as some unique options that you won't find anywhere else, as well as information to put you in touch with your favorite chain hotels to give you a feel for the full range of your options.

Please keep in mind that the small amount of space given to the off-site hotels' descriptions compared to the Disney hotels is not an endorsement of one over the other. It's just that there's more to discuss with the unique Disney hotels in terms of décor, atmosphere, and theme than there is with other accommodations. After all, there's only so many times you can say "big concrete building" before it starts getting a bit tiresome.

There are four major geographic concentrations of hotels catering to theme park visitors. They are Kissimmee/US 192, Lake Buena Vista/SR 535, Sea World/Convention Center/South International Drive, and Universal/North International Drive.

KISSIMMEE AREA HOTELS

Back when the Magic Kingdom first opened its gates in 1971, this was where the primary concentration of hotels was, on US 192 (W. Irlo Bronson Memorial Highway), on either side of the Disney maingate. Of course, a lot's changed in thirty years, and all of the properties in the area have been renovated since then, but this is still the most cluttered and dated-looking of the hotel clusters in the Disney area. It has also felt significant growing pains, as traffic on 192 can be as unpleasant as any commute around park opening times. However, at press time construction widening the road was well under way, signaling a light at the end of the tunnel.

Navigation in Kissimmee has gotten considerably easier with the addition of the huge, colorful mile markers on either side of the road. These 25-foot markers are easy landmarks, and many area businesses advertise their location in relation to them.

Kissimmee means "heaven's place" in the language of the Caloosa Indians who lived here centuries ago. Back before the advent of the automobile, the small town was known informally as the "cow capital" of the state. Ranching was big business here, and Kissimmee attracted cowboy passers-by, buttless chaps and all, with bars that would serve them while on horseback. The cowboys, that is, not the bartenders.

Today, what most travelers see of Kissimmee is nothing more than the glitzy, garish line of neon-accented motels, chain restaurants, and gift shops that is US 192. However, don't let the tackiness turn you off – you're in Disney World, after all – and there are good deals to be found among the 40,000 rooms, suites, and villas in the area.

Best Western Eastgate

5565 W. Irlo Bronson Memorial Highway, Kissimmee, FL 34746. Phone: 407/396-0707 or Tel. 800/223-5361. Rates: $33 to $89. Discounts: AAA, AARP, seniors, military, corporate.

This Best Western, located 3 miles east of WDW and across from Old Town, offers comfortable and spacious rooms, a landscaped courtyard, heated pool and spa, video arcade, free tennis, and an on site restaurant.

Best Western Suites & Resort on Lake Cecile

4786 W. Irlo Bronson Memorial Highway, Kissimmee, FL 34746. Phone: 407/396-2909 or Tel. 800/468-3027. Rates: $69 to $149. Discounts: AAA, AARP. Website: www.bestwesternhotelfl.com.

Located a little farther east, this Best Western offers inexpensive suite accommodations on the shores of picturesque Lake Cecile, with suites for parties of all sizes, including two-level family suites with two bathrooms, sleeping up to six people comfortably.

Comfort Suites Maingate Resort

7888 W. Irlo Bronson Memorial Highway, Kissimmee, FL 34747. Phone: 407/390-9888 or Tel. 888/390-9888. Rates: $70 to $135. Discounts: AAA, AARP, corporate, military, seniors. Website: www.formosagardens.com.

This 150-suite hotel, 3 1/2 miles west of WDW, offers free continental breakfast and free Disney shuttles. It's also within easy walking distance of an Outback Steakhouse, Subway, Taco Bell, and a Gooding's Super-market.

Courtyard by Marriott Orlando Maingate

7675 W. Irlo Bronson Memorial Highway, Kissimmee, FL 34747. Phone: 407/396-4000 or Tel. 800/568-3352. Discounts: Magicard. Rates: $69 to $150.

A mere mile and a half from the Disney maingate, this favorite of travelers everywhere offers a fitness center, pool, spa, tennis, and shuttle transportation to the parks.

Days Inn/Days Suites Maingate East

5820 W. Irlo Bronson Memorial Highway, Kissimmee, FL 34746. Phone: 407/396-7900 or Tel. 800/327-9126. Rates: $32 to $139. Discounts: AAA, AARP, corporate, military, Magicard. Website: www.thhotels.com.

This colorful complex right next to Old Town offers 404 standard guest rooms pretty much like you'll find at any other budget motel, but what's really special about this place is the presence of 600 huge 3-room suites with full kitchens, sleeping up to 6 people comfortably. There are also two restaurants where kids eat free, plus pools scattered throughout the complex.

Econolodge Maingate Hawaiian Resort

7514 W. Irlo Bronson Memorial Highway, Kissimmee, FL 34747. Phone: 407/396-2000 or Tel. 800/ENJOY-FL. Rates: $35 to $99. Discounts: AAA, AARP, corporate, military, seniors, Magicard. Website: www.enjoyfloridahotels.com.

Renovated in 1997, this colorful motel offers such perks as free kids' meals, free shuttle service, pool, hot tub, a full service restaurant with a breakfast buffet, a delicatessen, and room service by Pizzeria Uno.

Four Points by Sheraton Lakeside

7769 W. Irlo Bronson Memorial Highway, Kissimmee, FL 34747. Phone: 407/396-2222 or Tel. 800/848-0801. Rates: $65 to $150. Discounts: AAA, AARP, corporate, military, seniors. Website: www.orlandosheraton.com.

This Mediterranean-style hotel features 651 rooms in 15 two-story buildings scattered throughout 27 tropically landscaped acres, with over half the rooms featuring either pool, lake, or garden views. The hotel features three pools, complimentary use of four on-site tennis courts, an 18-hole miniature golf course, a fitness center, complimentary paddleboats, and five restaurants including a deli and Pizza Hut Express.

Holiday Inn Hotel & Suites Maingate East

5678 W. Irlo Bronson Memorial Highway, Kissimmee, FL 34746. Phone: 407/396-4488 or Tel. 800/366-5437. Rates: $59 to $225. Discounts: AAA, AARP, corporate, military, seniors, Magicard. Website: www.familyfunhotels.com.

The innovative features at this hotel are its KidSuites, which are themed areas within the two bedroom suites, which allows adults privacy by spiriting the kids away with video games, a VCR, bunk beds, and a fun phone. There is a full service restaurant where kids eat free and a food court featuring Little Caesar's pizza and more.

Hyatt Orlando

6375 W. Irlo Bronson Memorial Highway, Kissimmee, FL 34747. Phone: 407/396-1234 or Tel. 800/233-1234. Rates: $99 to $164. Discounts: AAA, AARP, seniors. Website: www.hyatt.com.

Convenient (1 1/2 miles from WDW) and modern, this 56-acre, resort features 900 rooms surrounding "Floribbean" courtyards, three restaurants, fitness, jogging, and tennis facilities, and special privileges at nearby golf courses.

Orange Lake Resort & Country Club

8505 W. Irlo Bronson Memorial Highway, Kissimmee, FL 34747. Phone: 407/239-0000 or Tel. 800/877-6522. Rates: $99 to $225. Discounts: Magicard. Website: www.orangelake.com.

Located 4 miles west of the Disney main gate on US 192, the Orange Lake's guests sleep comfortably in large villas while enjoying 90 holes of golf, tennis, swimming, restaurants, and more.

Radisson Resort Parkway

2900 Parkway Blvd., Kissimmee, FL 34747. Phone: 407/396-7000 or Tel. 800/634-4774. Rates: $59 to $129. Discounts: AAA, AARP, corporate, Magicard. Website: www.radisson.com.

With more of a resort atmosphere than many of the Kissimmee motels by virtue of its high-rise main building and smaller wings as well as nicely landscaped grounds, the Radisson is an attractive and inexpensive choice located just 1 1/2 miles from Disney. The hotel's amenities include a giant free-form pool with a waterslide, two whirlpools, two tennis courts, volleyball courts, jogging and fitness facilities, and dining options including a 50's-themed diner, a full-service family restaurant, sports bar, pool bar, and Pizza Hut pizza.

Travelodge Hotel Main Gate East

5711 W. Irlo Bronson Memorial Highway, Kissimmee, FL 34746. Phone: 407/396-4222 or Tel. 800/327-1128. Rates: $42 to $49. Discounts: AAA, AARP, corporate, military, seniors. Website: www.travelodge.com.

With 444 rooms across the street from Old Town at mile marker 10 of US 192, the Travelodge features a free scheduled shuttle to the Disney parks, two restaurants, a pool, whirlpool, sauna, and wading pool, along with a few other basics. One of the best choices for travelers on a limited budget for whom the basics will suffice.

LAKE BUENA VISTA AREA HOTELS

Up until a few years ago, Lake Buena Vista was a tiny stretch of real estate that you drove through on your way from I-4 to Downtown Disney, then known as the Disney Village. Recent development has given the area several prime choices of hotels, with lots of dining and shopping action to be had, along with easy access to Disney World and other Orlando attractions via nearby I-4. Hotels here are generally a little newer and a little more expensive than those located in Kissimmee, and about comparable to what you'll find around Sea World.

Buena Vista Suites

8203 World Center Drive, Orlando, FL 32821. Phone: 407/239-8588 or Tel. 800/537-7737. Rates: $95 to $189. Discounts: AAA, Magicard. Website: www.buenavistasuites.com.

Located near the intersection of South International Drive and SR 536 just 1 1/2 miles from Disney, this is an attractive and reasonably priced choice for families, as the two-room suites here sleep up to six and include a free full American breakfast buffet and free transportation to the Disney parks. This is one of the quieter and more under-developed areas in the region, so the throngs of fast food and cheap shopping are a bit more remote from this establishment. Kind of a double-edged sword, but having a one-mile drive to get a burger instead of a half-mile drive really isn't that much of a price to pay for the increased peace and quiet.

Caribe Royale Resort Suites

14300 International Drive, Orlando, FL 32801. Phone: 407/238-8000 or Tel. 800/823-8300. Rates: $159 to $199. Discounts: AAA, corporate, Magicard. Website: www.caribe-royale.com.

This resort and convention center, located at the south end of International Drive, opened in 1996 with three 10-story towers, catering to families, business travelers, and leisure travelers, respectively. The hotel offers over 1,200 two-room suites each with a pair of televisions, cable, and video games. King suites featuring whirlpool tubs are also available, as are two-bedroom villas with full kitchens, dining areas, and screened lanais or patios. Amenities include free transportation to the parks, complimentary breakfast buffet, and night-lit tennis courts.

Club Hotel by Doubletree

12490 Apopka Vineland Road, Lake Buena Vista, FL 32836. Phone: 407/ 239-4646 or Tel. 888/444-CLUB. Rates: $39 to $119. Discounts: AAA. Website: www.go2orlando.com/sponsors/clubhotel.

Imagine the colorful homage paid to dolphins and swans at the Disney resorts bearing those animals' names... now apply that homage to fruit salad, and you have a pretty good mental picture of what this hotel looks like. Renovated into its current state of tastefulness in mid-1999, this Doubletree, unlike most others, is not an all-suite resort. The rooms feature a light-hearted Caribbean motif and the location, within eyesight of Hotel Plaza Blvd., I-4, and the Crossroads shopping center, can't be beaten with a stick. They also offer an Au Bon Pain bakery and free transportation to the Disney parks.

Embassy Suites Resort Lake Buena Vista

8100 Lake Avenue, Orlando, FL 32836. Phone: 407/239-1144 or Tel. 800/257-8483. Rates: $149 to $239. Discounts: AAA, corporate, seniors. Website: www.embassy-suites.com.

Parents magazine recently listed Embassy Suites among the top hotels for families, thanks to spacious two-room suites that offer welcome breathing room from the ones you love, along with two TVs with cable and VCR, refrigerators and microwaves, and free transportation to the Disney theme parks. Like every Embassy Suites location, this hotel offers complimentary, cooked-to-order breakfast every morning and a reception every evening, and is located just outside Downtown Disney.

Grand Cypress Resort

One North Jacaranda, Orlando, FL 32386. Phone: 407/239-4700 or Tel. 800/835-7377. Rates: $275 to $540 for Hyatt rooms, $200 to $1500 for villas. Website: www.grandcypress.com.

The only hotel in Central Florida to be awarded five diamonds by AAA, the Grand Cypress scores a perfect ten with both its accommodations choices, the Hyatt Regency Grand Cypress and the Villas of Grand Cypress. The 1,500-acre resort includes 45 holes of golf, a golf academy, a racquet club, equestrian club, and several gourmet restaurants.

Hampton Inn Lake Buena Vista

8150 Palm Parkway, Orlando, FL 32836. Phone: 407/465-8150 or Tel. 800/370-9259. Rates: $65 to $109. Discounts: AAA, AARP. Website: www.hamptoninn.com.

Located right in the middle of Vista Centre and its multitude of restaurants and shops, the Hampton Inn offers low-cost rooms that are surprisingly stacked with amenities. Their rates include free local calls, free breakfast, and courtesy shuttles to the airport and theme parks, while their facilities include a pool, gym, and jogging trail.

Holiday Inn SunSpree Resort – Lake Buena Vista

13351 SR 535, Orlando, FL 32821. Phone: 407/239-4500 or Tel. 800/366-6299. Rates: $68 to $168. Discounts: AAA, corporate, Magicard. Website: www.kidsuites.com.

As you could probably surmise from the hotel's Web address, the Sunspree is very proud of having innovated the KidSuites concept, a room-within-a-room to allow parents that most precious of family vacation commodities – time away from the kids. In addition to the specially appointed rooms, the hotel offers a special check-in just for kids, a movie theatre in the lobby showing family flicks all day, Camp Holiday, a supervised activity program, an arcade, and a kids-eat-free program. There's a food court including a Little Caesar's, A&W, TCBY, and a deli as well, along with a fitness room, landscaped pool area, and complimentary theme park shuttles.

Marriott World Center

8701 World Center Drive, Orlando, FL 32821. Phone: 407/239-4200 or Tel. 800/621-0638. Rates: $145 to $399 for rooms, $199 to $376 for villas. Discounts: AAA, AARP, corporate. Website: www.marriott.com.

This AAA Four Diamond resort scores big with 18 holes of golf, twelve tennis courts, and a variety of restaurants ranging from casual to upscale. While not quite as posh as the Grand Cypress, the Marriott is a formidable full-service resort destination. All of its rooms include private balconies and sitting areas complete with a convertible loveseat. Additionally, the Sabal Palms, Royal Palms, and Imperial Palms are complexes of two- and three-bedroom villas located adjacent to the high-rise, part of Marriott's Vacation Club division.

Residence Inn by Marriott – Lake Buena Vista

8800 Meadow Creek Drive, Orlando, FL 32821. Phone: 407/239-7700 or Tel. 800/244-4070. Rates: $79 to $239. Discounts: AAA, AARP, corporate, military. Website: www.residenceinn.com.

Just three miles from the Magic Kingdom, the Residence Inn offers 688 spacious one- and two-bedroom suites with fully equipped kitchens, and separate living and dining areas. The resort's amenities include 3 pools, a lighted tennis court, and preferred access to 18 holes of golf at the World Center Marriott.

Sheraton Safari Hotel

12205 Apopka-Vineland Road, Lake Buena Vista, FL 32836. Phone: 407/239-0444 or Tel. 800/423-3297. Rates: $99 to $179. Discounts: AAA, corporate. Website: www.sheratonsafari.com.

A cool African theme sets this hotel apart from cookie cutter motels, along with such goodies as a Sony Playstation in every room, a full-service restaurant, deli, and bar, a heated outdoor pool with a 79-foot waterslide, a 24-hour fitness room, and complimentary transportation to the Disney parks.

Vistana Resort
8800 Vistana Center Drive, Orlando, FL 32821. Phone: 407/239-3100 or Tel. 800/877-8787. Rates: $99 to $239. Discounts: Magicard. Website: www.vistana.com.
The Vistana's large, cheery villas include full kitchens, living rooms with cable TV and VCR, washers and dryers, and more. Two bedroom villas include a whirlpool in the master bath. The resort's amenities include 13 tennis courts, 7 pools, 18 holes of miniature golf, three recreation centers, jogging facilities, and several restaurants.

SEA WORLD/SOUTH INTERNATIONAL DRIVE AREA HOTELS

International Drive runs from the Belz Factory Outlet complex south past Kirkman Road and Sand Lake Drive, all the way past the Bee Line Expressway, Sea World, and the Convention Center, to SR 536 and eventually all the way to US 192 in Kissimmee.

There's a significant difference in the atmosphere between the northern and southern portions of I-Drive. North of Sand Lake Drive, I-Drive is tackier and more cluttered and claustrophobic. South of Sand Lake Drive, the Plaza International area of International Drive is much newer, somewhat more subdued, and definitely easier on the eyes while at the same time offering easy access to theme parks, restaurants, and shopping.

Best Western Plaza International
8738 International Drive, Orlando, FL, 32819. Phone: 407/345-8195 or Tel. 800/654-7160. Rates: $50 to $95. Discounts: AAA, AARP, corporate, military, Magicard. Website: www.go2orlando.com/sponsor/bestwestern/internationaldrive.
This Best Western is conveniently located in the middle of International Drive, close to the Mercado and Pointe Orlando complexes and just 1/2 mile from the Convention Center. There's a variety of rooms available, including family suites, kitchenettes, and king Jacuzzi rooms, all of which have large-screen cable TV's equipped with pay per view movies and a Super Nintendo. The amenities here are pretty basic, with a pool, whirlpool, bar, café, and game room, but the price is right.

Courtyard by Marriott International Drive
8600 Austrian Court, Orlando, FL 32819. Phone: 407/351-2244 or Tel. 800/321-2211. Rates: $99 to $160. Discounts: AAA, AARP, corporate, military. Website: www.courtyard.com.
This AAA Four Diamond property, located just off International Drive, offers its standard business-traveler amenities, including work

desks, data ports, and voice mail in rooms, as well as a restaurant, pool, exercise room, and is located just across the street from Mercado and all of its dining, shopping, and entertainment options.

Doubletree Castle Hotel

8629 International Drive, Orlando, FL 32819. Phone: 407/345-1511 or Tel. 800/95-CASTLE. Rates: $119 to $229. Discounts: AAA, AARP, corporate, military, Magicard. Website: www.grandthemehotels.com/th.

Definitely one of the best options for lodging in the area, the Doubletree is an eye-catcher, that's for sure. Designed to resemble a medieval castle (sort of), the hotel carries out the theme with European artwork and authentic Renaissance era music inside. As for the rooms, they're stacked. Each has two queen-size beds, a six channel stereo system, 25" television with a Sony Playstation, and a refrigerator and coffeemaker. Add two excellent on-site restaurants (Vito's Chop House and Café Tu Tu Tango), a piano lounge, poolside bar and café, fitness center, and free transportation to Disney, Universal, and Sea World, and you've got a winner on your hands.

Embassy Suites International Drive South

8978 International Drive, Orlando, FL 32819. Phone: 407/352-1400 or Tel. 800/433-7275. Rates: $129 to $189. Discounts: AAA, AARP, corporate. Website: www.embassy-suites.com.

Located near Pointe Orlando and the Convention Center, this Embassy Suites location offers the amenities that made the chain famous – reasonably priced two-room suites, complimentary breakfast and cocktails, pool, exercise room, and a breathtaking atrium lobby. They also offer complimentary shuttles to WDW.

Fairfield Inn by Marriott

8342 Jamaican Court, FL 32819. Phone: 407/363-1944 or Tel. 800/228-2800. Rates: $69 to $79. Discounts: AAA, AARP, corporate. Website: www.fairfieldinn.com.

Marriott's no-frills Fairfield Inn offers the basics at a basic price. Continental breakfast is included, as is transportation to Universal and Sea World, making this of the better area choices for travelers on a tight budget.

Hampton Inn Convention Center

8900 Universal Blvd., FL 32819. Phone: 407/354-4447 or Tel. 800/ HAMPTON. Rates: $59 to $149. Discounts: AAA, AARP. Website: www.hamptoninn.com

This brand-spanking-new hotel offers pleasant accommodations and basic amenities geared more towards business travelers, but the complimentary continental breakfast and primo location, right behind Pointe Orlando, make it an excellent choice for vacationers as well.

La Quinta Inn International Drive

8300 Jamaican Court, Orlando, FL 32819. Phone: 407/351-1660 or Tel. 800/531-5900. Rates: $89 to $99. Discounts: AAA, AARP, Magicard. Website: www.laquinta.com

The La Quinta offers decent sized rooms, some with fridge and microwave, all with pull-out love seats and two double beds. It's set off International Drive, with much quieter surroundings and all the convenience of hotels on I-Drive itself. There's a pool, whirlpool, and kiddie pool, and breakfast is included in your room rate.

Omni Rosen Hotel

9840 International Drive, Orlando, FL 32819. Phone: 407/996-9840 or Tel. 800/204-7234. Rates: $190 to $230. Discounts: AAA, AARP, corporate. Website: www.omnirosen.com

This 24-story behemoth towers over International Drive next to the Convention Center. Primarily geared to conventioneers, this hotel features plush accommodations and fine dining at the Everglades Restaurant, specializing in fish, steak, and game, as well as a casual restaurant and a 24-hour deli.

Peabody Orlando

9801 International Drive, Orlando, FL 32819. Phone: 407/352-4000 or Tel. 800/732-2639. Rates: $270 to $330. Discounts: AAA, AARP, corporate. Website: www.peabody-orlando.com

The impressive Peabody, the only sister property to the Peabody Hotel in Memphis, offers luxurious accommodations ranging from standard rooms to colossal bi-level presidential suites, as well as a wealth of dining options such as the 24-hour B-Line Diner, home of the best damn omelets in the world, the spiffy Capriccio for Northern Italian specialties, and Dux, the only Mobil Four Star restaurant in town.

Quality Inn Plaza

9000 International Drive, Orlando, FL 32819. Phone: 407/345-8585 or Tel. 800/999-8585. Rates: $40 to $80. Discounts: AAA, AARP, military. Website: www.qualityinn.com

Right across the street from Pointe Orlando, this is a no-frills establishment that's easy on the wallet. The hotel includes a pool, game room, restaurant, bar, and gift shop, but little more, but with such a wide array of options right across the street, that's not such a hardship.

Radisson Barcelo Hotel
8444 International Drive, Orlando, FL 32819. Phone: 407/345-0505 or Tel. 800/333-3333. Rates: $105 to $125. Discounts: AAA, AARP, corporate, military. Website: www.radisson.com.

Located across from Mercado, guests at this hotel have access to the adjacent YMCA Aquatic Center, with two Olympic size swimming pools, 23 Nautilus machines, and racquetball courts. The rooms were renovated in 1997 and are spacious with two queen size beds, two phones, and two vanity areas in standard rooms. They offer free shuttles to Disney, Universal, and Sea World.

Renaissance Orlando Resort
6677 Sea Harbor Drive, Orlando, FL 32821. Phone: 407/351-5555 or Tel. 800/327-6677. Rates: $159 to $259. Discounts: AAA, AARP, corporate, military. Website: www.renaissancehotels.com.

Formerly the Stouffer Orlando, this hotel, just beyond the Sea World parking lot, is a luxurious hotel with plush rooms featuring views of Sea World or of the hotel's gorgeous atrium, which includes koi ponds and an aviary. The hotel's amenities include four restaurants and a recreation area with a pool, kiddie pool, whirlpool, tennis courts, volleyball, and a playground.

Sheraton World Resort
10100 International Drive, FL 32821. Phone: 407/352-1100 or Tel. 800/327-0363. Rates: $109 to $189. Discounts: AAA, AARP, corporate, military. Website: www.sheratonorlando.com.

Renovated in 1998, this peaceful 28-acre complex has long been one of my favorites. The 800 rooms here have been decorated in a Mediterranean motif, and come equipped with in-room movies, Nintendo games, refrigerators, irons, and ironing boards. The grounds include several pools, three tennis courts, a health club, and a miniature golf course, along with four bars and restaurants.

Sierra Suites – Pointe Orlando
8750 Universal Blvd., Orlando, FL 32819. Phone: 407/903-1500 or Tel. 800/830-4964. Rates: $89 to $189. Discounts: AAA, AARP, corporate, military. Website: www.sierra-orlando.com.

Nestled beside I-Drive's premier shopping destination, Sierra Suites is an attractive choice that opened in summer 1999, featuring two phone lines in each suite, plus direct modem outlets, free local calls, and VCRs.

Wyndham Orlando Resort

8001 International Drive, Orlando, FL 32819. Phone: 407/351-2420 or Tel. 800/421-8001. Rates: $89 to $139. Discounts: AAA, AARP, corporate, military. Website: www.wyndham.com

Formerly the Orlando Marriott, this hotel consists of 16 buildings across 48 acres at the corner of International Drive and Sand Lake Road, one block from I-4. Although that is one of the busiest intersections in the area, the Wyndham has a surprisingly away-from-it-all feel.

Wynfield Inn Westwood

6263 Westwood Blvd., Orlando, FL 32821. Phone: 407/345-8000 or Tel. 800/346-1551. Rates: $59 to $99. Discounts: AAA, AARP, corporate, military, Magicard. Website: www.wynfieldinn.com.

Located near Sea World, the Wynfield Inn offers basic amenities and comfortable accommodations at a reasonable price.

UNIVERSAL STUDIOS ESCAPE HOTELS

Upping the ante in its eternal battle against Disney, Universal has opened the Portofino Bay Hotel, the first of five planned hotels located on the property, designed to cement Universal's place as a world class destination.

Universal guests gain many of the same amenities offered to Disney guests and then some, such as courtesy water taxis and buses, early admission to theme parks, front-of-line access to selected attractions during the first hour of operation, priority seating at selected shows and restaurants, complimentary package delivery, special admission media, and the ability to charge purchases to your room with your resort ID.

HARD ROCK HOTEL

Coming December 2000

The second Hard Rock Hotel in the world – the first being in Vegas – will showcase the unique architectural style of a California mission with public areas decorated with artifacts from the Hard Rock's memorabilia collection. Amenities will include two restaurants, three bars, a fitness center, pool, and business center.

PORTOFINO BAY HOTEL

1000 Universal Studios Plaza, Orlando, FL 32819. Phone: 407/503-1000 or Tel. 888/U-ESCAPE. Rates: $265 to $1000. Discounts: AAA, AARP. Website: www.portofinobayhotel.com.

One of the most beautiful hotels anywhere, the Portofino Bay Hotel is patterned after the Italian seaside village of Portofino, with amazing attention to detail paid to the décor and architecture. Marble, topiaries, and huge chandeliers welcome you to the lobby, while the guest rooms are decked out with just as much thought as the atmosphere.

The Portofino offers special services including Curbside Check In, which simplifies the arrival process and makes the obligatory stop at the front desk a thing of the past. Smart Rooms ensure state-of-the-art safety, security, and convenience, from the guest key, which doubles as your resort ID, to automatic temperature adjustment and monitoring of room vacancy to eliminate service-related disturbances. There's also butler service for guests staying in Villa rooms and suites.

Rooms

The 750 rooms are luxurious, with either one king or two queen size beds, a large television complete with Sony Playstation, wet bar, two telephone lines with data ports, bathrobes, slippers, iron and ironing board, and coffee makers.

Villa rooms feature full butler service, complimentary breakfast and evening cocktails, turndown service, in-room fax machine, CD player, and a VCR.

Eat

The Portofino Bay features six restaurants in addition to 24-hour room service. The Trattoria del Porto offers three meals and an extensive antipasto/dessert bar. The Delfino River Restaurant offers Tuscan specialties overlooking the Portofino Harbor. Sal's Market Deli offers take out and a harborside café atmosphere. Splendido Pizzeria is a pool bar and grill featuring a wood fire pizza oven. The Gelateria and Caffe Espresso offer homemade ice cream, Italian pastries, and fresh brewed espresso and cappuccino.

Drink

The Thirsty Fish offers a light menu with appetizers, burgers, mozzarella sticks, and seafood along with a full bar. Bar American is a sleek, stylish bar offering the utmost in service and continental appetizers and seafood.

Be Merry

As if being right in the middle of Universal Studios Florida, Islands of Adventure, and CityWalk wasn't enough, the Portofino Bay Hotel boasts a world class spa complete with a full service salon, a children's activity center, an acqueduct-styled pool with a waterslide, another pool, 3 whirlpools, jogging, and 2 bocce ball courts. There's also a complete business center and coming soon five shops.

ROYAL PACIFIC RESORT

Coming Spring 2001

This 1,000-room property will be accented with lush tropical landscaping, waterfalls, and lagoons, evoking the feel of the South Pacific. A variety of dining options will include a restaurant, snack bar, and the Village Bazaar food court.

UNIVERSAL/NORTH INTERNATIONAL DRIVE AREA HOTELS

While the northern end of International Drive has more traffic and neon and less open space and landscaping than the southern half, this is a good place to find bargains on hotel rooms and souvenirs. This is also home to the area's biggest concentration of outlet shops, and offers easy access to Universal Studios, Islands of Adventure, and Wet 'N Wild, while Disney World is less than 10 minutes away.

Best Western Universal Inn

5618 Vineland Road, Orlando, FL 32819. Phone: 407/226-9119. Rates: $50 to $120. Discounts: AAA, AARP, corporate, military. Website: www.bestwestern.com.

Located next to Universal Studios Escape, this new (September 1998) motel offers 70 cheerful rooms in an unbeatable location. Breakfast is included in your rate.

Delta Orlando Resort

5715 Major Blvd., Orlando, FL 32819. Phone: 407/351-3340 or Tel. 800/268-1133. Rates: $69 to $89. Discounts: AAA. Website: www.deltaorlandoresort.com

This 25-acre resort near Universal contains 800 rooms, 3 pools, hot tubs and saunas, lighted tennis, basketball, and volleyball courts, several restaurants, and a 70's themed disco.

Hampton Inn Universal Studios

5621 Windhover Drive, Orlando, FL 32819. Phone: 407/351-6716 or Tel. 800/231-8395. Rates: $62 to $84. Discounts: AAA, AARP, corporate, military. Website: www.hamptoninn.com.

Two blocks from Universal, this hotel caters to those on a tight budget with pleasant, bright rooms and free continental breakfast every day along with a pool and exercise room.

Holiday Inn Express International Drive

6323 International Drive, Orlando, FL 32819. Phone: 407/351-4430 or Tel. 800/365-6935. Rates: $69 to $109. Discounts: AAA, AARP, corporate, military, Magicard. Website: www.enjoyfloridahotels.com

Providing basic accommodations and amenities in a cheery environment, the Holiday Inn Express offers 218 newly renovated rooms at the entrance to Universal Studios Escape, along with free shuttles to Disney, complimentary continental breakfast, and a multitude of restaurants and shops within walking distance.

Holiday Inn & Suites Universal Studios

5905 South Kirkman Road, Orlando,, FL 32819. Phone: 407/351-3333 or Tel. 800/327-1364. Rates: $123 to $159. Discounts: AAA, AARP, corporate, military, Magicard. Website: www.hiuniversal.com

Right across the street from Universal, many of the Holiday Inn's rooms boast a view of the park. There's a TGI Friday's on site, plus a swimming pool, fitness center, game room, and complimentary shuttles to Sea World and Universal.

Quality Suites Universal Studios

7400 Canada Drive, FL 32819. Phone: 407/363-0332 or Tel. 800/228-2027. Rates: $109 to $119. Discounts: AAA, AARP, corporate, military. Website: www.qualityinn.com

This cheery pink hotel is located within walking distance of Wet 'N Wild, just one block from International Drive and includes free theme park shuttle transportation, full American breakfast buffet, and nightly cocktails in its rates.

Radisson Twin Towers Hotel Orlando

5780 Major Blvd., Orlando, FL 32819. Phone: 407/351-1000 or Tel. 800/333-3333. Rates: $89 to $149. Discounts: AAA, AARP, corporate, military. Website: www.radisson.com

This landmark hotel opposite the entrance to Universal is the largest of Radisson's properties, with 760 rooms, a junior Olympic sized pool, sauna, steamroom, Jacuzzi, two restaurants, and a food court with TCBY, Pizza Hut, and Java Boost counters.

Sheraton Studio City
5905 International Drive, Orlando, FL 32819. Phone: 407/351-2100 or Tel. 800/327-1366. Rates: $110 to $229. Website: www.grandthemehotels.com/scr

This hotel is hard to miss, it's the only round 21-story tower on the block. Its rooms carry an art deco theme to reflect its Universal-inspired homage to the golden age of the movie biz. There's also a new restaurant, the Starlight Grille, a lounge, pool, fitness center, and gameroom. Transportation to Sea World and Universal is also included.

OFF THE BEATEN PATH

There are hundreds of hotels and motels scattered throughout the area. Most of the ones listed previously in this chapter cater primarily to the typical Disney guest – one whose vacation focus is on theme park touring, who really aren't looking for more out of a hotel than a comfortable, clean room, some basic amenities such as a pool and a dining room, and close proximity to the parks, amusements, attractions, dining, and shopping.

However, those of you willing to look a little bit deeper when choosing your accommodations can be rewarded with a level of luxury, service, and relaxation you just won't find in more Disney-centric hotels.

Celebration Hotel
700 Bloom Street, Celebration, FL 34747. Phone: 407/566-6000 or Tel. 888/499-3800. Rates: $135 to $440. Discounts: AAA, AARP. Website: www.grandthemehotels.com/ch.

This beautiful hotel is the focal point of the architecture in the small town of Celebration, a Disney-planned community just south of US 192 in the southeastern corner of Walt Disney World. The hotel features 1920's Florida architecture and is designed to convey the charm of America's small town inns. Each of the 115 rooms is individually furnished with unique furnishings, along with three phone lines, a Nintendo, and more. The amenities of the hotel include an 18 hole golf course, the 65,000 square foot Celebration Fitness Center and Day Spa, and a heated swimming pool and spa.

Chalet Suzanne
3800 Chalet Suzanne Drive, Lake Wales, FL 33853. Phone: 941-676-6011 or Tel. 800/433-6011. Rates: $159 to $219. Discounts: AAA, corporate, military. Website: www.chaletsuzanne.com.

This lovely bed-and-breakfast is located in Lake Wales, about 30 minutes from Disney. The inn, located on 28 acres of unspoiled country-side, has been welcoming guests since 1931 and offers 30 unique guest rooms, a swimming pool, and a private lake. They have also been named to Uncle Ben's Top 10 Country Inns of the Year award, while their dining room, which offers six-course dinners, has received numerous accolades. Their soup is so legendary that it's out of this world – for real – their Romaine soup flew on the Apollo missions.

Courtyard at Lake Lucerne
211 North Lucerne Circle East, Orlando, FL 32801. Phone: 407/648-5188 or Tel. 800/444-5289. Rates: $115 to $225. Discounts: AAA, AARP, corporate.

The largest bed and breakfast in Orlando, this establishment encompasses four unique historic houses surrounding a tropical courtyard. All rooms include complimentary breakfast, wine reception upon check in, and daily maid service. Each house has its own unique charm and décor, making this one of the most unique lodging experiences in Orlando. The Courtyard is located approximately 30 minutes north of Disney via I-4.

Cypress Glen
10336 Centurion Court, Lake Buena Vista, FL 32830. Phone: 407/909-0338 or 877-290-1980. Rates: $300 to $500. Website: www.cypglen.com.

"One of my business traveler guests once asked me, 'What do people who come here do?' And I answered, 'Make love.'" The Cypress Glen's charming innkeeper, Sandy Sarillo, related this conversation to me upon a recent visit to this lovely bed-and-breakfast. And there could quite possibly be no better place for amorous newlyweds or couples to get their schwerve on than here, in a luxurious, quiet art deco house just five minutes and WORLDS removed from Disney. Perfect for honeymooners, business travelers, and those who just plain need a vacation from their vacation, Cypress Glen only offers two rooms – but oh, my. The bathroom in the Sophia Suite is larger than most hotel rooms and features a whirlpool bath for two, a huge shower, walk in closets, exercise machines, refrigerator, and wet bar – and that's just in the bathroom!

Other amenities include the Taproom smoking lounge, complete with a fully stocked bar and assortment of cigars, a lushly landscaped swimming pool and Jacuzzi, the lavish breakfast spread and wine-and-cheese reception held daily, and to-the-hilt concierge service provided by Ms. Sarillo. "Pampered" does not even begin to describe the level of service she provides. Note that children under 16 are not permitted at Cypress Glen.

Grenelefe Golf & Tennis Resort
3200 SR 546, Altamonte Springs, FL 32703. Phone: 941-422-7511 or Tel. 800/237-9549. Rates: $99 to $190. Discounts: AAA, AARP, corporate, military. Website: www.grenelefe.com.

This full-service resort located in a suburb north of Orlando offers 800 rooms and villas strewn throughout an Audubon-protected retreat, each offering a water, forest, or fairway view. Beyond the three 18-hole golf courses here, there's 20 tennis courts with three different surfaces, 11 of which are lighted, a fitness center, marina with fishing, rec center, and kids' programs, along with three restaurants.

Meadow Marsh Bed & Breakfast

940 Tildenville School Road, Orlando, FL 34784. Phone: 407/656-2064 or Tel. 888/656-2064. Rates: $95 to $199 Website: www.meadowmarsh.net.

This 1877 Victorian, located on 12 acres of lush vegetation in the suburb of Winter Garden, offers suites with 2-person whirlpools or cozy bed chambers complete with antique bath fixtures. Facilities include a piano lounge, library, tea room, and a breakfast area where a full breakfast is served daily.

Mission Inn Golf & Tennis Resort

10400 County Road 48, Howey-in-the-Hills, FL 34737. Phone: 352-324-3101 or Tel. 800/874-9053. Rates: $120 to $450. Discounts: Corporate. Website: www.missioninnresort.com.

The Mission Inn is another full-service resort located 35 minutes from Disney, offering amenities including 36 holes of golf, eight tennis courts, fishing, sailing, powerboating, volleyball, hot air ballooning, canoeing, horseback riding, three restaurants, and two lounges. Accommodations are in deluxe hotel rooms, club suites, and villas.

Poinciana Golf & Tennis Resort

500 East Cypress Parkway, Kissimmee, FL 34746. Phone: 407/870-5412 or Tel. 800/331-7743. Rates: $90 to $160. Website: www.poincianaresort.com.

The Poinciana is a small resort, with only 56 rooms, plus another 70 suites and villas. However, it is loaded with amenities, such as tennis courts, and an 18-hole, 6,700-yard golf course designed by Robert Van Hagge and Bruce Devlin. This resort is nestled deep within the town of Kissimmee, an easy drive from Disney in an area much easier on the eyes than the tourist drags.

OTHER LODGING OPTIONS

There are well over 200 hotels, motels, and resorts in and around Orlando, with over 91,000 rooms between them. The ones listed above are by no means the only places in Orlando where you can find a decent place to stay the night. There are other easy ways to find a hotel room in the area.

Contact the chains with locations in the area. Some of the hotel chains advertise specials on their website, so it's a decent idea to check there for the best rates before you make your reservations. Area chains include:

- **Best Western**, *Tel. 800/780-7234, www.bestwestern.com*
- **Choice Hotels**, *Tel. 800/221-2222, www.hotelchoice.com* (includes Sleep, Comfort, Quality, Clarion, and Rodeway Inns plus Econolodge)
- **Days Inn**, *Tel. 800/325-2525, www.daysinn.com*
- **Doubletree**, *Tel. 800/222-TREE, www.doubletree.com*
- **Embassy Suites**, *Tel. 800/362-2779, www.embassy-suites.com*
- **Hampton Inn**, *Tel. 800/426-7866, www.hamptoninn.com*
- **Holiday Inn**, *Tel. 800/HOLIDAY, www.holidayinn.com*
- **Howard Johnson**, *Tel. 800/I-GO-HOJO, www.hojo.com*
- **Hyatt**, *Tel. 800/233-1234, www.hyatt.com*
- **Marriott**, *Tel. 800/228-9290, www.marriott.com* (includes Fairfield and Residence Inn and Courtyard by Marriott)
- **Radisson**, *Tel. 800/333-3333, www.radisson.com*
- **Ramada**, *Tel. 800/298-2054, www.ramada.com*
- **Red Roof Inn**, *Tel. 800/843-ROOF, www.redroof.com*
- **Sheraton**, *Tel. 800/325-3535, www.sheraton.com*
- **Summerfield Suites**, *Tel. 800/833-4353, www.summerfieldsuites.com*
- **Travelodge**, *Tel. 800/255-3050, www.travelodge.com*
- **Wynfield Inn**, *Tel. 800/346-1551, www.wynfieldinn.com*

Use an online search service. Sites like Expedia, Travelocity, and Preview Travel allow you to search for hotels with price, location, and amenity criteria that you select.

Use a hotel reservations service. These services offer rooms at dozens of accommodations, usually weighted somewhat on the budget end of the spectrum. They offer some good rates and good deals, but it's in your best interest to shop around. There's a few who operate via websites and telephone only, but some of those listed below also offer visitor information centers where you can purchase attraction tickets, reserve rooms, and gather information in the form of brochures, coupons, and publications.

Some reservations services include:

- **Accommodations Express**, *Tel. 800/249-3836, www.accommodationsexpress.com*
- **Central Reservation Service**, *Tel. 800/548-3311, www.reservation-services.com*
- **Discount Hotels America**, *Tel. 877/766-6787, www.discounthotelsamerica.com (12179 S. Apopka Vineland Rd., Tel.407/238-9293)*
- **Hotel Reservations Network**, *Tel. 800/964-6835, www.180096hotel.com*

- **Know Before You Go**, *Tel. 800/749-1993, www.1travel.com/knowbeforeyougo (8000 International Drive, Tel. 407/352-9813; 4720 W. Irlo Bronson Mem. Hwy., Tel. 407/396-5400)*
- **Vacation Relaxation**, *www.vacationrelaxation.com (7862 W. Irlo Bronson Mem. Hwy., Tel. 352/394-0018)*
- **Vacation Works**, *Tel. 800/396-1883, www.vacationworks.com (4834 W. Irlo Bronson Mem. Hwy., Tel. 407/396-1883)*

9. WHERE TO EAT IN & AROUND ORLANDO

Now that you've arranged the roof over your head, it's time to turn your attention to one of the other essentials of your trip... the eats. There are over 3,800 restaurants in and around Orlando, including dozens inside the theme parks.

This chapter covers some of the best choices for dining in and around Orlando, Kissimmee, and Lake Buena Vista. It also includes restaurants in Disney hotels and attractions such as Downtown Disney and CityWalk that do not charge admission for access to them; and dining at Church Street Station.

KEY TO ABBREVIATIONS & PRICES

B – Breakfast   L – Lunch   D – Dinner   S – Snacks
Budget – Meals under $10
Moderate — $10 to $20
Expensive: $20 to $35
Very Expensive — $35 and up.

Unless stated otherwise, dress at all restaurants is casual and reservations are not required. Also, all restaurants are located in Orlando unless listed. For 60-day advance reservations at any Disney restaurant, *call 407/ WDW-DINE.*

EATING IN THE THEME PARKS
Information on restaurants inside the Magic Kingdom, Epcot, Disney-MGM Studios, Animal Kingdom, Universal Studios Florida, Islands of Adventure, Busch Gardens, and Sea World can be found in the chapters covering those parks.

American

ALL STAR CAFÉ

Location: Disney's Wide World of Sports, Walt Disney World. Phone: 407/827-8376. Prices: Moderate. Meals: LD.

This theme restaurant, partially owned by Joe Montana, Tiger Woods, Ken Griffey Jr., Shaquille O'Neal, and Wayne Gretzky among others, features sports memorabilia, huge television screens showing sporting events, and standard American fare, such as salads, burgers, sandwiches, and pasta

ARTIST POINT

Location: Disney's Wilderness Lodge, Walt Disney World. Phone: 407/WDW-DINE. Prices: Moderate to expensive. Meals: BD.

Northwestern American fare is what you'll find at this excellent eatery, tucked in the Wilderness Lodge, five minutes' boat ride from the Magic Kingdom. The menu includes such items as cedar plank wild king salmon, dungeoness crab, rainbow trout, peppered tuna, roasted buffalo, grilled quail, prime rib, and pork chops. There's also a character breakfast buffet here daily.

BASKERVILLE'S

Location: Inside the Grosvenor Resort, 1850 Hotel Plaza Blvd., Walt Disney World. Phone: 407/828-4444. Price: Budget to moderate. Meals: BLD

Baskerville's surrounds a Sherlock Holmes museum and serves Sherlock's Breakfast, prime rib, fresh grouper, stir-fry vegetables with shrimp, chicken, or beef, and impressive specialty buffets, including an unlimited prime rib buffet held nightly for $14.95 and a breakfast buffet.

BENNIGAN'S

Locations and phone: 6324 International Drive (407/351-4435), 6109 Westwood Blvd. (407/352-5657), 5877 W. Irlo Bronson Mem. Hwy. (407/390-0687), 13520 South Apopka Vineland Rd. (407/938-9090). Price: Budget to moderate. Meals: LD.

Bennigan's is a bar and restaurant that locals and tourists alike enjoy for happy hour festivities twice daily (from 2 to 7pm and again 10pm to midnight) and casual American fare. Burgers, salads, and sandwiches dominate the menu.

BIG RIVER GRILLE & BREWING WORKS

Location: Disney's Boardwalk, Walt Disney World. Phone: 407/560-0253. Prices: Moderate. Meals: LD.

Mmm. Beeeeeer. All the brews available here are made on the premises, in a process that diners can check out, from the mill room and the brew house to the fermentation room, straight into your glass. The food here runs the gamut from the casual, with snacks like hot beer pretzels and burgers to things like pan roasted mahi mahi and strip steak.

THE BLACK-EYED PEA
Location: 5305 W. Irlo Bronson Mem. Hwy., Kissimmee. Phone: 407/397-1500. Price: Budget to moderate. Meals: BLD.

Southern specialties are dished up in this fun, family-style establishment. Entrees include chicken fried steak, meatloaf, pot roast, chicken breast tenderloins, rotisserie chicken, catfish, whitefish, and more, all accompanied by homemade cornbread and rolls.

B-LINE DINER
Location: In the Peabody Orlando, 9801 International Drive, Orlando. Phone: 407/345-4460. Price: Budget to moderate. Meals: BLDS.

Located in the swank Peabody, the B-Line offers good ol' American diner fare in a 1958 atmosphere open 24 hours a day. Full bar service and takeout are available. The omelets are phenomenal.

BOB EVANS RESTAURANT
Locations and phone: 4967 W. Irlo Bronson Mem. Hwy (407/396-7377), 6014 Canadian Court (407/352-2161), 7411 W. Irlo Bronson Mem. Hwy (407/396-8599). Price: Budget. Meals: BLD

The savior of many a hungry traveler, Bob Evans offers homestyle favorites at reasonable rates. Specialties include sandwiches, burgers, salads, chicken fried steak, meat loaf, fried chicken, and at breakfast, country skillets, fried mush, and omelettes.

THE BUBBLE ROOM
1351 S. Orlando Ave., Maitland. Tel. 407/628-3331. Prices: Moderate. Meals: L,D.

The Bubble Room's decor is a wild melange of junk and antiques from the 1930's and 40's. The menu is just as eccentric, with entrees with names like Hit the Deck, the Eddie Fisherman, and the Hedy Lam(b)arr.

CHILI'S
Locations and phone: 7021 International Drive (407/352-7618), 12172 S. Apopka Vineland Road, Lake Buena Vista (407/239-6688), 5340 W. Irlo Bronson Mem. Hwy., Kissimmee (407/396-4333). Prices: Budget to moderate. Meals: LD.

Southwestern specialties are served at this popular chain of restaurants. The ribs, fajitas, and nachos are particularly good.

DAMON'S

Location: Mercado, 8445 International Drive, Orlando. Phone: 407/352-5984. Price: Budget to moderate. Meals: LD.

Damon's offers some of the best barbecue fare in the area, including St. Louis-style pork ribs, steaks, chicken, prime ribs, and Damon's Onion Loaf, a big brick of golden-brown onion rings.

DAN MARINO'S TOWN TAVERN

Location: Pointe Orlando, 9101 International Drive. Phone: 407/363-1013. Prices: Moderate. Meals: LD.

This restaurant, owned by the Dolphins' legend, features burgers, steaks, pasta, and seafood in a friendly, upscale atmosphere.

DENNY'S

Locations and phone: 5855 W. Irlo Bronson Mem. Hwy., Kissimmee (407/396-0757), 11037 International Drive (407/238-0887), 9880 International Drive (407/351-5127), 7660 International Drive (407/351-1420), 5825 International Drive (407/351-1581), 7631 W. Irlo Bronson Mem. Hwy., Kissimmee (407/396-0757), 12375 SR 535, Lake Buena Vista (407/239-7900). Prices: Budget. Meals: BLDS.

Breakfast served all day along with burgers, sandwiches, and more at reasonable prices. Some locations are open 24 hours.

DUX

Location: In the Peabody Orlando, 9801 International Drive, Orlando. Phone: 407/345-4550. Price: Expensive to very expensive. Meals: D.

The Peabody's signature restaurant features a selection of American regional cuisine in an elegant setting from 6 to 11pm, Monday through Saturday. While mallards can be seen throughout the décor of the restaurant, don't look for any on the menu.

EMERIL'S RESTAURANT ORLANDO

Location: Universal Studios CityWalk. Phone: 407/224-2424. Prices: Moderate to expensive. Meals: LD.

This sophisticated, spirited restaurant was created by master chef Emeril Lagasse, he of *Emeril Live* fame and one of Food & Wine Magazine's top 25 chefs in the country. The focus here is on the open kitchen in the center of the restaurant, and the menu is dominated by Creole cuisine, such as Louisiana oyster stew, duck, and rib eye steak. There's also a full bar and cigar bar, as well as a retail outlet.

ESPN CLUB
Location: Disney's Boardwalk, Walt Disney World. Phone: 407/939-3463. Prices: Budget to moderate. Meals: LD.
One of your best bets for lunch or dinner while at Epcot or Disney-MGM is to leave the park and come here, conveniently located a boat ride away from both. The menu includes ballpark fare and family-friendly American food with a tongue-in-cheek flair straight out of SportsCenter. The menu includes a little bit of everything but your best bets are the Bloody Mary chili, "Overtime" fries (prepared like nachos), half-pound burgers, and delicious BBQ pork sandwiches. You can also find an arcade and souvenir stand here.

EVERGLADES
Location: Omni Rosen Hotel, 9840 International Drive. Phone: 407/354-9840. Prices: Moderate to expensive. Meals: D.
This Floridian restaurant offers such gourmet fare as venison pepper steaks, blackened lamb chops, and gator chowder, right next door to the Convention Center.

FRIENDLY'S
Locations and phone: 4753 S. Kirkman Road (407/295-6843), 8718 International Drive (407/345-1655), 3915 W. Vine Street, Kissimmee (407/846-4432). Price: Budget. Meals: BLDS.
Friendly's really does seem friendly, an envoy from home when you lose your luggage, ding your rental car door, and lose your reservation. Frozen yogurt, ice cream, sandwiches, soups, and salads are served.

HARD ROCK CAFÉ ORLANDO
Location: Universal Studios CityWalk. Phone: 407/351-ROCK. Prices: Budget to moderate. Meals: LD.
The world's largest installation of the Hard Rock, this restaurant recently moved its massive $3.5 million collection of rock and roll memorabilia and its surprisingly tasty menu of American fare to a new, 650-seat building at Universal Studios Escape, a building shaped like the Colisseum in Rome. As for the menu, it's strictly American, with sandwiches, salads, hamburgers, rib-eye steak, and barbecued ribs, pork, and chicken. There's also a gift shop where you can purchase the Hard Rock Café t-shirts that everybody in their brother seems to own.

HOLLYWOOD DINER
Location: 4561 W. Irlo Bronson Mem. Hwy., Kissimmee. Phone: 407/396-1212. Prices: Budget. Meals: BLD.
Bop on in to this 1950's-themed diner, offering ribs, pork chops,

steak, seafood, steamed shrimp, and various other blue-plate specials. There is also a sports bar here with six television screens.

HOOTERS
Locations and phone: 5300 Kirkman Road (407/354-5350), 2201 W. Vine Street, Kissimmee (407/932-2702), Church Street Market, 55 Church Street (407/649-4327), Pointe Orlando, 9101 International Drive (407/355-7711). Prices: Budget to moderate. Meals: LD.

Hooters offers tasty chicken wings, oysters, sandwiches, steaks, and ribs, but people seem to overlook the food when talking about Hooters. Everybody always seems to focus on the Hooters girls, waitresses in tank tops and tiny orange shorts. Happy hours are aptly named here, and there's rock music and an under-30 crowd after dark.

HOULIHAN'S FOOD AND SPIRITS
Location: 9150 International Drive. Phone: 407/363-0043. Prices: Budget to moderate. Meals: LD.

This pleasant bar and restaurant on International Drive by the Convention Center offers specialties like ribs, Santa Fe style chicken over linguine, Black Angus strip steak, and jambalaya.

HOUSE OF BLUES
Location: Downtown Disney West Side. Phone: 407/934-2583. Prices: Moderate. Meals: LD.

Along with the adjacent HoB nightclub and merchandise shop, there's the House of Blues restaurant, which is one of my absolute favorite places to chow down in Disney World or really anywhere else for that matter. The atmosphere is appropriately melancholy – a ramshackle building with a dark interior decorated with memorabilia from blues greats past and present.

The entertainment, provided by live blues bands, is top-notch – I had a real hard time dragging myself out of the restaurant – and you've got no right to sing the blues about the food, which includes standard fare like burgers and sandwiches but Creole and Cajun fare, in addition to creative twists on classic dishes, including a phenomenal spinach and artichoke dip served with blue and yellow corn tortilla chips, and the Caesar salad pizza, with romaine lettuce, fresh parmesan, tomatoes, and Caesar dressing on top of a mozzarella-covered crust. There's also a gospel brunch on Sundays with Gospel entertainment and prime rib, omelets, jambalaya, and award-winning bread pudding.

INTERNATIONAL HOUSE OF PANCAKES

Locations and phone: 9990 International Drive (407/352-9447), 6005 International Drive (407/351-0031), 7661 International Drive (407/351-4090), 6065 W. Irlo Bronson Mem. Hwy., Kissimmee (407/396-0406), 5184 W. Irlo Bronson Mem. Hwy., Kissimmee (407/396-2033), 12400 S. Apopka Vineland Road (407/239-0909)). Prices: Budget. Meals: LD.

Pancake breakfasts served all day, burgers, salads, and sandwiches are on the fare at this old standby.

JACK'S PLACE

Location: Clarion Plaza Hotel, 9700 International Drive. Phone: 407/352-9700. Prices: Moderate to expensive. Meals: D.

Jack's Place, named for Jack Rosen, whose caricatures hang on the wall, offers London broil, filet mignon, shrimp, prime rib, cedar plank salmon, pasta, escargots, and other American specialties. For dessert, go for fried ice cream.

JB'S SPORTS RESTAURANT

Location: 4880 South Kirkman Road. Phone: 407/293-8881. Prices: Budget. Meals: LD.

Rated the best sports bar in town by the Orlando Sentinel, this restaurant contains 11 satellite dishes and screens as large as 18 feet, with up to 30 games at one time, plus great drink specials Tuesdays, Wednesdays, and Thursdays.

JIMMY BUFFETT'S MARGARITAVILLE

Location: Universal Studios CityWalk. Phone: 407/224-2000. Prices: Budget to moderate. Meals: LD.

Changes in latitude, changes in attitude – that's the point of your vacation, right? So enjoy Floribbean cuisine while you're here — a cheeseburger in paradise perhaps, or conch fritters, calamari, and fins to the left, fins to the right, with various fish entrees, or enjoy sandwiches including the Third World fish sandwich and Cuban Meatloaf Survival Sandwich, and margaritas (duh) that'll make you ask yourself, "Why don't we get drunk?" Which you can do at three bars, Land Shark Bar, Volcano Bar, and 12 Volt Bar. There's a $3.25 cover charge after 10pm, when live performances start. I think I've run out of puns so I'll move on.

JOHNNY ROCKET'S

Location: Pointe Orlando, 9101 International Drive. Phone: 407/903-0763. Prices: Budget. Meals: LD.

This 50's style diner features burgers, shakes, and flavored Cokes on the first level of the Pointe Orlando shopping center.

JT'S PRIME TIME RESTAURANT AND BAR

Location: 16299 W. Irlo Bronson Mem. Hwy., Kissimmee. Prices: Moderate to expensive. Meals: LD.

This western-themed restaurant, located far west of Disney on US 192, offers steaks, rribs, chicken, and the house specialty, real smoked BBQ and offers early bird specials before 6:30 PM.

JUNGLE JIM'S

Locations and phone: Church Street Marketplace, 55 West Church Street, Orlando (407/872-3111), Crossroads, 12501 SR 535, Lake Buena Vista (407/827-1258). Prices: Budget. Meals: LD.

"Superpowerful" tropical drinks, specialty sandwiches, salads, and more are offered in this restaurant whose safari theme is complemented by stuffed animals and live birds.

MORRISON'S CAFETERIA

Locations and phone: 7440 International Drive (407/351-0051), Osceola Square Mall, 3831 W. Vine St., Kissimmee (407/846-6011). Price: Budget. Meals: LD.

Morrison's offers 100 simple, freshly-prepared menu selections daily.

MOTOWN CAFÉ ORLANDO

Location: Universal Studios CityWalk. Phone: 407/224-2500. Prices: Budget to moderate. Meals: D.

This restaurant pays tribute to the legends of R&B, artists like the Temptations, the Four Tops, the Supremes, and the Jason Five. There are two stages for live performances from the Motown Moments and other acts and a retro lounge on the third floor. The menu includes dishes like corned beef hash and eggs, meatloaf, chicken fried steak, and BBQ ribs, plus a full bar and retail outlet.

NASCAR CAFÉ ORLANDO

Location: Universal Studios CityWalk. Phone: 407/224-7723. Prices: Budget to moderate. Meals: LD.

This is the only officially NASCAR-sanctioned restaurant, and features cars, a surround sound video wall, and rare memorabilia and artifacts. The menu includes salads, fish, chicken, ribs, sandwiches, and burgers. There are also more than 20 arcade games including a virtual reality race simulator.

NBA CITY

Location: Universal Studios CityWalk. Phone: 407/224-2000. Prices: Budget to moderate. Meals: LD.

Yet another theme restaurant, this one capitalizes on the National Basketball Association and its teams and players, with four distinct areas: The CityWalk Cage is a two-level dining room with two nine-foot-by-twelve-foot video monitors. NBA City Playground features 2,100 square feet of interactive fun and games. NBA City Club showcases live and classic games in an upscale lounge environment. The NBA City Store features a plethora of NBA licensed apparel and memorabilia, including personalized jerseys. The menu includes contemporary American standbys plus interesting salads, sandwiches, pasta dishes, and more.

OMELET HOUSE
Location: 7618 W. Irlo Bronson Mem, Hwy, Kissimmee. Phone: 407/396-6957. Price: Budget. Meals: BLD.

This unpretentious restaurant serves up a dozen different omelettes, plus waffles and pancakes at breakfast. At lunch and dinner, sandwiches, steak, and family-style entrees make up the menu.

PASTAMORE
Location: Universal Studios CityWalk. Phone: 407/224-2244. Prices: Budget to moderate. Meals: BLD.

Pastamoré is a colorful family-style Italian eatery offering à la carte and family style menu items as well as takeout from their Marketplace Café. The menu includes pizza, chicken, steak, breakfast pastries, sandwiches, and gelato.

PAT O'BRIEN'S
Location: Universal Studios CityWalk. Phone: 407/224-2100. Prices: Moderate. Meals: LD.

This is an authentic replica of New Orleans' favorite watering hole, from the dueling pianos to the "flaming fountain" to the world-famous and rumfully delicious Hurricane drink. The menu includes Cajun style appetizers, entrees, and desserts, including catfish filets, jambalaya, shrimp Creole, and wings. Merchandise is available and there's nightly entertainment.

PEBBLES
Locations and phone: 17 W. Church St. (407/839-0892), Crossroads, 12551 SR 535, Lake Buena Vista (407/827-1111). Price: Moderate. Meals: LD.

Pebbles offers a wide range of foods ranging from casual hamburgers to gourmet delicacies like smoked duck with scallops and herb crusted chicken in a casual, fun California-themed atmosphere.

PERKINS FAMILY RESTAURANT
Locations and phone: 5170 W. Irlo Bronson Mem. Hwy., Kissimmee (407/239-0561), 7451 W. Irlo Bronson Mem. Hwy., Kissimmee (407/396-0845), Crossroads, 12559 SR 535, Lake Buena Vista (407/827-1060). Price: Budget. Meals: BLD.

Perkins, a family place open 24 hours, is well-known for their pancakes. Also featured are eggs Benedict, steak, burgers, and sandwiches.

PINEAPPLE PETE'S
Location: 7514 W. Irlo Bronson Mem. Hwy., Kissimmee. Phone: 407/296-2000. Prices: Budget. Meals: BD.

More geared towards an adult audience, Pete's offers breakfast and dinner buffets plus pool tables and dartboards in the lively bar.

PLANET HOLLYWOOD
Location: Downtown Disney West Side. Phone: 407/827-7827. Price: Moderate. Meals: LD.

The building is a landmark, a towering blue globe looming over Pleasure Island. The food is secondary to the atmosphere and the memorabilia hanging on the walls of the 400-seat restaurant, but like the Hard Rock Cafe, the food is surprisingly good. Expected and exotic burgers, sandwiches, salads, pizzas, pastas, and smoked and grilled meats are the primary specialties. Souvenirs are sold in a separate building, so those who were unable to be seated at the restaurant can buy t-shirts to make people think they ate there.

RACE ROCK ORLANDO
Location: 8986 International Drive. Phone: 407/249-9876. Prices: Budget to moderate. Meals: LD.

With celebrity owners like Kyle and Richard Petty, Jeff Gordon, Rusty Wallace, and Michael Andretti, Race Rock offers a huge collection of racing memorabilia (stock cars, funny cars, Indy cars, motorcycles, monster trucks, hydroplanes, and top fuel dragsters). As for the food, you'd be hard pressed to find bigger portions *anywhere*. A bowl of four onion soup could fill a gas tank on a stock car, and the nachos would feed a third world nation. There's a wide variety of entrees, sandwiches, and other goodies to choose from. While the décor and theme of the restaurant may not be to everyone's liking, the food certainly is.

RAINFOREST CAFÉ
Locations and phone: Disney's Animal Kingdom (407/938-9106), Downtown Disney Marketplace (407/827-8500). Prices: Moderate. Meals: BLD.

This wildly popular theme restaurant recently opened two locations in Disney World, one at the Marketplace and one just outside the gates to the Animal Kingdom. You don't need to buy an Animal Kingdom ticket to eat at the restaurant there, however. The restaurant combines a conservation theme and wild rainforest décor with unusual twists on classic food items, such as burgers (both beefy and meatless), pasta dishes, steaks, ribs, and much more. Breakfast is served at both locations as well.

SHONEY'S

Locations and phone: 7437 International Drive (407/248-9050), 5020 South Kirkman Road (407/352-1516), 6075 W. Irlo Bronson Mem. Pkwy., Kissimmee (407/396-4849), 7640 W. Irlo Bronson Mem. Hwy., Kissimmee (407/397-2779), 12204 S. Apopka Vineland Rd., Lake Buena Vista (407/239-5416). Prices: Budget. Meals: BLD.

Shoney's offers breakfast buffet plus burgers, sandwiches, steaks, chicken, seafood, and pasta at low prices.

SONNY'S REAL PIT BBQ

Location: 4200 Vine St., Kissimmee. Phone: 406-847-8888. Prices: Budget. Meals: LD.

Sonny's offers all-you-can-eat specials on BBQ chicken, beef, pork, and ribs Sunday through Wednesday of every week.

T.G.I. FRIDAY'S

Locations and phone: Crossroads, 12543 SR 535, Lake Buena Vista (407/827-1020), 5034 W. Irlo Bronson Mem. Hwy., Kissimmee (407/397-2200), 8126 International Drive (407/363-1414), 6424 Carrier Drive (407/345-8822). Price: Budget. Meals: LD.

The Great American Bistro, as Friday's is known, serves up tasty American favorites including sandwiches, steaks, burgers, and over 400 different drinks. Their appetizers, especially fried mozzerella and potato skins, are stellar. The International Drive location is a Friday's Front Row Sports Grill, a sports bar stacked with a full menu, 100 brands of domestic and imported beer, and 80 TVs, two basketball hoops, pool tables, video games, shuffle boards, darts, and memorabilia.

TONY ROMA'S – THE PLACE FOR RIBS

Locations and phone: 8550 International Drive (407/363-7427), 12167 Apopka Vineland Road, Lake Buena Vista (407/239-8040), Osceola Mall, 3415 W. Vine St., Kissimmee (407/870-9299). Price: Budget to moderate. Meals: D.

The Valhalla for rib lovers, varieties available include the original baby backs, Carolina honeys, Blue Ridge smokies, and Tony Roma's Red Hots. Also legendary here is the onion ring loaf.

TRADEWINDS

Location: RenaissanceResort, 6677 Sea Harbor Drive. Phone: 407/351-5555. Prices: Moderate. Meals: BLD.

Tradewinds, an open-air cafe in the luxuriant Stouffer Orlando, offers a pleasant dining experience across the street from Sea World, an excellent choice for a lunch to break up the day at the marine park.

WILDHORSE SALOON

Location: Downtown Disney Pleasure Island. Phone: 407/827-4947. Prices: Moderate. Meals: LD.

This country music club features live music and dance lessons nightly as well as award-winning BBQ and American goodies. The menu includes applewood smoked ribs, steaks, oak-roasted salmon, bourbon mustard pork chops, and various side-splitting combinations thereof.

WOLFGANG PUCK CAFÉ

Location: Downtown Disney West Side. Phone: 407/938-9653. Prices: Moderate to expensive. Meals: LD.

This open, airy edition of the world-famous chef's culinary playground features all the food that made Mister Puck famous – California-style pizzas and unique appetizers such as barbeque duck quesadillas, three different varieties of spring rolls, pad thai, blackened jumbo Gulf shrimp, free range chicken, ahi tuna, rotisserie lamb and chicken, Sonoma lamb chops, and half-pound burgers for your less adventurous (read: loser) companions. There are three different crème brulées to end your meal on the most decadent note possible. There's also a Wolfgang Puck Express with a limited menu with budget prices at Downtown Disney Marketplace.

Chinese

BILL WONG'S FAMOUS SUPER BUFFET

Location: 5668 International Drive. Phone: 407/352-5373. Prices: Moderate. Meals: LD.

Located at the corner of International Drive and Kirkman Road right by Universal Studios, this restaurant features a 100-item buffet for both lunch and dinner.

FORTUNE COURT

Location: 8607 Palm Parkway, Lake Buena Vista. Phone: 407/239-2399. Prices: Budget to moderate. Meals: LD.

The Fortune Court is a personal favorite of mine as far as Chinese food in Orlando is concerned, because the restaurant feels much more like a local place you pop into for wonton soup and an egg roll than a tourist-oriented dive less than a mile from Walt Disney World. Traditional Schezuan and Hunan cuisine is featured.

HAIFENG

Location: Renaissance Orlando Resort, 6677 Sea Harbor Drive. Phone: 407/351-5555. Prices: Moderate to expensive. Meals: D.

This restaurant offers gourmet Asian dishes and in intimate, classy atmosphere. The tastiest items on the menu include General Chow chicken, Mandarin lobster, Peking duck, and beef with orange peel.

MING COURT

Location: 9188 International Drive. Phone: 407/351-9988. Prices: Moderate. Meals: LD.

Now this is one joint nobody would dare call quaint. It's as flashy as Universal and Disney. It's virtually impossible not to see it. The emphasis of the innovative menu is on grilled Florida seafood and steak interspersed with regional Chinese cuisine. There's a dim sum bar and live Chinese music nightly.

TREY YUEN

Location: 6800 Visitors Circle. Phone: 407/352-6822. Prices: Budget. Meals: LD.

This restaurant is particularly convenient to Wet'n Wild, Universal, and the northern half of I-Drive. They offer a standard array of Chinese dishes plus special family combinations.

TWIN DRAGONS

Location: 4002 W. Vine St., Kissimmee. Phone: 407/846-6161. Prices: Budget. Meals: LD.

Given a Central Florida People's Choice Award and the Osceola Sentinel Reader's Choice Award, the Twin Dragons restaurant, located seven miles east of I-4, offers Cantonese and Schezuan cuisine. Lunch buffets and early bird specials are available.

Continental
ARTHUR'S 27

Location: 27th Floor, Wyndham Palace Resort, 19000 Hotel Plaza, Downtown Disney. Phone: 407/827-3450. Prices: Very expensive. Meals: D.

This elegant spot boasts an incredible view of all central Florida. An extensive wine list are available. The restaurant's skilled chefs can satisfy any dietary request with advance notice. Entertainment is provided by the Jazz Trio that performs on Friday and Saturday, the two nights that are most popular at the restaurant. AAA calls it a "unique culinary experience," with "artistic presentations impeccably served."

And they slapped Arthur's 27 with a Four Diamond Award. Orlando Magazine's readers named it one of the top three continental restaurants in the metropolis. It was given the Golden Spoon Award as one of the state's top 12 restaurants, four times. Reservations are required and should be made as soon as possible.

ATLANTIS

Stouffer Orlando, 6677 Sea Harbor Dr., Orlando. Tel. 351-5555. Prices: Expensive. Meals: D.

Elegant to the max, Atlantis offers stellar seafood and choice continental cuisine. Even better, for families with children, diners receive three hours of complimentary child care at the hotel's kids' club.

CHALET SUZANNE

Location: 3800 Chalet Suzanne Drive, Lake Wales. Phone: 941/676-6011. Prices: Expensive. Meals: D.

Chalet Suzanne is one of the finest restaurants in the area, offering soups that are absolutely legendary – so renowned that they flew on the Apollo 15 and 16 missions. Beside their house soup, the Romaine, they sell twelve different kinds of hot steamy goodness. The Chalet Suzanne has won the coveted Golden Spoon Award, given to the area's top restaurants, for over thirty years running. The restaurant is also on the National Register of Historic Places. It's located about 20 minutes from Disney. Take I-4 west to Exit 23, US 27, south to Route 17A.

CHATHAM'S PLACE

Location: 7575 Dr. Phillips Blvd. Phone: 407/345-2992. Prices: Very expensive. Meals: D.

Chatham's Place has an immense following who swear by their continental and American fare. Seafood, chicken, beef, and wild game dishes are featured. They've also received the Golden Spoon Award as well as accolades from Zagat and the Orlando Sentinel.

CITRICO'S

Location: Disney's Grand Floridian Resort, Walt Disney World. Phone: 407/WDW-DINE. Prices: Expensive. Meals: D.

This sunny, casual restaurant, which replaced Flagler's, overlooks the marina and provides a prime vantage point for the Magic Kingdom fireworks. The food is eclectic, with by French, German, Greek, Italian, Spanish, Californian, and Floridian influences. There's also an extensive wine list.

LA COQUINA

Locaiton: Hyatt Regency Grand Cypress, 1 Grand Cypress Blvd. Phone: 407/239-1234. Prices: Very expensive. Meals: D. Reservations are requested and dress is informal.

This top-notch restaurant in the area's finest hotel offers New World Cuisine, with entrees consisting of fish and shellfish plus meat and game, many with a citrus flair. There's also a champagne brunch on Sundays. They have won awards from Wine Spectator for the past five years due to their excellent wine cellar.

MAISON & JARDIN

Location: 430 South Wymore Road, Altamonte Springs. Phone: 407/862-4410. Prices: Expensive to very expensive. Meals: D and Sunday brunch.

The "Mason Jar," recipient of the Wine Spectator "Best of Award of Excellence" and Mobil Four Star awards, offering 40 wines by the glass and 800 by the bottle. The restaurant and its grounds are both beautiful, and the food is second to none. Dinner, cocktails, and Sunday champagne brunch are served. The restaurant is an excellent choice for a quiet, romantic night out.

SPOODLES

Location: Disney's Boardwalk. Phone: 407/939-3463. Prices: Moderate to expensive. Meals: BLD.

This restaurant has become a fast favorite for many Disney visitors, with innovative Mediterranean cuisine, including tapas (sampler sized appetizers), seafood (including 24-ounce French sea bass flown straight from the Mediterranean to you), pasta, chicken, beef, and lamb dishes. The lunch menu includes pizzas, sandwiches, and salads, while the breakfast buffet includes classic American fare plus Moroccan-style food including wraps and frittatas. Pizza takeout is also available by the slide and pie.

VICTORIA & ALBERT'S

Location: Disney's Grand Floridian Resort. Phone: 407/WDW-DINE. Prices: If you have to ask, you probably can't afford it. Meals: D. Reservations are required and the dress code is elegant.

The shining jewel of Disney's dining crown, this continental restaurant earned four stars from Mobil and four diamonds from AAA. The menu for the prix fixe seven-course dinner changes daily but can always be counted on to amaze. The service and atmosphere is equally dazzling, with a butler and maid for each table, German Schlott-Zweisel crystal, English Royal Doulton chinaware, and settings of Italian Sambonet silver, which are changed between each course, so no worries if you can't remember which fork is for the salad. Prices run $80 to $110 per person, an additional $30 to $45 to add wine pairings. Diners receive Godiva chocolates, long-stemmed roses and hand-printed souvenir menus to close out their experience.

To further amaze yourself, make your reservations extra early and request the Chef's Table. There is only one seating per night here, and as the name implies, it comes with personalized attention from the chef and staff while you dine in an alcove in the kitchen. It's $20 extra per person but nobody seems to complain. If you've got the scratch, you'd be hard pressed to find a better way to spend it.

French
LE COQ AU VIN
Location: 4800 S. Orange Ave. Phone: 407/851-6980. Prices: Moderate. Meals: LD.

This restaurant features hearty French classics, with the focus on seafood prepared with flair by chef Louis Perotte, who hails from France's west coast and brings with him the cooking styles of the region.

LE CORDON BLEU
Location: 537 West Fairbanks Ave., Maitland. Phone: 407/647-7575. Prices: Moderate to expensive. Meals: LD.

Le Cordon Bleu features a selection of clasic French entrees like chateaubriand, rack of lamb, stuffed mushrooms, and more. The pastries are decadent and delicious.

Indian
AKBAR PALACE
Location: 4985 W. Irlo Bronson Mem. Hwy., Kissimmee. Phone: 407/396-4836. Prices: Budget. Meals: D.

A variety of Indian specialties are offered here, including tandoori, chicken, lamb, beef, seafood, basmati, rice, and vegetarian dishes.

PUNJAB INDIAN RESTAURANT
Location: 7451 International Drive. Phone: 407/352-7887. Prices: Budget. Meals: LD.

New Punjab offers a taste of Indian specialties with and without vegetables. Take-out is available.

PASSAGE TO INDIA
Location: 5532 International Drive. Phone: 407/351-3456. Prices: Budget. Meals: LD.

Voted the best Indian restaurant in Orlando by the readers of the

Orlando Sentinel, Passage to India offers authentic Indian cuisine cooked to order, mild to spicy. There's an all-you-can-eat lunch buffet, and beer and wine are served.

SHAMIANA RESTAURANT
Location: 7040 International Drive. Phone: 407/354-1160. Prices: Moderate. Meals: LD.
This restaurant, on International Drive near Wet 'N' Wild, offers traditional Indian fare like tandoori chicken and curry dishes.

International
BAHAMA BREEZE
Location: 8849 International Drive. Phone: 407/248-2499. Prices: Budget to moderate. Meals: D.
This bar and restaurant features everything from steel drum bands to high energy house music along with free-flowing bars and island cuisine, including pizzas, salads, sandwiches, pastas, seafood, chicken, beef, and pork dishes with a Caribbean flair.

BOB MARLEY – A TRIBUTE TO FREEDOM
Location: Universal Studios CityWalk. Phone: 407/224-2262. Prices: Budget. Meals: D.
This restaurant and club pays tribute to the King of Reggae with a recreation of his Kingston, Jamaica home, plus video monitors telling Marley's story through images and music, and a Jamaican menu of appetizers, entrees, and desserts. Entrees include Jamaican beef patties and roasted plantains.

BONGO'S CUBAN CAFÉ
Location: Downtown Disney West Side. Phone: 407/828-0999. Prices: Moderate to expensive. Meals: LD.
This restaurant, owned partially by Gloria Estefan and her husband Emilio, contains two floors of dining along with a patio and a dance floor. The menu provides variety for everyone – fish, chicken, steak, and pork plus sandwiches at lunch, most notably the Cubano, the nation's greatest accomplishment since the cigar.

BRAZIL GRILL
Location: 7467 International Drive. Phone: 407/354-4669. Prices: Moderate. Meals: LD.
This restaurant, located a half mile south of Wet 'N' Wild, offers specialty cocktails and Brazilian cuisine, including a buffet served Saturday and Sunday nights after 7pm.

CAFÉ BRAZIL

Location: 6540 Carrier Drive. Phone: 407/363-7009. Prices: Moderate. Meals: BLD.

Located just off the north end of International Drive, this restaurant offers budget prices for the excellent, casual Brazilian fare they serve.

CAFE TU TU TANGO

Location: 8625 International Drive. Phone: 407/248-2222. Prices: Moderate. Meals: LD.

Orlando's installment of the popular concept restaurant, themed after a Spanish artists' loft, could very well be the most eclectic restaurant in the area. Comparable to a tapas bar, Tu Tu Tango offers appetizer-sized dishes designed for mixing and matching, sampling and sharing. The menu includes wide varieties of dips, soups, and finger foods ranging from standbys like spinach and artichoke dip to things like the beef napoleon and curry coconut tuna along with pot stickers, egg rolls, wings and ribs, quesadillas, and pizzas, all with a playful twist from the norm.

LATIN QUARTER

Location: Universal Studios CityWalk. Phone: 407/363-5922. Prices: Moderate. Meals: LD.

Serving the nuevo Latino cuisine of 21 different nations, this CityWalk restaurant is the place to live la vida loca, with tasty and creative spins on classic Latin creations, including quesadillas stuffed with portobellos, bell peppers, corn, ancho chilies, and cheese, ceviche, fried plantains with crab meat, Chilean salmon salads, and many other beef, pork, chicken, and seafood specialties. There's also a dance floor and stage, and there is a cover charge late in the evening, ranging from $4 to $10.

OHANA

Location: Disney's Polynesian Resort, Walt Disney World. Phone: 407/WDW-DINE. Prices: Expensive. Meals: D.

The main dining room at Disney's Polynesian-themed hotel offers a prix fixe meal consisting of huge courses of fruit, vegetables, and bread, followed by chicken wrapped in banana leaves, smoked seared salmon, and flame grilled sirloin steak. Drinks and desserts are available à la carte. While you dine you can enjoy hula lessons, coconut races, and storytelling.

Italian

BELLA ROMA

Location: 6423 International Drive. Phone: 407/352-9603. Prices: Budget to moderate. Meals: D.

Located two blocks from Wet 'n Wild, this restaurant offers fresh pastas and pizza, seafood, chicken, and veal dishes.

BERGAMO'S

Location: Mercado, 8445 International Drive. Phone: 407/352-3805. Prices: Moderate. Meals: D.

Bergamo's is a classy place located in the Mercado Mediterranean Village shopping center, featuring "a taste of Italy New York style." Complete with singing waiters. You may find a few surprises on the menu, which includes homemade pasta and traditional dishes, fresh seafood, and certified Angus steaks.

CAFÉ D'ANTONIO

Location: 691 Front Street, Celebration. Phone: 407/566-CAFE. Prices: Moderate. Meals: LD.

This restaurant offers fine Italian food a bit on the unusual side. If you can't make it any further into the menu at the Olive Garden than veal parmesan, this probably isn't the place for you. However, if you've got a sense of adventure, the entrees and pasta dishes won't disappoint.

CAPRICCIO

Location: Peabody Orlando, 9801 International Drive. Phone: 407/345-4450. Prices: Moderate to expensive. Meals: D.

Cappricio rounds out the trio of stellar restaurants in the Peabody Orlando, offering Northern Italian cuisine in an Italian modern setting, complete with display kitchen and brick pizza oven.

CHRISTINI'S

Location: 7600 Dr. Phillips Blvd., Orlando. Phone: 407/345-8770. Prices: Expensive. Meals: D.

Ivy Award winner Chris Christini has over 40 years of experience under his belt and still personally orchestrates his culinary team as they prepare pasta, chicken, seafood, and veal dishes ranging from well-interpreted staples like fettuccine Alfredo and veal piccata to the unusual, like three different varieties of seafood flambé and costata di vitello, a legendary 26 ounce veal chop. The restaurant has won dozens of awards, including the Wine Spectator Award and the AAA Four Diamond Award and has been named to the Distinguished Restaurants of North America list.

DOMINO'S PIZZA

Prices: Budget. Meals: L,D.

Call 896-3030 for pizza delivery anywhere in metro Orlando, 396-0550 for Kissimmee delivery.

EAST SIDE MARIO'S

Location: 8731 International Drive. Phone: 407/363-1190. Price: Budget. Meals: LD.

This new restaurant, located on the south end of International Drive, offers traditional Italian fare plus steak and ribs, going for a New York atmosphere. The desserts here are especially good.

ELEGANTE PIZZERIA & DELI

Location: 6400 International Drive. Phone: 407/226-1515. Price: Budget. Meals: LD.

Located on the north end of I-Drive, the standout choice at this industry-standard pizzeria is a Mediterranean pizza topped with artichoke hearts, tomatoes, and green peppers. Delivery is available.

ENZO'S

Location: 1130 South US 17-92, Longwood. Phone: 407/834-9872. Price: Expensive. Meals: LD.

Enzo's was named the top Italian restaurant in Orlando by the Orlando Magazine Readers' Choice Awards, and for good reason. This placid spot, overlooking a beautiful lake, serves up traditional specialties for lunch and dinner Tuesday through Saturday.

FLIPPER'S PIZZA

Locations and phone: 7480 Universal Blvd. (407/351-5643), 4774 Kirkman Road (407/521-0607), 6125 Westwood Blvd. (407/345-0113). Price: Budget. Meals: LD.

One of the better pizzerias in the area, Flipper's serves up salads, pasta, calzones, subs, and pizzas. New York, Chicago, and California style pies are available with over two dozen different toppings. Beer, wine, soda, and delivery are available as well.

FRANCESCO'S RISTORANTE ITALIANO

Location: 4920 W. Irlo Bronson Mem. Hwy., Kissimmee. Phoe: 407/396-0089. PricesL Moderate. Meals: D.

This family-owned restaurant offers hot and cold antipasto, pizza, calamari, octopus, veal, chicken, steaks, seafood, and pasta plus specialties of the house.

GIORDANO'S

Locations and phone: 12151 S. Apopka Vineland Road, Lake Buena Vista (407/239-8900), 7866 W. Irlo Bronson Mem. Hwy., Kissimmee (407/397-0044). Prices: Budget. Meals: LD.

This restaurant is renowned for its stuffed pizzas and also offers thin crust pizzas with a variety of adventurous toppings including spinach, shrimp, broccoli, and fresh garlic. Salads, sandwiches, and pastas are also available.

HOMETOWN PIZZA

Location: 4147 W. Vine Street, Kissimmee. Phone: 407/932-4411. Prices: Budget. Meals: D.

This restaurant offers pizza delivery along the Kissimmee tourist corridor, along with inexpensive calzones, pasta dishes, and more.

ITALIANNI'S

Location: 8148 International Drive. Phone: 407/345-8884. Prices: Moderate. Meals: LD.

Italianni's serves traditional dishes like spaghetti and meatballs and eggplant parmigiana as well as more exotic choices like salmon oreganato and lasagna a la ravina.

MICHELANGELO

Location: 4898 Kirkman Road. Phone: 407/297-6666. Prices: Moderate to expensive. Meals: LD. Reservations are requested.

This restaurant near Universal offers elegant Italian fare such as an excellent zuppa di pesce with shrimp, clams, mussels, scallops, and calamari over spaghetti and costata Michelangelo, a veal chop stuffed with prosciutto, mozzarella, and spinach. Classical and jazz entertainment is provided nightly.

THE OLIVE GARDEN

Locations and phone: 7653 International Drive (407/351-1082), Church Street Market, 55 West Church St. (407/648-1098), 5021 W. Irlo Bronson Mem. Hwy., Kissimmee (407/396-1680), 12361 Apopka Vineland Road, Lake Buena Vista (407/239-6708). Prices: Budget. Meals: LD.

The Olive Garden is a great choice for lovers of veal and chicken parmesan as well as for pizzas and other classic Italian dishes. The food is well prepared if not imaginative and the portions are colossal. The bottomless soup, salad, and breadsticks are a nice complement to any meal and also make for a filling, easy-on-the-wallet lunch. Sinful desserts include cannoli and tiramisu, and all items are available for takeout.

PACINO'S ITALIAN RISTORANTE
Location: 5795 W. Irlo Bronson Mem. Hwy., Kissimmee. Phone: 407/396-8022. Prices: Moderate. Meals: D.

Pacino's menu offers standard family-friendly Italian fare, with homemade pastas, sauces, bread, and desserts along with steak and seafood grilled on an open copper Sicilian grill.

PALIO
Location: Walt Disney World Swan. Phone: 407/934-3000. Prices: Moderate to expensive. Meals: D.

This fine Italian bistro is decorated with bright, vivid banners representing the Italian counties that competed in the races for which the café is named. Strolling mandolin players regale guests who dine on specialties including brick oven pizza, fettuccine Alfredo, linguini topped with shrimp and scallops, and an awesome stuffed veal chop.

PIZZA HUT
Locations and phone: 8699 Palm Parkway, Lake Buena Vista (407/239-0205), 5740 W. Irlo Bronson Mem. Hwy., Kissimmee (407/396-2207), 7060 International Drive (407/239-4456). Prices: Budget. Meals: LD.

Pizza Hut offers a variety of tasty if not overly authentic pizzas at several area locations, as well as through an increasing number of hotel restaurants. Contact your guest services desk for information and delivery numbers.

PIZZERIA UNO
Locations and phone: Crossroads, 12553 SR 535, Lake Buena Vista (407/827-1212), Church Street Marketplace, 55 West Church St. (407/839-1800), 8250 International Drive (407/351-8667), 5350 W. Irlo Bronson Mem. Hwy., Kissimmee (407/396-2755). Prices: Budget. Meals: LD (B at Kissimmee location only).

Pizzeria Uno offers Chicago-style deep dish pizzas and Italian specialties along with burgers and grilled items, giving this restaurant even broader appeal.

PORTOBELLO YACHT CLUB
Location: Downtown Disney Pleasure Island. Phone: 407/934-8888. Prices: Moderate to expensive. Meals: LD.

The atmosphere at this pleasant restaurant, located just outside Pleasure Island's admission gates, features a collection of oceanic memorabilia like model ships, photos, and pennants. The diners can sit indoors among brass, chrome, and mahogany reminiscent of the pleasure yachts of the 19th century or outdoors on a terrace suggestive of luxury cruise ships' decks. The frequently-changing menu includes classical Italian and seafood dishes including pizzas, pastas, salads, sandwiches, and steaks, but most notably is the stellar, fresh, warm, crusty Italian bead served with roasted garlic to spread like butter. One of the better dining choices in Disney World, the restaurant also boasts a critically acclaimed wine list.

ROMANO'S MACARONI GRILL
Locations and phone: 12148 S. Apopka Vineland Road., Lake Buena Vista (407/239-6676), 5320 W. Irlo Bronson Mem. Hwy., Kissimmee (407/396-6155). Prices: Moderate. Meals: LD.

This restaurant offers absolutely stellar pasta dishes and other classical Italian entrees, along with delicious peasant bread served with olive oil. Jugs of house Rosso Chianti, and Bianco wines are served as well, a Romano family tradition.

VENEZIA DUA
Location: Old Town, 5770 W. Irlo Bronson Mem. Hwy., Kissimmee. Phone: 407/396-6244 Prices: Budget. Meals: LD.

One of Kissimmee's best Italian restaurants, Venezia is located in the Old Town shopping center. They offer the standard Northern Italian specialties, but the thing that everybody talks about here is the stellar garlic bread.

Japanese
BENIHANA
Location: Hilton Hotel, 1751 Hotel Plaza Blvd., Downtown Disney. Phone: 407/827-4865. Price: Expensive. Meals: D.

The 1,000-year old art of cooking steak, shrimp, chicken, and vegetables at a teppan table is practiced here, much to the amazement of the diners at this branch of the prominent chain. The highlight is the Benihana Special: tender New York strip steak, cold water lobster tail, Japanese onion soup, Benihana salad, shrimp appetizer, Hibachi vegetables, rice, tea, and a special fresh pineapple dessert. There is a full bar and lounge.

KOBE JAPANESE STEAKHOUSE & SUSHI BAR
Locations and phone: 8350 International Drive (407/352-1811), 8460 Palm Parkway, Lake Buena Vista (407/239-1119), 2901 Parkway Blvd., Kissimmee (407/396-8088). Prices: Moderate. Meals: D.

The Kobe, its Vista Centre location easily visible from I-4, offers steak, chicken, lobster, shrimp, and scallops prepared on a Teppanyaki table.

RAN-GETSU
Location: 8400 International Drive. Phone: 407/345-0044. Prices: Expensive. Meals: D.
Ran-Getsu uses a garden atmosphere as a backdrop for tasty sushi, sukiyaki, tempura, and other traditional specialties. There's entertainment on weekends.

SHOGUN
Location: 6327 International Drive. Phone: 407/352-1607. Prices: Moderate. Meals: D.
Teppan table cooking is featured at this establishment.

YOJI
Location: 4592 W. Irlo Bronson Mem. Hwy., Kissimmee. Phone: 407/396-6858. Prices: Moderate. Meals: D.
This steakhosue offers sushi and sashimi plus teppan yaki food prepared right in front of your eyes, by mile marker 14 on US 192.

Mexican
ADOBE GILA'S
Location: Pointe Orlando, 9101 International Drive. Phone: 407/903-1477. Prices: Budget. Meals: LD.
This lively hole-in-the-wall-looking bar and restaurant located in the Pointe Orlando shopping center offers tons of frozen drinks, 75 different varieties of tequila, a dirt cheap menu consisting of tacos, quesadillas, tostadas, and Gila wraps, and Tejano, Conjunto, country, and top 40 music.

DON PABLO'S
Location: 8717 International Drive. Phone: 407/345-1345. Prices: Budget. Meals: LD.
Located right next to the Official Visitor Center, Don Pablo's offers large portions of affordable Mexican classics like tacos, burritos, taquitos, enchiladas, and combination dinners cooked in an open kitchen.

JOSE O'DAY'S
Location: Mercado, 8445 International Drive. Phone: 407/363-0613. Prices: Moderate. Meals: LD.
This cool, casual restaurant in the Mercado shopping village serves up traditional Mexican specialties in a casual, friendly atmosphere at times enlivened by a mariachi band. The fajitas and chimichangas are particularly irresistible.

JUAN & ONLY'S CANTINA, BAR, & JAIL
Location: Walt Disney World Dolphin. Phone: 407/934-3000. Prices: Moderate. Meals: D.

It's safe to drink the water at this kitschfully seedy restaurant, but it's a better idea to sip a margarita. They're rather legendary here. Also worth investigation are the fajitas and the blue and red corn tortilla chips, served with fresh pico de gallo. Especially convenient for Disney-MGM guests, it's just a boat ride away form the gate.

MAYA GRILL
Location: Disney's Coronado Springs Resort. Phone: 407/WDW-DINE. Prices: Moderate to expensive. Meals: BD.

This restaurant is operated by the same family that runs the San Angel Inn restaurants in Epcot and in Mexico city, and provides a taste of authentic Mayan cuisine. No fajitas and burritos here, instead you'll find creative and authentic dishes such as grilled achiote chicken breast, pumpkin seed encrusted snapper, and ropa vieja. There's also an all-you-can-eat breakfast buffet.

Steak & Seafood
ATLANTIC BAY SEAFOOD GRILL
Location: 2901 Parkway Blvd., Kissimmee. Phone: 407/238-2323. Prices: Moderate. Meals: D.

Atlantic Bay, located between the Hyatt Orlando and Arabian Nights, offers live Maine lobster, seven varieties of fresh fish daily, oysters on the half shell, prime rib, steak, pasta, and poultry. An all-you-can-eat seafood bar and early bird specials are available.

BLACK ANGUS
2001 W. Vine Street, Kissimmee. Tel. 846-7117. Prices: Budget. Meals: B,L,D.

Black Angus sells certified Black Angus steaks, all-you-can-eat dinner specials, breakfast buffets, and salad and fruit bars. The breakfasts here are bounteous and low-cost. Karaoka is also featured from 9:30 p.m. until 1:30 a.m. every night except Monday.

BOSTON LOBSTER FEAST
Location: S. Orange Blossom Trail at Sand Lake Road. Phone: 407/438-0607. Prices: Expensive. Meals: D.

This restaurant offers all the Maine lobster you can eat for $19.95, including a forty-item buffet of clam chowder, lobster bisque, peel-and-eat shrimp, oysters, mussels, seafood Alfredo, crab claws, London broil, and much more.

BROWN DERBY

Location: 6115 Westwood Boulevard, Orlando. Tel. 352-4644. Prices: Budget to moderate. Meals: L,D.

At the corner of Westwood and I-Drive, the Girves Brown Derby offers a varied selection of steaks and seafood.

THE BUTCHER SHOP STEAKHOUSE

Location: Mercado, 8445 International Drive, Orlando. Tel. 363-9727. Prices: Expensive. Meals: D.

The Butcher Shop is one of Mercado's classiest options, serving steaks from 14-ounce filets to 28-ounce T-Bones. Also served are prime rib, fresh fish, and chicken, cooked to perfection over hardwood grills. If you wish, you can take your raw cut of beef to the pit in the center of the restaurant and cook it to your own taste.

CALIFORNIA GRILL

Location: Disney's Contemporary Resort, Walt Disney World. Phone: 407/ WDW-DINE. Prices: Expensive. Meals: D.

Located on the 15th floor of the Contemporary Resort, this elegant restaurant features spectacular views of the Magic Kingdom and arguably, WDW's best food. The menu includes sushi and sashimi, spit fired chicken, salmon, tuna, grouper, pork, and beef entrees, prepared with a flair you won't find elsewhere. The desserts are phenomenal as well.

CAP'N JACK'S OYSTER BAR

Location: Downtown Disney Marketplace. Phone: 407/WDW-DINE. Prices: Moderate to expensive. Meals: LDS.

This popular lounge and restaurant sits on a dock over the shores of Buena Vista Lagoon, offering more tasty frozen margaritas than you can shake a straw at, plus lobster tails, crab claws, oysters, clams on the half shell, shrimp, seafood marinara, Maryland crab cakes, and ceviche, along with prime rib and pot roast.

CAPTAIN NEMO'S

Location: 5469 W. Irlo Bronson Mem. Hwy., Kissimmee. Phone: 407/239-7729. Prices: Moderate. Meals: D.

Nemo's offers standard steak and seafood dishes plus happy hour and plenty of sports action on the satellite dishes.

CATTLEMAN'S STEAKHOUSE

Location: 2948 Vineland Road, Kissimmee. Phone: 407/238-2333. Prices: Moderate. Meals: D.

Conveniently located at the corner of U.S. 192 and S.R. 535, the

Cattleman's offers a selection of charbroiled, corn-fed beef, including a 32-ounce Porterhouse steak.

CHARLEY'S STEAK HOUSE

Locations and phone: 2901 Parkway Blvd., Kissimmee (407/396-6055), 8255 International Drive (407/363-0228). Prices: Moderate. Meals: D.

Charley's selects their steaks from three-year-old grain-fed steer, ages them for four to five weeks, and broils them over a 1,100-degree wood fire. Specialties include porterhouse, T-bone, Alaskan king crab, lobster tail, and 12-ounce filet mignon.

CHARLIE'S LOBSTER HOUSE

Location: Mercado, 8445 International Drive. Phone: 407/352-6929. Prices: Moderate to expensive. Meals: D.

Charlie's brags the "best crab cakes in town," and who's to argue? Other fruits of the Florida and New England waters include live Maine lobsters prepared eight different ways, chowders and bisques, clams, oysters, steaners, mussels, shrimp, scallops, crab legs, twelve varieties of fresh fish, steaks, surf and turf, and more.

THE CRAB HOUSE

Locations and phone: 8291 International Drive (407/352-6140), 8496 Palm Pkwy., Kissimmee (407/239-1888). Prices: Moderate. Meals: D.

The specialties at this restaurant include ocean-fresh fish, garlic and steamed crabs, live Maine lobster, shucked oysters and clams, and much more. There is also an all-you-can-eat seafood and salad bar.

DARRYL'S

Locations and phone: 8282 International Drive (407/351-1883), 5260 W. Irlo Bronson Mem. Hwy., Kissimmee (407/396-1901). Prices: Moderate. Meals: LD.

Famous for its inventive stuffed baked potatoes, this restaurant also features beef, seafood, and some pasta dishes, including a good selection on the children's menu.

FLYING FISH CAFÉ

Location: Disney's Boardwalk, Walt Disney World. Phone: 407/939-3463. Prices: Expensive. Meals: D.

In a town that seems to have more seafood restaurants than it does residents, this one truly stands out. With breathtaking and refreshingly low-key décor, the centerpiece of the restaurant is the open kitchen. The restaurant offers a tasting menu for you indecisive types plus à la carte options including oak grilled wahoo, potato wrapped red snapper, and fennel crusted yellowfin tuna. There are also a few beef, pork, and pasta entrees on the menu.

FULTON'S CRAB HOUSE

Location: Downtown Disney Pleasure Island. Phone: 407/934-2628. Prices: Expensive to very expensive. Meals: LD.

The posh Empress Lilly, formerly home to three upscale restaurants, has been renovated and transformed into the more family-friendly Fulton's. The menu includes such specialties as crabs (duh), tuna filet mignon, Maine lobster, crab cakes, and more. There's a handful of landlubber entrees as well, and the menu changes daily to reflect market availability.

GOLDEN CORRAL

Location:8032 International Drive. Phone: 407/352-6606. Prices: Budget. Meals: BLD.

Cheap, decent food served up buffet style three times a day.

HEMINGWAY'S

Location: Grand Cypress Resort, 1 Grand Cypress Blvd. Phone: 407/239-3854. Prices: Expensive. Meals: LD.

The upscale Hemingway's overlooks the Hyatt Regency's elaborate swimming pool from atop a rocky bluff, and the Key West atmosphere plays host to seafood, game, and steaks.

KEY W. KOOL'S OPEN PIT GRILL

Location: 7725 W. Irlo Bronson Mem. Hwy., Kissimmee. Phone: 407/396-1166. Prices: Moderate. Meals: D.

This restaurant features authentic USDA prime choice meats and seafood, cooked right in front of your eyes on the Open Pit Grill. The signature dish of the house is a 32 ounce Porterhouse steak.

MAGIC MINING CO. STEAKS AND SEAFOOD

Location: 7763 W. Irlo Bronson Mem. Hwy., Kissimmee. Phone: 407/396-8986. Prices: Moderate. Meals: D.

This is a landmark — it's got a small, waterfall-crossed mountain rising above it. The food is hearty, including top sirloin, prime rib, T-bone, lobster, grilled shrimp, baby back ribs, jackleg chicken, and more.

MONTY'S CONCH HARBOR

Location: Pointe Orlando, 9101 International Drive. Phone: 407/354-1122. Prices: Moderate to expensive. Meals: LD.

Monty's specialty is the stone crab, but there's much more to choose from, from conch fritters and grilled salmon to "she crab" soup and BBQ baby back ribs.

MORTON'S OF CHICAGO

Location: 7600 Dr. Phillips Drive. Phone: 407/248-3485. Prices: Expensive. Meals: D.
This restaurant has showcased great steak without the bull since 1978. The restaurant is known for its USDA prime aged beef, seafood including whole baked Maine lobster flown in fresh daily, hand picked vegetables, and elegant desserts.

THE OCEAN GRILL

Location: 6432 International Drive. Phone: 407/352-9993. Prices: Moderate. Meals: D.
The fare at this friendly spot on International Drive (by Wet'n Wild) includes soups, salads, pasta, shrimp, steak, and seafood prepared in a range of styles from Southern to Chesapeake to New English to Pacific. If you enjoy lobster, and lots of it, the restaurant offers fresh, in fact, live, Maine lobster ranging from one to four pounds. $8.95 early bird specials are available as well.

OUTBACK STEAKHOUSE

Locations and phone: 7804 W. Irlo Bronson Mem. Hwy., Kissimmee (407/396-0017), 4845 S. Kirkman Road (407/292-5111). Prices: Moderate. Meals: LD.
Favorite of hearty eaters everywhere but nowhere more than on John Madden's tour bus, the Outback offers great steaks, succulent ribs, and of course the legendary Bloomin' Onion in an Aussie setting.

PONDEROSA STEAKHOUSE

Locations and phone: 6362 International Drive (407/352-9343), 5529 S. Kirkman Road (407/345-0200), 7598 W. Irlo Bronson Mem. Hwy., Kissimmee (407/396-7721), 5771 W. Irlo Bronson Mem. Hwy., Kissimmee (407/397-2477), 14407 International Drive (407/238-2526), 8510 International Drive (407/354-1477). Prices: Budget. Meals: BLD.
Ponderosa offers up steaks, seafood, ribs, chicken, salads, and the All-You-Can-Eat Grand Buffet, including spaghetti, soups, chili, tacos, chicken, potatoes, and more.

RED LOBSTER

Locations and phone: 5936 International Drive (407/351-9313), 9892 International Drive (407/345-0018), 5690 W. Irlo Bronson Mem. Hwy.,

Kissimmee (407/396-6997), Crossroads, 12557 SR 535, Lake Buena Vista (407/827-1045). Prices: Budget to moderate. Meals: LD.
This popular national chain offers steak, chicken, pasta, and seafood entrees.

SHULA'S STEAKHOUSE
Location: Walt Disney World Dolphin. Phone: 407/934-3000. Prices: Expensive to very expensive. Meals: D.
Where else would legendary football coach Don Shula open up a steakhouse but in the Walt Disney World Dolphin hotel? It's the 14th restaurant in Shula's Florida chain, replacing Harry's Safari Bar & Grille in December 1999. The signature dish is a 48-ounce porterhouse. Those who can eat the whole thing in one sitting are immortalized on a plaque in the restaurant. Hey, we all have to have goals in life.

SIZZLER
Locations and phone: 7602 W. Irlo Bronson Mem. Hwy., Kissimmee (407/ 397-0997), 12195 S. Apopka Vineland Rd., Lake Buena Vista (407/238- 1551), 9142 International Drive (407/351-5369), 6308 International Drive (407/248-9711). Prices: Budget. Meals: BLD.
Sizzler offers steaks, salads, chicken, fish, and the famed Buffet Court. The breakfast buffets here are also well worth the trip.

STEAK AND ALE
Locations and phone: 5855 american Way (407/352-0422), 6115 Westwood Blvd. (407/352-0526). Prices: Budget to moderate. Meals: D.
This understated and thankfully theme-less steakhouse offers excellent steaks, most notably the nine-pepper filet and Bourbon Street steak. Also worth checking out is the Cajun chicken pasta.

WESTERN STEER
Location: 6315 International Drive. Phone: 407/363-0677. Prices: Budget. Meals: BLD.
This hearty eaters' haven offers all-you-care-to-eat buffets at all three meals, plus steaks and seafood.

WILD JACK'S STEAKS & BBQ
Location: 7364 International Drive. Phone: 407/352-4407. Prices: Budget to moderate. Meals: LD.
The food at this Wild West-themed restaurant is better and more imaginative than most, with red chile crusted New York strip steak, adobo pork chops, New Mexico salmon, and more, along with better-than-average appetizers.

Thai
SIAM ORCHID
Location: 7575 Universal Blvd. Phone: 407/351-0821. Prices: Moderate. Meals: D.

The Siam Orchid, regarded by some as the most exotic – and best – restaurants in the International Drive area, with a comfortable, intimate setting in which diners feast on delectable Thai cuisine such as Siam wings, curry puffs, basil seafood, and orchid roast duck.

10. SPORTS & RECREATION

In the first part of this chapter you'll find the more popular sports and activities available in WDW, followed by the many possibilities in the greater Orlando area.

Walt Disney World's 43 square miles include five golf courses, numerous tennis courts, boating, swimming, and health clubs. You can ride a horse just as easily as you can ride Star Tours, and you can play baseball, basketball, skee ball, and almost anything else imaginable.

BASEBALL & SOFTBALL - Diamonds, located in Fort Wilderness, are only open to WDW Resort guests. Bring your own equipment.

BASKETBALL - Basketball courts can be found throughout the camping loops of Fort Wilderness, but are open to resort guests only.

BIKING - Riding a bike is a good way to get around Fort Wilderness or the Disney Institute. There are paths and not-too-busy roads in both places. Rental is $4 an hour or $9 a day for regular bikes, $6 an hour or $10 a day for tandems. Included in some vacation plans. Call 824-2742.

BOATING - Walt Disney World has the world's fifth largest navy and the single largest pleasure boat fleet in the nation. Boating can be done at many locations in the World, and on a variety of craft, ranging from sailboats to speedboats to canoes. Pay for your boat rental with the American Express card and receive a 10% discount. You've got the following options:

Canoes can be rented for traveling down the placid canals of Fort Wilderness. Cost is $5 per hour, $12 per day. Available at the Bike Barn. Outrigger canoes are available at the Polynesian Resort's marina, six people can ride and paddle each of these Hawaiian contraptions through Seven Seas Lagoon. Cost is $14 an hour.

Parasailing can be done at the Contemporary Resort. Cost is $80 for one rider, $120 for tandem. Riders get seven to ten minutes of airtime.

Pedal boats are available at the marinas of the Contemporary, Grand Floridian, Polynesian, and Fort Wilderness Resorts for use on Seven Seas Lagoon and Bay Lake; at the Caribbean Beach Resort's marina on Barefoot Bay; at the Yacht and Beach Club Resorts' Bayside Marina; the waterways of Port Orleans, Coronado Springs, and Dixie Landings; and the Dolphin and Swan's Crescent Lake. The cost is $6 a half hour or $10 an hour.

Pontoon boats (large, motorized, canopied boats) cost $40 an hour and are good for families and other large groups. Available at the Contemporary, Fort Wilderness, Grand Floridian, and Polynesian Resorts.

Rowboats are found at the Yacht and Beach Club marina for $6 a half hour.

Sailboats are available at the Marketplace and all resort marinas. The cost varies from $13 to $18, dependent on the type of boat: Sunfish, Capris, and Hobie Cat 14s and 16s are all available.

Toobies, large innertubes with motors, are available at the Port Orleans, Dixie Landings, and Caribbean Beach Resorts.

Wakeboarding is $130 per hour for up to four people.

Water skiing boats complete with instructor, driver and equipment can be rented at the Contemporary marina. Price is $130 per hour for up to five guests.

Water Sprites are the small, two-man speedboats that can be found cruising virtually all of the waterways in the World. They are available at all of the marinas for $13 a half hour. The little craft are very popular in the early afternoon, so plan accordingly.

FISHING - You can fish on a guided trip, complete with gear, driver/ guide, and refreshments. Trips leaving the Magic Kingdom or Epcot resorts run $160 per group, up to five people. Lake Buena Vista excursions run $137 for two hours. Excursions on Lake Sully are $175 for two hours. *Call 407/WDW-PLAY for more information or the necessary reservations.*

Or, if you prefer going solo, check out the canals in Fort Wilderness and the Disney Institute. No license is required, you can keep what you catch. Rods and reels are available for rent at Fort Wilderness's Bike Barn, and gear is for sale at the Trading Posts in the Fort. Included in some vacation plans.

See the extensive *Fishing* section later in this chapter for details on guides outside of WDW.

VOLLEYBALL - Courts are scattered throughout Fort Wilderness, and on the beaches at Contemporary Resort, Coronado Springs Resort, and the Yacht and Beach Club Resorts. Equipment is provided.

GOLF

With the addition of the **Bonnet Creek Golf Club**, there are now 99 holes of golf inside the Walt Disney World complex. There are 45 holes at Shades of Green, 18 at Disney Institute, and 36 at Bonnet Creek. The golf here is so spectacular that it is an annual stop on the PGA Tour.

Recently, Walt Disney World was recognized as one of the top golf meeting resorts in the United States and was presented with an ACE Award honoring outstanding golf meeting resorts in a competition sponsored by Successful Meetings magazine. Resorts were rated on difficulty of their golf courses, quality of golf professional staffs, meeting facilities, accessibility, and hospitality. Only 100 resorts nationwide were nominated for the award.

Shades of Green - This hamlet just west of the Grand Floridian Resort houses the original WDW links. The Magnolia offers 18 holes at distances ranging from 6,642 to 7,150 yards and the Palm, rated one of the nation's top 100 courses by Golf Digest Magazine, has 18 holes measuring 5,398 to 6,957 yards. Both are par-72 layouts, both designed by Joe Lee. The Palm differs from the Magnolia in that the fairways at the former are shorter, narrower, and wooded, and the Palm has nine water hazards. There are driving ranges at both courses.

Also located here is Oak Trail, a nine-hole, 45-acre course designed specifically for the beginner. There are water hazards and bunkers on the par-36, 2,913-yard course, and the cost for 18 holes here is substantially lower than at the other courses. This is a walking course only.

Disney Institute - Tucked away between the quiet villa retreat and the shores of Buena Vista Lagoon is the 18-hole Lake Buena Vista course. Also designed by Joe Lee, the par-72 links range in distance from 5,315 to 6,829 yards. This is a particularly pretty course as it winds through the Fairway and Treehouse Villas, the Vacation Club Resort, and scrubby forests and streams.

Bonnet Creek Golf Club - In January 1992, this pair of courses, located next to Fort Wilderness at the northeast corner of the World, opened with great fanfare. To reach the Bonnet Creek Country Club, call your hotel's Guest Services desk to get directions or arrange for private van transportation. **Osprey Ridge** was designed by Tom Fazio and is a rather unusual course. Start with the natural terrain that surrounds the links. "Some of the factors that have us excited about the project are the vegetation, the water areas, and the wetlands which will become part of the background and framing for the holes," Fazio said. The par-72 Osprey Ridge ranges from 5,305 yards from the forward tees, 7,150 from the pro tees. The men's yardage is 6,705.

Environmentally conscious duffers will be glad to know that the circulating 18-hole design of the course uses the existing land patterns to their fullest while preserving all of the adjacent wetlands and other natural areas. Other things that make the Ridge unique are its paths, winding through remote areas and the use of high ridges and mounding, with some tees, greens, and viewing areas 20 to 25 feet above grade. The ridge that gives the course its name has quite a bearing on play.

Eagle Pines, designed by Pete Dye, is another 18-hole, par-72 affair. But this one differs quite a bit from Osprey Ridge. First of all, the course is laid out with a low profile, to be at the same level as or lower than the surrounding land. Second, the yardage is substantially shorter: 5,134 from the women's tees, 6,029 from the men's, and 6,842 from the professional tees. Also, in an interesting touch, the areas outside the fairways are not rough, but pine straw. The low, dished fairways are surrounded with tall, spindly pines, giving it a secluded feel. Note that this is a traditional course in the sense that golfers can return to the clubhouse after the out nine.

Golf Instruction

One-on-one instruction with PGA professionals is available by appointment only at the rate of $50 per half hour for adults and $30 per junior (17 and under). *Call 407/WDW-GOLF.*

National Car Rental Golf Classic

Each October, the PGA pulls into Lake Buena Vista to hold its annual pro-am tournament on the three older courses. To play alongside the pros, you need to join the Classic Club, which will set you back approximately $5,000. If you just want to watch the tournament, shell out $15 to $25 per day or $50 for a weekly badge. Clubhouse access is $75 for the week. Note that if you're planning on golfing on your WDW vacation and are not a member of the Classic Club, this is a week to avoid. *Call 407/ WDW-GOLF for details.*

Practical Information

Balls: Buckets of balls for use on the driving range go for $4 apiece.

Carts: Included in greens fees, not permitted at Oak Trail.

Club rental: Titleist DTR clubs are available for $25.

Fees: Greens fees for the 18 hole courses are $100 to $155 for WDW resort guests (depending on course and time of year), $105 to $160 for day guests. Twilight specials ranging from $50 to $80 are available. Oak Trail charges $32 for adults, $20 for juniors under 17 for nine holes, $48 and $30 respectively for 18.

Lockers: Available at all three clubhouses.

Reservations: WDW Resort guests can reserve tee times up to 60 days in advance, day guests 30 days in advance, by calling *407/WDW-GOLF*.
Shoe Rental: Available for $8.

HIKING

Winding throughout the resort are some pleasant trails including the Wilderness Swamp Trail, the Marshmallow Marsh Trail, and more, in Fort Wilderness. Contact Guest Services for information.

HORSEBACK RIDING

Trail rides depart from the middle of Fort Wilderness every day at 9, 10:30, noon, and 2pm daily. The horses are gentle and the ride is relaxing and slow. The cost is $13 per person. Children under 9 are not allowed to ride, but pony rides can be arranged at the petting farm at Fort Wilderness. *For reservations and information, call 407/824-2832 up to five days in advance.*

MINIATURE GOLF

Disney offers 72 holes of miniature golf, 26 each at the Winter Summerland and Fantasia Gardens courses. The eponymous course at **Fantasia Gardens** challenges guests with interactive obstacles pulled straight from the film. The key word there being "interactive," especially when you walk past the brooms carrying buckets of water and absent mindedly think to yourself, "Wasn't there a flood in this scene?" You'll never view water hazards the same way again. The Fantasia Fairways course offers par-three and par-four holes from 40 to 75 feet long. Fantasia Gardens is located across from the Disney-MGM Studios, within walking distance of the Epcot resorts. **Winter Summerland** combines the festive North Pole-themed Winter course with the beachy keen Summer course, evoking thoughts of Santa's 11 months off.

Winter Summerland is located, appropriately, next to the similarly-confused Blizzard Beach water park. Both courses are open 10am to 11pm Greens fees are $9.25 for adults and $7.50 for kids 3 to 9. There's a 50 percent discount on a second round played the same day. *Call 407/WDW-PLAY for details.*

SWIMMING

You wouldn't expect to find beaches in the middle of Florida, but here they are. There are strands of powdery white sand at the Contemporary, Polynesian, Grand Floridian, Fort Wilderness, Caribbean Beach, Yacht and Beach Club, Swan, and Dolphin Resorts. The most notable of these is the long, placid Fort Wilderness beach, on lovely Bay Lake.

TENNIS

All told, there's 32 tennis courts at WDW resort hotels: 8 between the Dolphin and Swan, 6 at the Contemporary, 4 at the Disney Institute, and 2 each at the Yacht and Beach Club, Old Key West, Boardwalk, and Fort Wilderness Resorts, plus a few others scattered throughout the resort.

Instruction

Lessons are available from Peter Burwash International, the world's leader in tennis management services. A variety of clinics is offered as well as private instruction. *Call 407/WDW-PLAY for more information.*

Youth Tennis Camp

The Contemporary Resort offers two separate tennis camps, one for children 4 to 8, the other one, for kids 7 to 16. The younger children play with lower nets, smaller racquets, and foam balls for a week of daily 45-minute lessons. The cost is $50. The older children play regulation tennis with regulation equipment for a week for $125, including all court time.

Practical Information

Balls: Can be purchased for $5 a can, or used ones rented for $4 per bucket.

Fees: Courts at the Contemporary, Grand Floridian, and Disney Institute charge $15 per hour. There is no charge for the other courts.

Hours: The tennis courts are open from 8am to 10pm. All are lighted for play after dark.

Lockers: Complimentary, available at all tennis court areas.

Pairing service: "Tennis Anyone" will find you a playing partner if you need one. *Call the Contemporary Pro Shop at 407/824-3578.*

Racquet rental: Available for $4 an hour, free at the Old Key West and Boardwalk courts.

Reservations: *Call 407/WDW-PLAY*

ADDITIONAL ACTIVITIES IN DISNEY WORLD

Arcades - Video gamerooms are located throughout the World. There's the Penny Arcade on Main Street, U.S.A. (see MAGIC KINGDOM), with old and new coin-operated machines. But outside the parks, the biggest of the bunch is the Food 'n Fun Center on the first floor of the Contemporary Resort. Open 24 hours a day, the complex includes computerized games old and new, pinball machines, a movie theater, and a snack bar.

Campfire Program - At Fort Wilderness, WDW resort guests (no day guests, sorry) are treated to a free campfire program, complete with

Disney movies, singalongs, and appearances by Chip 'n' Dale.

Croquet - There's a regulation croquet court at the Beach Club. Equipment is available for loan at no charge, just see the people at the Ship Shape Health Club.

Electric Water Pageant - This is a dazzling display of a fusion of light and water as a 1,000-foot procession of illuminated creatures that appear to be swimming. Usually, the floating parade can be viewed from the Polynesian at 9 PM, from the Grand Floridian at 9:20, from Fort Wilderness at 9:45 PM, 10:05 from the Contemporary, and 10:20 from the Magic Kingdom when it's open late.

Hayrides - Another one of those neat Fort Wilderness amenities, guests can board a hay wagon for a ride from Pioneer Hall to Bay Lake and back. The round-trip takes an hour and costs $6 per person ($4 for kids 3 to 12). Kids under 12 must be accompanied by an adult.

Horseshoes - A round of horseshoes on the agenda? Facilities are scattered throughout Fort Wilderness.

Marshmallow Marsh Excursion - Held during the summer only, guests take a canoe down a crystalline Fort Wilderness canal, followed by a short walk to a hamlet in the woods where a marshmallow roast is held. From this spot, you can also watch the Elecric Water Pageant floating by. The cost is $8, $6 for kids 3 to 12.

Movies - There's a movie theater at the Fiesta Fun Center in the Contemporary, showing Disney classics three times an evening. Also, the campfire program at Fort Wilderness (see above) includes a Disney film. If you'd prefer a first-run film, there's the AMC 24 Complex *(Tel. 407/827-1300)* adjacent to the Pleasure Island nighttime entertainment complex. Note that you do not have to buy a Pleasure Island ticket to enter the movie theater.

FISHING

Florida is renowned for its bass fishing. Many guides and fishing camps can be found in the area. Here is a sampling of them.

- **A#1 Bass**, *Tel. 800/707-5463, 352/394-3360 (Clermont)*
- **A Pro Bass**, *Tel. 800/771-9676, 407/877-9676 (Winter Garden)*
- **Bass Anglers**, *Tel. 407/656-1052 (Windermere)*
- **Bass Challenger**, *Tel. 800/241-5314, 407/273-8045 (Orlando)*
- **Black Hammock**, *Tel. 407/365-1244 (Oviedo)*

- **Cutting Loose**, *Tel. 800/533-4746, 407/629-4700 (Winter Park)*
- **Fishing Connection**, *Tel. 800/583-2278, 407/469-2279 (Monteverde)*
- **Florida Deep Sea**, *Tel. 727/360-2082 (St. Petersburg Beach)*
- **Incentive Fishing**, *Tel. 407/676-1948 (Melbourne)*
- **J&J Guides**, *Tel. 407/935-9016 (Kissimmee)*
- **Sea Venture**, *Tel. 800/455-0333, 407/453-6764 (Merritt Island)*
- **Shiner King**, *Tel. 800/882-8333, 407/390-9400 (Kissimmee)*

GOLF

There is a wide assortment of golf courses in central Florida which are open to tourists, besides the five courses in Walt Disney World. Listed below is a sampling of the clubs:

Celebration Golf Course

Location: 701 Golf Park Drive, Celebration. Phone: 407/566-4653. Length: 4,921 to 6,786 yards. Par: 72. Greens fees: $35 to $90, twilight rates are available.

This Robert Trent Jones/RTJ Jr. course, built in 1996, features both open and narrow fairways with Bermuda grass just 5 minutes from Disney World in Celebration and has become very popular, hosting 45,000 rounds per year. A bonus if you're golfing with your young'uns, greens fees are only $25 for those 16 to 17 years old and $10 for 15 and unders.

Dubsdread

Location: 549 West Par Avenue, Orlando. Phone: 407/246-2551. Length: 5575 to 6055 yards. Par: 71, 72 from women's tees. Greens fees: $28 to $31, depending on season.

One of the oldest courses in the area, the tradition-steeped Dubsdread is one of Orlando's most popular courses. The course is owned and operated by the city of Orlando and hosts its annual amateur championship. Greens are small and well-bunkered, while the fairways are tight, emphasizing control over distance.

Falcon's Fire

Location: 3200 Seralago Drive, Kissimmee. Phone: 407/239-5445. Length: 5417 to 6901 yards. Par: 72. Greens fees: $78 to $127, twilight rates available.

Strategic bunkering and an abundance of water hazards enhance the challenge of this course, convenient for and popular with both residents and tourists. The course is suitable for players of all skill levels.

International

Location: 6351 International Golf Club Road, Orlando. Phone: 407/239-6909. Length: 5100 to 6776 yards. Par: 72. Greens fees: $59 to $101.

This Joe Lee-designed course is located conveniently off the southern end of International Drive. Thre are six lakes and oak and cypress forests. Architect Lee called this course "a challenge, but a fair one."

Kissimmee Bay Country Club

Location: 2801 Kissimmee Bay Road, Kissimmee. Phone: 407/348-4653. Length: 5171 to 6846 yards. Par: 71. Greens fees: $38 to $76, depending on season.

Golf Digest nominated this course as one of America's best new courses and was twice ranked among the top fifty in the state by Golfweek. The fast greens are double-cut daily.

Kissimmee Golf Club

Location: 3103 Florida Coach Drive, Kissimmee. Phone: 407/847-2816. Length: 5083 to 6537 yards. Par: 72. Greens fees: $35 to $61, twilight rates available.

Adjacent to the Kissimmee Municipal Airport, this course has long been a favorite for locals and visitors alike. Facilities include a lounge, pro shop, and the county's largest driving range.

Marriott's Orlando World Center

Location: World Center Drive, Orlando. Phone: 407/238-8660. Length: 4988 to 6307 yards. Par: 71. Greens fees: $65 to $85.

Another Joe Lee course, this one surrounding the 27-story resort hotel mixes brawn and beauty to challenge both beginners and scratch players. Water hazards dot 16 holes and there are 85 different locations to beach your shot.

Metrowest Country Club

Location: 2100 South Hiawassee Road, Orlando. Phone: 407/299-1099. Length: 5325 to 7051 yards. Par: 72. Greens fees: $75 to $123.

Designed by Robert Trent Jones Sr. and operated by Arnold Palmer's company, MetroWest features 100-foot elevations that roll around water hazards and expansive bunkers.

Orange Lake Country Club

Location: 8505 W. Irlo Bronson Mem. Hwy., Kissimmee. Phone: 407/239-1050. Length: 5,525 to 7.072 yards. Par: 72. Greens fees: $45 to $94 for the Resort course, $65 to $138 for the Legends course.

The Resort course, designed by Joe Lee, winds through woodlands of oak, cypress, and pine and past marshlands, lakes, and abundant wildlife. Golf Week Magazine named this one of Florida's top 50 courses. The Arnold Palmer-designed Legends course, which opened in late 1998, features nine holes of Scotland style holes and nine inspired by the woodlands of North Carolina, with multi-tiered greens and spacious fairways.

Poinciana Golf & Recreation Club
Location: 500 East Cypress Parkway, Kissimmee. Phone: 407/933-5300. Length: 4,988 to 6,700 yards. Par: 72. Greens fees: $31 to $65.

This Devlin/Von Hagge course offers a peaceful and natural resort setting with slightly rolling fairways of both the open and narrow variety, plenty of water, and an abundance of doglegs.

Ventura Country Club
Location: 3201 Woodgate Blvd., Orlando. Phone: 407/277-2640. Length: 4392 to 5467 yards. Par: 70. Greens fees: $40.

Despite its length, this is considered a challenging course, as water comes into play on 14 of the 18 holes, and 49 sand traps dot the landscape.

GOLF RESERVATION SERVICE
OUTSIDE DISNEY WORLD
Linksinfo (Tel. 800/546-5746) offers complete, up-tp-date golf course information and tee time reservation for over 1,000 courses across the state. Tee Times USA (Tel. 888/GOLF-FLORIDA, www.teetimesusa.com) offers on line and centralized telephone tee time reservations plus golf packages.

MINIATURE GOLF
Pirate's Cove *(8601 International Drive, Orlando, FL 32819, 407/352-7378; Crossroads Shopping Center, Lake Buena Vista, FL, 407/827-1242; and 2845 Florida Plaza Blvd., Kissimmee, FL 32741, 407/396-7484)* is truly a work of art. The three, 36-hole complexes feature lushly landscaped holes, some of them intricate works that take up an entire hillside, flanked by waterfalls, streams, bridges, boulders, caves, and dungeons, all to carry out the pirate theme. Music is piped in, and signs along the holes tell the stories of Blackbeard and Captain Kidd. Hole-in-one prizes are given daily, and snacks and beverages are sold.

In particular, the International Drive location is absolutely spectacular and rated as not to be missed. The courses are fastidiously manicured, and has more atmosphere. Why? It might have something to do with the fact that it looks out to the Spanish mission-style Mercado Mediterranean Village. With the combination of the miniature golf and the shopping village, one could easily spend an entire evening on that one block.

Other miniature golf courses in the area are **Pirate's Island** *(4330 W. Irlo Bronson Mem. Hwy, Kissimmee, FL 34746, Tel. 407/396-4660)*, another pirate-themed course; **Congo River Golf & Exploration Co.** *(6312 International Drive, Orlando, FL 32819, Tel. 407/352-0042; 4777 W. Irlo Bronson Mem. Hwy, Kissimmee, FL 34746, Tel. 407/396-6900)*, two courses based on the Stanley and Livingstone expeditions; **River Adventure Golf** *(4535 W. Irlo Bronson Mem. Hwy, Kissimmee, FL 34746, Tel. 407/396-4666)*, and **Bonanza Golf** *(7771 W. Irlo Bronson Mem. Hwy, Kissimmee, FL 34746, Tel. 407/396-7536)*.

A step above miniature golf is pitch-and-putt golf: **Million Dollar Mulligan** *(2850 Florida Plaza Blvd., Kissimmee, FL 34746,Tel. 407/425-5505)* offers 9 holes of pitch and putt plus a unique hole-in-one contest.

SPECTATOR SPORTS
Baseball

Several teams have their spring training facilities in the area. The **Houston Astros** hold theirs at the Osceola County Stadium Complex in Kissimmee. Tickets are $7 to $12 and can be ordered by calling *407/933-6500*. The **Atlanta Braves** hold theirs at Disney's Wide World of Sports complex. Tickets are $10.50 to $15.50 and can be ordered by calling *407/839-3900*. The **Cleveland Indians** train at Chain of Lakes Complex in Winter Haven, by Cypress Gardens. Tickets run $5 to $12 and can be ordered by calling *813/287-8844*. The **Kansas City Royals** train at the Baseball City complex about 15 minutes south of Disney. Call *407/839-3900* to order tickets at $6 to $10 a pop.

During the regular season, the nearest hardball action can be found at Tropicana Field in St. Petersburg, where the **Tampa Devil Rays** play. Tickets are $3 to $20 and can be ordered by calling *813/282-7297*. The **Florida Marlins** play at Pro Player Stadium in Miami. *Call 305/350-5050 for ticket information.* They sell for $7 to $21. Info on both teams can be found at www.majorleaguebaseball.com.

As for the minor leagues, the Devil Rays' AA-level affiliate, the **Orlando Rays,** play at Tinker Field in O-town. Call *407/649-RAYS* to order tickets ($2 to $7). The **Kissimmee Cobras** are Houston's A-level affiliate. *Call 407/933-5500 for ticket info ro check out www.minorleaguebaseball.com.*

Basketball

The often-mediocre **Orlando Magic** play NBA games at the Orlando Arena, located in the downtown area, at 600 West Amelia Ave. Tickets are $10 to $64 and can be ordered by calling *407/839-3900*. Check out www.orlandomagic.com for more.

The WNBA's **Orlando Miracle** also play at the O-rena. Ticket prices were not available at press time, but you can call *407/916-WNBA* or surf to *www.wnba.com/miracle* for up-to-date information.

Football

There's an arena football team here, the **Orlando Predators**. They also play at the O-rena. Consult www.orlpredators.com or call *407/648-4444*. NFL action can be found an hour west of Orlando, where the **Tampa Bay Buccaneers** play. *Check out www.buccaneers.com or call 800/795-2827 for tickets, schedules, and info.*

Golf

Orlando hosts several major PGA tournaments. They are the **Bay Hill Invitational**, presented by Office Depot, held at Arnold Palmer's Bay Hill Country Club less than a mile from the junction of Sand Lake Road and International Drive. The tournament, which takes place every March, solicits some of the top names in the sport. *Daily and tourney-long tickets are available, call 407/351-2800.*

Hockey

The NHL's **Tampa Bay Lightning** play at Tampa's Mark Center. *Call 813/287-8844 or check out www.tampabaylighning.com for info.* Tickcts are $16 to $60.

The **Orlando Solar Bears** of the International Hockey League play at the O-rena. Tickets are $8 to $29. *Surf to www.solarbears.theihl.com or call 407/872-PUCK.*

11. THE MAGIC KINGDOM

Most people think that Walt Disney World is composed of **The Magic Kingdom** and nothing else. Well, WDW encompasses 28,000 acres of Florida land, of which the Kingdom takes up only 98. Still, this is the most recognizable part of the Vacation Kingdom and the foremost drawing card for many families.

Many children prefer the Magic Kingdom to the other parks, and visiting this park first may pose a problem. Younger kids who visit the MK first expect the same thing from EPCOT and the Studios and tend to dislike the somewhat cerebral theme of the other parks. This problem can be alleviated by visiting EPCOT first, then MGM, and the MK. The Magic Kingdom is best described by the dedication, by Roy O. Disney, on October 25, 1971:

Walt Disney World is a tribute to the philosophy and life of Walter Elias Disney and to the talents, the dedication, and the loyalty of the entire Disney organization that made Walt Disney's dream come true. May Walt Disney World bring joy and inspiration and new knowledge to all who come to this happy place... a Magic Kingdom where the young-at-heart of all ages can laugh and play and learn together.

GETTING AROUND

To get to the Magic Kingdom from:

• Polynesian Resort, Contemporary Resort, Grand Floridian Resort: Take the monorail or motor launch.
• TTC: Take the monorail or ferry.
• Epcot: Take the monorail to the TTC and transfer to the monorail or ferry.
• Fort Wilderness or Wilderness Lodge: Take the motor launch.
• All other WDW resort areas: Take the bus.

WDW VITAL STATISTICS

Walt Disney World, P.O. Box 10,040, Lake Buena Vista, FL 32830-0040.

On the Internet: *www.disneyworld.com*

Tel.: *407/824-4321.*

Hours: *Vary, see Chapter 4. Gates open at 8:30 AM, attractions at 9 AM.*

Admission: *$44 for adults, $35 for kids. See section on "Admission Media" for full details.*

Parking: *$6.*

Time to See: *A minimum of a day and a half during quiet seasons, two days during the busier times of the year.*

When to See: *Tuesday, Wednesday, Friday, and Sunday are the least crowded days here.*

Don't Miss: *Space Mountain, Splash Mountain, Big Thunder Mountain, Country Bear Vacation Hoedown, Diamond Horseshoe Revue, Pirates of the Caribbean, Jungle Cruise, Haunted Mansion, It's a Small World.*

All off-site hotels, via I-4: Take exit 25B (U.S. 192 West, Magic Kingdom) and keep your eyes peeled for signs. You can't miss it, but if you begin to pass concentrations of motels, restaurants, and kitschy souvenir shops, you just did the impossible. Feel free to laugh at yourself.

PARKING

The Magic Kingdom's parking lot can accommodate 12,156 vehicles. The cost is $6, free for resort guests (remember your ID!) and there is no cost for leaving and returning or switching parks on the same day (retain your receipt!). But the three most important points regarding WDW parking are: 1. Write down where you park! 2. Write down where you park! 3. Write down where you park!

The parking sections are named after Disney characters, and each row is numbered. Write it down! That one point can not be stressed enough! Note that the handicapped can park in a special lot adjacent to the TTC.

ADMISSION

WDW passes and tickets are available at the TTC, the park's main entrance, and at most hotels' guest services desks. Prices are subject to change, and usually rise in the spring of every year. *Call 407/W-DISNEY for current pricing information.*

- **One-day ticket** allows admission to ONE of the major theme parks only. $44 for adults, $35 for kids 3 to 9.
- **Park Hopper Passes** include four or five days' unlimited admission to the Magic Kingdom, Epcot, Disney-MGM Studios, and the Animal Kingdom plus use of the Disney transportation system. You can go from one park to another in the same day. Four-day passes are $167/$134, five-day passes are $199/$159.
- **Park Hopper Plus Passes** include unlimited admission to the four major theme parks plus give you your choice of admissions to Pleasure Island, River Country, Typhoon Lagoon, Blizzard Beach, or Disney's Wild World of Sports. Five day passes (including two of the above options) cost $229/$183. Six day passes (including three options) cost $259/$207 and both include use of the WWD transportation system.
- **Annual Passes** are good for admission to all four parks and is valid for 365 days from the date that you claim your pass at one of the four parks. Cost is $324/$275 and includes complimentary parking and use of the WWD transportation system.
- **Premium Annual Passes** include admission to the four theme parks, Pleasure Island, the Disney water parks, and the Wide World of Sports for a year, plus parking and transportation. Cost is $434/$369.
- **Unlimited Magic Passes** are available to guests staying at Disney hotels and include unlimited admission to ALL Disney attractions for the length of your stay. See Chapter 8 for details on this pass.

Note that these prices do not include 6% Florida sales tax. *To order, call 407/W-DISNEY or go online at www.disneyworld.com.* You can also order through any Disney Store location.

MONEY

Walt Disney World accepts American Express, MasterCard, Visa, and the Disney Credit Card, as well as travelers' checks and cash, even at counter-service eateries. There are SunTrust ATMs located in all four theme parks.

DRESS CODE

Shirts and shoes must be worn, as a rule. However, this rule is broken as often as it is obeyed during the summer.

REFURBISHMENT & INTERRUPTION OF ATTRACTIONS

Since WDW stays open 365 days a year, attractions may be closed from time to time for upkeep. Known as "rehab," this can be annoying if you have your mind set on a ride that happens to be down that month. You can soften the blow beforehand by calling 407/824-4321 and finding out what's closed before you get to the park. Also, note that continually moving attractions like Peter Pan's Flight and Spaceship Earth may be halted momentarily to allow handicapped passengers to board.

PACKAGE PICKUP

Each theme park offers package pickup service, where rather than lugging your purchases around all day, you can send them to a centralized package pickup center near the entrance to the park. Disney resort guests can have their packages sent directly to their hotels. Note that package pickup locations are most crowded between 5 and 6pm and/or one hour before the theme parks close.

DISNEY'S FASTPASS

This system allows you to bypass the line at selected major attractions in the theme parks, by issuing guests a reserved time when they can return to the attraction and walk right on. Just bring your admission media to the Fastpass Distribution Centers at each participating attraction and stick it in the machine to get your time.

At press time this was being used at Space Mountain, Splash Mountain, and the Many Adventures of Winnie the Pooh in the Magic Kingdom, Honey I Shrunk the Audience and Test Track at Epcot, the Rock and Roller Coaster, Star Tours, Tower of Terror, and Voyage of the Little Mermaid at the Studios, and Countdown to Extinction, Kali River Rapids, and Kilmanjaro Safaris at the Animal Kingdom.

PRACTICAL INFORMATION

Alcoholic Beverages: Forbidden in the Magic Kingdom.

Baby Services: Changing and nursing facilities are located next to the Crystal Palace Restaurant on Main Street, U.S.A.

Baby Strollers: Can be rented for $6 a day at the Stroller Shop, on the right side of the entrance plaza.

Banking: There are SunTrust ATMs located on Main Street USA and in Adventureland.

Cameras: The Kodak Camera Center on Main Street has a full array of cameras for rent, film, videotapes, and two-hour development (see below).

Cigarettes: Not sold in the park.

First Aid: Next to the Crystal Palace is the First Aid Center.

Foreign Language Assistance: Maps and assistance are available at Guest Relations.

Hearing-impaired Guests: A Telecommunications Device for the Deaf (TDD) is available at City Hall.

Information: City Hall is the place to go for info on the day's entertainment schedule.

Kennel: Pets are not allowed in WDW Resorts or attractions. There is, however, an air-conditioned kennel next to the TTC. Reservations are not needed.

Lockers: Available for $.25 or $.50, at the TTC and under the Main Street Railroad Station.

Lost and Found: Claim or report missing items at City Hall on Main Street.

Lost Children: Report to Baby Services or City Hall. Smoking, eating, and drinking: Not allowed in any attractions.

Transportation: Information is available at the TTC.

Visually-impaired guests: Complimentary tape cassettes and players are available at City Hall. A deposit is required, though.

Wheelchair Guests: Wheelchair rental is available at the Stroller Shop. Disabled Guests Guidebooks are available at City Hall.

At the foot of Main Street is the entrance to the park and about 99.9% of Magic Kingdom visitors stroll up the street, laden with shops and eateries, all from the turn of the century. Speculation has led us to believe that Main Street in Disneyland was directly based on Marceline, Missouri, Walt Disney's hometown.

The street has a certain air of Victorian splendor to it, and there are many necesseties located here. There's a bank, the City Hall Information Center, first aid and baby centers, and Guest Relations.

TIPS

Attractions - The attractions on Main Street are not among the most popular in the World, but many are still worth your time. If you're not going to watch the afternoon parade, stay away from Main Street between 2:30 and 3:30. The best bet for visiting Main Street is to arrive before opening time, when the entire concourse can be experienced at a leisurely pace while waiting for the other "lands" to open.

Dining - While the Magic Kingdom is not noted for its food (actually, it's more of an ignominy), Main Street has several of the parks better dining options. Also, they are among the few in the park that offers full breakfasts. The best bets are Tony's Town Square Cafe, the Plaza

Restaurant, the Crystal Palace, and the Main Street Wagons.

Shopping - The best selection of souvenirs of all sorts in the park can be found lining the Street. However, for souvenirs like stuffed animals, toys, key-chains, and the like, you'd be better off visiting Mickey's Character Shop at the Marketplace. However, shops of note are the Harmony Barber Shop, House of Magic, Main Street Confectionery, and Crystal Arts. Stop by before 2:30, after which the parade will trap anyone on the Street, followed by a mass exodus of the park, which continues on until about 5 PM.

ATTRACTIONS
WALT DISNEY WORLD RAILROAD

Rating: 5 1/2. A great way to associate yourself with the park's sights. Location: The first thing you see when you enter the park. Duration Of Ride: 19 minutes, round trip. Best Time To Go: Before 11 AM.

The Walt Disney World Railroad offers visitors a great way to get from point A to point B without tiring out. The four locomotives, the Lilly Belle, Roy O. Disney, Walter E. Disney, and the Roger Broggie, were all built in Philadelphia between 1916 and 1928, and were once hauling freight cars filled with jute, sugar and hemp across Yucatan jungles.

Disneyland visitors will be disappointed to know that the WDW Railroad lacks the Grand Canyon Diorama and Primeval World sections that the Disneyland Railroad has. As for the stations: the Main Street U.S.A. is closest to Town Square and the entrance; the Frontierland station is closest to Liberty Square and Adventureland; and the Mickey's Starland station, wedged in between Fantasyland and Tomorrowland. The circuit tour is about 1.5 miles long and is great for people who want to sit down and enjoy a breeze while getting somewhere. Trains arrive at each station every five to seven minutes. Note that ines are often shortest at Main Street.

MAIN STREET CINEMA

Rating: 5. Pleasant, a great way to get out of the searing afternoon heat. Location: At the middle of Main Street, east side. Duration Of Show: Continuous presentation. Best Time To Go: Anytime except the half-hour on either side of the parade time. Most pleasant between noon and 2:30 when the heat is at its worst and other attractions are packed.

This attraction, by virtue of its inconspicuous location and its image, is never crowded. Kids and adults alike revel in six separate films being shown at once. Five of them are silent, but the sixth, the theater's piece de resistance, was the first cartoon with sound. This particular movie, Steamboat Willie, introduced to the world a mouse named Mickey, who met another mouse called Minnie, and the rest, as they say, is history.

PENNY ARCADE

Rating: 4 1/2. Beguiling, though not necessarily unforgettable. Location: At the north end of Main Street. Best Time To Go: If you arrive before the park opens, or before 2:30.

Disneyland patrons are intrigued (or disheartened) by the presence of several ordinary arcades in that park. WDW has an arcade as well, though this one actually relates to the land it is situated in. Anyone with a penchant for video games will be fascinated by the Victorian era machines located here. The cost ranges from one to twenty-five cents.

There are Minute-o-scopes (circa 1900), viewing devices operated by turning them by hand; and Cali-o-scopes, their newer siblings, the PianOrchestra player-piano, and the usual array of pinball and video game machines. Worth at least a look.

MAIN STREET VEHICLES

Rating: 5 1/2. A delightful way to travel up Main Street. Location: Town Square. Duration Of Ride: Varies. Best Time To Go: Anytime.

Enjoy a breezy ride up Main Street in a horse-drawn trolley, a refitted and modernized horseless carriage, jitney, an open-sided double-decker omnibus, or a bright red fire engine. Not worth the wait if the line is long.

SHOPPING

EMPORIUM

This is the Magic Kingdom's largest gift shop, and located on Town Square in an easily discernible location, lures many a visitor to its realm. Due to its size and proximity to the lockers (beneath the station), this is a good place to pick up stuffed animals, toys, t-shirts, sweatshirts, towels, handbags, hats, and Mousketeer ears, many adorned with Mickey, Minnie, or the WDW logo. Also, the store sells gifts, books, film, records, and sundry items. Very crowded in the late afternoon.

HARMONY BARBER SHOP

Here, you can get an old-fashioned shave or haircut. Appointments are necessary and available by calling 824-6550, The trims come with musical accompaniment courtesy of the Dapper Dans, the Kingdom's own barbershop quartet. Also, nostalgic items like moustache cups and shaving gadgets are available for purchase.

DISNEY CLOTHIERS

If it's meant to be worn, and if it bears any likeness of Mickey, Minnie, and the WDW logo, it can be purchased here. Possibly the nicest souvenirs for Disney film buffs are the black satin jackets and golf shirts depicting

Fantasia's Sorcerer's Apprentice, portrayed by the one and only Mouse. Fashions for men, women, and children are sold here.

HOUSE OF MAGIC

Demonstrations of necromancy here, like disappearing cards, water pouring from empty jugs, coins passing through paper, and other tricks make the clientele long to purchase a starter Blackstone kit, or other tricks, gimmicks, gifts, gags, books, and joke items.

MAIN STREET BOOK STORE

Here, items purveyed include books (many of which feature Disney art), magazines, stationary, writing utensils, paper plates, napkins, wrapping paper, and greeting cards.

DISNEYANA COLLECTIBLES

This small market offers a selection of rare and new Disney memorabilia, including limited edition plates, cels, and animation art. Two features distinguishing this from the many other WDW outlets may make this a mandatory stop. First of all, the necessary reservations for the Diamond Horseshoe Jamboree can only be made here (and on a first-come, first-serve, same-day basis). Secondly, when the weather turns foul, this is where the Disney characters seek refuge.

KODAK CAMERA CENTER

Cameras and paraphernalia are available for sale or rental, including 35mm cameras plus film, repairs (only minor ones), and camcorders.

CAMERA RENTAL RATES

	Per Day	Deposit
Disc Cameras:	Free	$50
35mm Cameras:	$5	$145
Camcorders:	$40	$400

The refundable deposit can be charged to MasterCard, American Express, and Visa cards. Also available is two-hour express photo processing. Just drop off your film at the drop-off center and pick them up here before you leave.

MAIN STREET CONFECTIONERY

The sweet tooth in everyone urges a visit to this elysium of chocolates, pastilles, jelly beans, nougats, mints, marshmallow crisps, and peanut brittle the house specialty. A good place to get that sugar rush.

UPTOWN JEWELERS

Here, a myriad of trinkets and baubles are available for purchase, ranging from ceramic Mickeys and Donalds for a few bucks to watches and jewels for a few thousand. Of interest are 14-karat gold and sterling silver charms featuring that mouse guy, Tinkerbell, the WDW logo, and Cinderella Castle. Timepieces are also stocked here, including Mickey Mouse watches and those that play the theme to "It's a Small World."

DISNEY & CO.

This quaint Victorian shop sells a variety of Disney T-shirts, sweats, hats, stuffed animals, pens, bags, and other souvenir items, albeit a smaller selection than the Emporium.

MAIN STREET MARKET HOUSE

This authentic turn-of-the-century general store sells snack and sundry items like pickles, honey, teas of all sorts, and tobacco products. Souvenir matchbooks given out with each purchase.

CRYSTAL ARTS

This shop sells a variety of cut-glass bowls and vases, plates and glasses, all created by a glass-blower here. Engraving is also available, and either the glass-blower or the engraver can always be seen working his magic.

SERVICES

AAA HOSPITALITY CENTER

Located on the east side of Main Street, this kiosk offers travel tips and services, including hotel reservations and complimentary towing for those who need it.

MAGIC KINGDOM BABY CENTER & FIRST AID

At the north end of the Street, the Baby Center offers changing and nursing facilities, as well as a place to prepare formula or purchase essentials like bottles, diapers, and baby food. First aid is located in the same building as the Baby Center.

STROLLER SHOP

Adjacent to the entrance, this offers rental strollers and wheelchairs. However, the price tag is $6 for a stroller. Bring your own if at all possible.

CITY HALL INFORMATION CENTER

City Hall offers information on the day's entertainment, Magic Kingdom guidebooks, lost-and-found facilities, and transportation info.

On the left side of Town Square. The characters tend to hang out next to this building.

GUEST WINDOW
Information and ticket upgrades are available here.

LOCKERS
Souvenirs and stuff can be stored in the lockers directly underneath the Main Street Railroad Station.

The first bridge on the left from the Hub leads here, the home of tropical vegetation and the World's best adventure rides. The landscape resembles that of a rain forest more than a one-time Florida swamp. The architecture is particularly faithful to the theme, as every building looks like it could have come out of Indiana Jones or Romancing the Stone.

Imported items are the major bill of fare at the shops here, featuring the products of Africa, India, the Caribbean, Honk Kong, and Bangkok. Many rate this as their favorite land.

TIPS
Attractions - This land has some of Disney's best creations, and inevitably long lines. The queues at the Swiss Family Treehouse and Jungle Cruise are notoriously slow, however, the Pirates of the Caribbean waiting area is more like a show in itself! Best bet: get Adventureland out of the way early in the morning or late in the afternoon.

Dining - Adventureland's only restaurants are rather ordinary fast food eateries. However, Aloha Isle is a good bet for a cool snack.

Shopping - There is a large concentration of shops at Caribbean Plaza, at the exit from "Pirates." The shops there and at Adventureland Bazaar hold a great deal of interesting goods, including many imports from Asia and Africa.

ATTRACTIONS
SWISS FAMILY TREEHOUSE
Rating: 7. Lets your imagination run wild! Location: Next to the Hub. Duration of Tour: Varies, but usually 10-15 minutes. Best Time To Go: Before 11:30 AM. Comments: Stairs! Lots and lots of stairs! If you can't handle the climbing, you may want to skip this one.

A spectacular re-creation of the Robinsons' lost paradise. It has everything the marooned family could want in treetop living. Patchwork quilts, mahogany furniture, candles stuck in abalone shells, and a system of running water in each room. Pulleys carry buckets full of water from below and pour them into pipes of hollowed-out wood and carry it into, oh, never mind. It's just one of those things you have to see to understand.

Some people think that the Treehouse is boring. Some even consider it a labor to climb the many steps. Granted, it may be a challenge, but the Robinson domicile at the top is worth it! Also, enjoyment of the exhibit is increased greatly by visitation in the morning, when you aren't likely to be tired out by hiking up a lot of steps. If you can't get there early (this attraction crowds up fast!), visit around 5:30.

JUNGLE CRUISE

Rating: 9. Disney's pride and joy, one of the best attractions in the park. Don't miss it. Location: Next to the Swiss Family Treehouse. Duration Of Ride: 10 minutes. Best Time To Go: Early morning or late afternoon. Comments: Another attraction that gets crowded fast. Most enjoyable during the day.

For those souls who dream about going on a safari, this is your chance. You can visit the African veldt, a southeast Asian jungle, the Amazon rain forest, and the Nile valley, all without leaving central Florida.

Audio-Animatronics (Disney's sophisticated robotic system) animals representing their habitats are found along every step of the journey. The populace of the Jungle includes a family of bathing elephants, hippos, lions, and cannibals, also of interest is a section of the cruise that plunges cruisers into a dark Cambodian temple, home to a ferocious white tiger! And if you were wondering, the tropical vegetation is real and not robotic and is kept warm in the winter by 100 heaters hidden in the rocks.

Best of all, the boats, bearing great alliterative names like Amazon Annie, Nile Nellie, and Senegal Sal, are not on a track but are piloted by real people, and the Jungle, inspired by the film The African Lion, is the only ride in the Magic Kingdom to be narrated by a human. The pun-heavy prattle covers topics like previous guests who didn't make it, the headhunters, and the rest of the sights. The scenes are about as genuine as you can get, and some kids are squeamish at first, but most soon sit back and enjoy the ride. Some of it is gruesome and odd, but it is all fun.

Disney's Fastpass system was recently installed here, allowing you to reserve your time on the ride and bypass most of the line.

"TROPICAL SERENADE" (ENCHANTED TIKI BIRDS)

Rating: 6. Under new management; definitely an improvement over the old model. Location: Across from the Jungle Cruise and next to the Adventureland Bazaar. Duration of show: 15 minutes. Best time to go: mid-afternoon.

The addition of the Tiki Room's "new owners," Iago from Aladdin and Zazu from The Lion King, has breathed new life into a show that had remained constant and constantly boring since it first debuted in 1964. Now the birds sing songs including "In the Still of the Night," "Hot Hot Hot," "Do the Conga," and "Get on Your Feet." Hollywood-savvy guests will enjoy the irony of the pre-show, with two bickering birds who work as talent agents – named William and Morris. Har har har.

PIRATES OF THE CARIBBEAN
Rating: 10. Unbelievable! DO NOT MISS IT!!! Location: At the far end of Adventureland. Duration Of Ride: 7 1/2 minutes. Best Time To Go: In the morning or late afternoon. Comments: This ride is tame, except for a steep flume-like drop.

As you walk through the queueing area, you immediately feel like you should be wearing an eyepatch and a pegleg. At the entrance, a parrot wearing a hat and patch sits, singing "Yo Ho," the first of many of this attraction's citizens to croon that tune. Then, you walk through stucco-walled rooms to a dark, dank, humid passageway through pirate dungeons. One cell has two prisoners hunched over a checkerboard. As you approach the loading area, you pass a cannon, a stack of cannonballs nearby. You may hear sentries yelling, "Sound the alarm" as you board your craft and set sail. The only sound is the water, for a while, then the lonely cry of a seagull, whose only companionship is a skeleton, posthumously defending his treasure on a desert island. The ship then sails right in the crossfire of the pirates and the law-abiding citizens. Cannons fire, sending up spouts of water as the ship sails on.

The pirates are coming! The pirates are coming! The pirates- oh, never mind, they're already here and they've taken over the town. A woman looks out of her window to survey the situation, but is quickly "discouraged" by bullets that shatter the flowerpots on either side of the windowsill.

Pirates pillage, pirates burn. One mildly sexist scene portrays the auction of village wenches, another pictures a lustful pirate chasing a young lass. As the scenes progress, the tide turns. The buccaneers drink and share their potables with, among other things, a couple of pigs. They can be seen getting chased with broomsticks by their women, and eventually, fighting over their treasure. These Audio-Animatronic figures are remarkable for their individuality, personality, and immaculate detail (One buc even has wiry hair on his legs). Especially uncanny are the movements and noises (attitudes?) of the chickens, dogs, and pigs found throughout the attraction.

There's one steep drop - a pitch-black plunge down a chute to the accompaniment of a roaring waterfall. But it's over before you know it.

And the horrible sights are animated by the omnipresent choruses of "Yo Ho, Yo Ho, a pirate's life for me." This song is something of a pirate standard, seemingly used in every pirate movie in the history of film.

One of the best things about this attraction is the speed of the lines. Despite the popularity of this attraction, their is rarely a wait over half an hour, and then only during peak seasons. If you only have the chance to experience a few rides, put this at the top of your list.

SHOPPING

ZANZIBAR SHELL COMPANY

Here's the place to find goods imported from exotic ports of call like Hong Kong, Beijing, and Singapore.

ELEPHANT TALES

Forgot your khakis? Need a new pith helmet? A variety of safari garments for both men and women is available here, plus jewelry, accessories, and stuffed animals.

TRADERS OF TIMBUKTU

Traders sells a variety of African imports, including striking ethnic jewelry (including that made of sharks' teeth), wood carvings, and khakis. Apparel is also available.

TIKI TROPICS SHOP

Jewelry, shoes, shorts, and T-shirts are sold here.
island supply

Surf gear is sold here, including T-shirts, shorts, bathing suits, jewelry, and surfboard wax.

HOUSE OF TREASURE

Here, kids can find their fantasy with pirate hats, swords, eye patches, toy rifles, and other memorabilia. HINT: If you are flying back home, pack any toy guns, knives, and swords in your luggage. Otherwise, you might encounter trouble from airport security.

THE GOLDEN GALLEON

Blackbeard's crew ne'er saw so much gold as is in this small shop. The treasure here is all nautical in its motif, ranging from model ships to ships' wheels, brass schooners, and racing yachts, plus fashions with maritime themes.

PLAZA DEL SOL CARIBE
This emporium sells candy, clothes, silk flowers, gift items, pinatas, pottery, and straw bags.

LAFFITE'S PORTRAIT DECK
Kids love to dress up as pirate lads and lasses, then pose with chests of treasure. Souvenir 8x10 photos of your child as a buccaneer make for lasting memories.

LA PRINCESA DE CRISTAL
Pretty much the same wares are sold here and in the Crystal Arts shop on Main Street, albeit in a completely different atmosphere. Glass blowing, cutting, and engraving are the skills practiced here. If you have more than one day to spend here, it is enjoyable to spend a few minutes watching the master craftsmen at work.

CROW'S NEST
Cameras, film, and accessories are available here. This is also a drop-off point for the Photo Express service.

Out of the jungle and into the Old West, Frontierland is like some great old Western "B" movie come to life, with cacti, red concrete paths, sandstone mountains, rickety wooden structures, and a distinctively rugged feel throughout. Buildings have unpainted barn sides, stone, or clapboard, and all have a weathered look.

TIPS

Attractions - Four of WDW's best experiences are located here: Big Thunder Mountain Railroad, Diamond Horseshoe Revue, Country Bear Vacation Hoedown, and Splash Mountain. It is recommended to tour Frontierland early in the morning.

Dining - Eating and entertainment can be combined at the Diamond Horseshoe. All of the Frontierland eateries are decent, and the churros and turkey legs sold by wagons are worth note. However, there is no full-service restaurant on the Western front.

Shopping - A good place if you got a hankerin' fer Western goods, cowboy hats, leather, toy guns, and other Southwestern and Indian crafts.

ATTRACTIONS

BIG THUNDER MOUNTAIN RAILROAD

Rating: 10. Another not-to-be-missed attraction, this is a wild ride through through a beautifully themed mountain. Location: A landmark in itself, it can be seen from most of the park. Duration Of Ride: 3 1/2 minutes. Best Time To Go: Early morning or early evening. Comments: Children must be 3' 4" to ride. People in line may switch off at the ride. Kids 7 and under must be accompanied by an adult.

The lines wind up a path, through what appears to be a gold-mining operation. As you enter the main building, you overlook some hot springs and the railroad below. Occasionally, a geyser erupts. Then, you make your way down the ramp and to the boarding area. Those under the height requirements or those who just chickened out can get off here. But the rest of us board mine trains for a journey through the Gold Rush Days.

The trains set off, entering a cave filled with cool mists, shrieking bats, and falling rocks. As you ascend, notice the rumble as rocks shimmy and slowly fall towards you. Waterfalls and phosphorescent pools also can be seen. As you exit the dark cave, the trains slowly gain speed and zoom down the hill!

The scenery is excellent, especially the flooded-out town of Tumbleweed, in which a man sits, wearing his pajamas and a puzzled look as a Professor Cumulus Isobar's rainmaking machine sputters and pops, the flood beneath him, as he lays in a bathtub. All told, more than 20 Audio-Animatronics goats, people, chickens, and donkeys populate this section of the Old West. The trains careen around, dodging dinosaur remains and whipping by the Gold Dust Saloon (where a party still rages on), and eventually back to the loading platform.

Overall, the ride itself is tame as roller coasters go (there are no loop-de-loops, steep drops, or terribly sharp curves like in the Python or the Great American Scream Machine), as any thrill ride zealot will tell you, but this is an adventure. Where as the forementioned rides just zoom about the air with no real purpose, Big Thunder takes riders on a quest through a mining town, complete with about $300,000 worth of mining equipment - the real Mccoy. Even if you loathe roller coasters, give this one a whirl. It's so tame that it barely qualifies as a roller coaster, and it's so striking that it would be a crime to miss it.

Some statistics of note: Big Thunder took 15 years of planning and two more to build it, contains 650 tons of steel, 4,675 tons of cement, and 16,000 gallons of paint, and at a height of 197 feet, it is Florida's third highest peak.

Try riding the Railroad after dark. The experience is completely different from (and somewhat more convincing than) a daytime tour.

TOM SAWYER ISLAND

Rating: 5. Relaxing, but you could forgive yourself for skipping this if you don't have any kids with you. Location: A landmark, can be seen from almost anywhere in Frontierland or Liberty Square. The raft docks, are next to Big Thunder Mountain and Splash Mountain. Best Time To Go: Anytime. Most enjoyable early in the day or mid-afternoon. Comments: Attraction closes at dusk.

Kids love this attraction, where they take a raft across the Rivers of America to an island loaded with caves to explore, bridges that lead to Fort Sam Clements, and there, a dozen or so air guns that they can fire at nearby mountains, passing steam ships, or the occasional tourist.

This attraction, which may seem boring to adults if toured early in the day, makes for a good out-of-the-way retreat for the heat of the afternoon. While the kids are off burning blood sugar like water, the grown-ups can relax at Aunt Polly's with a sandwich and a cool glass of lemonade. There are maps posted for those who manage to get lost. In busy seasons, a second raft landing may be brought into use.

COUNTRY BEAR VACATION HOEDOWN

Rating: 9. A Disney classic, good rhythmic fun. Don't miss it! Location: In the center of Frontierland. Duration Of Show: 15 minutes. Best Time To Go: Before 11:30 AM or after 5 PM. Comments: The show changes twice annually: at Christmas and again in the summer.

Everybody seems to love the Country Bear Vacation Hoedown (formerly the Jamboree), which would account for the fact that this show almost always has a substantial wait. Also, Grizzly Hall, the theater in which the Hoedown plays, is smaller than adequate to accommodate the crowds who flock here.

Here, 'da bearsss' perform like never before in a musical revue filled with fun. Led by Henry, the master of ceremonies, they kick up a storm. One bear has a knack for impersonating Elvis Presley, while three other bruins, Bubbles, Beluah, and Bunny, harmonize "Wish They All Could Be California Bears". Other performers include the heartthrob Teddi Barra, who sings in the rain a la Gene Kelly (complete with raincoat and galoshes), a country-western band known as the Bear Rugs: Zeb, Zeke, Ted, Fred, and Tennessee, Liver Lips McGrowl, Wendell, Gomer the pianist, Trixie the Tampa Temptation (a torch-song crooner), Melvin the Moosehead, and Big Al, who is nothing short of a cult hero at WDW. His face can be seen on postcards, T-shirts, and other memorabilia. He's one of only a handful of Audio-Animatronics characters to have a following.

FRONTIERLAND SHOOTIN' ARCADE

Rating: 4 1/2. Not worth it if you only have one day to spend at the Kingdom. Location: Near the passageway to Adventureland. Best Time To Go: Any time. Comments: Costs 25¢ per play.

At this attraction, you can be the Lone Ranger, Clint Eastwood, or your favorite Western hero as you pick up a Hawkins 54-caliber buffalo rifle (modernized: they shoot infrared beams now) and can blow away any or all of almost a hundred targets each one procuring a different reaction. Digital sound effects add to the realism of this arcade.

DIAMOND HORSESHOE JAMBOREE

Rating: 10. Great fun for any and all. Don't miss it! Location: At the border with Liberty Square. Duration Of Show: 30 minutes. Best Time To Go: Whenever your reservations are for. Comments: That's right, reservations. If you don't have 'em, you can't get in. Book your time at the Disneyana Collectibles shop on Main Street.

This show has rapidly become a Disney favorite, although seeing it is a real pain in the butt. First, you must go to Disneyana Collectibles on Main Street, make the necessary arrangements, then show up about thirty minutes before showtime to be admitted to the theater, fifteen minutes for food orders to be taken and filled, then finally, the show.

The show, composed in the same style as the Hoop-Dee-Doo Revue, features a troupe of live actors and actresses who sing, dance, and joke their way through the wholly entertaining show. The cast is energetic and brims with youthful exuberance, and overall, the show rarely fails to amuse. If you want to avoid wasting time but still want to see the Diamond Horseshoe, arrive before the rest of the park opens, go to Disneyana, and make your reservations before 9 AM. If you want, you can combine the show and lunch by choosing the 12:15 seating.

About lunch: a small selection of sandwiches, soft drinks, freshly baked pies, and snacks is available before the show.

SPLASH MOUNTAIN

Rating: 10. Unforgettable! Don't miss it! Location: A landmark, next to Big Thunder Mountain. Duration Of Ride: 10 minutes. Best Time To Go: As soon as the park opens. Comments: Kids must be 3' 6" tall to ride, kids under 7 must be accompanied by an adult. The last drop is not nearly as bad as it looks.

When this opened up, it became the fastest ride in Walt Disney World outrunning the Humunga Cowabunga and Space Mountain by a good ten miles an hour. It's also been the most highly touted of all the Magic Kingdom expansion projects, and that, coupled with its Anaheim predecessor's popularity, should make the latest Disney mountain adventure by far the resort's busiest ride.

In Splash Mountain, guests board log flumes and are set off on a ten-minute adventure chronicling Br'er Rabbit's wily escape from Br'er Fox and Br'er Bear. Riders are diverted by some of Song of the South's (Splash Mountain's origin) Oscar-winning music, including "Everybody's Got a Laughing Place" and "Zip-A-Dee-Doo-Dah", that ever-popular Disney anthem. Over 100 Audio-Animatronic animals populate Splash Mountain to tell the tale of those wacky briar patch animals. The flume ride itself is about half a mile long, travelling through bayous and over waterfalls, culminating in a 52-foot, 45-degree drop off Chickapin Hill, reaching a top speed of about 40 MPH. The logs then hit the water with a huge splash and seemingly sink into the lake.

Compared to the California version, this Splash Mountain is described as the "new and improved model," with more emphasis on the highly themed show areas and a slower pace through the mountain, making it easier to follow the story.

Note that you will get wet. No matter where in the log you sit, you will step off Splash Mountain dripping, soaked, saturated, and otherwise, wet. If the idea doesn't really appeal to you, you can fashion yourself a rain poncho out of a garbage bag, or buy one from the Emporium on Main Street.

If you are really intent on riding Splash Mountain without crowds, it is imperative that you arrive at the MK before official opening time. Walk up Main Street and turn left at the Crystal Palace Restaurant. In front of the Palace is the bridge leading to Adventureland. It is not the bridge at the Hub. Get as close as possible to the barrier rope. When the rope is dropped, walk quickly or run to the passageway just across from the Swiss Family Treehouse. There will be phones and restrooms there. Go through this passageway and turn left. You should have a clear view of Splash Mountain across the waterfront. Run for it!

Disney's Fastpass system was recently installed here, allowing you to reserve your time on the ride and bypass most of the line.

WALT DISNEY WORLD RAILROAD

This station, situated as a transition area between Splash Mountain and Big Thunder Mountain, was recently rebuilt, having been shut down to allow for the construction of Splash Mountain. *See the entry for the Railroad under MAIN STREET U.S.A. earlier in this chapter.*

SHOPPING

FRONTIERLAND TRADING POST

This shop sells a variety of souvenirs with a Western theme. You can get provisions like venison chili, buffalo, and boar meat, or cowboy can't-live-without's like six-shooters, rifles, and toy horses, or Indian sundries like peace pipes and tom-toms. Also, clothes from the frontier are available, like ten-gallon hats, moccasins, brass belt buckles, sheriff's badges, and Western jewelry.

TRICORNERED HAT SHOP
Indian headdresses, ten-gallon hats, and a variety of other headgear are sold here alongside leather goods.

FRONTIER WOOD CARVING
This is the spot to get personalized wooden gifts.

PRAIRIE OUTPOST AND SUPPLY
Here, one can procure various Southwestern gift items, art, and apparel.

BIG AL'S
Big Al, the bruin with a cult-like following, has his own shop, where harmonicas, toy guns, coonskin caps, rock candy, and big lollipops can be found, along with the big bear's image on almost everything.

You are transported from the Gold Rush-era West to the Colonies around 1776. The buildings are clapboard and brick, with weathervanes and gingerbread moldings.

One of Liberty Square's foremost pieces of work was crafted by Mother Nature: it's the Liberty Tree, a 130-year-old live oak. It was found at the property's southern fringe and was transported to its present location twenty years ago. Thirteen lanterns hang on the tree, one for each of the original colonies.

TIPS

Attractions - The attractions here include a boat ride, a tour of a haunted mansion, and a show featuring every single U.S. President. Like Main Street, if you opt to experience any of the land's adventures at parade time, don't expect to be able to get to the hub. However, you can get through to Fantasyland.

Dining - If you care to sit down and relax in a full-service restaurant, the Liberty Tree Tavern may be your cup of Boston Tea Party. It serves good food and is often overlooked at lunch. If faster fare appeals to you more, the Columbia Harbour House offers the best light fare in the park.

Shopping - Colonial-era antiques are the main bill of fare here.

ATTRACTIONS

THE HALL OF PRESIDENTS

Rating: 7 1/2. Very moving. Location: Between the Columbia Harbour House and the Liberty Tree Tavern. Duration Of Show: 23 minutes. Best Time To Go: Anytime. Comments: Many kids are not mature enough to appreciate the show.

The two attractions in WDW that focus on the U.S. (this and the American Adventure at EPCOT) make you proud to be an American. I know, it's trite and cliche, but it's true. This attraction traces its origins back to Great Moments with Mr. Lincoln, one of the Disney-designed pavilions at the 1964-65 World's Fair in Flushing, New York. The attraction of the same name can be found today on Main Street U.S.A. in Anaheim's Disneyland.

The first portion of the show is a 70mm film about the magnitude of the Constitution throughout history, narrated by Maya Angelou. Then, Audio-Animatronic Abe Lincoln and Bill Clinton deliver speech preceded by a roll call. All the presidents are here, from George Washington to Clinton, who was installed just after his inauguration. The detail is almost frightening, as the chief executive officers fidget, nod, and whisper. Each president is dressed in the costume of his period, from his hairstyle to his shoes to the fabric of his pants. Even their personal effects were painstakingly researched and recreated, like Washington's chair and FDR's leg brace. This is the epitome of the trademark Disney attention to detail.

If you are a history buff or just someone who feels especially proud of his red, white, and blue heritage, you will particularly appreciate this show. However, if you only have limited time and have seen the American Adventure, you can skip it, although not without a few pangs of guilt. However, small (and some not-so-small!) kids find the show boring, so if that's a major consideration, you can skip it. And don't worry if there's a substantial line here: it turns over 700 people every 25 minutes.

LIBERTY SQUARE RIVERBOAT

Rating: 5 1/2. Scenic, but not special. Location: On the bank closest to the Hall of Presidents. Duration Of Ride: 16 minutes. Best Time To Go: Anytime. Comments: If you're the type who's prone to seasickness, don't worry - the boat travels on a rail.

This is a steamboat ride down the half-mile Rivers of America, aboard the Richard F. Irvine, named for a key WDW Imagineer. It is a real steamboat in all aspects except one: it travels around Tom Sawyer Island on a guide rail. From the boat, you will pass Tom Sawyer Island and Fort Sam Clemens, Big Thunder and Splash Mountains, and props that enhance the Wild West theme. It's a relaxing way to beat the heat on a sticky afternoon.

MIKE FINK KEELBOATS

Rating: 5 1/2. Very similar to the Riverboat. Location: On the bank closest to the Columbia Harbour House. Duration Of Ride: 9 1/2 minutes. Best Time To Go: Morning or late afternoon. Comments: Closes at dusk.

This attraction is a boat journey that goes along the same path as the Liberty Square Riverboat. The only major differences are the loading speed (considerably slower than the Riverboat) and the fact that the top decks of the two ships, the Berthe Mae and the Gullywhumper, are exposed to the elements.

THE HAUNTED MANSION

Rating: 9. Great Disney entertainment! Don't miss it! Location: By the entrance to Fantasyland. Duration Of Ride: 7 minutes. Best Time To Go: Anytime.

This attraction is one of my favorites for several reasons: the awesome special effects, the eerie sets in which the special effects are rigged, and the legend that surrounds the Mansion. One of the best things about the Haunted Mansion is the way that you experience something new every single time you ride it. Like the movies The Naked Gun and Airplane, there's a lot of details in the margins that you probably won't notice the first time, or even the second. Another thing that makes the ride so appealing is the fact that you can experience it as often as you like the lines move like greased lightning.

First, you are led into a portrait hall (known in inside circles as the Stretching Room) by cast members dressed as morticians. They grumble instructions, never smiling and never meeting your eyes. Then comes the classic spiel about how there are no windows and no doors, while either the floor sinks or the ceiling rises (they won't tell me!) and you are loaded into your "doom buggies". A gleefully evil voice tells you how to behave to coax the spirits into sight, and sure enough, your car is lurching forward between tableaus of dancing ghosts and organ players who look less than human.

One of the nicest touches in this ride is located at the very end, and it's more fun as a surprise, but let it suffice to say that any warnings about hitchhikers should be heeded.

SHOPPING

UMBRELLA CART

If it starts raining as you find yourself between Cinderella Castle and the Hall of Presidents, this is the place to pick up personalized umbrella.

OLDE WORLD ANTIQUES

Who comes to Disney World to buy antique furniture? I don't personally know anyone who does, but if you are one of those people, you can pick up furniture and decorative items crafted from mahogany, pine, oak, brass, pewter, and copper.

This isn't exactly the Price Club, so don't expect to get a steal on a particular item. Some even poke into four digits. All of the antiques, though, are in good shape. If the idea of buying family heirlooms at WDW doesn't appeal to you, take heart. The shop also deals clothing, perfume, and accessories.

SILVERSMITH

This market sells jewelry and housewares are sterling silver or silver-plated. Incidentally, the name "J. Tremain" listed as the shop's proprietor comes from Johnny Tremain, a silversmith's apprentice who joined the Boston Tea Party and the basis for the 1957 Disney movie of the same name.

HERITAGE HOUSE

Here, you can purchase parchment replicas of historical documents. Pewter items are also available, plus a good assortment of other housewares.

ICHABOD'S LANDING

This shop, found on the return path from the Haunted Mansion, is geared towards guests just coming back from that major attraction. Gags items are sold as well, but a better selection can be had at Main Street's House of Magic.

THE YANKEE TRADER

Cookware makes up the majority of the items for sale here, ranging from the mundane (cookie cutters, spatulas, and egg-timers) to the wild (souffle dishes and escargot holders). There are also cookbooks, including collections of recipes from days long gone. Also, Smucker's sells all of its varieties here. How many are there? Take a guess. Got it? Good. Now triple it.

SILHOUETTE CART
Profiles are for sale here, created while you wait.

THE COURTYARD
Topiaries, wind chimes, flowers, and garden merchandise are sold here.

This is where dreams come true and fairy tales are personified. This is truly the heart and soul of WDW. This is where Disney's classic films, Peter Pan, Alice in Wonderland, 20,000 Leagues Under the Sea, Cinderella, Dumbo, Snow White, and The Wind in the Willows come to life. Sleeping Beauty's father is also here (in Cinderella's Castle! What's the deal with that, hmm?). This is many children's favorite land, although there are only two or three memorable attractions here. The buildings in which the adventures here are housed resemble an Alpine village, complete with a Swiss-made air gondola.

Planned for Fantasyland is a ride based on the Disney smash movie The Little Mermaid, which will be the first new attraction in the land since 20,000 Leagues Under the Sea (1971).

TIPS

Attractions - Most of the attractions here appeal to younger children more than any other land. If you have children under the age of ten, KEEP A CLOSE EYE ON THEM HERE, for all the rides here can captivate a child into "better-dealing" his parents for Dumbo or Snow White.

Dining - The only table-service restaurant in the land, King Stefan's Banquet Hall, offers a chance to check out Cinderella Castle and meet the lady herself. Other than that, it might be a good idea to avoid Fantasyland food.

Shopping - Most of the shops here sell character merchandise and are worth only a cursory glance, but the King's Gallery, in Cinderella Castle, is an exception.

CINDERELLA CASTLE & THE HUB
The Castle is the symbol of all Walt Disney World, but it comes as a surprise to many visitors that they cannot freely tour Cinderella Castle and that there is no ride or show in it. Still, it is arguably the most beautiful building in the whole World, and one of the most-photographed in the

real world (as in the Earth!). The gold, grey, and blue spires of the castle reach 189 feet over Main Street (100 feet higher than Sleeping Beauty Castle in Disneyland) and serve as the final bridge between the melancholy burden of reality and quixotic fantasy.

Some trivia and history for you. How many stones were used to build Cinderella Castle? The same number that you had for lunch today. Zero. It's all fiberglass and steel. What do you mean, you ate stone for lunch? The architecture of the castle was borrowed from French palaces around the end of the 1100s, but with flavors of Mad King Ludwig of Bavaria's mansion and the castle from the Disney film.

Cinderella Castle is also, for lack of a better term, the brain of the Magic Kingdom. It is here that the nerve center of the park is located, both above ground and below it. If you were to travel up past King Stefan's Banquet Hall on the second floor, there are broadcast rooms, security centers (guardhouses, if you will), and an apartment meant for but never occupied by the Disneys. Below ground Disney employees change out of their "real people" outfits (yes! they are real people, not Audio-Animatronics) and into a Mickey suit or khakis and a pith helmet. They then travel through underground corridors to their designated "land" and inconspicuously melt into the scenery.

What makes the castle Cinderella's besides the name? Certainly not the restaurant inside. King Stefan was Sleeping Beauty's father, not Cinderella's. However, there is a series of five mosaic murals depicting the familiar tale. The panels, measuring 150 square feet apiece, were designed brilliantly by artist Dorothea Redmond and constructed by master craftsman Hanns-Joachim Scharff. They contain over one million tiny bits of Italian glass in 500 colors, plus bits of real silver and 14-karat gold.

There are also coats of arms here. They belong to prominent families in WDW history. The hostess of King Stefan's has a book telling whose is whose on the walls. An interesting note: many of the families represented on the walls of the Castle can also be found inscribed on the windows on the second story of Main Street.

The Hub is a small island at the dead center of the park. From here, you can directly reach every land but Frontierland and Mickey's Starland. As you enter the Hub from Main Street U.S.A. in the south, going clockwise: the first path leads to Adventureland and Frontierland, the second to Liberty Square and Frontierland, the third to Fantasyland via Cinderella Castle, the fourth to Fantasyland and Tomorrowland.

ATTRACTIONS
MAD TEA PARTY
Rating: 4 1/2. Strictly Coney Park, not the kind of ride Disney excels at. Location: On the border with Tomorrowland. Duration Of Ride: 1 1/2 minutes.

Best Time To Go: Anytime in the morning or evening. Comments: May induce motion sickness.

Here, you sit in oversized teacups that circle around each other on a sheltered platform. The ride is loosely based on the scene in Alice In Wonderland where the Mad Hatter holds his un-birthday party. If you take away the teacup decorations and the central teapot with the mouse inside this is just a larger version of the Tilt-A-Whirl, a common ride found at every amusement park and carnival in the country. However, it is a fun ride and definitely one worth experiencing if there's not much of a line. You say you like spinning around and projectile vomiting? Me too! Well, here's how to twist your way into a nauseous seventh heaven. See the wheel in the center of the cup? Spin it. But hold onto the booook.....

SNOW WHITE'S ADVENTURES
Rating: 5. Good. Location: By the carousel. Duration Of Ride: 2 1/2 minutes. Best Time To Go: Before 11 AM, after 6 PM.

This ride is good, but not one of Disney's best. Although it is in the same genre of ride as Mr. Toad, Snow White is much better, by virtue of more realistic effects and thicker tension. This ride was recently changed, some of the dark, Tim Burtonesque feel of the ride removed and Snow White placed in the attraction for the first time. Previously, the ride told her story in the first-person.

"LEGEND OF THE LION KING"
Rating: 5 1/2. Well-executed, but ill-advised. Location: By the carousel. Duration Of Show: 18 minutes. Best Time To Go: Anytime after noon.

In this attraction, scenes from Disney's record-shattering Lion King are recreated, using non-computerized "Humanimals" controlled by live human beings. The animateers are so talented you'll swear it's Audio-Animatronic. However, the script is taken verbatim from the movie, boiling the movie down to a 18-minuts Cliffs notes version. You can go to Blockbuster Video and rent the Lion King for $3. There's no need to pay $40 and waste precious vacation time to watch it.

DUMBO, THE FLYING ELEPHANT
Rating: 4. Undistinguished, but great fun for everyone who's ever longed to ride a flying elephant. Location: At the center of Fantasyland. Duration Of Ride: 1 1/2 minutes. Best Time To Go: Before 10 AM or after 5 PM.

Young kids absolutely love this ride, while anyone over thirteen is likely to find it dull and childish. As if the idea of cruising above the Magic Kingdom in an aerodynamic grey elephant wasn't attractive enough, there are buttons inside each elephant that raise or lower them. Cool!

Little kids will insist on riding this, but its lines are probably the slowest-moving in all WDW. Go early in the morning. In fact, if you arrive before 10 AM, you might even be able to let the kids ride it twice. However, if there are no young children in your party, skip it.

CINDERELLA'S GOLDEN CARROUSEL
Rating: 6. Beautiful. Location: Center of Fantasyland. Duration Of Ride: 2 minutes. Best Time To Go: Anytime in the morning or evening.

This is one of those attractions, like the Swiss Family Treehouse, that places the emphasis not on action but on beauty and attention to detail. Probably the most picturesque merry-go-round you will ever see, the Carrousel is an authentic item, built in Philadelphia in 1917. Originally dubbed "Liberty", it had 72 horses and several stationary chariots on a 60-foot platform. "Liberty" was discovered at Olympic Park in Maplewood, New Jersey.

Refurbishments replaced the chariots with fiberglass horses, and the mechanics were completely modernized. Each of the 90 white horses is different, each with personality-lending details. Also, eighteen separate scenes, each six square feet, were hand-painted by Disney artists. The horses glide effortlessly around with accompaniment from a band organ that plays classic tunes from Disney movies. This ride is especially breathtaking at night.

IT'S A SMALL WORLD
Rating: 8 1/2. Happy, cheerful, colorful, and innocent. Don't miss it. Location: On the west side of Fantasyland. Duration Of Ride: 11 minutes. Best Time To Go: In the afternoon.

Saccharine overload! It really is a Small World after all, according to the cutesy, if not sappy, lyrics to the theme song that plays all through the boat ride. You board pastel-hued boats and set sail through rooms filled with Audio-Animatronics dolls representing almost every culture group in the world. There are also nursery rhyme characters.

You can find can-can dancers, Tower of London guards, leprechauns, Dutch kids with wooden clogs on their feet, Thai dancers, snake charmers, kite flyers, hula-dancing Polynesians, Don Quixote lookalikes, and countless others. The costumes are particularly faithful, and the overall effect is glowing and alive with warmth. This ride is particularly relaxing, and the oft-times mammoth lines move quickly, so there's rarely much of a wait. Also, "Small World", as it is commonly called, offers a great video taping opportunity.

Oh, did I neglect the music? *It's a Small World*, the ride's theme song, is possibly one of the most-recognized Disney songs ever. It was composed by Richard and Robert Sherman, the brother team who brought us Mary Poppins and other Oscar-winning music. Ride it, but be prepared: you

WILL hum the song afterward. It's state law.

PETER PAN'S FLIGHT

Rating: 9. Fantasyland's best ride. Location: At the border with Liberty Square. Duration Of Ride: 3 minutes. Best Time To Go: Morning or evening.

The legend of Peter Pan is one of a rare breed, one that has been shown as a full-length animated feature, a live action film, and a stage musical. Riders here view Pan from the perspective of the cartoon. You board a replica of Captain Hook's pirate ship, suspended from above, and sail off through Peter's cries of "Here we go!" as the Darling children fly with him to Neverland.

The flight over London is breathtaking, as the Thames, Big Ben, and Parliament pass underneath. Other highlights are the sword fight between Pan and Captain Hook and the finale: the crocodile holding Hook between his jaws. All of the characters are here, including the Darlings, Mr. Smee, Tinkerbell, and Tiger Lily. WDW's most underrated attraction.

THE MANY ADVENTURES OF WINNIE THE POOH

Rating: 5 1/2. Cute but skippable. Location: Where Mr. Toad used to live. Duration of Ride: 2 minutes. Best Time to Go: Before 11am or after 5pm.

In the space formerly occupied by Mister Toad's Wild Ride is this ride, which uses the same mechanism and track to tell the story of Winnie the Pooh and the Blustery Day. Featuring Eeyore, Piglet, Kanga, Roo, and all the other characters from the Hundred Acre Wood, it's sure to please those with a fetish for Pooh – and you know who you are. Also, Disney's Fastpass system was recently installed here, allowing you to reserve your time on the ride and bypass most of the line.

SHOPPING

THE MAD HATTER

This shop, located just outside Magic Journeys, sells Mouseketeer ears, hats, and ready-to-wear clothing.

tinkerbell toy shop

Peter Pan's sidekick hosts this boutique, jam packed with Disney memorabilia including wind-up toys, stuffed animals, games, clothing, and Madame Alexander dolls. This is also where you can replace a stolen stroller or wheelchair.

THE KING'S GALLERY

One of only two ways that you can check out the Castle (the other being King Stefan's Banquet Hall), this is the only Fantasyland shop worth devoting substantial amounts of time to, as it offers an exceptional selection of unique gifts and medieval souvenirs. Included are all sorts of

European clocks, tapestries, suits of armor, decorative boxes, swords, beer steins, chess sets, and handcrafted jewelry. A visit this magical shop is a must unless you are pressed for time.

MICKEY'S CHRISTMAS CAROL

Who can forget Mickey Mouse's heart-wrenching Bob Cratchit and Scrooge McDuck's miserly Ebenezer Scrooge in the annual Disney TV special? Well, there aren't any spirits here (supposedly!), but instead, the Magic Kingdom's year-round Christmas shop, selling ornaments, stockings, and such. You can't help but feel merry as you walk around this store.

THE ARISTOCATS

Fantasyland's foremost Disney souvenir shop, selling the usual selection of T-shirts, stuffed animals, keychains, china figurines, and so on.

ROYAL CANDY SHOPPE

In addition to a small selection of Disney memorabilia, this shop sells sundries, film, and candy.

KODAK KIOSK

This booth, which also serves as a drop-off point for two-hour Photo Express service, offers film and information.

NEMO'S NICHE

Another booth, just outside "Leagues", has film, stuffed animals, and information.

In 1988, a three-acre section of the Grand Prix Raceway was transformed into an attraction commemorating the Mouse's 60th birthday. The architecture of this town, Duckburg, is cartoonish: the only buildings constructed to scale are Mickey's House and Hollywood Theatre. Everything is like a 3D cartoon cel, from Daisy Duck's Millinery to Scrooge McDuck's Bank. On the whole, this is a fun place for kids of all ages.

TIPS

Attractions - All of the attractions here are skippable unless you've got young children.

Dining - A cart patrols the land with ice cream and drinks.

Shopping - Mickey stuff is sold off a cart.

ATTRACTIONS

WALT DISNEY WORLD RAILROAD

This station was created in 1988, along with then-known-as Mickey's Birthdayland. *See the entry for the Railroad under MAIN STREET U.S.A. earlier in the chapter.*

MICKEY'S HOUSE & STARLAND SHOW, & MICKEY'S HOLLYWOOD THEATER

Rating: 7. A lot of zip-a-dee-doo-dah fun. Location: Next to the railroad. Duration Of Show: 14 minutes. Best Time To Go: In the afternoon.

Walk through Mickey's Mouse House, full of Disney memorabilia and Mickey's personal effects, and into a tent in the backyard (doesn't everybody have a tent in their backyards?) where cartoons featuring (guess who!) Mickey are shown. After watching them for a while, you are escorted into the main theater where a character show is presented.

The show features afternoon heroes like Darkwing Duck of the show of the same name, Scrooge McDuck and Launchpad McQuack of DuckTales, Louie and Baloo of TaleSpin, and Chip and Dale of Chip 'n' Dale Rescue Rangers in a madcap mystery that involves a plane crash and an explosion. Typical family fun. The show ends in an audience sing-along.

After the show, you are escorted into another tent, called Mickey Mouse Club Funland, which has interactive video stations that can put you on TV, a hallway filled with boxes that make different noises when opened, much like at the Loony Bin at the Disney-MGM Studios. More in the category of "Stuff They Took from the Studios," Mickey's Walk of Fame, based on its Hollywood namesake, has stars with the characters' names. When you step on the star, you hear his or her voice. By and large, though, this attraction is for kids. And though classified as a separate attraction, here we lump Mickey's Hollywood Theater together with the Starland Show. This is a tent that you enter to find Mickey's dressing room and the chance to pose for pictures and get autographs.

His dressing room is filled with Mouse stuff, like his Sorcerer's Apprentice hat from Fantasia. Groups of about four families each are escorted into the room, where the Mouse waits. Each group spends about five minutes with Mickey.

MINNIE'S COUNTRY HOUSE

Rating: 6. Kind of funny in that tongue-in-cheek sort of way Location: Next to Mickey's House. Best Time To Go: Anytime.

Minnie, the "cartoon Martha Stewart," opens up her house to visitors. She's gettting ready to publish her latest issue of Cartoon Living Magazine, and the house is strewn with memorabilia from the "magazine" and various awards that Minnie has won for her involvement with the Fair. Cute, kind of amusing. Check it out.

THE BARNSTORMER AT GOOFY'S WISEACRES FARM
Rating: 4. Not much here. Location: Across from Mickey's Hollywood Theatre. Duration of ride: 1 minute. Best Time To Go: Anytime.

This is a kiddie-sized roller coaster featuring everyone's second favorite doofus (behind David Schwimmer), Goofy. The theme is this: you're flying a crop duster plane through Goofy's Wiseacres Farm in such a manner that would pale the FAA. Fun for kids, but not particularly compelling for those old enough to enjoy the real roller coasters.

DONALD'S BOAT
Rating: 5. Cute. Location: Across from Mickey's Hollywood Theatre. Best Time To Go: The hotter, the better.

Donald Duck's boat is an interactive fountain moored in a duck pond of blue "Saf-Deck." Fountains hidden throughout the boat and pond squirt unsuspecting tourists.

SHOPPING
MERCHANDISE CART
Mickey Mouse memorabilia and gifts.

Formerly a dull and monochromatic mass of concrete, Tomorrowland has been revamped and the focus changed from a "serious" look at the "real" future to the future envisioned by Jules Verne and other sci-fi writers. It's now a sleek and somewhat sexy, neon-lined intergalactic spaceport. Dated attractions like Mission to Mars were replaced or renovated. The total effect of the renovations is a new community feeling in Tomorrowland, which the old one lacked. Every other "land" had this feeling, so the renovations merely bring Tomorrowland up to par.
Overall Tips

Attractions - When Splash Mountain opened, it replaced Space Mountain as the biggest draw in the park. So crowds there will be a little thinner. However, most of the other attractions rarely have long lines, so they are best visited during the hot, crowded part of the day.

Dining - Surprisingly, some of the best fast food restaurants in the Magic Kingdom are here. The Plaza Pavilion is the best of the bunch, Cosmic Ray's Starlight Cafe is good and quick

Shopping - None of the shops in Tomorrowland are worth a separate trip, but some are worth a look if you've got the time and the desire.

ATTRACTIONS

THE EXTRATERRORESTRIAL ALIEN ENCOUNTER

Rating: 8. Wild, adrenal fun. Location: At the entrance to Tomorrowland. Duration Of Show: 12 minutes. Best Time To Go: From 11:00 to 4:30.

Replacing the tired and obsolete Mission to Mars, this collaboration with George Lucas places guests in the midst of a teleportation experiment gone terrifyingly wrong.

The Tomorrowland Interplanetary Convention Center hosts a presentation from X-S Tech. In the lobby, a short trade show-type promotional film is shown for businesses including Cryo Cybernetics, Electro Robotics, and Planetary Restructuting.

In the main show room, we meet X-S Tech's sinister chairman, L.C. Clench, not-too-bright teleportation technician T.O.M. 2000, and Skippy, the cutest alien this side of E.T. X-S technicians then lock guests in their chairs and scan their genetic makeup to find a suitable guinea pig for the intergalactic teleportation. Then, Chairman Clench comes in and demands to be the one to travel. What follows is the most terrifying experience ever unveiled in the Magic Kingdom, as a deadly alien appears in the auditorium and starts wreaking havoc.

This show follows the technology used in 3D movies at EPCOT and Disney-MGM, combining film entertainment, live characters, and special effects to scare the living daylights out of you.

THE TIMEKEEPER

Rating: 7 1/2. Hyperkinetic humor. Location: At the entrance of Tomorrowland. Duration Of Show: 20 minutes. Best Time To Go: Between 11:00 and 4:30. Comments: The audience must stand during the show.

The Timekeeper replaces American Journeys with a show that combines Circle-Vision 360 technology with Audio-Animatronics figures and special effects that simulate time travel both backwards and forwards. The production stars the eponymous Timekeeper, the hyperactive robot creator of the time machine (played to the hilt by Robin Williams) and 9-Eye (Rhea Perlman), a camera-equipped robot who serves as the eyes and ears, and occasionally the wisecracking mouth, of the expedition back in time to pick up Jules Verne and H.G. Wells and then catapult them centuries into the future. Robin Williams is deliciously off-center in his performance, as always. It's loads of fun for kids of all ages.

TOMORROWLAND TRANSIT AUTHORITY

Rating: 6. Relaxing, a change of pace. Location: Below the AstroOrbiter.
Duration Of Ride: 10 minutes. Best Time To Go: Anytime.

The TTA Metroliner Blueline track can be seen winding all throughout Tomorrowland, but if you wish to ride, you have to go to the boarding area, near the AstroOrbiter. The ride is a scenic overview of Tomorrowland, passing each of the attractions. There is a pleasant computer narration, and the 10 mile per hour ride is good for getting acquainted with the layout of Tomorrowland, checking out the crowds at Space Mountain, and getting a view of the actual ride, the rockets zooming through the blackness. Environmentalists take heart! This ride produces very little noise and is propelled by a electromagnets, uses limited power, and does not pollute.

ASTRO ORBITER

Rating: 3 1/2. Boring, not worthwhile. Location: A landmark. Duration Of
Ride: 1 1/2 minutes. Best Time To Go: Before 11 AM or after 5 PM. Frightening?
Only to those afraid of heights.

These shuttles, modeled after Buck Rogers', make up a midway ride primarily for those kids between Dumbo and Space Mountain. Small aircraft circle a model rocket connected by large metal arms, and the height of your vehicle's flight can be altered. The shuttles rotate eleven times a minute for a top speed of 26 MPH, rising up to 80 feet.

It's too tame for most people over twelve and is more time-consuming than most other attractions, because you have to go up an elevator, then get in line for a minute-and-a-half journey. Skip this one or ride it during the morning, evening, or special events.

WALT DISNEY'S CAROUSEL OF PROGRESS

Rating: 6. A delightful way to spend a few air-conditioned minutes. Location:
At the southeast corner of Tomorrowland. Duration Of Show: 18 minutes. Best
Time To Go: Between 11:30 and 4:30.

This is a happy show depicting the advancement of technology throughout the twentieth century, recently updated and rescripted to include innovations like virtual reality, voice-activation, and high-definition television.

The show stars a typical family going from generation to generation. The Audio-Animatronics folks here tell how we evolved from ice cubes and fans to air conditioning, from radio to television, and so on and so forth. This show is worth seeing, especially in the hot hours when other attractions are filled.

SPACE MOUNTAIN

Rating: 10. One of the Magic Kingdom's premier attractions. Don't miss it! Location: A landmark. Duration Of Ride: Almost 3 minutes. Best Time To Go: As soon as the park opens or in closing hour, or between 6 and 7 PM. Comments: Children must be 3'8" tall to ride, those under seven must be accompanied by an adult. Not recommended for expectant mothers, those with heart, back, or neck problems, or those prone to motion sickness. Frightening: A ride much wilder than Big Thunder Mountain, and in the dark to boot, frightens many.

Space Mountain is a psychological thrill ride. While the thrill in conventional roller coasters lies in the actual twists, turns, drops, and loops, Space Mountain tries to terrify by sending you off through passageways of flashing lights, strobes, and strange sounds, and eventually into a cavernous place where the only thing you can see is the dark shape of a head in front of you. Not to say that the ride isn't savage, it is; just ask anyone who ate a good, hearty breakfast just before boarding. Roller coaster enthusiasts are likely to find the ride, only measuring 28 miles an hour at its fastest, tamer than the special effects, and this roller coaster can't be described as diabolical like some others, though those not weaned on the Great American Scream Machine and the Cyclone may disagree with me on that point.

The tension begins to mount in the queueing area, where on either side of the passageway, bent-plastic windows give a strange perspective into space, with stars aplenty. When you get to the boarding area, look up and you will see shooting stars, created by a light shining off a disco ball, and meteors, reportedly projections of chocolate chip cookies. As the shuttles take off, you hear screams in the distance. And you begin to wonder if this was such a great idea. If you wimp out in line, just ask the Disney personnel to show you to the "ride bypass" (more commonly known as the chickens' exit) and they will do so.

If you choose to remain (and good for you), put any loose articles in a safe place unless you want to see it under the track. You will eventually be loaded onto a shuttle, six rows. Unlike most roller coasters, only one person sits in each row. That way, there's nobody to lean on when the butterflies hit. But you start climbing up the track, with flashing signs on the side of the track tell you how many seconds to liftoff. But once you do, hold on!

Like Splash Mountain, there will always be people who are Space Mountain groupies who line up at the central Hub thirty minutes before park opening to wait for the rope to drop so they can make for the large white dome to be the first one on the ride. Well, I've got a secret for you. There's a way to beat them there! They're all lining up at the Hub, so you go up past the Plaza Restaurant and stop under the arch reading The Plaza Pavilion Terrace Dining. Here, you'll be cool, comfortable, ready, and 100 yards closer to Space Mountain than your counterparts at the Hub. Feel free to laugh at them. Now, as soon as the Disney employee takes down the barrier rope, walk, jog, or disregard his instructions discouraging running, as fast as you can to Space Mountain.

Some families come upon an unforeseen problem when visiting this attraction. Let's say there's a family, Mom, Dad, and little Joey. Mom and Dad are both dead set on riding Space Mountain. But alas, little Joey is not tall enough to ride. So what can you do? Get in line twice? You don't have to! Just get in line, and tell the first attendant that you see that you want to switch off. He will radio to a second attendant and tell him to expect you. When you reach the second attendant, one parent will go on ahead while the other waits with the kid(s). After the first parent gets off the ride, another attendant will lead him/her up a staircase to the boarding area. There, the parents swap custody of little Joey, the second one rides, and the first parent and Joey go to the unloading area and meet again. Happy happy joy joy! This technique can also be used on Big Thunder Mountain and Splash Mountain, both in Frontierland.

Also, Disney's Fastpass system was recently installed here, allowing you to reserve your time on the ride and bypass most of the line.

TOMORROWLAND SPEEDWAY
Rating: 5. Not worth the wait. Location: A landmark, next to Space Mountain. Duration Of Ride: About 4 minutes. Best Time To Go: Morning or evening. Comments: Children must be 4'4" tall to ride alone.

What this attraction has to do with the future, I can't seem to figure out. But in any case, this ride is perpetually crowded. Kids really love it, but unfortunately, those under 4'4" can't ride because they can't steer and reach the pedals at once. The first time I went on this ride, I was just over the height limit and I kept on smacking the steel guide rail, again and again (I still haven't heard the end of it). Adults find this one boring, teenagers could take it or leave it, mostly dependent on whether or not they have their drivers' licenses yet. The track makes for a rather dull ride, as the cars' top speed is a gut-wrenching 7 miles an hour and you can't bump the car in front. Skip it if there's a line.

If your kid is too small to drive, get in the car together. Let your child sit on your lap and steer while you work the pedals. This gives the illusion of driving to your kids.

BUZZ LIGHTYEAR'S SPACE RANGER SPIN
Rating: 6 1/2. Interactive fun for the whole family. Duration of Ride: 6 minutes. Best time to go: Before 11am or after 5pm.

This ride follows the adventures of Buzz Lightyear's Space Rangers (that's you) in their fight to save the world from the evil intergalactic

Emperor Zurg, who's plotting to take over the world by stealing batteries. You ride in cars that rotate 360 degrees and come equipped with lasers with which you can blast the enemy into submission. Your car keeps score of your progress, and as I found out... shooting aliens isn't as easy as it looks.

SHOPPING

MICKEY'S STAR TRADERS

This large shop, located near the Grand Prix Raceway, offers a very good selection of stuffed animals, clothes, collectibles, film, and sunscreen.

SKYWAY STATION SHOP

Next to the Tomorrowland station and across from Space Mountain, this sells selected Magic Kingdom memorabilia.

MERCAHNT OF VENUS

This is the only shop in Tomorrowland selling something other than character merchandise and park mementos, instead, kitschy futuristic gifts, toys, games, fashions, jewelry, and the like. Strollers and wheelchairs can be replaced here.

GEIGER'S COUNTER

Situated in the booth next to StarJets are clothing, gifts, snacks, and hats.

FILM & GLOW KIOSK

Film and camera merchandise all day long, plus glow-in-the-dark merchandise after dark. Also, this is a Photo Express drop-off point.

ENTERTAINMENT IN THE MAGIC KINGDOM

There is always some sort of live entertainment going on around the Magic Kingdom, and here is a basic outline of entertainment during a typical week. All of the entertainment below is subject to change or cancellation.

ALL-AMERICAN COLLEGE MARCHING BAND

College students from around the country perform throughout the park during weekday afternoons and early evenings. The program occurs during the summer.

BANJO KINGS
A band plays 20's songs on banjos and washboards.

CHARACTERS
There are designated character viewing areas in each of the lands of the Magic Kingdom, where you can meet Mickey, Minnie, Goofy, Donald, and the rest of the gang. Check the park guide maps for exact locations.

COKE CORNER PIANIST
There's a ragtime piano player outside the Refreshment Corner restaurant who performs throughout each day.

THE DAPPER DANS
This barbershop quartet can usually be found either at the Harmony Barber Shop or up and down Main Street, on foot or a four-seater bike. The flawless harmonies emanating from the men in straw hats and striped vests are enjoyable, and they enhance the reality of Main Street's Victorian atmosphere. For info on the Harmony Barber Shop, see *Main Street U.S.A.* at the beginning of the chapter. They perform various times throughout the day.

DIAMOND HORSESHOE JAMBOREE
This is a dance hall show in Frontierland during the afternoon. Reservations are required, go to the Disneyana Collectibles store on Main Street. For a detailed description of the Jamboree, see the *Frontierland* section earlier in this chapter.

DISNEYMANIA
Some of the newest Disney characters join up with the old favorites and the Kids of the Kingdom in a musical show at the Castle Forecourt Stage. Performed at various times during each day.

DISNEY'S MAGICAL MOMENTS PARADE
This parade, running at 3 in the afternoon daily, features floats and characters from classic Disney films like Beauty and the Beast, the Little Mermaid, and Cinderella.

DISNEY WORLD IS YOUR WORLD
Disney characters and the Kids of the Kingdom present a musical celebration of Walt Disney World, twice a day, two days a week at the Tomorrowland Theater.

FLAG RETREAT

Each day at ten minutes after five o'clock, a small color guard, accompanied by the WDW Marching Band, takes down the American flag that flies in Town Square. A flock of homing pigeons is then released. They fly to their home, behind the castle, in about twenty seconds.

FRONTIERLAND

Shootouts are staged here. If you happen to be around when one does go down, I hope you brought your Kevlar.

GALAXY SEARCH

Disney characters and the Galaxy Palace Dancers participate in an intergalactic talent show. All it's missing is Ed McMahon.

J.P. AND THE SILVER STARS

Hey, mon, thees ees the place for listening to an authentic Caribbean steel drum band. At Caribbean Plaza, performances run several times a day five days a week.

MAIN STREET ELECTRICAL PARADE

Back by popular demand, the Disneyland installation of the MSEP has moved east, displacing SpectroMagic with its 500 miles of wiring, 530,000 light bulbs, 850 rechargeable 65-pound batteries, and favorite characters like Mickey, Minnie, and Cinderella.

ONE MAN'S DREAM

This show, which has been running in Tokyo Disneyland for five years now, pays homage to 65 years of musical highlights from favorite Disney films like Peter Pan, Snow White, the Jungle Book, and Lady and the Tramp.

TINKER BELL'S FLIGHT &
"FANTASY IN THE SKY" FIREWORKS

Tinker Bell flies from Cinderella's Castle to trigger a spectacular four-minute fireworks display. 150 shells are set off, a rate of one every two seconds. Performed at 10 PM during peak seasons and the summer.

HINT: Everyone assumes that the best vantage point for Fantasy in the Sky is right at Cinderella Castle. Not so. Since the fireworks are unleashed from behind 20,000 Leagues Under the Sea, excellent views can be had from the cafe tables in Fantasyland.

WALT DISNEY WORLD MARCHING BAND CONCERTS
This band performs at Town Square twice six mornings a week, and on occasion at Fantasy Faire.

PARADE VIEWING
Most people who decide to watch a parade, either the Surprise Celebration Parade orMain Street Electrical Parade, choose spots on Main Street U.S.A. or the central Hub, totally clogging those areas. True, some of the best vantage points are along this section of the parade route (the ones from the train platform are magnificent), but they must be grabbed as much as forty-five minutes early. In Liberty Square and Frontierland are many excellent vantage points that are often overlooked:
• At Sleepy Hollow, in Liberty Square close to the Hub, you can arrive ten to twenty minutes early, buy some refreshments, and take a table by the rail.
• Any spot on the pathway between Sleepy Hollow and the Castle on the Liberty Square side of the moat.
• The covered walkway between Liberty Tree Tavern and the Diamond Horseshoe Saloon.
• The raised platform in front of the Frontierland facade.
• The central hub, between the Adventureland and Liberty Square bridges.
• Waterfront at the Rivers of America.

DINING IN THE MAGIC KINGDOM

Note: alcoholic beverages are not served in the Magic Kingdom. Reservations are available 30 days in advance, 60 days for WDW Resort guests, for all full-service restaurants.

In Main Street, U.S.A.
TONY'S TOWN SQUARE CAFE
Location: East side of Town Square. Prices: Moderate. Cuisine: Italian. Meals: B,L,D.
Everybody remembers that scene from Lady and the Tramp where the two dine on spaghetti and meatballs outside Tony's Restaurant. Well, Tony's has leapt from the silver screen to the Magic Kingdom. The restaurant is elegantly Victorian, with polished brass, many windows, beautiful woodwork, and a terazzo-floored patio overlooking Main Street.

The food is very good here, especially at breakfast. The specialties include at breakfast, egg dishes, waffles, Tony's Italian Toast, cereal, biscuits, and danishes. At lunch, the fare includes salads, sandwiches, and pasta. At dinner, served after 3:30, there's pizza, lasagna, shrimp scampi, tortellini, ravioli, grilled chicken, steak and lobster, and grilled seafood. After your meal, unwind and "wetta you whistle" with a cup of espresso or cappucino and an Italian pastry with spumoni. This is a great spot to watch the SpectroMagic and Remember the Magic Parades. Arrive early and ask to be seated in the glassed-in area.

MAIN STREET BAKE SHOP
This cozy little shop offers pastries, cakes, pies, and lots of cookies. The freshly-baked cinnamon rolls are a real treat. Beverages and fresh strawberries (when in season) are also served (B,S).

PLAZA ICE CREAM PARLOR
Sealtest ice cream cones are served. For the health-conscious, there's fat-free ice cream (S).

THE PLAZA RESTAURANT
Location: At the Plaza. Prices: Budget. Cuisine: American. Meals: L,D.
This Art Nouveau building houses the restaurant that offers the biggest ice cream sundaes in the World. Other frozen treats available arc floats and shakes. The entrees here include sandwiches, big seven-ounce hamburgers, turkey burgers, pot pies, fruit and cheese platters, and quiche.

CASEY'S CORNER
Diners here sit outside and listen to the ragtime pianist on the porch while they munch hot dogs (with or without cheese), brownies, soft drinks, and coffee (L,D,S).

THE CRYSTAL PALACE
Location: By the Adventureland Bridge. Prices: Moderate. Cuisine: American. Meals: B,L,D,S.
This restaurant is a beautiful landmark, its Victorian architecture imitating similar structures that once stood in New York and San Francisco's Golden Gate Park. The restaurant is particularly brilliant after dark, when rows of white lights outline the profile of the restaurant. Inside, the tropical atrium helps to create a harmonious transition betweeen Main Street U.S.A. and Adventureland.

The food is good, and the breakfasts are the Kingdom's best. There's scrambled eggs, biscuits, sausage, hot cakes, French toast, bacon, ham,

Danish, and cereal. For lunch and dinner, the fare includes prime rib, spit-roasted chicken, baked fresh fish, pasta dishes, salads, and sandwiches. Dixieland jazz entertainment is offered.

In Adventureland

ALOHA ISLE
This counter offers pineapple spears, juice, and Dole Whip, a soft serve combining vanilla and pineapple ice cream (S).

EL PIRATA Y EL PERICO
A very good fast food joint offering nachos, tacos, taco salads, and hot dogs with toppings like chili and cheese (L,D,S).

THE OASIS
Snacks and soft drinks are sold from this kiosk outside the Jungle Cruise and Swiss Family Treehouse (S).

In Frontierland

DIAMOND HORSESHOE JAMBOREE
Location: Next to the Liberty Tree Tavern. Prices: Budget. Cuisine: Fast food. Meals: L, S.
This Old West vaudeville hall hosts a show five times a day. The food is secondary to the entertainment, in the form of a singing and dancing troupe of actors. You don't have to eat anything to view the show, but if hunger strikes, you can get cold sandwiches, potato and corn chips, freshly baked pies, soft drinks, and fruit punch.

PECOS BILL CAFE
Here, tacos, nachos, hot dogs, cheeseburgers, and barbecue chicken sandwiches are served up in a rustic Old West atmosphere, with a stick-and-twig ceiling. There is outdoor seating at the Cafe (L,D,S).

AUNT POLLY'S LANDING
This is an ideal place for adults to sit and rest while the kids burn energy on the rest of Tom Sawyer Island. The fare is limited to sandwiches served with an apple and a cookie, pies, iced tea, lemonade, and soft drinks (L,S).

SUNSHINE TREE TERRACE
Snacks, frozen yogurt, and soft drinks are served here (S).

TURKEY LEG WAGON

This riverfront cart offers beverages and big, filling, juicy smoked turkey legs that are great bets for no-frills, no-fuss meals or snacks. Chicken noodle soup is also available (L,D,S).

In Liberty Square
LIBERTY TREE TAVERN

Location: Next to the Diamond Horseshoe Jamboree. Prices: Moderate. Cuisine: American. Meals: L,D.

One of the classiest places in the Magic Kingdom, this quaint colonial inn looks like something out of a history book. The atmosphere includes wooden Venitian blinds, oaken floors, and two-tiered chandeliers. It's the kind of place where you can picture secret meetings about the Boston Tea Party taking place.

The food is colonial as well, and quite palatable. Lunch entrees include sandwiches, seafood, hamburgers, and prime rib. For dinner, you can have pasta, chicken, lobster, prime rib, and filet mignon. The best of the desserts are red velvet cake and cream cheese mousse.

SLEEPY HOLLOW

Here, by the water, you can fill your stomach with hot dogs, Disney Handwiches, and hot and cold beverages. Great chocolate chip cookies and brownies round out the menu (L,D,S).

COLUMBIA HARBOUR HOUSE

The seating sections of the restaurant offer the atmosphere of a New England dining room and a sailing ship, depending on where you sit. The menu includes clam chowder, a stellar Monte Cristo sandwich (deep-fried and loaded with turkey, ham, and cheese), a fruit plate, fried shrimp and chicken strips (together or separately), salad, and sandwiches. This restaurant's always a good bet (L,D,S).

In Fantasyland

The eateries here are mediocre and perpetually crowded. Eat elsewhere if you can.

CINDERELLA'S ROYAL TABLE

Meals: B,L,D. Cuisine: American. Location: Cinderella Castle. Prices: Expensive.

For many children, the chance to eat inside Cinderella Castle is the highlight of an entire vacation. The excitement trebles when the blonde princess herself sweeps in, dressed to the nines. She poses for pictures and greets children, many of whom are tempted to salaam wildly on the ground while chanting "We're not worthy! We're not worthy!" (While Cinderella converses with your awestruck children, try not to wonder what she's doing in a restaurant named after Sleeping Beauty's father.) The fare at the Magic Kingdom's most pricey restaurant is a tad disappointing. At lunch, there's prime rib sandwiches, fish sandwiches, chicken, and club sandwiches. At dinner, house specialties include beef, fresh fish, and a fried chicken breast with fettucine, ham, spinach, and cheese.

The "Once Upon a Time" breakfast is held here every morning, featuring Cinderella, Snow White, Alice, and friends.

HOOK'S TAVERN
Soft drinks and chips are sold here (S).

PINOCCHIO VILLAGE HAUS
Overlooking the loading area of It's a Small World, this restaurant serves up hot dogs, burgers, chicken, club sandwiches, and pasta salad. The restaurant is decorated with cuckoo clocks, brick ovens, and murals depicting characters from Carlo Collodi's classic tale (L,D,S).

THE LITTLE BIG TOP
Soft drinks, milkshakes, and snacks are on the menu at this establishment. Open seasonally (S).

ENCHANTED GROVE
Citrus drinks and soft serve are offered here (S).

LUMIERE'S KITCHEN.
Here, across from 20,000 Leagues..., kids can get a Disney Afternoon box meal, with grilled cheese or chicken nuggets, cookies, and a prize. Selections for grown-ups include hot dogs, hamburgers, sandwiches, chips, and beverages (L,D).

SCUTTLE'S LANDING
This is the spot for refreshing shaved ice treats and caramel apples (S).

MRS. POTTS'S CUPBOARD
Next to Lumiere's, this place is great in the heat of a summer afternoon, you can get Sealtest ice cream cones, hot fudge sundaes, and root beer floats here (S).

In Tomorrowland
COSMIC RAY'S STARLIGHT CAFE
The offerings at this restaurant include hamburgers, hot dogs, minestrone and chicken noodle soups, barbecued pork loin sandwiches, marinated grilled chicken sandwiches, and fruit salad. This restaurant has little of a wait due to its immense size (L,D,S).

THE LUNCHING PAD AT ROCKETTOWER PLAZA
The usual array of snacks, hot dogs, and soft drinks is offered here (L,D,S).

AUNTIE GRAVITY'S GALACTIC GOODIES
Frozen yogurt, fruit juices, and soft drinks are served here (S).

THE PLAZA PAVILION
Halfway decent Italian fast food is served up in this spot adjacent to the Hub Waterways. There's a surprisingly good deep dish pizza by the slice, skinless chicken parmesan sandwiches, meatball subs, Italian hoagies, and pasta salad. Ice cream cups and beverages are on hand to finish up the meal (L,D,S).

12. EPCOT

On October 1, 1982, Epcot opened on 260 acres of land between the Magic Kingdom and the Downtown Disney area. Epcot is a sort of permanent world's fair type installation comprised of two sections, **Future World** and **World Showcase**.

The former features pavilions that pay tribute to various aspects of modern civilization and the earth, such as agriculture, communications, energy, and medical science. The latter contains eleven pavilions representing the cultures of different nations from around the world through food, architecture, entertainment, and shopping.

Planning for Epcot (short for Experimental Prototype Community of Tomorrow) began in 1964, when Walt Disney described the concept:

"Epcot will take its cue from the new ideas and new technologies that are new emerging from the creative centers of American industry. It will never be completed, but will always be introducing and testing and demonstrating new materials and systems. And Epcot will be a showcase to the world for the ingenuity and imagination of American free enterprise."

GETTING TO & AROUND EPCOT

To get to Epcot from:

- Magic Kingdom, Polynesian Resort, Contemporary Resort, Grand Floridian Resort: Take the monorail to the TTC and switch to the Epcot Center line.
- TTC: Take the monorail.
- Fort Wilderness: Take the bus to the TTC and switch to the monorail.
- Disney-MGM Studios Theme Park: Take the motor launch or bus.
- Epcot Resorts: Take the motor launch or tram or simply walk.
- All other WDW Resort Areas: Take the bus.
- Off-site Lake Buena Vista hotels: Take 535 to International Drive. Go towards I-4. It will change to Epcot Center Drive. Take the jughandle

to parking lot.

• Off-site Kissimmee hotels: Take U.S. 192 to World Drive (maingate). Take World Drive to Epcot Center Drive. Take the jughandle to the parking lot.

• Off-site International Drive hotels: Take International Drive south to SR 536/SR 417 (World Center Drive and the Central Florida Greeneway, respectively) and turn right. Take SR 536 straight into Disney World and follow signs.

• Off-site hotels via I-4: Take I-4 to exit 26B (Epcot Center). Take the jughandle to the parking area.

EPCOT VITAL STATISTICS

Walt Disney World, P.O. Box 10,040, Lake Buena Vista, FL 32830-0040.

On the Internet: *www.disneyworld.com/*

Tel.: *407/824-4321.*

Hours: *Vary. Gates open at 8:30 AM, Future World attractions at 9 AM, World Showcase at 11 AM.*

Admission: *$44 for adults, $35 for kids. See section on Admission Media for full details.*

Parking: *$6.*

Time To See: *A minimum of one day.*

When to See: *Tuesday and Friday are the crowded days here.*

Don't Miss: *Spaceship Earth, Ellen's Energy Adventure, GM Test Track, Body Wars, Cranium Command, Honey, I Shrunk the Audience, Mexico pavilion, Wonders of China, The American Adventure, Impressions de France, O Canada!*

PARKING

The Epcot Center parking lot can accommodate 11,391 vehicles. The cost is $6, free for resort guests (remember your ID!) and there is no cost for leaving and returning or switching parks on the same day. Be sure to keep your receipt. Also, it is vital that you write down where you park!

The parking sections are named after themes of the Future World attractions. Write the section down! This cannot be stressed enough. Note that the handicapped can park in a special lot next to the entrance plaza.

ADMISSION, MONEY, REFURBISHMENT AND INTERRUPTION OF ATTRACTIONS, PACKAGE PICKUP, DRESS CODE & FASTPASS – see Chapter 11.

PRACTICAL INFORMATION

Alcoholic Beverages: Allowed, sold at most table-service establishments.

Baby Services: Changing and nursing facilities are located at the Odyssey Complex.

Baby Strollers: Can be rented for $6 a day at the Stroller Shop, on the left side (as you enter) of Spaceship Earth.

Banking: ATMs are located at the main entrance, by the Odyssey bridge, and at Germany in World Showcase.

Cameras: The Camera Center, presented by Kodak, has a full array of cameras for rent, plus film, videotapes, and two-hour development (see below).

Cigarettes: Not sold in the park.

First Aid: Located at the Odyssey Complex. Foreign Language Assistance: Personal translator units, available at Guest Relations at Innoventions East, translate some theater presentations into Spanish, French, or German. WorldKey Information Satellites also provide information in Spanish. Maps and assistance are available at Guest Relations.

Hearing-impaired Guests: Written descriptions for most attractions are available at Guest Relations. A Telecommunications Device for the Deaf (TDD) is available at Guest Relations.

Information: Guest Relations offers all sorts of info plus entertainment schedules.

Kennel: Pets are not allowed in WDW resorts or attractions. However, there is an air-conditioned kennel by the east side of the Entrance Plaza (left side as you face the gates). Reservations are not needed.

Lockers: Available for $.25 or $.50, these are located on the west (right, as you face it from outside the gates) side of the Entrance Plaza, at Bus Services, and at the International Gateway.

Lost Children: Report to Baby Services or Guest Relations.

Reservations: Can be made up to 30 days in advance for day guests, 60 days for those staying at WDW resorts.

Smoking, eating, and drinking: Not allowed in any attractions.

Visually-impaired guests: Complimentary tape cassettes and portable tape recorders are available at Guest Relations. A deposit is required, though.

Wheelchair guests: Wheelchair and motorized three-wheeled convenience vehicle rentals are available in limited quantities at Stroller & Wheelchair Rental at Spaceship Earth. The standard kind of wheelchair is available for rent at the International Gateway. Disabled Guests Guidebooks are available at Guest Relations.

FUTURE WORLD

This section of Epcot Center features themes of humanity's achievements in various areas of technology, and offers a somewhat academic view of the world as it was, is, and might be. Many people confuse Future World and Tomorrowland. Tomorrowland, in the Magic Kingdom, is whimsical and amusing, but not intended to be taken seriously as a vision of the future. Future World is. Also, the latter is less science-fiction and more real-future in its architecture.

Future World is lined up for major expansion, including the addition of a Space pavilion in which flight simulators and special effects will send guests into orbit via a thrill ride a la Body Wars.

Note that Future World pavilions open at 9 AM and close two hours before the rest of the park, except for Spaceship Earth and Innoventions, which are open until the rest of the park.

TIPS

Attractions - Future World is most crowded during the morning and least crowded from about 2:30 on. The Wonders of Life pavilion is almost always crowded, and Journey into Your Imagination is very popular also.

Dining - The two full-service restaurants here (the Garden Grill and Coral Reef) are very good, but very popular and hard to book. The fast food quality is stellar here as compared to the Magic Kingdom's eateries; the Odyssey Restaurant and Sunshine Season Food Fair are good choices.

Shopping - Future World shopping has little more to offer than Disney and Epcot memorabilia plus future-themed gifts, toys, novelties, and the like.

ENTRANCE PLAZA
Shopping
GIFT STOP

On the right side of the entrance plaza, this small stop offers guest mementos and convenience items.

Services
LOST & FOUND/PACKAGE PICKUP

This building, adjoining the Gift Stop, is where found articles and cumbersome packages are forwarded to.

PET CARE KENNEL
  Pets may not be brought into Epcot Center, but can be boarded for $4 per day, per pet, and may not be boarded overnight here. Restrooms and phones are located here.

SPACESHIP EARTH

  Rating: 10. It's Epcot's crowning achievement, so don't miss it. Location: A landmark, at the park's entrance. Duration of Ride: 16 minutes. Best Time to Go: Before 9:15 AM or after 5 PM. Comments: Guests move forward in a dark, enclosed area in slow-moving cars up a steep incline, and ride backward for the slow return.

  This is the recognized symbol of Epcot, much like Cinderella's Castle is in the Magic Kingdom. Measuring 180 feet in height and 164 feet in diameter, this geosphere is visible from either coast on a clear day. It is kept aloft by six huge pylons sunk 100 feet into the ground. Here you'll find two shops, one of the park's top rides, and Global Neighborhood, a hands-on exhibit area featuring the latest communications technology products.

  You board small cars ("time machines") and venture deep into the bowels of the Spaceship Earth geodesic sphere. Actor Jeremy Irons ("The Lion King," "Die Hard with a Vengeance") narrates as you begin your ascent through a black tunnel. Lightning flashes at the end of the tunnel and fans blow air in your face to give the illusion of speed. Finally, you arrive at the Cro-Magnon age, 40,000 years ago. Eerie holographic projections of cavemen and wooly mammoths melt and metamorphose as if blown by a breeze. The displays are dark and black-lighted, and a strange soundtrack presents a foreboding atmosphere. Scenes then show the advent of communication, from Egyptian hieroglyphics (real!) and a pharaoh dictating a letter (taken from an actual letter from an Egyptian ruler), to cave drawings to ancient peoples chewing the fat as they imprint symbols on stone tablets, to the Phoenician merchants who introduced the written alphabet in the ninth century before Christ.

  Traveling on through the ages, you see a performance of Oedipus Rex, witness the fall of Rome (during which you will smell smoldering wood through the rubble it's not your imagination, it's a Disney effect called "smellitzer" that shoots aromas at you at appropriate times), where you may notice the graffiti on the walls... identical to that in real Pompeii. There's Audio-Animatronic monks and scholars trying to hand-copy precious documents and scriptures, one of whom has fallen asleep and can be heard snoring and seen breathing. A working Gutenberg press sits in one scene, its operator thoughtfully examining a page of a replicated Bible from California's Huntington Library. Particularly impressive is the robotic Michaelangelo who lays on a scaffold, putting the finishing touches on the awesome Sistine Chapel ceiling.

From there, we zoom into the information age. A man stands by a rumbling printing press, his hands and clothing slathered with ink. Then, to the finished product: a pile of newspapers, and a newsboy holding one up and crying "Extra, extra, New York's daily." There's a radio studio, and then a movie marquee. Past that, several movies are played on the screens. Some of the radio broadcasts include The Lone Ranger and the Max Schmeling-Joe Louis rematch in 1938, and a commentary by Walter Winchell. The TV segments include Ozzie and Harriet, the 1964 NFL championship game, and the Ed Sullivan show. There are then displays showing computers in the home and office, and an AT&T phone system.

But most stirring of all is the finale at the top of the Spaceship, a huge dome filled with tiny stars and one small blue-green sphere swathed in clouds. The effect is produced by a "star ball," created by Disney when the Imagineers discovered that the dome was too large for traditional planetarium equipment. Following this sweeping view, time machines pass innovative, interactive communications at work — bringing life-saving medical technology to wilderness homes, helping archaeologists share discoveries with home base instantly, creating electronic bridges that aid mutual understanding. Projected onto screens overhead are images of newscasts, superdefinition TV, and virtual reality classrooms.

This is arguably the best attraction in Future World, and everybody seems to love it. Thus, it is almost always crowded. But the lines move quickly and see it you must, so go early or late.

Exhibit
AT&T'S GLOBAL NEIGHBORHOOD
This hands-on exhibit area features cutting-edge AT&T technology and games that illustrate and detangle the information superhighway.

Shopping
GATEWAY GIFTS
Located on the west side of Spaceship Earth, this shop offers a variety of souvenirs and sundries, mainly t-shirts, mugs, toys, games, books, ceramic figurines, suntan lotion, Pepto-Bismol, tissues, and so on and so forth. There are restrooms and phones located alongside this shop.

CAMERA CENTER
Kodak film, video tape, camcorder and camera rental, and two-hour film processing are offered here. Minor camera servicing and photography tips are also available. Located next to the camera center on the east side of Spaceship Earth, are restrooms and phones.

Services
STROLLER & WHEELCHAIR RENTAL

Wheelchairs and a limited supply of motorized vehicles are available for rent, as are strollers. Sundries, guest convenience items, and Epcot Center mementos are sold here.

INNOVENTIONS

Innoventions is a must-see for those who insist on staying on the crest of the technological wave at all times, as it showcases new technologies in an entertaining and educational way as you wander along "The Road to Tomorrow." Although exhibits are constantly changing, here's an idea of what you can expect to find.

Exhibits
NETWORKED LIVING

IBM's exhibit offers a glimpse at the future of computing and the Internet with demonstrations of voice recognition software and other cutting edge happy fun goodness, as well as the opportunity to send an email postcard to anyone worldwide.

ULTIMATE HOME THEATER EXPERIENCE

Lutron highlights technologies such as HDTV, state of the art lighting and surround sound, and much more. Couch not included.

BEAUTIFUL SCIENCE

Monsanto's tribute to the life sciences shows how scientists are working to solve world food and health problems while sustaining the planet. Particularly interesting here is the Tunnel of Bugs, which is exactly what it sounds like.

VIDEO GAMES OF TOMORROW

Sega uses this pavilion as an excuse to show off its eye-popping Dreamcast system and games ("Awww Mom, do we have to?") while offering a behind-the-scenes peek at the technologies that drive the video game revolution.

THE BROADBAND CONNECTION

This "game show," presented by AT&T pits a telephone, television, and personal computer against one another in the never ending battle for bandwith, here camouflaged as a love connection program. Cute.

MEDICINE'S NEW VISION

Inside this indoor dome you'll see how radiological technologies will change the way we view medicine in the next millennium. There's also interactive games for your enjoyment and enlightenment. Presented by RSNA.

THE KNOWLEDGE VORTEX

Xerox's pavilion showcases advances in information technology, things like "digital paper," super-compressed data, and other things to help you capture, organize, and share information.

FORESTS FOR OUR FUTURE

Here you can learn about the steps being taken to sustain our forests, visit a mock up of a field research station, or test your knowledge with some "tree"via. Ha. Presented by the Technical Association of the Pulp and Paper Industry (TAPPI).

INNOVENTIONS INTERNET ZONE

What look at the technology that shapes our lives would be complete without the internet? Here children can play interactive on line games, play "virtual tag," or send video postcards via email. Presented by Disney.com.

COMMUNICATIONS DREAM FORUM

Motorola's exhibit, hosted by a clairvoyant robot named Starnac, features some weird, wild stuff. There's a presentation on a high-definition screen plus interactive fun in the Reality Lab.

HOUSE OF INNOVENTIONS

This "smart home" features cutting-edge home technologies such as robotic pet dogs and Internet-ready refrigerators that track what's inside and automatically order replenishments. Presented by Panja.

WEB SITE CONSTRUCTION ZONE

Here you can set up your family's web page with customized content on Go.com.

FUTURE CARS

General Motors' exhibit here is a "future car" showroom, including all-electric vehicles and fuel cell-powered vehicles.

Shopping
MOUSEGEAR
This shop, located on the East side of Innoventions, features Epcot's best selection of character merchandise and park mementos. There's the usual watches, hats, pencils, bumper stickers, and books, plus more exotic toys, models, watches, and holograms.

ART OF DISNEY
Animation cels, sculptures, and Disney collectibles are sold at this store at Innoventions' West side.

ICE STATION COOL
Coca-Cola's refreshing exhibit lets you walk through an ice-cold cavern complete with snow (gotta love liquid nitrogen) to find yourself in a shop featuring all sorts of Coca-Cola merchandise, plus the opportunity to enjoy free samples of soft drinks from around the world. A godsend in the warmer seasons, you can find Ice Station Cool easily – just look for the glacier poking out of the side of the West Side building.

Services
GUEST RELATIONS
The guest services headquarters, moved from Spaceship Earth to accommodate the AT&T Global Neighborhood, is now located in Innoventions East. This is the headquarters for WorldKey interactive terminals for making dining reservations; guided tour information; lost children, personal translator units; foreign currency exchange; disabled guest information; taped narrations for guests with sight impairments, written descriptions of attractions for hearing-impaired guests; Disney Dollar exchange; Disney resort reservations; Disney Vacation Club information; and information on behind-the-scenes programs.

EPCOT OUTREACH
If you have a question that's been bothering you all day, take it here. Attendants armed with computers can answer any sort of question you might have about Epcot Center. The information, found in encyclopedias, periodicals, and wire services, is all accessible through the computer system. If the personnel can't answer your question, they can call the Disney Archives in beautiful downtown Burbank, California. Whether your inquiry is purely trivial or vital, they can usually help you out.
teacher's center
Here, educators can preview films, videos, multi-media kits, educational software, and other educational media. Also, they can receive

complimentary lesson plans, geared to all age groups, on all Future World themes.

ELLEN'S ENERGY ADVENTURE

Rating: 9. Striking, brilliant, not to be missed. Location: A landmark, next to Wonders of Life and Innoventions East. Duration of Show: 26 1/2 minutes. Best Time To Go: Before 10:30 or after 4:30. Frightening: The dinosaurs scare some younger kids.

This attraction has been recently renovated and revamped. The new pre-show features comedienne Ellen DeGeneres, who is watching Jeopardy and flubbing all the questions in the Energy category. Her neighbor, Bill Nye (the Science Guy) comes over to borrow supplies for an experiment, and is appalled by her lack of knowledge.

To inspire her, he shows her an eccentric, eight-minute presentation. In it, vivid images of falling water, fire, burning coal, piles of logs, all illustrating today's energy sources. But the renown here lies not in the film but the screen on which it is projected. As its creator, Czech filmmaker Emil Radok, calls it, this "kinetic mosaic" is made up of 100 triangular panels that rotate on computer-given cues.

Then, guests enter a seemingly normal theater with a capacity of nearly 580 and slide into bench seats. They watch as Ellen falls asleep in front of the TV and dreams that she is on Jeopardy, facing off against Albert Einstein and her college roommate (played by Jamie Lee Curtis). Ellen's roommate is winning big, Einstein's at zero, and Ellen's in the red at the end of the first round. Thankfully, Bill arrives and whisks Ellen off for a crash course in the history of fossil fuels.

This is the part of the attraction that most wows visitors. We're talking Jurassic Park come to life. The theatre splits into smaller cars that slowly enter a world where the air is rich with sulfur and the sky flashes with lightning. The profile of a brontosaur is visible in the distance. Fog fills the warm, dank air and lava bubbles next to the cars. The lava is so realistic that few guests are convinced when informed that its main ingredient is hair gel. Audio-Animatronic dinosaurs battle on a rocky ledge, a mighty allosaurus against the armored stegosaurus. There are 250 prehistoric-looking trees, all manmade, and various other creatures of the era, from millipedes to pteranodons. An elasmosaurus sticks his head out of a lagoon. The dinosaurs here are frighteningly realistic, some of Disney's best Audio-Animatronic figures. And sure enough, Ellen manages to get trapped by one of them, and it's Science Guy to the rescue. Ellen returns from the past in time to win Double Jeopardy.

This is one of Future World's most popular attractions, for good reason. I don't recommend seeing this in the morning. It gets crowded in a hurry (by 10:30), and there are other attractions that are best experienced in that time period because they're crowded the whole day. However, crowds here seem to disappear at about 4:30, so try it then.

WONDERS OF LIFE

Epcot Center's newest pavilion, this $100 million dome houses ten attractions and exhibits related to health and the human body, all presented in a smoke-free environment. This pavilion also includes the park's only thrill ride, plus one of its most entertaining multimedia productions. Outside the pavilion, be sure to notice the 72-foot tall DNA molecule.

Attractions
"BODY WARS"

Rating: 9 1/2. Spectacular ride and effects! Location: As you enter the pavilion, it's on the far side of the dome. Duration of Ride: 5 minutes. Best Time To Go: As soon as the park opens. Comments: Guests with heart, back, or neck conditions as well as expectant mothers and those prone to motion sickness pass up this ride. Frightening: Visually and physically, this is as intense as any ride in WDW.

Get ready for the ride of someone else's life! Here, you are set in one of four 40-passenger flight simulators and "miniaturized" in order to be injected into a patient, where you pick up the intrepid Dr. Lair who has been examining a splinter imbedded just under the skin. A normal day in the office for anyone, right?

But something is bound to go awry, as is the Disney thrill-ride tradition, and the ship piloted by actor Tim Matheson almost reaches Dr. Lair, played by Elizabeth Shue, when whoosh, these white blood cells scream onto the scene like bats out of hell, and next thing you know, you're chasing after her in a wild ride through the circulatory system.

Along the way, a contaminant in this particular human's body (that contaminant being you) is assaulted by white blood cells, is pumped throughout the body, and into the heart, where it runs out of energy. The technicians sitting safely outside this guy's body can be heard screaming over the intercom "You're out of power! We can't beam you out of there if you have no power," and you're either terrified or overjoyed at this, when your pilot and the doctor come up with an idea. You ride the bloodstream up to the brain, where the electrical impulses allow them to beam you out and return you to normal.

This is a very rough ride, so be sure to buckle your seat belt when they instruct you to do so, even though the cars only travel a few feet in any direction, and it is known for its ability to cause motion sickness. In fact, they sometimes have to shut down one of the cars to remove, ahem, a souvenir left by the last motion-sick rider.

If you start feeling queasy, close your eyes. Much of the thrill is visual, so if you take out one sense, it'll feel better. But if you get off the ride and feel like you're gonna blow chunks, there are restrooms just outside the attraction.

CRANIUM COMMAND

Rating: 9. Funny, entertaining, don't miss it. Location: As you enter the pavilion, it's on the far side of the dome. Duration of Show: 20 minutes. Best Time To Go: Before 11 AM or after 3 PM.

Okay, troopers, don your battle helmets! Batten the hatches! You are about to join an Audio-Animatronic Cranium Commando named Buzzy, who has a tough job ahead of him in order to earn his stripes. He has to pilot a twelve-year-old boy through his daily routine. Gasp! A cartoon character named General Knowledge barks out the assignment to Buzzy in the witty pre-show. Buzzy balks at the idea, but changes his mind when threatened of being put inside the head of a chicken. Note that if you miss the preshow, you'll have a harder time understanding the rest of the presentation. If you arrive as the preshow is ending, it'd probably be a better idea to wait for the next show.

Two hundred guests at a time are led into the semi-circular theater where the main presentation takes place. Buzzy sits in a contraption that allows him to oversee various organs of the body, all of whom are depicted by actors. The left brain is represented by Charles Grodin, the right brain is portrayed by Jon Lovitz, formerly of Saturday Night Live, the stomach is played by George Wendt (Cheers' Norm Peterson), the heart is pumped up by Kevin Nealon and Dana Carvey as their Saturday Night Live duo. Hans and Franz, and Bob Golthwait is a hyperactive adrenal gland.

Anyhow, this unlikely team wakes up inside the head of this 12-year-old, goes to school without eating his breakfast, fights off bullies, impresses a beautiful female classmate, and does all the other things that twelve-year-old boys do. It is easy to get into the story and relate to Buzzy's charge, but if you've forgotten what it was like to be twelve, you may be less enchanted.

"THE MAKING OF ME"

Rating: 6. A worthwhile film. Location: At the center of the pavilion. Duration of Show: 14 minutes. Best Time To Go: After 4:30 PM. Comments: Since this deals with the sensitive subjects of human reproduction and birth, parents may want to use discretion when deciding whether their family should view it.

Glenn Gordon Caron directed this funny film starring Martin Short as a man who ponders his conception, and not being one to leave us hanging, travels back in time to watch his parents date, fall in love, marry, and eventually decide to have him. There is actual footage of a developing fetus and yes, the birth. The sexual information necessary to a production like this is handled tastefully, and although it is considered controversial for a company like Disney, most guests take it in stride.

This quality film is shown in a tiny room which only seats 100 people at a time, not nearly the number of fans it draws, so unless you can visit after 4:30 PM, you're likely to hit a long line.

"GOOFY ABOUT HEALTH"

Rating: 5 1/2. Pleasant. Location: In the center of the pavilion. Duration of Show: 10 minutes. Best Time To Go: Anytime. Comments: Guests can come and go as they please.

Who'da thunk it? Your pal and mine, Goofy, smokes. He also drinks, doesn't sleep regularly, doesn't eat right, never exercises, and lives a stressful life. But on this seven-screen production, Goofy changes his ways and becomes a healthy guy. This production, which plays continuously in a 100-seat theater, mixes long-lost Goofy cartoons and newly-made footage to illustrate the road to good health.

ANACOMICAL PLAYERS

Rating: 6. Enjoyable. Location: In the center of the pavilion. Duration of Show: Varies, usually about 15 minutes. Best Time To Go: Anytime. Comments: Guests can come and go as they please.

The show here features live improv actors and audience participation in a 100-seat theater in the center of the pavilion. The humor is corny, but it's always there and always fun. Consult the Epcot Entertainment schedule, or the WorldKey system for scheduled performance times, usually six or seven times every day.

Exhibits

MET LIFESTYLE REVUE

Here, touch-sensitive screens let you type in statistics about your health habits, and the computer tells you how you're doing and how you could improve your life, reduce your stress level, and live longer. That's always fun.

COACH'S CORNER

If you play tennis, golf, or baseball, you'll want to stop by. You'll be put into a cage where you take a swing with a club, racquet, or bat, and a well-known professional athlete tells you (via videocameras, tapes, and Disney cast members who urge you to "say hi to Gary Carter") what's wrong with your swing.

Should you listen? I think that Gary Carter, Chris Evert, and Nancy Lopez know what they're doing. So just sit there and listen to what they have to say. The instant replay of your swing in slow motion is also pretty cool.

FRONTIERS OF MEDICINE

The only 100% serious exhibit here, Frontiers of Medicine, located near the exit from Body Wars, lets guests check out cutting-edge technology and educational, scientific exhibits. These are changed on a somewhat regular basis.

SENSORY FUNHOUSE

Lots of hands-on exhibits dealing with one of the five senses and the tricks they can play on your mind. While you're here, check out the 50-foot mobile swinging in the air. You may have trouble getting kids to leave this exhibit.

WONDERCYCLES

These are stationary bikes with a computer screen that tells you your speed, how far you've traveled, and how many calories you've burned. On this same screen, travel footage is played as you pedal. You can choose from an everyday town, the Rose Parade, or Disneyland. However, if you've just ridden Body Wars, you might consider giving your stomach a few minutes off before jostling it again on a bike.

TEST TRACK

Rating: 7 1/2. Fun but by no means worth the typical 90 minute-plus wait. Location: In the old World of Motion pavilion at the edge of Future World. Duration of Ride: 5 1/2 minutes. Best time to go: First thing in the morning. Frightening: At points. Mostly it's just adrenaline. Guests must be 40" tall to ride.

This much-hyped attraction replaced the venerable World of Motion, and is themed after the rigorous testing that prototype automobiles go through. While an intriguing theory, the ride itself is for the most part disappointing.

Following a pre-show you board a six-passenger car and climb thee stories at a 15 degree pitch for the Hill Climb Test. The Suspension Test sends your car over various rough road surfaces. Next, the brake test demonstrates the effect of anti-lock brakes, sending you into a tailspin without and to a complete stop with. The Environmental Chamber test exposes the car to searing heat, frigid cold, and then an acidic mist. The Ride Handling test sends you up and down a "switchback" hill and into the path of an oncoming truck and then through a crash barrier in the Barrier Test. Fun for the whole family. Up to here, the ride is pretty tame, and is mostly forgettable. At this point during my first ride, I was ready to declare it the dud of the year.

However, they save the best for last on this ride, and the best here is the High Speed Test, where you race around the exterior of the building in open air at 65 mph, navigating 50 degree banked curves along the way. It's exhilarating but before you know it, you've reached the end of the mile-long ride.

This ride is insanely popular and often has 90-minute waits during times of the year when you can walk onto any other ride on the premises. Honestly, I don't feel like the ride is good enough to justify the wait. But you're going to ignore me and ride it anyway, because it's the Next Big Thing at Disney. So here's how to do it with the minimum of a wait. You can either get there first thing in the morning, reserve a Fastpass time, or opt to ride alone. There is a separate entrance for single riders, who fill in available spaces on the cars. Your wait in the single rider line varies but is almost always shorter than the main line.

ODYSSEY COMPLEX

This pavilion consists of the park's most attractive fast-food restaurant, the Odyssey Restaurant, and three services, listed below. The complex is accessible by three bridges: one from the Test Track pavilion, one by World Showcase Plaza, and one by World Showcase's Mexico pavilion.

Services
FIRST AID

If you need this kind of help, it's comforting to know that there are Registered Nurses staffing this establishment.

BABY SERVICES

Open from one hour before the park opens to two hours after it closes, the Baby Services amenities include nursing and changing facilities, and a shop selling formula, baby food, and diapers.

LOST CHILDREN

Located alongside Baby Services, this is where young people who've been lost are taken by Disney staff who find them. Since it's rather unlikely that your kids could find their way there on their own, tell them that if they are separated from you, they should go to anyone with a Disney name tag. If you're all the way to Spaceship Earth or the Japan pavilion before you discover the loss of your charge, go to a phone and call 560-7928 or report it to Guest Relations or any WorldKey terminal.

JOURNEY INTO YOUR IMAGINATION

Outside this pavilion are waterfalls and fountains that defy logic one waterfall shoots water up and over a cliff face instead of the other way around. A fountain shoots blobs of water at regular intervals, most kids can't help but smack the blobs. My personal favorite is the Leap Frog Fountain, which winds across a landscaped courtyard, shooting streams of water from one planter to the next to the next, even over paths (and often guests' heads as well!). One of my favorite WDW photos is of my youngest brother catching the one-inch stream in the face!

The pavilion itself is impressive, with the pair of mirrored-glass pyramids serving as a backdrop for the monorail and the crystal-like structures by the Upside Down Waterfall.

JOURNEY INTO YOUR IMAGINATION

Rating: 5. The new and "improved" version just doesn't cut it. Location: On the right side of the pavilion as you approach it. Duration of Ride: 8 minutes. Best Time to Go: Before 11am or after 5pm.

Fresh off a rehabilitation, this classic ride was revamped completely. Gone is the whimsical red-bearded Dreamfinder, and with the exception of a small cameo during the ride and a small role in the pre-show, so is the lovable Figment. Instead, John Cleese reprises his role as Dr. Nigel Channing, the chairman of the Imagination Institute. This ride takes you behind the scenes of the Institute for a look at some of the experiments taking place there. Some of the experiments include Up Is Down, where gravity seems to reverse itself, Color of Sound, which represents sound visually, and more. The clinic "scans" your imagination once at the beginning of the ride and once at the end of it, to illustrate the results of these mental stimuli upon your imagination. Unfortunately, the ride just ain't all that inspiring.

With the removal of the original Journey Into Imagination ride, Horizons, and the World of Motion, Disney seems to be phasing out the whimsy in Epcot center in favor of a more serious tone. And I for one miss the whimsy.

HONEY, I SHRUNK THE AUDIENCE

Rating: 10. Wild! Location: Just to the left (east side) of the pavilion. Duration of Show: 23 minutes. Best Time To Go: In the morning or evening. Frightening: The special effects and high volume may be too intense for small children.

Rick Moranis stars with John Cleese of Monty Python fame in this hysterical, completely unexpected spinoff of the movies "Honey, I Shrunk the Kids" and "Honey, I Blew Up the Baby." Without giving away any of the delightful surprises this movie holds, let me just say that it will leave your knees shaking with excitement. In-theater technology, computer-enhanced 3D effects, and "sneaky tricks" combine to make this the most incredible movie experience around.

The plot, or more accurately, the pretense of the film is a ceremony honoring Professor Wayne Szalinski (Moranis) as "Inventor of the Year." Demonstrating his incredible shrinking machine, he accidentally shrinks the audience to the size of a bread box. The unsuspecting vacationers are then beseiged by tennis shoes, huge dogs, scurrying mice, and no longer-small bratty children. This unforgettable interactive theatre production makes previous 3D look and feel archaic in comparison, and accordingly, is very popular. It is most crowded during the afternoon hours.

Exhibit
WHAT IF LABS

This "creative playground of the future" allows kids from one to one hundred to flex their imaginary muscles at interactive displays that will amaze, amuse, and entertain. Located at the exit from Journey Into Your Imagination, it can also be accessed from outside the pavilion.

THE LAND

This pavilion, covering six acres and containing two stories, is shaped like a greenhouse and contains a real greenhouse with actual cultivation going on inside it. The Garden Grill, a full-service eatery, is often overlooked for lunch, but the Sunshine Season Food Fair below, an attractive food court with several separate stands, is not.

However, it's one of the best places in Epcot for families of finicky eaters to go. The attractions, though, are often thronged with crowds at mealtimes.

Attractions
"CIRCLE OF LIFE"

Rating: 7 1/2. Compelling, humor-filled. Location: On the entry/exit level of the pavilion. Duration of Show: 18 1/2 minutes. Best Time To Go: Anytime.

The stars of Disney's animated megahit "The Lion King" return in this new adventure, delivering a parable about environmental conservation in the face of overdevelopment and industrialization.

Now king of the Pridelands, Simba (voice of Matthew Broderick) walks in just as a cry of "Timber!" echoes, followed by the splash of a fallen tree. It seems that carefree slackers Timon and Pumbaa (Nathan Lane nad Ernie Sabella) have begun clearing the savannah to construct "Hakuna Matata Lakeside Village" — a timeshare community!

Simba then relates a story told by his father of a creature that forgets that everything is connected in the great Circle of Life. "That creature," he explains, "is man." The 70mm footage that follows was taken from the "Symbiosis" film that previously occupied this theater.

This film is especially notable for its presentation. The subject matter is serious, but the view is far more optimistic than many environmental films, and it encourages the notion that individual people can make a difference. Also, I found it daring that a company as vast and commercial as Disney would send such an anti-development message.

This film is more popular than its predecessor, but can still be seen virtually anytime without much of a wait.

FOOD ROCKS

Rating: 7. Cute and nostalgic. Location: On the lower level of the pavilion. Duration of Show: 15 minutes. Best Time To Go: Before 11 AM or after 3 PM.

Audio-Animatronics whimsy, rock and roll, and a nutritional message come together (apologies to the Beatles) in this attraction, which replaces the Kitchen Kabaret but keeps the same cartoonish feel and theme of good nutrition. Various kitchen utensils and food items perform parodies of music including Queen's "Bohemian Rhapsody," the Police's "Every Breath You Take," the Beach Boys' "Good Vibrations," Peter Gabriel's "Sledgehammer", Cher's "Shoop Shoop Song," Little Richard's "Tutti Frutti," Chubby Checker's "Do the Twist," Neil Sedaka's "Breaking Up Is Hard to Do," and the Pointer Sisters' version of "Respect." As "Fud Wrapper," Tone Loc hosts and sings a takeoff on "Funky Cold Medina." Tone Loc, Checker, Sedaka, Little Richard, and the Pointer Sisters all performed the parodies of their music. It's a lot of fun, especially for those who grew up with the music of the artists featured.

This attraction tends to get thronged during lunch and dinner hours, mainly due to its location adjacent to the Sunshine Season Food Fair.

LIVING WITH THE LAND

Rating: 7. Relaxing, informative. Location: On the lower level of the pavilion. Duration of Ride: 12 minutes. Best Time To Go: Before 11 AM or after 3 PM.

The only ride in Epcot Center narrated by a real live human being, the boats of Listen to the Land first pass through Audio-Animatronics scenes of the African veldt, the American prairie as it used to be, and a turn-of-the-century farm. Then, the boats proceed into greenhouses. As opposed to the "biomes" explored in the first segment of the ride, the plants are real here. Many different modern systems of agriculture are demonstrated here.

For example, there are plants thriving in a desert atmosphere, feeding off of drip irrigation that provides the exact amount of nutrients and water needed. Other vegetables are suspended in a drum that revolves, reproducing the effects of gravity. This is a technique that could be employed in outer space in the future. Other plants are hung from the ceiling and are conveyed through sprays that provide the necessary nutrition. There are also hydroponics, the one method of farming whose name really sticks in your mind. At the end of the ride is a fish farm that breeds a great assortment of seafood. Many of the products of the greenhouse are served in restaurants in Future World.

This attraction is one of Future World's most popular attractions, and is crowded most of the time. However, an early-morning or evening visit may allow you to walk right on. Avoid it during mealtimes, though, when the entire pavilion is teeming with people.

Services
BEHIND THE SEEDS

If you are intrigued by the agricultural technology presented in the Listen to the Land boat ride, sign up for the our-long "Behind the Seeds" tour. It departs every half-hour from 9:30 to 4:30, and cover technologies displayed in the Living with the Land boat ride in greater detail. In addition, guests can view a new biotechnology lab where tissue culture and genetic engineering are being studied.

Also, guests can visit an integrated pest management lab, offering a look at the science of controlling insect and disease pests in plants. The cost is $5 for adults, $3 for kids 3 to 9. Sign up at the tour podium near the Green Thumb Emporium.

Shopping
GREEN THUMB EMPORIUM

This shop, next to Food Rocks, sells placemats, refrigerator magnets, books, topiaries, hydroponic plants, and mementos.

THE LIVING SEAS

Rating: 4 1/2. An excellent concept flawed in execution. Location: A landmark. Duration of Ride: 3 minutes. Best Time To Go: After 3 PM.

This $100 million pavilion, the second addition to Future World, features a restaurant and a multi-faceted attraction/exhibit. Outside, be sure to notice the striking designs on the exterior walls and the waves that crash behind the "Living Seas" sign outside every few seconds.

Whoever had the idea it was to create an attraction with lots of live marine mammals, fish, and crustaceans should be commended. However, most people consider the Living Seas a disappointment because the ride portion of the attraction is over almost as soon as it has begun.

The first parts of the attraction, serving as an introduction to the rest of it, are a 2 1/2-minute multi-media presentation and a 7-minute film that laud the pioneers of undersea research and describe the oceans as a resource. These are too academic to be thoroughly enjoyed.

Guests then board "hydrolators," elevators that simulate a plunge of many fathoms while in truth, descending about 2 inches. The illusion is created by the vibrating of the 20-passenger hydrolators and the bubbles that are pumped through the water screens outside their windows.

Finally, you reach the Caribbean Coral Reef Ride and board gondolas for an all-too-short ride between sections of the 5.7 million gallon tank. This section of the tank simulates the Caribbean, and some of the 5,000 specimens include bass, barracudas, sharks, dolphins, sea lions, diamond rays. An interesting note: the navy here includes divers in JIM suits, two one-man submarines, and two robotic submersibles. The divers can talk to guests about their operations by wireless radios.

The ride ends at Sea Base Alpha. This is the major portion of the attraction, so it's a shame that many visitors exit the pavilion here and miss the exhibits. The six stations include JIM suits that guests can try on, a module dedicated to the study of aquatic mammals, another featuring a show in which Jason, an Audio-Animatronic submersible (named for the sub which helped Dr. Robert Ballard find the sunken Titanic) explains the history of robotics in deep-sea exploration, one detailing the oceanic food chain, and more.

Shopping
LIVING SEAS SHOP
Here, at Sea Base Alpha, a small selection of guest convenience items, gifts, and mementos from the Living Seas.

WORLD SHOWCASE

The other half of Epcot is a celebration of the cultures and people of the world community. The architecture, culture, history, and people of eleven nations are featured. However, since there are very few attractions, adults and older children are more likely to appreciate World Showcase, while younger children may find it boring.

World Showcase, on the whole, is least crowded in the morning and early afternoon, when the majority of guests are checking out the pavilions at Future World. Entertainment, in the form of guest artisans, native musicians, dancers, and actors is often featured at all eleven pavilions.

Just opened is Millennium Village, a collection of exhibits, food, and crafts from over 20 nations never before represented at World Showcase. Note that World Showcase opens daily at 11am. Note that World Showcase pavilions open at 11am.

TIPS

Attractions - The only attraction in World Showcase that draws large lines is the Maelstrom in Norway. The others can all be experienced with little of a wait. World Showcase is least crowded during the morning.

Dining - All of the national pavilions have at least one restaurant faithful to the country. Many demand reservations, but some others do not. The best are Le Cellier in Canada, Au Petit Cafe in France, Biergarten in Germany, and the Cantina de San Angel in Mexico.

Shopping - Browsing the World Showcase shops is always fun. The most interesting of the shops are Mitsokushi in Japan, Norway's The Puffin's Roost, and China's Yong Feng Shangdian.

Transportation

The "Friendship" boats crisscross World Showcase Lagoon at regular intervals, from two docks on either sides of Showcase Plaza, with their destinations Germany and Morocco. Double-decker buses circle the lagoon, stopping outside Canada, France, Italy, and Mexico. Both suspend operation during events on or around the lagoon.

Shopping in Showcase Plaza
DISNEY TRADERS

Located on the left side of Showcase Plaza, this is the place for Disney character souvenirs, decorative gifts, and clothing representing the nations of World Showcase. Sundry items are also available.

PORT OF ENTRY

Across from Disney Traders, this shop offers film, guest convenience items, and one-of-a-kind gifts from countries all around the world, including several not in World Showcase.

MEXICO

This pavilion is housed inside a pyramid whose Meso-American likenesses date back to the third century A.D. As you walk inside, it immediately becomes dusk. The air is filled with the excitement of a Mexican mercado (marketplace) and the romance of the San Angel Inn.

The inside is beautiful on a grand scale and amazing in its intricate detail. Although not an attraction, I consider the inside of the pavilion not to be missed, even if you have no intention of riding El Rio del Tiempo.

Attraction
EL RIO DEL TIEMPO

Rating: 7. Excellent, well-tailored blend of film and Audio-Animatronics. Location: In the back of the pavilion. Duration of Ride: 7 minutes. Best Time To Go: After 6 PM.

A slow, pleasant boat ride suggestive of It's a Small World in the Magic Kingdom. As you embark, you pass the San Angel Inn and a glowing volcano for a journey through the past and present of Mexico. There are artifacts and scenes representing the Mayan, Aztec, and Toltec peoples, meshed with video screens that give the attraction a more serious feel. There are dolls of children at play, reminiscent of Small World.

The monitors also depict Mexico today, with cliff divers, speed boats, flying dancers, and a shopping mercado. The finale of the ride is a breathtaking fireworks display created by fiberoptics.

Exhibit
ART OF MEXICO

This exhibit, subtitled "Reign of Glory," is a celebration of pre-Colombian art including vases, masks, and sculpture. Note that if a line for El Rio extends outside the pyramid and you only want to see the art, it is acceptable to bypass the line and just go in.

Shopping
PLAZA DE LOS AMIGOS

Just inside the pavilion (past the art collection), this is an excellent place to pick up baskets, clothing, papier mache, and pre-Colombian artifacts. Paper flowers, wooden trays and bowls, and pinatas are available here.

ARTESANIAS MEXICANAS

Ceramics and gifts of a different type are sold here, including onyx ashtrays, plaques, chess sets, and bookends.

LA FAMILIA FASHIONS

Ready-to-wear fashions, jewelry, and accessories for women and children are featured here.

EL RANCHITO DEL NORTE

Gift items and souvenirs from Northern Mexico are purveyed at this shop, alongside World Showcase Lagoon. You can also watch artists create rings here.

NORWAY

World Showcase's newest pavilion is one of its best, featuring an adventure boat ride similar to Pirates of the Caribbean, one of the World's most exciting restaurants, and a vivid blend of architectural styles. The Restaurant Akershus is named for the Norwegian castle of the same name, built in Oslo's harbor in the 1300s and still standing today, a wood-stave church mimicking the Gol church built around the year 1250. Incidentally, when Viking kings adopted Christianity and spread it throughout Scandinavia, the presence of churches of this type was confined to Norway. Very few still exist.

Outside the Maelstrom is a lovely courtyard surrounded by more traditional buildings. On the lagoon sits the Norseman, a 50-foot ship duplicating a thousand-year-old Viking ship. This was given to the pavilion by a Norwegian maritime group.

Attraction
MAELSTROM

Rating: 6 1/2. Exciting, promising, but too short. Location: In the rear of the courtyard. Duration of Ride: 4 1/2 minutes. Duration of Show: 5 minutes. Best Time To Go: After 6 PM. Frightening: A three-headed troll and a steep, backwards drop frighten some kids.

Maelstrom puts you on a 16-passenger boat with a dragon's head carved onto it for a journey through the mythology and the reality of Norse culture. After passing a 10th century Viking village, you meet up with a three-headed troll who obviously got up on the wrong side of the bed. The troll puts a spell on you and you speed towards a waterfall that looks like you will be dumped into the courtyard below, but at the last moment, the boat reverses direction and accelerates down a chute into the wind-swept North Sea. You pass a drilling platform and get out of your boat in a recreation of a harbor village.

Here, you wait to be admitted to a theater that shows a short but powerful presentation on how the sea affects Norwegian life. This film is shown through the perspective of a young boy visiting a museum.

Exhibits
"TO THE ENDS OF THE EARTH"

This is an impressive display of 20th century artifacts from two polar expeditions.

TRAVEL INFORMATION

If the pavilion's sights, sounds, smells, and tastes whet your palate for a sojourn in the Land of the Midnight Sun, representatives of the

Norwegian Tourism Board will be more than happy to provide you with necessary information.

Shopping
THE PUFFIN'S ROOST

The only shop in the pavilion stocks all sorts of imports, including clothing, jewelry, pewter candlesticks and tableware, glassware, blankets, wood carvings, decorative gifts, candy, and toys like the famous and popular-once-more trolls and Playmobil sets.

CHINA

As aesthetically pleasing as any of the other pavilions, China features a half-sized replica of Beijing's Temple of Heaven, a pond, and a courtyard suitable for resting up with a red bean ice cream or a Chinese beer while others in your party shop. The premier cinematic exhibit in E[cot Center can be viewed in the Temple of Heaven, called Wonders of China; this CircleVision 360 film is described below.

Attraction
WONDERS OF CHINA

Rating: 9 1/2. Exciting, breathtaking scenes. Not to be missed. Location: In the Temple of Heaven. Duration of Show: 19 minutes. Best Time To Go: Any time of the day. Comments: The theater has no seats.

After the original World Premiere CircleVision, American Journeys, the Disney film-sters hauled their 700-pound, 9-camera contraption to the People's Republic of China. Ports of call on this whirlwind journey include the Forbidden City of Beijing, the vast plains of Inner Mongolia, the 2,400-year-old Great Wall, Shanghai, European in its look, Ghangzhou, a developing economic center, and many others. The film is dramatic and well-done, worth a visit. To see without a crowd, see this before noon or after six.

Exhibit
HOUSE OF WHISPERING WILLOWS

This is a display of art and artifacts native to China, changed periodically, usually every six months, but at latest the featured exhibit was Artistry In Time, a collection of magnificent timepieces from the eighteenth century. On loan from the People's Republic of China.

Shopping
YONG GENG SHANGDIAN

This huge emporium sells all sorts of Chinese memorabilia, including silken robes, prints, paper umbrellas and fans, purses, glassware, and as you climb up the price ladder, dolls, jewelry, figurines, rugs, porcelain masks, carved chests, and antique tables and chairs. For the younger set, toys include nunchuks, ninja swords, and toy snakes. The selection of Chinese goods is better than that found anywhere else.

GERMANY

Of of the five World Showcase pavilions that have no formal attractions, Germany is the most festive. The village, its architecture an amalgam of several sources, including towns on the Rhine, in Bavaria, and the north of the nation, with some influence from Frankfurt and Rothenberg.

The centerpiece on the plaza, St. Georgsplatz, is the Biergarten, an Olde World tavern where authentic German fare and authentic German entertainment are presented. The merry atmosphere is helped by communal seating and huge steins of beer. There is a half-hour-long dinner show performed several times a night. Street entertainment is also offered. There are several WorldKey terminals outside the pavilion.

Shopping

SUSSIGKEITEN

If you are planning to blow your diet, this is as good a place as any. H. Bahlsen chocolates, tons of cookies of all sorts: chocolate, butter, and a spicy cookie crisp called Lebkuchen, a traditional Christmas treat, nuts, almond biscuits, caramels, and that everlasting standby, the Gummi Bears imported from the Black Forest area.

WEINKELLER

The translation of this shop's title is evident as soon as you walk in: wine cellar. Most of the 250 varieties of H. Schmitt Sohne wine sold here are of the white variety. Prices range from the humble to the humbling, and tastings are held daily. In addition to the grape, beer steins, wine glasses, goblets, decanters, and assorted cheeses are available.

GLAS UND PORZELLAN

Art is the featured attraction here, with Goebel giftware, ceramic figurines including those of M.I. Hummel, plus renderings on paper. Of particular interest is an informative display of how the figuines are manufactured, including the ceramics at each stage of production. Wheelchairs and strollers can be replaced here.

DIE WEINACHTS ECKE

This shop celebrates Christmas 365 days a year, with nutcrackers and other traditional German gifts and ornaments made by companies from all over Germany. Replacement batteries for WDW rental video cameras are also available.

VOLKSKUNST
The main objects in this small shop are clocks of all sorts, chiefly cuckoo clocks, plus beer steins and a variety of gift items, scarves, nutcrackers, and incense burners in the guise of small wooden dolls. Ceramics are also sold here.

DER BUCHERWURM
English-printed books on Germany, ashtrays, spoons, and vases adorned with the images of German cities, sundries, film, and hand-painted Faberge eggs, created by a master egg-painter are offered here.

DER TEDDYBAR
Toys and more toys! The fanciful creations here are all traditional playthings to German youth, including building blocks, LGB-brand miniature trains, a spectacular collection of dolls, and stuffed animals, including teddy bears.

KUNSTARBEIT EN KRISTALL
Glassware is featured here.

GERMANY CART
Close to the Lagoon, this offers t-shirts, pins, souvenirs, novelties, and film.

ITALY
Italy, like its next-door neighbor in World Showcase, Germany, is a festive pavilion featuring fine dining, shopping, and street entertainment. A campanile atop the detailed replica of the Doge Palace towers over the pavilion, along with pedestals on which St. Mark the Evangelist and his lion companion stand, as in the square named for the apostle in Venice. In the Lagoon, there are peppermint-striped poles to which gondolas are tethered, and around the piazza, a fountain and cheery landscaping liven up the atmosphere.

Shopping
DELIZIE ITALIANE
If you didn't stop at Sussigkeiten or Patisserie Boulangerie and your kids are sore at you for it, a visit here will smooth out any rough edges

between you. Luscious Perugina chocolates, cookies, and candy are sold here.

LA GEMMA ELEGANTE

The jewelry sold here ranges from the inexpensive to the exorbitant, and includes gold and silver chains, Venetian-glass beads, pendants, earrings, and mosaics.

IL BEL CRISTALLO

This pretty shop purveys Capodimonte ceramic flowers and figurines, Venetian glass objets d'art like paperweights, lead crystal bowls and candlesticks, alabaster figurines, and inlaid wood music boxes.

ITALY CART

Visit this cart if you have a sudden urge to buy T-shirts, magnets, souvenirs, and novelties of the pavilion.

THE AMERICAN ADVENTURE

Rating: 10. Arguably EPCOT's best attraction. Not to be missed. Location: The centerpiece of the pavilion. Duration of Show: 29 minutes. Best Time To Go: Before noon and after 3:30 PM.

When a dinner party is held, the host sits at the head of the table. In this World Showcase, it is only fitting that America serve as the centerpiece. With a facade comprised of 110,000 bricks, the pavilion's main building houses a fast food restaurant, a shop, and the title attraction.

American history is celebrated here, in a moving presentation hosted by Mark Twain and Benjamin Franklin. As you rise on the escalator to the theater, you pass under forty-four flags that had flown over what is now the United States. When you enter the theater, check out the statues representing the spirits of America.

The show then begins with the Pilgrims' arrival at Plymouth Rock. It then progresses to view the soul of the country at various points in its history. In one scene, a Ben Franklin robot walks up a flight of stairs to visit the author of the Declaration of Independence, Thomas Jefferson. All over, the realism is incredible. Mark Twain smokes a cigar. Audio-Animatronic figures of Nez Perce Chief Joseph and Susan B. Anthony repeat the words of the originals. The voices of the robot Will Rogers and Franklin Delano Roosevelt are their own, the price of gas in the Depression scene is an accurate eighteen cents.

The sets are as impressive as the cast, including a nearly life-size replica of Independence Hall in Philadelphia, Philly's Centennial Exposition, and a roadside gas station during the Depression, where one man strums a banjo, humming "Brother, Can You Spare Me a Dime?" while another bemoans the cost of gasoline. Their antique radio plays a speech from FDR. Incidentally, this last scene was inspired by a photo in Life magazine.

The musical accompaniment, provided by the Philadelphia Symphony Orchestra, is among the best in the World, and the finale, "Golden Dream," is absolutely breathtaking, presented along with video clips of among other people and events, the moon landing of the Eagle, John F. Kennedy's inaugural speech and Dr. Martin Luther King's "I have a dream" speech. This moving, stately conclusion often brings people to tears.

According to the Disney public relations department, this attraction has been revised over one thousand times during its lifetime and is extremely popular and thus, quite crowded between noon and 3:30pm, so plan to witness the production outside those hours. Even during peak hours, the huge capacity of the theater effectively manages crowds. And even when there is a wait, it is bearable thanks to the entertainment provided by the carillon and the Voices of Liberty chorus. Not to be missed.

Exhibit
"PATCHWORK QUILTS: A FOLK ART TRADITION"
Quilts from the turn of the century are on display here.

Shopping
HERITAGE MANOR GIFTS
Hand-crafted goods and pre-1940s Americana items including glassware, food, toys, porcelain, and items of wood and cloth. Replicas of historic documents like the Constitution and the Declaration of Independence are available. This shop also serves as a drop-off point for two-hour photo processing.

AMERICAN ADVENTURE CARTS
Souvenirs from the American Adventure pavilion such as shirts, magnets, pins, and some sundries.

KODAK KIOSK
Camera accessories, film, and two-hour photo processing service are available.

JAPAN
A five-story, blue-roofed pagoda, modeled after an eighth-century building in the Horyuji Temple in Nara, majestically overlooks the rest of

Japan, easily distinguished from the other World Showcase countries by the torii gate at the edge of the Lagoon. The bright red torii was designed like the one at the Itsukushima Shrine in Hiroshima Bay. Perhaps the most beautiful and soothing part of the pavilion is the lovely garden, with streams and waterfalls, boulders, evergreens, and a small pond filled with koi, Japanese goldfish. At the present time, the only attractions in Japan are the architecture and landscaping. However, there is talk of adding a Mount Fuji thrill ride based on Disneyland's Matterhorn Mountain.

Exhibit
BIJUTU-KAN GALLERY
"Echos Through Time" is on exhibit here, featuring traditional and contemporary Japanese art forms. The exhibits are changed periodically.

Shopping
MITSUKOSHI DEPARTMENT STORE
This branch of the 300-year-old "Japanese Sears" is the largest shop in Epcot Center, offering traditional Japanese items, including a vast selection of dolls whose prices range from $3.50 to $3,500, kits for cultivating bonsai trees, bowls and vases for flowers, china, kimonos, T-shirts, porcelain, wind chimes, jewelry, stationery, and snack items.

MITSUKOSHI KIOSK
Mementos, toys, and gifts are available in a more limited selection than at the department store.

MOROCCO
You can almost hear Peabo Bryson singing "A Whole New World" as you enter the courtyard of a replicated Arabian village. If you look carefully at any of the pieces that make up the 9 tons of tile, you would notice a flaw or imperfection with every single piece. This was done purposely by the Moroccan artists imported to Epcot to construct the pavilion because the Koran, the Islamic holy book, says that only Allah may create perfection. This touch adds to the authenticity and the apparent age of the pavilion, including the Koutoubia Minaret, the landscaped Medina, and the Bab Boujouloud gate, all imitations of the real articles.

Exhibits
GALLERY OF ARTS AND HISTORY
An ever-changing collection of Moroccan art, artifacts, and costume

is on display on the left side of the courtyard, in the building closest to the lagoon.

FEZ HOUSE
This is an early example of Moroccan architecture.

TRAVEL INFORMATION
The Moroccan National Tourist Office hosts this information outlet, with a Royal Air Maroc desk for booking a flight, literature on the country, and a continuously-playing slide show on Moroccan peoples and landscapes.

Shopping

CASABLANCA CARPETS
Wall hangings, prayer rugs, throw pillows, and Berber and Rabat carpets. And no, Aladdin, they do not fly.

JEWELS OF THE SAHARA
Sold here is an assortment of hand-crafted Berber jewelry of silver and gold with glass, amber, and beads.

FASHIONS FROM FEZ
Contemporary women's clothing, accessories,

MARKETPLACE IN THE MEDINA
Wicker, leather, and straw objects are offered here, mainly baskets, handbags, wallets, and lampshades.

TANGIER TRADERS
Contemporary fashions, leather purses, and accessories like fezzes, woven belts, leather sandals, and traditional Moroccan clothing.

THE BRASS BAZAAR
Pottery is sold alongside with pitchers, planters, vases, trays, and serving sets of brass and copper.

MEDINA ARTS
A selection of crafts from all over Morocco plus jewelry, sweatshirts, blouses, and film.

BERBER OASIS
Located in a tent by the Lagoon, this shop sells baskets, leather, brass, jewelry, and curios.

FRANCE

From Morocco's rugged mystique, we then progress to the charm of France. This interpretation of the country features narrow street, quaint sidewalk cafes, fountains, and shopping boutiques. The architecture is turn-of-the-century Paris and is towered over by a replica of the Eiffel Tower, which, ironically, is visible from everywhere in World Showcase except the France pavilion.

There is a small enclave by the river connecting the International Gateway to the Epcot Resorts, this enclave housing a beautiful, small park inspired by A Sunday Afternoon on the Island of La Grande Jatte, Georges Seurat's famed painting. The park is relaxing and peaceful, but if exciting and breathtaking is more your cup of tea, try the gorgeous film playing at the Palais du Cinema theater towards the rear of the pavilion.

Attraction
IMPRESSIONS DE FRANCE

Rating: 8 1/2. Excellent, not to be missed. Location: The rear of the pavilion. Duration of Show: 18 minutes. Best Time To Go: Before 11am and after 7pm.

Many people lump Impressions de France together with the two CircleVision 360 films. There are some similarities, like the travelog presentation with superb musical accompaniment, but the differences are major: while the CV360 films cover all 360 degrees, the huge screen on which Impressions de France is shown covers only 200 degrees. Because viewers need not stand to see a full circle, the Disney people installed seats in the theater, a godsend for families who've been trekking around the world and praying for a chance to sit.

The film is absolutely stunning, featuring picturesque footage from Versailles, the Eiffel Tower, Mont St. Michel, Cannes, the Alps, and 43 other locations. A highlight, for sure, is the beautiful music, played by the London Philharmonic Orchestra and composed in the classic style by Frenchmen who lived in the late 1800s and early 1900s, including Jacques Offenbach, Charles-Camille Saint-Saens, Claude Debussy, and Erik Satie. To view this production without much of a wait, visit in the morning or evening.

Shopping
PLUME ET PALETTE

French art, including elegant prints of countryside scenes, oil paintings, sparkling crystal creations, Limoges porcelain miniatures, tapestries, and china boxes.

LA MODE FRANCAIS
This shop sells French fashions and accessories.

GUERLAIN BOUTIQUE
Perfumes and cosmetics are sold here.

LA SIGNATURE
French apparel, fragrances, and bath products are offered in this intimate, tasteful shop.

LA MAISON DU VIN
French wine of all sorts is sold here, with prices ranging from a few bucks a bottle upwards to $300 for a rare vintage. Wine tastings are held here. There is a nominal fee, but you get to keep the glass. Wine accessories are also sold here.

GALERIE DES HALLES
The largest shop in France, this market offers cookies, chocolate, souvenirs, books, toys, and ready-to-wear items.

ART FEST
Portraits are inked out here.

FRANCE CART
Vastly overpriced T-shirts, flags, sweatshirts, magnets, and other knick-knacks. Film and sundries are also sold here.

INTERNATIONAL GATEWAY
This is Epcot's second entrance, designed for guests coming from the Epcot Resorts and the Disney-MGM Studios Theme Park. The World Traveler shop here is one of the best bets for Epcot mementos.

Shopping
SHOWCASE GIFTS
This small shop sells convenience items, sundries, film, and Epcot Center mementos and also houses the package pickup.

WORLD TRAVELER
A good selection of Epcot Center mementos, character merchandise, and Disney ready-to-wear, plus sundries, film, cameras, camcorder rental. A drop-off point for two hour photo processing.

STROLLER & WHEELCHAIR RENTAL
Convenience items, film, keepsakes, and sundries.

UNITED KINGDOM

You can picture Chevy Chase saying "Hey look, kids, Big Ben, Parliament!" (as in National Lampoon's European Vacation movie) as you wander the streets of a quaint British town here in Florida. There are no attractions per se in the UK pavilion, but a walk through the shops here is a most pleasant way to spend a few minutes, or hours.

The entertainment is provided here by the Old Globe Players, an improvisational street theater troupe.

Shopping
THE TEA CADDY

Every dog must have his every day, every Brit must have his tea, and if you want to pick up some R. Twining and Co. tea bags or loose leaves, both mundane and exotic, this is an excellent place. Hard candies, biscuits, shortbread, teapots, and accessories are also available.

Incidentally, the design of this shop resembles very much the architecture of Stratford-upon-Avon, Shakespeare's birthplace.

THE MAGIC OF WALES

The items presented in this small shop all hail from the corner of the United Kingdom known as Wales. The Welsh handicrafts, gifts, and mementos include jewelry, pottery, slate, and other hand-crafted items.

THE QUEEN'S TABLE

Royal Doulton china, figurines, crystal, and statuettes, ranging from five dollars to five digits. A very pretty shop.

PRINGLE OF SCOTLAND

Socks, scarves, hats, and ties are all sold here with various plaids on them, if you're the kind of guy who'd feel uncomfortable in a "skirt", plus lots of woolens, sweaters and golf clothes.

LORDS AND LADIES

Gift items like tobacco, bath products, fragrances, pipes, plaques, mugs, chess sets, coins, stamps, and record albums are sold in this shop.

THE TOY SOLDIER

British kids play, too! And here, you can check out the tools that they use to have a good time. There are wooden boats, toys, games, coloring books, books, stuffed animals, and a vast variety of dolls.

U.K. CART
A cart on the Promenade selling souvenirs.

MILLENIUM VILLAGE

Just in time for Y2K, this indoor pavilion celebrates diversity and multiculturalism with interactive displays from dozens of nations. Upon entering the pavilion, cast members representing Ethiopia, Indonesia, Israel, Kenya, Namibia, New Zealand, India, and South Africa recall their nations' **"Gifts to the World."** Moving inside, you reach the **Carnival**, a midway of interactive games teaching facts about Brazil, Scotland, Saudi Arabia, Eritrea, Sweden, and more.

Walk a little further to find shops featuring hand made art and artifacts from nations like Chile, Denmark, Thailand, Lebanon, Peru, Egypt, Greece, Korea, and Venezuela. There's also a food court with eight different regions represented.

CANADA

Canada's landscape features the Victorian Gardens, an attractive little park based on the Butchart Gardens in British Columbia, a replicated Quebec hotel, towering elegantly over the pavilion, a stream, waterfall, and a small Rocky Mountain. The pavilion represents French Canada, the Canadian Rockies, the gardens of the city, and other areas.

Attraction
O CANADA!
Rating: 8 1/2. Well done, not to be missed. Location: At the very back of the pavilion. Duration of Show: 18 minutes. Best Time To Go: After 3:30 PM. Comments:The theater has no seats.

Believe it or not, the theater housing the CircleVision 360 is inside a mountain. But the attraction is not the theater but the splendid film, dramatic and awesome at points. All of Canada's famed landmarks are featured, plus some not-so-famous hamlets where wilderness is still king. There is also footage of the Royal Canadian Mounted Police (better known as Mounties), pristine woodlands, a rodeo, the Calgary Stampede, and Montreal with all its Old World charm.

This film is very well done, but since it is right at the center of the park, seeing it without a crowd can be difficult unless you check it out in the late afternoon or early evening.

Shopping
NORTHWEST MERCANTILE
Canada's largest shop sells stereotypical items like lumberjack shirts,

maple syrup, and sheepskin. There are also real Native American artifacts alongside kitschy items like toy tomahawks, fur vests, moccasins, and headdresses. Other items sold here include toys, clothes, gifts, and crafts. Film can be dropped off here for two-hour processing.

LA BOUTIQUE DES PROVINCES
Hand-crafted item, figurines, jewelry, fashions, accessories, dolls, and gift items from French Canada are offered here.

WOOD CART
Souvenirs of Canada are sold at the edge of the lagoon.

ENTERTAINMENT IN EPCOT

In Epcot Center, especially **World Showcase**, live entertainment is king. At the various "countries" expect either live and native entertainment or piped-in music.

ALFREDO'S RESTAURANT (ITALY)
Strolling musicians and singing waiters entertain nightly at World Showcase's most popular restaurant.

ALPINE TRIO (GERMANY)
This group brings the spirit of *gemutlitchkeit* (coziness) to the courtyard seven times daily.

ANACOMICAL PLAYERS
An improvisational acting troupe produces funny, lively sketches about health and life six times a day every day. Inside the Wonders of Life pavilion.

CALEDONIA BAGPIPES (CANADA)
A band consisting of two pipers and a drummer entertains while illustrating Canada's rich British heritage. They perform seven times a day, five days a week.

CANADIAN COMEDY CORPS (CANADA)
Eh? Comedic actors and musicians from the land that brought us Dan Aykroyd, John Candy, and Mike Myers.

CHARACTERS

The Disney characters were once painfully missing from all of Epcot Center, as their presence was seen as incompatible with the Epcot theme. Now, they are here en force. They can be found wandering Future World, but in a higher concentration in World Showcase, in which they wear costumes representing the nations in which they appear.

The characters can also be found in the Stargate Restaurant between 9 and 10am, and in a show at the Odyssey Restaurant performed four times throughout the day. They can also be found in the American Adventure garden from 12:15 to 3pm. To see the whole gang at once, try Showcase Plaza at 1:05 and 4:55 daily for the Character Carnivale.

COMMEDIA DI BOLOGNA (ITALY)

A troupe of actors invitest the audience to help recreate folk tales in this commedia dell'arte. The fifteen-minute shows are held in the Italy courtyard six or eight times each day.

COURTYARD ENTERTAINMENT (MOROCCO)

The unique sounds of Moroccan music are heard in the courtyard at selected times of the day five days a week.

EPCOT CENTER WORLD DANCERS & WORLD DANCERS BAND

A show highlighting dances from all around the world goes up in front of the footlights of the America Gardens Theater by the Shore four times a day, five days a week.

FANTASY DREAMMAKER (JAPAN)

A man named Nasaji Teresawa performs his 2,400-year-old craft: molding bits of rice toffee into swans, unicorns, and other creatures... blindfolded!

FESTIVAL MARRAKESH (MOROCCO)

Check this out for music and dance in the courtyard.

FUTURE CORPS

A marching band plays contemporary music in the traditional style of a drum and bugle corps.

FUTURE WORLD BRASS

These brass and percussion musicians play a wide variety of songs, including many Disney classics. Performed outside CommuniCore East.

GENROKU HANAMAI (JAPAN)
This ensemble presents classical music and dance outside the pagoda.

I CANTANAPOLI (ITALY)
An Italian quartet fills the courtyard with song.

ILLUMINATIONS
This not to be missed show could easily be the highlight of any Epcot Center visit. This show, presented at closing time nightly, features fireworks, dancing fountains, lasers, fiber optics, and lights, all woven together with classical music. Music from each nation plays as white lights outline the pavilion. Lasers shine high overhead, fireworks explode, and messages trail across the globe in the center of the lagoon.

The experience is unforgettable and serves as the exclamation point to a day at Epcot. There are some superb, often overlooked points from which viewing IllumiNations and other lagoon events is convenient and hassle-free. See sidebar below for viewing tips.

ILLUMINATIONS VIEWING TIPS

The absolute best viewing spots for IllumiNations are at Showcase Plaza, as anyone could tell you. But these spots are often snatched well ahead of time. There are other, more comfortable spots which are often overlooked. These include:

• If you arrive about 45 to 60 minutes beforehand, grab a table on the lakeside terrace of the Cantina de San Angel outside the Mexican pavilion. You can buy a churro and a margarita to tide you over until the show begins.

• There is a small park between the International Gateway and the United Kingdom pavilion, adjacent to the Rose and Crown dining complex. The park has benches, a perfect view, and virtually no crowds.

• The Promenade between China and Germany offers an excellent view.

• The outdoor terrace at the Rose & Crown Pub in the United Kingdom. Again, you can relax with a drink and a snack... and be seated.

• Italy's gondola landing often goes all but unnoticed.

• The boat dock outside of Germany is another good spot.

• If you can, get a lagoon-view table at the Mitsukoshi Dining Rooms and you will be able to see the program in spite of the torii gate at the water's edge.

• The bridge connecting the U.K., France, and the International Gateway hides a small island with an excellent, though slightly obstructed, view of the proceedings.

MARIACHI COBRE (MEXICO)
The traditional sounds of mariachi music is performed on the pavilion steps or inside the pavilion at Plaza de los Amigos.

MARIMBA MAYALANDIA (MEXICO)
Marimba music is performed in the Plaza de los Amigos and the Cantina de San Angel.

NORDAVIND (NORWAY)
Traditional songs of Norway, sung outside the Restaurant Akershus.

OKTOBERFEST MUSIKANTEN (GERMANY)
Inside the Biergarten Restaurant, experience a rollicking fest atmosphere with a dinner show, complete with sing-alongs, yodelers, dancers, and musicians.

OLDE GLOBE PLAYERS (UNITED KINGDOM)
See a troupe of actors present comedy with special guest stars from the audience.

ONE WORLD TAIKO (JAPAN)
This group presents the stacatto rhythms of traditional Japanese music.

RESTAURANT MARRAKESH (MOROCCO)
Belly dancers and musicians perform throughout the day.

SOLID BRASS
A wacky quintet performs classical music all around the Promenade over the course of the day three days a week.

TAPESTRY OF NATIONS
This parade is held twice daily at three different locations around World Showcase Lagoon and features stilt walkers, 18-foot puppets, 30-foot torch towers, fifteen massive rolling drum floats, over 150 costumed performers, and an original score composed by Gavin Greenaway.

TRIO BAL MUSETTE (FRANCE)
A group strolls the courtyard playing songs like "Alouette", "Frere Jacques" and "Sur le Pont d'Avignon" along with some you may not be familiar with.

VALHALLA (NORWAY)
Valhalla features the spirit of Scandinavia and brings it to life with traditional song and dance.

VOICES OF LIBERTY (AMERICAN ADVENTURE)
This is a near-perfect choir whose lovely melodies can be heard inside the rotunda of the pavilion.

YUEN CHEN CHIN (CHINA)
Native Chinese song, dance, magic, and solo flute are all performed under the Great Arch.

SPECIAL GUESTS
Past guest performers at Epcot Center have included "The President's Own" United States Marine Band, ring carvers from Mexico, a Hummel figurine painter and an egg-painter from Germany, a sculptor from Italy, brass artisans and carpet makers from Morocco.

Special guests are listed in the weekly entertainment program.

DINING IN EPCOT

Epcot is home to many of Disney's finest restaurants, mostly those in World Showcase. Reservations are available 120 days in advance, for all full-service restaurants. *Call 407/WDW-DINE.*

In Future World
ELECTRIC UMBRELLA RESTAURANT
Lunch and dinner see this Innoventions East restaurant serving salad, cheeseburgers, and chicken breast sandwiches. The chicken and burgers here are good and come with fries. A topping bar lets diners put lettuce, tomatoes, onions, pickles, bacon bits, barbecue sauce, and hot cheese on their sandwiches, a definite plus. Guests can choose to eat indoors or on a canopied patio outside (L,D,S).

DESSERTS AND THINGS
Beverages, frozen yogurt, cones, and sundaes are offered here, along with hot dogs and nachos outside of Innoventions East. Open seasonally (L,D,S).

PASTA PIAZZA RISTORANTE

The menu at this restaurant, in Innoventions West, includes fried flounder, fried shrimp, fried chicken strips, subs, pizza, pasta, lasagna, salads, and antipasto. At breakfast, omelettes, French toast, and pastries are featured (B,L,D).

FOUNTAIN VIEW EXPRESSO AND BAKERY

Chic as the neon-tinted design of the Innoventions West pavilion in which it is located, this snack bar offers fresh-baked pastries along with espresso, cappucino, and other specialty coffees (B,S).

PURE 'N SIMPLE

The kitchen in the Wonders of Life pavilion features fresh ingredients and no frying. Menu items include Beta-Carotene Salad (spinach, carrots, greens, tomatoes, and broccoli, topped with a cantaloupe vinaigrette,) hot-and-sour soup, the Sub-Fat-Sub (loaded with tuna bologna, lettuce, tomato, and cheese on a sub roll, 95% fat free), venison chili, turkey and vegetable hot dogs, low fat hot dogs, and bran waffles with fruit toppings. Beverages sold include fruit juices, mineral water, frozen nonfat yogurt, yogurt shakes, and smoothies (L,D,S).

ODYSSEY RESTAURANT

The menu at this, the largest eatery in Future World, includes hot dogs, hamburgers, and chicken, tuna, and ambrosia salad platters. There is a topping bar for burgers and sandwiches. The fresh pies baked here are a delicious end to any meal. The restaurant is situated right between the Test Track pavilion and the Mexico pavilion.

The Disney characters can be found here various times throughout the day, check the entertainment schedule for details. (L,D,S).

THE GARDEN GRILL

Location: On the second floor of the Land pavilion. Prices: Moderate. Cuisine: American. Meals: BLD.

Newly renovated, the Garden Grill is a revolving restaurant that overlooks the Living with the Land boat ride, whose greenhouses provide much of the produce served here. Family-style character meals are served at breakfast, lunch, and dinner. The breakfast menu includes standard offerings like eggs, bacon, and breakfast breads, while lunch and dinner offer home grown gardens salads, pork roast, BBQ grilled flank steak, catfish sticks, and a children's menu.

SUNSHINE SEASON FOOD FAIR

This pleasant, newly renovated food court would be a good bet for families who can never agree on where to eat. The only problem is during peak seasons, the seating in the center of the pavilion fills up quickly.

At the Bakery, the breakfast menu includes danish, bagels, cinnamon rolls, and muffins. After breakfast, the fare changes to apple pies, cheesecake, chocolate cake, brownies, cookies, date-nut bread, and cheese bread. At the Beverage House, there are vanilla, chocolate, and strawberry shakes, chocolate milk, hot chocolate, coffee, tea, sodas, buttermilk, vegetable juice, peach nectar, and both alcoholic and non-alcoholic margaritas. The Barbecue Store sells barbecued beef, pork, and chicken breast sandwiches, plus spit-roasted chicken, beans, and cornbread.

The Cheese Shop features quiches, fruit and cheese platters, baked macaroni and cheese, fettucine with chicken, vegetable lasagna, and of course, cheese. The Ice Cream Stand has cups, cones, and shakes. At Picnic Fare, one can nibble on cheeses, sausages, and fresh fruit. At the Potato Store, steaming baked potatoes are served up with bacon and cheddar, beef in wine, or sour cream and chive sauces. The Sandwich Stand has beef and cheese, seafood, club, grilled chicken breast, and meatball sandwiches, along with Disney Handwiches. From the Soup and Salad Stand, you can have fruit salad, chicken salad, pasta salad, and New England clam chowder.

Beer and wine are sold as well, but they are not permitted outside the building. Soda and French fries are sold at most counters as well (B,L,D,S).

CORAL REEF
Location: The Living Seas. Prices: Expensive. Cuisine: Seafood. Meals: L,D.
Here, guests overlook the 5.7 million gallon aquariums of the Living Seas while dining on seafood dishes. The view is impressive and the food is excellent (executive chef Keith Keogh won the Florida Seafood Chef of the Year award twice), but it is mostly overpriced. The menu includes citrus and red snapper, lobster, Manhattan clam chowder, clams, oysters, shrimp, scallops, seafood fettucine, lobster Bisque, tuna, snapper, and grilled swordfish steak. For "landlubbers", there's New York strip steak and broiled chicken breast. The atmosphere is surprisingly ambient, with each table individually lighted by ceiling-mounted spotlights. The decor is oceanic tones and is accented by a six-million-gallon fish tank.

The bottom line on the Coral Reef is this: it's an excellent restaurant, but really overpriced. First of all, you can get the same view for free at the Living Seas ride upstairs. Second, there are other seafood joints in Orlando which are much cheaper and easier to get into, and finally, there are seafood restaurants where you live. Go for something more unusual.

In World Showcase
SAN ANGEL INN RESTAURANTE
Location: Mexico pavilion. Prices: Moderate. Cuisine: Trad Mexican. Meals: L,D.

This is undeniably the most romantic restaurant in Epcot Center, as the dining area overlooks the tranquil Rio del Tiempo where the boats from the attraction sail past a volcano, through a jungle, and onwards. The atmosphere is that of a tranquil Mexican village, with the shops of the plaza making a pleasant backdrop.

As far as the food is concerned, the quality, variety, originality, and value of the menu all score a solid A+. For those of you (much like myself) weaned on tacos, burritos, and nachos from Taco Bell, the menu almost comes as a shock. Those items are offered here alongside exotic regional specialties made of pork, sausage, lobster, chicken, red snapper, beef tenderloins, chicken, and shrimp. Up on your college prep Spanish? The names of the specific offerings include carne asada tempiquena, huachinango a la Veracruzana (red snapper poached with wine, onions, tomatoes, and peppers), mole poblano (it's not mole like the rodent, it's mole like the chocolate sauce, served over chicken), queso fundido (corn or flour tortillas with cheese and sausage with guacamole), and pollo en pipian (chicken strips served with a pumpkin seed sauce).

For dessert, there's flan, rice pudding, crepes or vanilla ice cream with caramel, each a delectable treat. The beverages served include lemon water, soft drinks, margaritas, and Mexican beer (both Tecata and Dos Equis brands). If you only have one restaurant to experience in EPCOT Center, put this towards the top of your list.

CANTINA DE SAN ANGEL
The tables at this counter-service restaurant on the waterfront at the Mexico pavilion offer the single best vantage for IllumiNations, offers nachos, tacos, burritos, chicken tostadas, ensalada, and churros, a sweet, deep-fried, cinnamon-rolled pastry. Dos Equis and Tecate beers are served with margaritas and soft drinks. To snag a table here for IllumiNations, arrive 45 minutes in advance (L,D,S).

RESTAURANT AKERSHUS
Location: Norway pavilion. Prices: Moderate. Cuisine: Norwegian. Meals: L,D.

The restaurant sits inside the castle Akershus, whose namesake sits on the harbor in Oslo. It's an impressive building and surprisingly intimate inside. The hot and cold buffet (known as koldtbord) includes hearty, traditional fare like salmon, herring, lamb, pork, beef, venison, Norwegian cheeses, vegetables, hard-boiled eggs, salads, breads, meatballs, casseroles, and other seafoods. Additional dishes are offered at the dinner buffet. Norwegian desserts, wines, spirits, Ringnes beer are offered a la carte alongside soft drinks. The desserts include ring cake; veiled maidens, a delectable concoction of tart apples, cream, and bread crumbs; and when in season, cloudberries, delicate fruits native to the Norwegian Mountains. Hostesses are available to answer questions about the menu.

KRINGLA BAKERI OG KAFE

This pleasant, open-air restaurant in the Norway pavilion's courtyard sells desserts called kringles, which are pretzels with raisins, almonds, and a sweet icing; sugar-dusted, jam-topped, heart-shaped waffles called vaflers; kranesake, almond-pastries; school bread filled with custard and coated with icing and coconut; and delectable cloudberry horns.

Open-faced sandwiches with salmon, ham, beef, or turkey, called smorbords, are also sold here. Diners can wash them down with cold Ringnes beer (L,D,S).

LOTUS BLOSSOM CAFE

This counter-service, 200-seat Chinese restaurant offers guests a chance to munch egg rolls, stir-fried beef or chicken, sweet and sour chicken, pork fried rice, and soup. Red bean ice cream, Chinese beer, and soft drinks are served as well (L,D,S).

NINE DRAGONS RESTAURANT

Location: China pavilion. Prices: Moderate to expensive. Cuisine: Chinese. Meals: L,D.

This is one of the newer EPCOT restaurants but unfortunately, it chooses to give diners Americanized versions of their dishes instead of an authentic representation like those found in Morocco and Norway. Other Chinese restaurants in Orlando are less expensive. However, the service is attentive, and if you want to eat overpriced Chinese food, this is as good a place as any. The chefs in charge here come from the world-famous Beijing Hotel, and the cuisine is regional: Szechuan, Cantonese, Kiangche, and Mandarin.

The entrees include Canton beef, boneless braised duck, shrimp ambrosia, sweet and sour pork, lemon chicken, Kang Bao chicken, and beef and jade tree. Stir-fried meats, veggies, spare ribs, dumplings, soups, and pickled cabbage are also available. Chinese teas, beers, and wine are served. Finish a meal with red bean ice cream, pastries, or toffee apples.

BIERGARTEN

Location: Germany pavilion. Prices: Moderate to expensive. Cuisine: German. Meals: L,D.

This is considered by many to be EPCOT's premier dining experience, between the tasty and authentic German specialties dished up, the relatively low price, and the Oktoberfest entertainment. The restaurant, located at the rear of the St. Georgsplatz, features a half-hour long dinner show with yodelers, dancers, singers, and an oompah band, all clad in lederhosen.

The show is performed throughout the evening and diners are encouraged to join in the festivities. The menu includes veal shank, sauerbraten, smoked pork loin with red cabbage, grilled bratwurst, spitted chicken, bierwurst, bauernwurst, jaegerwurst, potato salad, winekraut, breaded veal, seafood stew, roast beef loin, and for dessert, German chocolate cake.

Germany is possibly best known for its beer. Here, you can get yourself a 33-ounce stein of Beck's, or if you're in a wining mood, glasses of H. Schmitt Sohne wines. The dining is communal (eight to a table) and friendly, the atmosphere is rowdy and festive, making this an excellent choice for anyone, especially families and singles.

SOMMERFEST

This courtyard stand in the Germany pavilion offers soft pretzels, bratwurst sandwiches apple strudel, Black Forest cake, soft drinks, Beck's beer, and H. Schmitt Sohne wines (L,D,S).

L'ORIGINALE ALFREDO DI ROMA RISTORANTE

Location: Italy pavilion. Prices: Moderate to expensive. Cuisine: Italian. Meals: L,D.

The most popular World Showcase restaurant, Alfredo's is generally considered one of its safest, if not best, bets. The atmosphere is as festive as the Biergarten, with strolling accordionists and waiters and waitresses who burst into Italian traditional, opera, and classical songs. The scenery is beautiful, decorated with murals that give the impression of real scenery instead of the two-dimensional flats on the walls.

The cuisine is traditional and lesser-known Italian, and excellent. The house specialty is terrific fettucine Alfredo, whose creator, Alfredo DiLelio, the establishment is named for. The rest of the menu is more than 20 entrees deep, with seafood, veal, chicken, and pasta dishes, accented by sauces including house tomato, pesto, and carbonara. This is EPCOT Center's most popular ethnic eatery, and sometimes fails to live up to overinflated expectations (brought about by the booking difficulty). But it is still a worthwhile choice, as most families can find menu items they will enjoy, the kids menu is extensive enough to satisfy picky eaters. Italian wines, beers, and spirits are available. For dessert, there's spumoni, gelati, tortoni, and ricotta cheesecake, served alongside steaming cappucino or espresso.

The only fault to be found with Alfredo's is that tables are packed in like sardines and the restaurant is almost always crowded, so dine early or late.

LIBERTY INN

Families with children and others unwilling to try the ethnic cuisines elsewhere gravitate to this restaurant at the American Adventure pavilion to eat good old American fast food. There's hot dogs, hamburgers, chicken breast sandwiches, fried chicken, salads, barbecue beef, roast chicken, baked macaroni and cheese with ham, French fries, and chili. There are also freshly baked cookies, apple pies, and dessert cups (L,D,S).

TEPPANYAKI DINING ROOM

Location: Japan pavilion. Prices: Lunch: Moderate to expensive. Cuisine: Japanese. Meals: L,D.

Sadly, these five rooms offer not a chance to sample authentic cuisine like that in Germany, France, and Mexico, but instead, teppan table cooking like that found at Benihana's. The chefs chop, toss, juggle, sizzle, and stir-fry chunks of steak, chicken, vegetables, and seafood on the tables. If you want teppan cuisine, your money would be better spent elsewhere. If you want to try authentic cuisine representing the nations, your time would be better spent elsewhere.

TEMPURA KIKU

Location: Japan pavilion. Prices: Moderate. Cuisine: Japanese. Meals: L,D.

This corner of the Mitsukoshi dining complex serves up tempura, those tasty, battered-and-deep-fried chunks of beef, chicken, seafood, and vegetables. Sushi and sashimi appetizers are also available, along with Kirin beer, sake, plum wine, and Japanese spirits.

MATSU NO MA LOUNGE

This lounge, located in the Mitsukoshi dining complex on the second story of the Japan pavilion, offers exotic drinks, sushi, tempura, and Kabuki beef or chicken. The lounge provides a sparkling view of World Showcase Lagoon and the nightly IllumiNations display (L,D,S).

YAKITORI HOUSE

This stand in the quaint Japanese courtyard sells skewered chicken and beef, teriyaki and yakitori dishes (sandwiches or beef and chicken with rice), seafood salad, plus sweets and beverages. It's a good place to pick up a bite to eat in between meals or for a quick, no-fuss meal (L,D,S).

WAFFLE/ICE CART

A best bet for a snack. When it's hot, you can get four kinds of ice slush concoction called kaki-gori. When the mercury dips, the shop changes to sell hot waffles with red bean paste (S).

RESTAURANT MARRAKESH

Service: Table-service. Meals: L,D. Cuisine: Moroccan. Location: Morocco pavilion. Prices: Expensive. Reservations: Suggested.

This excellent restaurant provides an exotic taste of Morocco available in few other locations anywhere in the nation. The surroundings are foreign and as zestful as the food. Entertainment is provided by beautiful belly dancers and a live three-piece Moroccan combo or piped-in music.

The food is served up in tasty, heaping portions and the menu includes cous cous, a filling dish of steamed semolina topped with vegetables, chicken, beef, or lamb, harira soup flavored with saffron, braised or roast lamb, chicken or shrimp brochette, shish kebab, baked grouper, and bastila, layers of filo dough filled with chicken, almonds, saffron, and cinnamon. Sampler platters are also available. The children's menu includes chicken and Kefta brochette (skewer-grilled minced beef). Mint tea, Moroccan wine and spirits, and desserts are also available.

Since the piquant Moroccan cuisine is virtually unknown to most people, this restaurant rarely fills up. So you can sometimes get in without a reservation. Also, Marrakesh is roomy, so diners won't get the claustrophobic feeling found in other World Showcase eateries.

LES CHEFS DE FRANCE

Location: France pavilion. Prices: Expensive. Perhaps the most expensive place in WDW. Cuisine: Trad. French. Meals: L,D.

The master chefs here are a renowned trio: Roger Verge, Paul Bocuse, and Gaston LeNotre. Bocuse and Verge each operate three star restaurants, Bocuse's in near Lyon, Verge's on the Riviera, while LeNotre operates six Paris bakeries and is generally acknowledged as one of the world's top pastry chefs. The three collaborated on the menu and often make visits to Chefs de France to make changes to it.

The atmosphere is Victorian-era continental, accented with wood paneling, brass light fixtures, etched glass, linen table cloths, and a dilligent staff dressed in formal wear. The dinner menu is traditional French, starting with the appetizers of foie gras, vichysoisse (chilled potato soup), Lyon-style onion soup, leek soup, salmon souffle with tarragon and white butter sauce, and escargot (snails in garlic butter and hazelnuts). The entrees include grouper in lobster sauce, roast duck with wine sauce and prunes, chicken fricasee, veal, beef tenderloin, seafood stew, beef stew, and the house specialties: roast red snapper wrapped in potato with red wine lobster sauce on a bed of braised cabbage, and beef in red burgundy wine with onions and mushrooms.

The menu is considerably lighter (both in fare and cost) at lunchtime, including cheeses, pates, succulent quiches, croissants stuffed with ham and cheese, seafood casserole, prawns, scallops, sauteed fish, chicken breast, or strip steak, and braised beef.

Save room for the famous LeNotre pastries and a hot mug of cafe filtre, a strong, thick coffee similar to Italian espresso. One of the best bets for dessert is the chocolate cake layered with chocolate mousse. Beer, spirits, and wine from the modest cellar are offered as well. At dinner time, it is imperative that you make reservations days in advance (if you're staying inside WDW) or as soon as the park opens.

BISTRO DE PARIS

Location: France pavilion, second floor. Prices: Expensive. Cuisine: French provincial. Meals: D, lunch seasonally.

Originally designed to handle the overflow from Chefs de France, this restaurant, located upstairs from "Chefs", has come into its own. The menu (also created by Verge, Bocuse, and LeNotre) includes hearty provincial specialties like grilled beef tenderloin with mushrooms, glazed onions, and a green peppercorn sauce, Southern France seafood casserole in garlic sauce and croutons, chicken breast in puff pastry, steamed filet of grouper, braised beef, chicken crepes, grilled lamb, quail, salmon, swordfish, scallops, blue crabs, and sauted duck. The children's menu includes fish sticks, chicken breast casserole, or ground beef steak. There is an unassuming wine list, and beer and spirits are also served.

The only other EPCOT restaurant this romantic is the San Angel Inn in the Mexican pavilion. If you have children, you might want to get a babysitter or one of the kids' clubs to take charge of them for the evening you reserve a table, as it is not very suitable for kids. Note that guests sometimes book this restaurant by mistake, thinking that they were reserving a table at Chefs de France. They lose their reservation when they go to the wrong restaurant. Do that and you'll be told "au revoir". Just remember, les Chefs are downstairs, the bistro is on top.

BOULANGERIE PATISSERIE

This magnificent little shop at the back of the France pavilion sells some of the best pastries known to man. Popular for breakfast, lunch, and dessert, the fare includes quiche, croissants stuffed with ham and cheese or chocolate, a delectable strawberry-topped cheesecake called schuss, and more goodies to wreck any diet. Absolutely not to be missed (B,L,D,S).

ROSE & CROWN DINING ROOM AND PUB

Location: On the promenade, across from the United Kingdom pavilion. Prices: Moderate. Cuisine: British. Meals: L,D,S.

This promenade restaurant, along with the pub of the same name, is a pleasant place to dine. The view of World Showcase Lagoon is unsurpassed, and the food is consistently good. There's Scotch eggs (hardboiled, stuffed in sausage, chilled, and served with mustard), steak and kidney pie, chicken and leek pie, broiled fish, roast beef with gravy and mashed potatoes, fish and chips, a vegetable and cheese plate, prime rib, roast lamb, mixed grill (broiled pork loin, beef tenderloin, and veal kidney), and meat pies (try not to think about the story of Sweeney Todd as you eat).

Afterwards, get on a sugar high with sherry trifle (made of pound cake, whipped cream, custard, strawberries, and sherry) and raspberry fool (raspberry puree and whipped cream.

The pub offers snacks like Stilton cheese, fruit platters, miniature chicken-and-leek or steak-and-kidney pies, and Scotch eggs. A variety of brews from the isles is available, including English Bass Ale, Scottish Tennent's Lager, and Irish Guiness Stout and Harp Lager. Also available are English mixed drinks. The Pub also boasts a magnificently panoramic vista of World Showcase Lagoon and the nightly Illuminations show.

HARRY RAMSDEN'S

This new counter-service eatery on the World Showcase Promenade in the United Kingdom area offers heaping platters of fish and chips along with baked potatoes along with Bass Ale and Guiness (LDS).

GIFT OF CUISINE

Located in the rear of the Millennium Village pavilion, this food court offers international fare at prices conducive to snacking and sampling. The menu includes meat and vegetable sandwiches and black forest roulade at the Europe stand, Thai chicken curry, spring rolls, and rice pudding at the Asia stand, Polynesian pulled pork, shrimp and pineapple salad, and Hawaiian haupia cake at the Pacific rim outlet, lamb kefta, baklava, and a mid-eastern sampler at the Middle East pavilion, peanut crusted chicken, geeme kerrie, and coconut pie in Africa, BBQ beef and nova scotia lox sandwiches, along with apple blossoms at the North America stand, jerk beef and island chicken sandwiches with guava puffs in the Caribbean area, and empanadas, Nicaraguan flank steak, and flan at the Latin America stand. Regional beverages, both alcoholic and non-alcoholic, are also available. (LDS).

LE CELLIER
   Location: Canada pavilion. Prices: Lunch: Budget. Cuisine: Canadian. Meals: L,D,S.

Specialties from Canada make up the menu at this stone-walled cafeteria, which actually does resemble the medieval wine cellars for which it is named. It's a good bet for a quick, hot meal, except when the lunch rush inundates the restaurant, when the restaurant loses speed. Menu items include Canadian cheddar cheese soup, sandwiches, cheese and fruit platters, sauteed poached salmon, prime rib, chicken and meatball stew, huge slabs of delectable Quebec pork-and-potato pie called tourtiere, cold meat and cheese platter, seafood stew over rice, and braised cabbage roll with minced pork.

There is also Labatt's beer, Canadian wine, and soft drinks. The desserts include British trifle and maple syrup pie, great for inflicting a killer sugar rush on yourself. The dinner menu is close to that offered at lunch, but includes a few more items.

13. DISNEY-MGM STUDIOS THEME PARK

In May 1989, the Disney-MGM Studios Theme Park opened to great fanfare and was immensely popular, not only among tourists, but also with the locals. Crowds thronged the place during normally quiet seasons and the park often reached capacity by noon.

As a result, Disney decided to double the size of the park created to commemorate the "Hollywood that never was and always will be," a 1930s Hollywood facade with real production facilities, an animation studio, and a whole array of other attractions.

GETTING TO & AROUND DISNEY-MGM

To get to the Studios from:
• EPCOT Center: Take the bus. Or, take the International Gateway exit, walk to the Beach Club Resort, and catch a motor launch. Be prepared to show the attendant your multi-day passport.
• EPCOT Resorts: Take the motor launch.
• All Other WDW Resort Areas: Take the bus.
• Off-site hotels: Take I-4 to exit 26A and follow the signs.

PARKING

The Studios lot costs $6, free for resort guests who choose to drive (be sure to remember your I.D.) and there is no cost for leaving and returning on the same day. Keep your reciept and write down which section you parked in.

ADMISSION, MONEY, REFURBISHMENT/INTERRUPTION OF ATTRACTIONS, PACKAGE PICKUP, and DRESS CODE. See Chapter 11.

GUEST SERVICES

Inside the main entrance on the left, Guest Services is the park's headquarters for entertainment schedules, lost children, lost and found,

DISNEY-MGM VITAL STATISTICS

Walt Disney World, P.O. Box 10,040, Lake Buena Vista, FL 32830-0040.

On the Internet: *http://www.disneyworld.com/*
Tel.: *407/824-4321.*
Hours: *Vary. Attractions open at 9 AM.*
Admission: *$44 for adults, $35 for kids. See section on Admission Media for full details.*
Parking: *$6.*
Time To See: *Eight hours.*
When to see: *Sundays and Wednesdays are crowded here.*
Don't Miss: *Great Movie Ride, Star Tours, The Magic of Disney Animation, Jim Henson's Muppet*Vision 4D, Backstage Studio Tour, Inside the Magic, Twilight Zone Tower of Terror, and Rock'n'Roller Coaster.*

foreign language maps, information for disabled guests, taped narrations for guests with sight impairments, TDD (telecommunications device for the deaf), assistive listening devices, Disney Dollar exchange, information on private parties, and behind-the-scenes educational and professional programs.

PRODUCTION INFORMATION WINDOW

Just inside the main entrance on the right, this booth offers free tickets to tapings of televsion shows under production. Tickets are disbursed on a first-come, first-served basis, so it would be best to pick up tickets early.

PRACTICAL INFORMATION

Alcoholic Beverages: Allowed, sold at most table-service establishments and a few lounges.

Baby Services: Changing and nursing facilities are located at Main Entrance Guest Services Building. Diapers, food, formula, and other items are available for purchase.

Baby Strollers: Can be rented for $6 a day in Oscar's Super Service inside the Main Entrance.

Banking: There are SunTrust ATMs at the main entrance and by Star Tours.

Cameras: The Darkroom, presented by Kodak, has a full array of cameras for rent, film, videotapes, and two-hour development (see below).

Cigarettes: Not sold in the park.

First Aid: Located outside the Guest Services building.

Foreign Language Assistance: Foreign language maps and assistance are available at Guest Services.

Hearing-impaired Guests: A Telecommunications Device for the Deaf (TDD) is available at Guest Services.

Information: To get facts about attractions, shows, and dining, visit the Guest Information Board at the end of Hollywood Boulevard at Sunset Plaza. For an entertainment schedule, visit Guest Services or most shops.

Kennel: Pets are not allowed in WDW Resorts or attractions. There is, however, an air-conditioned kennel outside the left side of the Entrance Plaza. Reservations are not needed.

Lockers: Available for 25¢ or 50¢, these are located next to Oscar's Super Service on the right side of the Entrance Plaza.

Lost Children: Report to Guest Services or call *407/560-4654*.

Reservations: Accepted at four restaurants in the park. May be made at the door or, for WDW resort and Hotel Plaza guests, up to thirty days in advance by calling *407/WDW-DINE*.

Smoking, eating, and drinking: Not allowed in any attractions.

Visually-impaired guests: Complimentary tape cassettes and portable tape recorders are available at Guest Services. A deposit is required, though.

Wheelchair guests: Wheelchair rentals are available in limited quantities at Oscar's Super Service. Disabled Guests Guidebooks are available at Guest Services.

ATTRACTIONS

ROCK 'N' ROLLER COASTER STARRING AEROSMITH

Rating: 8 1/2. Disney's best roller coaster. Location: Past the Tower of Terror. Duration of Ride: 2 minutes. Best Time to Go: As early as possible. You must be 48" high to ride.

Disney's first roller coaster venturing out of the realm of the tame, the Rock and Roller Coaster is one of the best things that Disney has done in years. That being said, it's still not all that much of a thrill for coaster junkies, especially those who've already experienced Islands of Adventure's Hulk Coaster.

The pre-show winds through G-Force Records' offices, with displays showing the history of recorded music, from wax canisters to minidiscs. You then arrive at Aerosmith's Los Angeles studio where they are finishing up recording. They're about to head out to a concert, and guess what, you're invited. Their manager balks. Aerosmith insists. How kind of them. Next thing you know, you're boarding a long roller coaster train in the shape of a super-stretch limousine. You move around the boarding area, which resembles an underground garage, and wait at a red light. You can hear the engine running until the light turns green. Tires squeal and you're off, flying from 0 to 60 in 2.8 seconds and 5 G's with "Sweet Emotion" or one of four other Aerosmith tunes blaring from 120 onboard speakers. The coaster features two rollover loops and a corkscrew as well as black light décor recalling California landmarks such as the Hollywood Hills, masterfully carrying the theme throughout the entire attraction. The only downside to the attraction is its length – it's just under two minutes from beginning to end, and unlike the Hulk Coaster, which isn't all that much longer, this ride *feels* short.

Note that Fastpass is in use at this attraction.

TWILIGHT ZONE TOWER OF TERROR
Rating: 9. Mind-blowing. NOT TO BE MISSED! Location: A landmark visible for miles around, it is located at the end of Sunset Blvd. Duration of Ride: 8 minutes, including pre-show. Best Time to Go: As soon as the park opens. Comments: Expectant mothers, those with back, neck, or heart conditions, and those prone to motion sickness are advised against riding. Children under 3 can't ride, children under 7 can not ride without a parent. Frightening: Even if you know what's coming, you'll find yourself screaming when it happens.

"Tonight's story on 'The Twilight Zone' is somewhat unique and calls for a different type of introduction," Rod Serling tells you. So begins Disney's newest, most amazing, frightening, wild attraction, the Tower of Terror.

The storyline is promising. In an 88-second pre-show, Rod Serling and a sound-alike (Serling died in 1975 – his introduction was taken from a 1961 episode) explain to you that in 1939, a Hollywood couple, a bellboy, a child actress, and her governess boarded the elevator in the Hollywood Tower Hotel and as the elevator rose, it was struck by a bolt of lightning. The elevator vanished and its occupants with it. As the protagonist in "tonight's Twilight Zone," you must venture up to the top of the hotel in service elevators to find out what exactly happened on that stormy night.

Unfortunately, the ride does not follow through on the storyline as much as it could, glossing over the disappearance. There is one stop in a corridor in which spectral images of the missing passengers gesture to you and then disappear into the starry night, followed by the entire corridor. It's amazing. The next stop is the "fifth dimension." where holographic projections, lights, mirrors, and other effects simulate "The Twilight Zone."

Your elevator door closes. When it opens again, you see a wall for just a split second. Brace yourself. You're about to eat it. Your elevator drops, and miraculously catches... and you're propelled – I mean FAST – to the 13th floor, with a vantage of the whole park. Enjoy it while it lasts – you'll soon be dropped like a one night stand, destination, the ground. Or is it? Your elevator will once again rise to the 13th floor and drop again. Honestly, I lost count of how many times I was sent earthbound. Eventually, I did land, and so will you. Adrenalized, dazed, and staggering back into line to ride again – or even better, to the Fastpass distribution center, which will allow you to reserve your time on this ride and then go elsewhere to play.

Especially notable is the Disney attention to detail, which totally outdoes itself here. Everything from the angle of the hotel to the scorchmarks where the missing wing was to the dust in the lobby to the darkened boiler room where you board the service elevators, to the sardonic tone of the Serling sound-alike's warning about haunted hotels after the drop makes this by far the scariest place in Florida.

There is quite a bit of memorable stuff about this attraction, from the special effects in the tower to the seamlessly-produced video (directed by Joe Dante, who directed the 1983 Twilight Zone motion picture), but what you will remember is the drop.

Oh, and you may want to take the stairs back to your hotel room.

THE GREAT MOVIE RIDE
Rating: 9 1/2. Not to be missed. Location: At the Chinese Theater at the end of Hollywood Boulevard. Duration of Ride: 19 minutes. Best Time To Go: Before 10 AM or after 5 PM. Frightening: Some segments are visually intense.

As you enter a full-scale replica of Grauman's Chinese Theater, you wend your way past props from classic films, like the ruby slippers from the Wizard of Oz. As you near the trams, you watch trailers from classic MGM films on a huge screen. Finally, you reach the boarding area, behind it, a painted backdrop with spotlights and a sign reading "Hollywoodland" underneath a sunset. You get into cars piloted by real live men and women and head off past the corner of Hollywood and Vine and under a marquee promising "A spectacular journey into the movies! A cast of thousands! A sweeping spectacle of thrills! Chills! Romance!"

Musicals are the first genre of movie explored, as sixty of Disney's less sophisticated Audio-Animatronics women dance atop a revolving cake (from the Busby Berkeley musical *Footlight Parade*). Then, you go to a rainy night where Gene Kelly croons "Singin' in the Rain." Kelly inspected his Audio-Animatronic likeness before it was shipped to Florida. Then to a Disney flick, *Mary Poppins*, where Julie Andrews floats, singing "Chim Chim Cher-ee" while Dick Van Dyke dances on a rooftop.

Ya then progress to a back alley where a coupla gangsters ("business-men, please") prepare for an ambush but then decide "Nah, they're just a bunch of rubberneckin' tourists." But a shootout occurs and you are forced to detour into the Wild West. There, John Wayne sits on a horse, brandishing a rifle while he talks to the audience. A little later, a bank heist goes down and the robber's Audio-Animatronic accomplice fires at the crowd. The bank blows up, and the flames can be felt as you ride by. Overhead, hay begins to smolder.

Now, there are two different things that happen in the gangster/western scene. In the bank heist or the shootout, your driver-emcee-actor stops the car and goes in to investigate. But then, a robber or gangster runs out, brandishing a tommygun or a rifle and commandeers the vehicle. She/he leaves the driver and takes off with you as hostages. You then head into the spaceship Nostromo (of *Alien* fame), where Sigourney Weaver's Ripley stands with weapon in hand, sweating and leaning against the wall of a corridor, then... gross, what is that? It's one of the title creatures, dripping with pus and lunging at you from the side. Another one swings at you overhead.

You pass under and reach Harrison Ford and John Rhys-Davies lifting up the ark from *Raiders of the Lost Ark*. Snakes! Why do they have to be snakes? You will then reach an Egyptian scene with a huge gem on an idol. Greed gets the better of your "host" and the criminal runs up to grab the gem, not hearing a belated warning about a curse. The crook reaches the gem, grabs it and smoke begins to envelop him/her. The smoke clears and the crook is gone. A monk throws off his robe, revealing your original driver, yelling a cheery "Remember me?"

Tarzan swings on a vine, Cheetah and Jane sit below, a reassuring sign. You leave the jungle but you're not out of the jungle yet. Where are you? Casablanca. The plane's engine sputters, the propellors whirl, and Rick bids Ilsa farewell. Then, it's off to a happy place. You hear Munchkins sing "Ding dong, the witch is dead," and the subject of the song's sister pops out of a puff of smoke, threatening your driver. You leave the frightened Munchkins and follow the yellow brick road ("Why didn't I think of that?" the driver says after asking the Munchkins for directions), where you see Dorothy, Toto, the Tin Man, Scarecrow, and Cowardly Lion gaping at the Emerald City.

The finale of the ride is an impressive montage of 90 Academy Award-winning films squeezed into three minutes. This tribute was created by Oscar-winner Chuck Workman. As you exit, the driver yells after you to remember them "when Oscar time comes around!"

Not to be missed. Ride this in the first hour after opening or in the evening if you wish to avoid crowds. If the line extends outside the theater, you will have a twenty-five minute wait or more.

BEAUTY AND THE BEAST

Rating: 7 1/2. The inspiration for the Broadway musical. Location: At the Theater of the Stars, on Sunset. Duration of Show: About 25 minutes. Best Time To Go: Anytime.

This new live show relives the romance between Belle and the Beast, along with the rest of the characters from the movie, Lumiere, Chip, Mrs. Potts, and the rest. The music from the film is featured.

DOUG LIVE!

Rating: 6. As charming as the TV show on which it is based. Location: In the old Superstar Television building at lakeside. Duration of show: 30 minutes. Best Time to Go: Anytime.

Bluffington comes to life in this live action show featuring the characters from Disney's Doug, an animated miniseries and motion picture. It's a multimedia presentation combining live actors, animated scenes, and music. The storyline follows 12 1/2 year old Doug Funnie and his sidekicks, Skeeter, Patti Mayonnaise, and Porkchop, plus adversary Roger Klotz. Doug has won tickets to the Beets' farewell concert, and wants to ask Patti, who's going with Roger. The show follows Doug's attempts to win Patti's heart, and is a charming attraction that will amuse and entertain children of ALL ages.

SOUNDS DANGEROUS

Rating: 6 1/2. Entertaining but not on the same level as its predecessor, Monster Sound. Location: At lakeside, in the old Monster Sound venue. Duration of show: 12 minutes. Best Time to Go: Mid to late afternoon.

Replacing Monster Sound, this attraction stars Drew Carey as a police officer who wears a hidden camera and attempts to bust a jewel smuggling ring. All of it is captured on a hidden camera for a show called Undercover Live – at least until Drew breaks the camera, and all that's left is the sound. You're in a darkened auditorium, listening to headphones. That's still quite a bit, as binaural technology allows guests to spatially place the sounds. Often funny, this is a worthy if not equal successor to Monster Sound. Note that most of it takes place in total darkness.

INDIANA JONES EPIC STUNT SPECTACULAR!

Rating: 7 1/2. Spectacular action sequences, but dry narrative. Location: Lakeside Circle, by the dinosaur. Duration of Show: 22 minutes. Best Time To Go: After 10 AM. Frightening: Visually intense at points.

This show demonstrates how fights, explosions, and other movie magic are safely performed. The show opens with a Harrison Ford lookalike in the scene from Raiders of the Lost Ark where Indy gently replaces a golden idol with a bag of sand, then is chased down an incline by a huge, 12-foot high stone ball and is seemingly run over. But no, the director yells "cut" and the stuntman pops up. The production crew explains how movie stunts are done and then proceeds to make a fiery demonstration thereof. The two other scenes are the Cairo marketplace where Indy is ambushed by sword-wielding acrobats, and then to a scene with an attempted escape with a Nazi plane, the runaway truck, and the explosive finale. There are machine gun battles and a climax of unbelievable magnitude.

In case you were wondering, everything is real. You will realize that after the first explosion when heat hits your face. The stuntmen have been hurt on more than one occasion, but the production usually goes off without a hitch. The one and only flaw of this production is the slow pace of the narration between the action sequences. A retooled script could breathe new life into the show.

At the beginning of the show, ten extras are selected from the audience to perform in the show, but don't worry, there is absolutely no danger for nine of the extras. The tenth is used to demonstrate how to "take a punch." But don't worry, this one's a plant. You'll know which one he is because of the comments about his wardrobe. Look on your entertainment schedule or on the board outside the attraction for showtimes, plan on arriving 30 minutes beforehand and you will have little or no wait. If before the house is opened, the line extends to the dinosaur at the shore, you probably will not be seated in the next show.

STAR TOURS

Rating: 10. Absolutely spectacular! Not to be missed. Location: Next to New York Street. Duration of Ride: 7 minutes. Best Time To Go: Soon after the park opens. Comments: Expectant mothers, those with back, neck, or heart conditions and those prone to motion sickness are advised against riding. Children under 3 can't ride, children under 7 can not ride without a parent. Frightening: Visually and physically intense.

A model Ewok village and an Imperial Walker tower over front of Disney's most breathtaking work, a sensational flight simulator adventure called Star Tours. The ride is based on the Star Wars trilogy and was created by Disney and George Lucas. As you enter the queueing area, you pass dozens of Audio-Animatronics droids, including C3P0 and R2D2, who now work for an intergalactic travel agency. The displays on either side of the queue are fascinating and make long waits in line somewhat bearable. Threepio, Artoo, and the other robots converse while they, among other things, prepare the Starspeeders for takeoff.

You enter the Starspeeder and buckle up. Then, you meet your pilot, a rookie robot played by Pee-Wee Herman. Your trip gets off to a bumpy start almost immediately as you make a wrong turn and almost smash the ship before you even take off. But you eventually get your bearing and fly straight to the Moon of Endor. But unfortunately, you wind up taking a detour through an asteroid field and into a comet. As you smash through the wall of the comet, you are out in open space, just you, the pilot, and an Imperial TIE fighter! The tie fighter fires on you and you somehow wind up in the tractor beam of the Death Star. But a Rebel pilot steers you out of the tractor beam and leads you on an attack on the Death Star. After one more near miss, your Starspeeder docks and you get off saying with a huge grin on your face, "Let's do it again!" as you exchange high-fives.

This is one of the most popular rides in the Disney-MGM Studios and is crowded from the second the park opens. If you are not at the gate by 9:15, expect a sizable wait. If you only had one ride to experience in Walt Disney World, this is it. Not to be missed.

JIM HENSON'S MUPPET*VISION 3D
Rating: 10. Hilarious, not to be missed. Location: In the New York area. Look for the balloon overhead. Duration of Show: 17 minutes. Best Time To Go: In the morning or after 3 PM.

This wild insanity of an attraction goes WAY beyond 3D, as the film is supplemented by the presence of Audio-Animatronic figures, live characters, and dazzling, live special effects like bubbles raining down on the audience or a gentle spray of water when Fozzie Bear shoots water from a corsage, plus a theater that actually changes as the show goes on. The plot of the story is thin, but done in spectacular fashion.

After an explanation of the technology behind Muppet*Vision from Dr. Honeydew (with the perpetual abuse of his assistant, Beaker), the Muppets attempt to mount a musical production, but run into the usual Muppet mishaps, prompting Bean Bunny to run away with Waldo, the computer-generated "spirit of 3D." The Muppets roam the theater looking for them. Bean pops up in the upper balcony and there is a happy, albeit destructive ending at the hands of the Swedish Chef, who happens to be working the projector as well as a cannon.

At the beginning of the film, Kermit assures the audience that at no time will they "be resorting to cheap 3D tricks." The words barely get out of his mouth. At the end of the show, the two famous critics, Waldorf and Stadler, who are sitting in one of the balconies, ask if they should get up and go to the bathroom before the next show. The answer: "We can't! We're bolted to the seats!"

The pre-show is equally amusing, held in a warehouse filled with crates to be delivered to the Muppets. The Muppets cavort about three television screens overhead, preparing for the show. Disney prepared for the large crowds who frequent the theater by making it large enough to accommodate them. The only time when you may experience a wait of more than twenty minutes is immediately after the nearby Indiana Jones Epic Stunt Spectacular! discharges an audience.

HONEY, I SHRUNK THE KIDS MOVIE SET ADVENTURE

Rating: 6 1/2. Original, great for young kids. Location: Next to New York Street. Best Time To Go: Before 10:30 AM or after dusk.

This is a playground based on the motion picture Honey, I Shrunk the Kids. There are 20-foot tall blades of grass, rolls of film to play in, huge bugs, enormous Legos, and a garden hose that drips on unsuspecting passers-by. It's fun, but nonessential, and worth skipping if there are no children in your party.

VOYAGE OF THE LITTLE MERMAID

Rating: 7. Dazzling special effects help capture the feel of the movie. Location: Just inside the Studio Arch. Duration of Show: About 15 minutes. Best Time To Go: Anytime.

This show features songs from the movie, puppets, live actors, and Audio-Animatronic characters, including a 12-foot high Ursula singing "Poor Unfortunate Soul." Ariel and Sebastian sing other songs from the movie. Special effects are also featured, like wind, rain, bubbles, and a black-light scene.

THE AMERICAN FILM INSTITUTE SHOWCASE

Rating: 6. Informative, nostalgic. Location: The New York Street area. Best Time to Go: Anytime.

On permanent display are set pieces, costumes, and props worn, handled, and used by today's biggest stars in today's biggest movies.

BACKLOT TOUR

Rating: 9. Informative, fast-paced, not to be missed. Location: Inside the Studio Arch. Duration of Tour: 30 minutes. Best Time To Go: Anytime. Frightening: The Catastrophe Canyon sequence is somewhat intense.

You board a shuttle and venture inside the production of movies. After passing the Bungalows, where production facilities for several projects, including the New Mickey Mouse Club, are contained, you reach your first destination: Costuming, where skilled designers create the clothes worn by the stars. The costumes on display include those worn by Bob Hoskins in "Who Framed Roger Rabbit?," Julia Roberts in "Pretty Woman," Warren Beatty and Madonna in "Dick Tracy", and Michael Jackson in "Captain EO." Next to Costuming is the Scenic Shop, where sets needed for the various productions are designed and constructed.

Then, the tram passes the topiary, camera, prop, and lighting department, where the pieces are stored until needed. You then ride past famous homes, including those of the Golden Girls and Vern from the film "Ernest Saves Christmas", and other houses with a real "lived-in" look. But as you turn around and view the "homes" from behind, you realize that they can't be lived in, they're only facades. As soon as you're out of camera view, the house's exterior vanishes. You pass the Boneyard, where vehicles used in films like the ship from "Flight of the Navigator" and the trolley from "Who Framed Roger Rabbit?" are stored.

Then, it's off to Catastrophe Canyon. The guide warns you at the beginning of the tour, "Those of you on the right side of the cars are going to get a little wet, those of you on the left are going to get soaked." This is the place he meant. You enter an oil drilling operation, only to be hit by rain, earthquakes, fires, explosions, and flash floods (sounds like California!) and then suddenly, it's over, just as quickly as it began. You've survived. As you pass around behind Catastrophe Canyon, you see the inner workings of it. Impressive.

Your last port of call is New York Street, where a technique called forced perspective turn two blocks of two-dimensional "buildings" into a cityscape. You depart the trams here. You may continue with the second part of the tour, Inside the Magic, eat, drink, shop, go to the bathroom, or just save the second half for later. Check the Entertainment Schedule so you won't miss the last departure.

BACKSTAGE PASS

Rating: 9. Not to be missed. Location: By New York Street. Duration of Tour: 60 minutes. Best Time To Go: Anytime.

The second segment of the tour, this part done on foot, begins at the Water Effects Tank, where blue screens, simulated strafing attacks and depth charges, explosions, and other effects combine to turn one person from the audience into a certain Captain Duck and star in a short film. You then enter the prop room, where props on display include the chessboard from Star Wars, the gold-plated Johnny Five from Short Circuit 2, and a few of the characters from Captain EO.

Then it's into the Special Effects Workshop and Shooting Stage, where technicians and children from the audience combine to show how models, blue screens, and editing create a scene. The demonstration recreates the scene from Honey, I Shrunk the Kids where two kids fly on a giant bee. The three Soundstages, on which filming may be done at any time, are the next stop. You overlook from a sound-proof chamber high above, so filming can continue uninterrupted. Note that no photography or videotaping is allowed in the soundstages (for legal reasons).

In the Audio department, technicians complete the job after the photography is complete. Then, at Post-Production, C3PO, R2D2, and George Lucas explain what happens in editing. The final stop is the Walt

Disney Theater, where a behind-the-scenes 14-minute featurette on the making of Alan Parker's "Evita," starring Madonna and Antonio Banderas.

THE MAGIC OF DISNEY ANIMATION
Rating: 10. Whimsical, fun, not to be missed. Location: Next to the Backstage Studio Tour. Duration of Tour: 36 minutes. Best Time To Go: Before 11 AM or after 5 PM.

This is a self-guided, walking tour that begins in the pre-show area, where 13 of the Oscars won by the Disney animators and cels from classic films are all on display. You enter a theater for "Back to Neverland," an uproarious film starring Robin Williams and Walter Cronkite, an unlikely pair if ever there was one. Williams becomes a cartoon character, one of the Lost Boys from Peter Pan, and plays it to the limits. At one point, he turns himself into a variety of objects, including Mickey Mouse ("I can even be a corporate symbol!"), and gets stern admonitions from Cronkite throughout. By the way, this 8-minute film was difficult to complete because Cronkite kept on cracking up.

Then, you follow Williams and Cronkite through the Animation Department for a step by step explanation of the animation process. Animators are at work here from 9 AM until 5 or 6 PM, so try to visit between these hours. The various chapters in the story are displayed on overhead monitors. You can linger as long as you like in this part of the tour to watch the animators at work. The tour finishes up at the Disney Classics Theater, where a montage of clips from animated films from Snow White to Beauty and the Beast are shown. After that, you are released into the Animation Gallery, where limited-edition cells, lithographs, and animation art can be purchased.

BEAR IN THE BIG BLUE HOUSE – LIVE ON STAGE
Rating: 6. Delightful for the littl'uns. Location: Animation Courtyard. Duration of Show: 15 minutes. When to Go: Anytime.

This live performance features characters from the Disney Channel show of the same name and is very well suited for younger children. Bear, Ojo, Tutter, Treelo, Pop, and Luna are all in attendance here and regale your children with songs from the television show.

SHOPPING
OSCAR'S CLASSIC CAR SOUVENIRS
A "gas station" selling automotive memorabilia like key chains, models, and mugs. The 1947 Buick is authentic (and not for sale), and the gas tanks bear the name Mohave Oil Co., the same moniker found at Catastrophe Canyon. Lockers, wheelchair and stroller rental, infant

products, and postage stamps are available at Oscar's Super Service, adjacent to the shop.

MEMORABILIA

A kiosk on the left side of the Entrance Plaza selling souvenirs like toys, hats, books, key chains, sunglasses, film, and sundry items.

SID CAHUENGA'S ONE OF A KIND

Sid and his wife Rose have a house filled with antiques and curios. Autographed photos, movie posters, and movie magazines, and other collectibles are sold here.

CROSSROADS OF THE WORLD

Mickey stands watch on top of his kiosk, right in the middle of Hollywood Boulevard, sells sundries, film, sunglasses, and raingear. Information is also available here.

THE DARKROOM

Film, videotapes, and cameras for sale; cameras and camcorders available for rent. Two-hour photo processing is available.

COVER STORY

Here, you can get your mug on the front cover of magazines like Sports Illustrated, Time, Life, Cosmopolitan, and more. Costumes and accessories are provided.

TOY STORY PIZZA PLANET ARCADE

It seems a little out of place, but there's a Toy Story-themed gameroom arcade and pizzeria across from Muppet*Vision 3D.

THE STUDIO STORE

Located near Voyage of the Little Mermaid, this store sells memorabilia and gift items inspired by new and classic Studio releases.

IT'S A WONDERFUL SHOP

It's a Christmas store, in the snow-dabbled New York area. It's a take-off of It's a Wonderful Life... get it?

SUNSET BOULEVARD SHOPS

On Sunset Blvd., this is the place for unique gifts including custom watches, menswear, housewares, and collectibles.

TOWER HOTEL GIFTS

At the exit of the Twilight Zone Tower of Terror, this is the place to purchase Twilight Zone and Tower of Terror memorabilia as well as photos of your elevator at the beginning of the drop.

STAGE 1 COMPANY STORE

This shop features Muppet and Sesame Street gifts, toys, and apparel in the New York area.

ONCE UPON A TIME

Timeless vintage Disney Character merchandise.

LEGENDS OF HOLLYWOOD

Books, videos, and posters of legendary films. On Sunset Boulevard.

CELEBRITY 5 & 10

This replicated five-and-dime Hollywood-themed ready-to-wear, magnets, jackets, teddy bears, and movie-themed items, including a director's clapboard.

SWEET SUCCESS

"Starry-eyed hopefuls come here for a special taste of Sweet Success," the Studio Guidebook says of this specialty candy shop. Plush M & M toys are also sold here.

L.A. CINEMA STORAGE

Guests can star in a video screen test here, as well as shop for Disney clothing, accessories, and movie/show memorabilia.

MICKEY'S OF HOLLYWOOD

This is the best place in the Studios to get Disney character merchandise, and Disney and Studio ready-to-wear, books, wallets, tote bags, and watches.

LAKESIDE NEWS

Comic books, movie magazines, and souvenirs are offered.

KEYSTONE CLOTHIERS

Disney jackets, jewelry, and fashions, all with a Hollywood twist, are sold here.

GOLDEN AGE SOUVENIRS

This shop, located alongside Echo Lake, sells radio and television program gifts plus Disney Channel memorabilia.

ENDOR VENDORS

Endor Vendors gets the nod as my personal favorite shop in the Studios. Anyone who enjoyed the Star Wars movies, Timothy Zahn's new trilogy, or just the Star Tours attraction that discharges passengers here will enjoy browsing this shop.

Books, models, toys, games, gifts, and clothing are sold here, many of which bear the Star Wars or Star Tours logos. Be sure to notice Darth Vader's ominous body in the wall between Star Tours and here.

ANIMATION GALLERY

At the end of the Magic of Disney Animation attraction, this shop sells original Disney animation cels, exclusive limited edition reproductions, books, and figurines, including an exclusive commemorative cell.

THE WRITERS' SHOP

Featuring books, gifts, snacks, and celebrity book signings.

FOTOTOONS

Here, you have an opportunity to pose in photographs with famous cartoon characters. Finished Fototoons can be picked up here, or after closing, at Cover Story.

THE COSTUME SHOP

This unique boutique is where you can pick up gifts celebrating the great villains from Disney animated classics, from Snow White's Wicked Witch to Aladdin's Jafar.

STAGE ONE COMPANY STORE

Items sold here include gifts, gadgets, and mementos highlighting everything from Mickey Mouse to Miss Piggy.

INDIANA JONES ADVENTURE OUTPOST

Alongside the amphitheater that houses the Epic Stunt Spectacular!, this shop sells "adventure gear" and "artifacts" with the Indiana Jones logo.

ROCK AROUND THE SHOP

At the exit to the Rock and Roller Coaster, this shop features studio and ride memorabilia plus Aerosmith music, videos, attire and gifts.

ENTERTAINMENT IN THE DISNEY-MGM STUDIOS

There's some great entertainment in the Disney-MGM Studios complex. Below you'll find a brief list of the possibilities:

MULAN PARADE

Disney pays tribute to their latest animated flick every day at 3:30pm, as this parade, featuring live actors and dancers as well as animatronics and floats, winds its way down Hollywood Boulevard. Disney tends to replace this parade every time they release a new animated film, so by the time you read this Mulan may already be history. Thank goodness they only throw parades for their animated films, I think that a Flubber parade would probably be a bit hard to handle.

CHARACTERS

Disney characters can be found on Mickey Avenue and at the Chinese Theatre. Mickey himself hangs out in the animation courtyard. The Toy Story characters hang out on Mickey Avenue across from the entrance to the Backlot Tour.

FILMING

Crews may be producing shows at any given time, many of which welcome a studio audience. If you are interested in being in the house for one of these or want information on filming currently going on, visit the Production Information Window or Guest Services, both at the main entrance.

The Studios' resume includes, for television: Adventures in Wonderland, Body by Jake, Wheel of Fortune, and You Asked For It; for theaters: Beauty and the Beast, Honey, I Blew Up the Baby, and Flipper: The Movie.

FANTASMIC!

This show, imported from Anaheim, bring to life some of the most memorable villains from "Fantasia," "Aladdin," "Pocahontas," and many more with fireworks, music, water screens, and larger-than-life characters. Note that you need to arrive at the theatre, tucked away behind the Tower of Terror, at least 45 to an hour minutes in advance to guarantee a good seat for the 25-minute show. If there are two shows in a night (during peak seasons), see the second. It'll be much less crowded. Seating begins up to two hours before showtime, and yes, people are lined up when the doors open. The theatre contains two snack bars and restroom facilities, and there's vendors selling refreshments and toys.

STREET SHOWS

On Hollywood Boulevard, the Screen Extras Band, Tubafours Quartet, and Streetmosphere characters entertain daily. In the Studio Courtyard, the Disney characters are on hand daily, while the Toon Town Trio plays five days a week. On the Backlot, a piano player plunks the ivories on weekdays and Ace Ventura and the Hollywood Hitmen Band perform daily.

DINING AT DISNEY-MGM STUDIOS

You can make reservations in person or up to 30 days in advance by calling *407/WDW-DINE.*

THE HOLLYWOOD BROWN DERBY

Location: At the end of Hollywood Boulevard. Prices: Moderate to expensive. Cuisine: American. Meals: L,D.

1930s Hollywood is represented here, as the spirit of the original Vine Street establishment has been transplanted to Florida. The Studios' signature restaurant is one of Disney's best reproductions. There's the Wall of Fame, covered with caricatures faithfully remade from the originals. Louella Parsons and Hedda Hopper even hang out here, or at least actresses representing them. The atmosphere is such that you are tempted to just scan the restaurant from stars.

The fare is American, including the house specialty, the Cobb salad, named for the original restaurant's owner, Bob Cobb. The salad is comprised of chopped salad greens, tomato, bacon, turkey, egg, avocado, and blue cheese. Shrimp and lobster varieties of the salad are also available. Other menu items include rotisserie chicken, filet of red snapper, baked grouper, sauteed veal, mixed grill, sandwiches, gumbo, corned beef and cabbage, stuffed chicken breast, roast chicken, filet mignon, strip steak, and Fettucine Derby with chicken, Parmesan cheese sauce, and red and green peppers.

STARRING ROLLS BAKERY

This bake shop, adjacent to the Hollywood Brown Derby, offers great breakfasts and pastries. Starting at 8:30 AM, there are Danishes, rolls, croissants, fruit tarts, and bear claws. After breakfast, there are sinfully delicious cookies, cakes, and pies. Coffee, tea, and assorted soft drinks are also sold. Since this spot opens half an hour before the rest of the park, it's a good pick for a quick, easy breakfast (B,S).

50'S PRIME TIME CAFE

Location: South of Echo Lake, on Vine Street. Prices: Moderate. Cuisine: American. Meals: L,D.

This restaurant, my pick as the best one in the Studios, dishes up nostalgia in heaping platefuls along with good, homey dishes. The atmosphere is enhanced by Fiesta Ware plates, and TV trays straight from a 50's sitcom kitchen. Televisions show clips from classics like Leave It to Beaver. The waitresses insist on being called "Mom," they check for dirty fingernails before dinner, and then announce to the fellow diners when one of the "kids" clears a plate.

The menu consists of tasty offerings that June Cleaver might have served her families. There's meat loaf with mashed potatoes, broiled chicken, gigantic sandwiches, chicken pot pies, Swiss steak, burgers, shrimp, beef tenderloin, grilled salmon, and salads.

The entrees are accompanied by ice cream sodas, root beer floats, milkshakes, beer, wine, and spirits. Afterwards, you can try strawberry-rhubarb pie, S'mores, sundaes, and more.

TUNE IN LOUNGE

Located alongside the 50s Prime Time Cafe, this whimsical lounge features fiercely personal nostalgia, with the furniture and decor of Beaver Cleaver's childhood living room. Appetizers and drinks are served (S).

MAMA MELROSE'S RISTORANTE ITALIANO

Location: In the New York area, by the Studio Showcase. Prices: Lunch: Moderate. Cuisine: Italian/Regional American. Meals: L,D.

This new restaurant is described as "where Italy meets California in the heart of the Backlot". That's pretty accurate. The menu includes brick oven pizza with a variety of toppings (including lobster!), chicken marsala, seafood pasta, lasagna, chicken, veal, and steak dishes.

SCI-FI DINE-IN THEATER RESTAURANT

Location: Behind the Monster Sound building. Prices: Moderate. Cuisine: American. Meals: L,D.

A soundstage between Monster Sound and New York Street now houses a drive-in where it is always nighttime. Diners enter through the ticket lobby and sit in classic automobiles and watch a 45-minute montage of clips and trailers from movies like Attack of the 50-Foot Woman,

Invasion of the Saucer People, and other classic "B" science fiction and horror films. The atmosphere is enhanced by waitresses dressed like carhops.

As for the menu, it's secondary to the entertainment. It includes funky-sounding dishes like the "Monster Mash", a turkey Sloppy Joe; "Revenge of the Killer Club Sandwich", with smoked turkey, roast beef, turkey ham, Swiss cheese, and all the trimmings, served on seven-grain bread; "Tossed in Space", a chef's salad; "They Grow Among Us", a fruit platter; "The Red Planet", vegetables with linguine; "Meteoric Meatloaf", made of smoked meat; "20,000 Leafs under the Sea", a salad of greens, marinated vegetables, fruits, scallops, shrimp, and roast garlic dressing.

Desserts include the "Cheesecake That Ate New York", a banana split called "Twin Terrors", "When Berries Collide", a strawberry shortcake, and "Science Gone Mad", comprised of fruit cobblers. Beer, wine, and soft drinks are also served.

HOLLYWOOD & VINE
Location: Next to the 50's Prime Time Cafe. Prices: breakfast is budget. Cuisine: American. Meals: B,L,D.

This is the Crystal Palace of the Studios, with good, unpretentious American dishes served up in a cafeteria setting. The atmosphere inside includes 8-foot murals depicting Hollywood landmarks like the original Hyperion Avenue Disney Studios, Columbia Ranch, the Warner Brothers Studio, and the Cathay Circle Studio. This is the only full-service restaurant in the Studios serving breakfast. The fare early in the day includes pastries, French toast, pancakes, lox and bagels, fruit, cereals, and the Hollywood Scramble: two eggs, bacon or sausage, grits or hash browns and a biscuit.

The lunch menu includes tortellini, baby back ribs, pork chops, spit-roasted chicken, chopped sirloin, fresh seafood, and seafood and chef's salads. The dinner menu includes salads (chicken breast or seafood), prime rib, pork chops, veal shank, and grilled sirloin. Desserts are available, as are beer and wine.

ECHO PARK PRODUCE
This stand at lakeside offers fresh fruit and vegetables as a viable snack alternative to the ice cream and popcorn purveyed elsewhere in the park (S).

ECHO LAKE CAFE
Location: On Echo Lake, a landmark. Prices: Budget to moderate. Cuisine: Sandwiches and salads. Meals: L,D,S.

This diner takes residence on Lake Echo in the "California Crazy" architecture form of a tramp steamer, the *S.S. Down the Hatch*. Min and Bill serve up "Cucamonga Cocktails" of marinated shrimp and fresh veggies, San Pedro Pasta, a tri-colored pasta dish with crab legs and shrimp, fruit plates, and submarine sandwiches including tuna salad, turkey, and the Santa Monica Sub, consisting of provolone, salami, and mortadella.

COMMISSARY

This huge (550-seat) new restaurant offers healthier fast food, churned out from the open kitchen. The menu includes salads, stir-fried vegetable dishes, chicken breast sandwiches, burgers, chicken teriyaki, and vegetarian chili (L,D).

BACKLOT EXPRESS

Here, by the Star Tours attraction, up to 600 people can sit and eat hot dogs, hamburgers, charbroiled chicken with salsa and tortillas, chef's salad, fresh fruit, chili, and for dessert, apple pie, and cake. Beer and wine are offered by the glass. The atmosphere is that of a scenic shop for a movie studio. Props are scattered throughout, and the paint shop section features furniture spattered with paint. An outdoor seating area features plants, trees, and potted plants (L,D,S).

STUDIO CATERING CO.

This massive restaurant looks like the paint shop of a studio and features sandwiches – roast beef and swiss, turkey and cheddar, Italian, or club (LDS).

DINOSAUR GERTIE'S ICE CREAM OF EXTINCTION

The huge brontosaurus that looms over Lakeside Circle chews on greens and conceals a stand offering ice cream and yogurt bars, ice cream sandwiches, frozen bananas and soda (S).

TOY STORY PIZZA PLANET

This backlot restaurant, themed after the computer-animated 1996 Disney hit movie, also includes an arcade. Salads, espresso, and cappucino are also served (L,D,S).

SUNSET RANCH MARKET

This outdoor food court on Sunset Boulevard consists of several stands. World War II icon Rosie the Riveter hosts one of them, Rosie's Red Hots, serving both traditional and unusual hot dogs, including foot longs, red hots, and turkey hot dogs. Catalina Eddie's Frozen Yogurt serves sundaes, soft-serve cones, and stir-frozen fruit. The Anaheim Produce Company sells fresh fruit. Drinks are also available (L,D,S).

14. DISNEY'S ANIMAL KINGDOM

Disney's fourth Florida theme park, the **Animal Kingdom**, opened amid great hoopla in April 1998. The theme park combines classic Disney atmosphere with the excitement and wonder of a zoological park. The park is themed to tell the story of all animals, real, imaginary, and extinct, with attractions, dramatic landscapes, and close encounters with exotic creatures.

The 500-acre park is home to over 1,000 live animals representing 200 different species, representing one of the largest zoo migrations in history. Many of the animals can be viewed running free in the 100-acre grassland and forest designed to replicate the African savannah.

There are six themed lands to the Animal Kingdom. The Oasis is the entry land, offering essential services and a smooth, tropical transition from the outside world to the adventure inside. Safari Village sits on the island in the middle of the Discovery River and serves as the hub between the lands. It's also home to the Tree of Life, the icon attraction of the park – like Cinderella Castle or Spaceship Earth are to their respective parks. Dinoland U.S.A. celebrates America's fascination with dinosaurs, showcasing interactive adventures and thrill rides in a kitschy roadside attraction sort of way. Camp Minnie-Mickey features live shows featuring characters from the Lion King and Pocahontas along with Disney characters waiting to meet your kids. Africa plays host to a walk-through safari attraction, a jeep adventure, and a train to Conservation Station, an interactive, educational pavilion devoted to teaching about saving the earth and its inhabitants. Asia features the Kali River Rapids flume ride and another walk-through.

Touring this park requires an entirely different mindset than the other Disney parks. This one is less about relentless go-here-see-this-do-this-turbo-death-race-kamikaze touring and more about stopping and smelling the flowers. There are only a few major attractions here where you'll encounter any kind of a wait, and if you're in such a hurry to put those particular notches in your belt, you'll miss what makes this park special – the lush vegetation and the amazing menagerie of animals who roam the park.

GETTING TO & AROUND THE ANIMAL KINGDOM

To get to the Animal Kingdom from:
- All Disney resorts and theme parks: Take the bus.
- Lake Buena Vista and International Drive area: Take I-4 to Exit 26B.
- Kissimmee area: Take US 192 to the main gate.

PARKING

The Animal Kingdom's lot has ample parking available, at $6 a pop.

ADMISSION, MONEY, REFURBISHMENT/INTERRUPTION OF ATTRACTIONS, PACKAGE PICKUP, and DRESS CODE. See Chapter 11.

PRACTICAL INFORMATION

Alcoholic Beverages: Allowed, sold at the Rainforest Café and Dawa Bar.

Baby Services: Changing and nursing facilities can be found behind Creature Comforts in Safari Village.

Banking: There's an ATM on the right side of the entrance plaza.

Cameras: Film processing is available at Garden Gate Gifts.

Cigarettes: Not sold in the park.

First Aid: Located behind Creature Comforts in Safari Village.

Foreign Language Assistance: Maps and assistance are available at Guest Relations.

Hearing-impaired Guests: A TDD is available at Guest Relations.

Information: Guest Relations at the front entrance is your one-stop-shop here.

Kennel: Located at the main entrance. Reservations are not required.

Lockers: Available for $.25 or $.50, on either side of the main entrance.

Lost and Found: Behind Creature Comforts in Safari Village.

Transportation: Information is available at Guest Relations.

Wheelchair guests: Wheelchairs are available for rent at Garden Gate Gifts.

TIPS

Attractions: Fastpass is available at Kali River Rapids, Countdown to Extinction, and Kilimanjaro Safaris. Use them. Do this and there aren't many lines left for you to wait in. See "It's Tough to Be a Bug" early, because this ride, being the focus of attention and physical center of the park, is crowded pretty much all day.

Dining: Rainforest Café is the only full service restaurant in the park. Good bets elsewhere include the character breakfast at Restaurantosaurus and pretty much everything at Tusker House Restaurant and Flame Tree Barbecue, whose aroma is particularly difficult to resist.

Shopping: Mombasa Marketplace offers authentic African gifts, while Beastly Bazaar offers memorabilia featuring "A Bug's Life" characters. Out of the Wild in Conservation Station is another good bet for some unique conservation-themed gifts.

THE OASIS

This placid, tropical garden serves to ease your transition from the urban world, with lush vegetation, flowers, waterfalls, streams, rocky grottos, and colorful wildlife such as wallabies, tree kangaroos, anteaters, giant sloth, Chinese deer, exotic birds, and more. There aren't any attractions per se here, but walking around the maze of trails is as good a way as any to spend a half-hour. Don't even think about skipping this land in your rush to do everything else.

Services

Behind Garden Grove Gifts are wheelchair and stroller rental, a kennel, ATM, and lockers. Guest Relations, on the other side of the entrance plaza, has a TTY phone, more lockers, and all the information you could possibly need during your day here.

Shopping
GARDEN GROVE GIFTS

This shop, located at the entrance to the park, offers the services listed above plus package pickup, film processing, and some character and park merchandise.

SAFARI VILLAGE

The central hub of the Animal Kingdom, this land has counter-service restaurants and shops at every turn, along with trails where you can see wildlife such as lemurs, kangaroos and capybaras, and the Tree of Life, the

14-story landmark that best represents the mood of the park. This artificial tree is the icon of the Animal Kingdom, with representation of over 325 animals carved into the massive branches and roots.

Attractions
IT'S TOUGH TO BE A BUG
Rating: 8 1/2. Fun, funny, utterly charming. Location: Inside the Tree of Life. Duration of Show: 15 minutes. Time to Go: Early in the day.

The queue for this 3D multimedia presentation winds through the roots of the Tree of Life, to the theatre inside. Theatre buffs will appreciate posters from the Tree of Life Repertory Theatre's past productions, shows like "A Cockroach Line," "My Fair Ladybug," and even "The Dung and I." While waiting to enter the theatre, guests are entertained by musical numbers from the aforementioned shows, sung by buzzing, humming insects.

The auditorium itself is a hoot, with the nooks and crannies on the underside of the tree exploited for the venue. The show stars Flik and Hopper (Dave Foley and Kevin Spacey) from "A Bug's Life." Flik emcees a talent show designed to show humans, who Flik declares "honorary bugs,' life from a bugs-eye point of view. The irritable Hopper objects, vehemently. The 3D film is accented by animatronic characters and effects built in to each seat in the house, effects realistic enough to make you feel like you're having a close encounter of the six-legged kind.

This is a fun and witty spin-off of "A Bug's Life," although the tone here is a bit more scholarly than that of the movie. The special effects are really good, a step up from the similar technology at "Honey, I Shrunk the Audience." This is definitely one of the best attractions in the park.

Shopping
BEASTLY BAZAAR
Safari hats, personalized keychains, mugs, shot glasses, and character merchandise from "A Bug's Life," "Tarzan," and of the park itself.

DISNEY OUTFITTERS
Animal-themed gifts, housewares, watches, and apparel are sold here.

ISLAND MERCANTILE
This large shop features figurines and themed merchandise from each of the lands plus personalized mugs, keychains, plush toys, pins, and a bit of apparel.

CREATURE COMFORTS

This store offers kids' apparel, toys, books, videos, and plush toys.

With the quirky design of a roadside attraction – Dinoland offers an array of entertaining looks at the ancient creatures that continue to fascinate us for millennia – the dinosaurs. The Cretaceous trails in Dinoland allow you to walk through a collection of plants that are survivors of the Cretaceous period.

Attractions
COUNTDOWN TO EXTINCTION

Rating: 9. Pretty intense, and with humor too. Duration of Ride: About 7 minutes. Best Time to Go: Very first thing in the morning, or at the time on your Fastpass. Frightening: Yes, intense motion and effects.

You board time machines and hurtle back in time to the late Cretaceous period – just minutes before the cataclysmic asteroid hits the earth and puts the dinosaurs in the history book. Your mission, bestowed by a not-quite-by-the-book is to retrieve a herbivore and bring him back with you. Unfortunately, you're threatened by both the Carnotaurus, a fierce meat eater, and by the asteroid itself. You race around an apocalyptic scene tracking a homing beacon placed on the dino and barely escape with your lives. Some of the effects are similar to those found in the Indiana Jones ride at Disneyland. While rough, it's not nearly as bumpy a ride as flight simulator rides, it's still more than enough of a jolt for those with less of a taste for the action. As you exit the ride, be sure to check out the video monitors overhead — they show the amusing coda to the story of the attraction.

TARZAN ROCKS!

Rating: 7. Entertaining and well-received. Location: Along the riverside. Duration of Show: 30 minutes. Best Time to Go: Anytime.

This live action show features the music and characters of Disney's recent animated feature Tarzan. Tarzan, Jane, and Terk are joined by a cast of "jungle gymnasts" in a four-act show featuring five songs from the soundtrack, including "You'll Be in My Heart." The cast of 27 sings, dances, and performs stunts such as rappelling over the audience and an airborne ballet. Lively and amusing, this show is performed several times a day at the 1,500 seat Theatre in the Wild, by the water.

THE BONEYARD
Rating: 7. Clever. Location: Just on the Dinoland side of the river. Best Time to Go: Anytime.

This creative, interactive playground lets kids wander through a dig site, slide down oversized bones, play xylophones on other bones, and participate in fossil digs.

DINOSAUR JUBILEE
Rating: 8. Real funny. Location: Between Tarzan and Countdown. Duration of Show: 20 minutes. Best Time to Go: Morning.

Fossils are on display here, and Disney cast members leads tours through a few times a day. Their narration is lively and their humor warped, making this attraction a sleeper favorite.

Exhibit
FOSSIL PREPARATION LAB
Paleontologists in residence work in this airy-windowed office next to Dinosaur Jubilee. At press time University of Chicago experts were preparing the largest and most complete T-Rex skeleton ever found.

Shopping
CHESTER AND HESTER'S DINOSAUR TREASURES
Themed after a tacky 50s gift shop, this shop sells dinosaur toys of all kinds, books, models, t-shirts, hats, magnets, bean bag dolls, and other goodies.

CAMP MINNIE-MICKEY

This land, geared more strictly towards children, features shows based on The Lion King and Pocahontas as well as extensive opportunities to meet Disney characters.

Attractions
FESTIVAL OF THE LION KING
Rating: 7. A consistent fan favorite. Location: At the far end of the land. Duration of show: 25 minutes. Best Time to Go: Anytime.

This stage show featuring a talented cast of trapeze artists, singers, dancers, and actors, draws heavily from the Broadway production of The

Lion King to produce a moving, beautiful, colorful show that deserves the word 'festival' in its title.

COLORS OF THE WIND

Rating: 6. Enjoyable, especially for animal lovers. Location: On the near side of the land. Duration of show: 20 minutes. Best Time to Go: Anytime.

Pocahontas and Grandmother Willow search for the protector of the forests in this charming children's show featuring a host of live animals.

CHARACTER GREETING TRAILS

This is the place to meet Mickey, Minnie, Pluto, Goofy, and other Disney friends.

This land features a walk-through safari, a jeep safari, and exceptional shopping, as well as the opportunity to learn about conservation.

Attractions
KILMANJARO SAFARIS

Rating: 10. Not to be missed. Location: To your left as you walk into the land. Duration of ride: 26 minutes. Best Time to Go: Early in the morning.

One of the only attractions in Disney world with both live narrator/guides and not-on-a-track vehicles, the Safaris put you in a jeep and take you across the African savannah where you'll see elephants, giraffes, apes, lions, and more. Who knows, you might even get to chase a poacher across the forest. This is the best ride in the park, hands down. Charismatic cast members, breathtaking vistas, and endearing animals all combine to make this ride a truly memorable experience. Note that this ride is best when experienced early in the day, as many of the animals are most active then, and in fact sleep during the hotter parts of the day.

PANGANI FOREST EXPLORATION TRAIL

Rating: 9. This is why you're here. Location: On the outskirts of Africa. Best Time to Go: Morning.

One of the many walking trails at the Animal Kingdom, this one allows you to wonder at animals native to Africa, including mountain lions, gorillas, hippos, birds, and more. Be sure to take your time walking through this exhibit, as sometimes the animals are not readily visible at first glance. Patience is rewarded, though, as guests can see animals in their natural habitats doing all kinds of animal things. Particularly interesting is a wall containing a blind mole rat colony, as well as underwater viewing of hippopotami. Keep in mind that animals are generally most active early in the day, and many of them sleep away most of the afternoon. So plan accordingly.

CONSERVATION STATION

Rating: 6 1/2. Informative and pleasant. Location: A train ride away from Africa. When to Go: In the afternoon.

Guests board trains in the Africa pavilion for a five-minute ride through the backstage area of the park, where animal care facilities are located, to arrive at Conservation Station, a big, airy pavilion with tons of interactive activities and educational experiences with a conservation theme. Serving as the nerve center for the park and the hub of its global conservation efforts, Conservation Station offers guests the opportunity to take control of cameras strategically placed in the animals' homes, watch real research, veterinary care, and food preparation. There's also the Affection Section petting zoo.

Shopping

DUKA LA FILMU

Stock up on film here for your safari.

MOMBASA MARKETPLACE/ZIWANI TRADERS

These colorful shops sell carved wood items, apparel, and books with an African theme as well as plush toys and safari wear.

OUT OF THE WILD

Conservation Station's gift shop offers unique gifts including Forest Pure lotions and shampoos, candles, and a small selection of toys, snacks, and apparel.

The Animal Kingdom's most recent addition, this land recalls the hustle and bustle of India with a white water rafting ride, another walk-through safari, and a bird show.

Attractions
KALI RIVER RAPIDS

Rating: 6 1/2. This type of ride is done much better elsewhere. Location: Far end of Asia. Length of Ride: 10 minutes. When to Go: During the heat of the afternoon, with a Fastpass.

This is a white water rafting ride similar to those found in many other theme parks, putting eight guests in a circular raft bound for swirling white water. The ride starts promisingly, with the rafts being elevated up an incline shrouded by mist... once you reach the top of the attraction and start floating downstream, it goes a bit... shall we say... downhill. While most Disney rides have a nicely developed story behind them, this one is but skin and bones, one scene showing deforestation by logging companies, followed by a scene of an overturned logging truck set ablaze... and that's pretty much it. The ride is all too short, all too plain, and nowhere near wet enough. Popeye and Bluto's Bilge Rat Barges at Islands of Adventure is a far better incarnation of this kind of ride. Note that Fastpass is in use at this attraction.

MAHARAJAH JUNGLE TREK

Rating: 9. Another breathtaking walk through beautiful scenery and endearing animals. Location: By the bridge to Safari Village. When to Go: Morning.

The second walk through safari, this one sends you through the Royal Forest of Anandapur, a fictional Asian nation with some serious wildlife. The animals cavorting here include Malaysian simians, Vietnamese white cheeked gibbons, Komodo dragons, endangered Malayan tapirs, Rodrigues fruit bats and Malayan flying foxes, six tigers, a field of elk and antelope, as well as a bird sanctuary. Between the animals and the intricate ruins along the trail, this is one of the most breathtaking spots in the Animal Kingdom.

"FLIGHTS OF WONDER"

Rating: 6. Stupid animal tricks have never been this much fun. Location: By the bridge to Safari Village. When to Go: Anytime.

This show features a colorful variety of birds and showcases their natural behaviors, along with lively narration from cast members. "Flights of Wonder" takes place at Caravan Stage, a theatre carved out of the stone ruins and includes barn owls, West African crowned cranes, parrots, and birds of prey and follows the adventures of Luke and the Phoenix, who are on the hunt for lost treasure.

Shopping
MANDALA GIFTS

This fun shop offer authentic African and African-themed gifts including wind chimes, carved wood items, print shirts and dresses, candles, and more.

DINING IN THE ANIMAL KINGDOM

RAINFOREST CAFÉ
Location: Just outside the park's gates. Prices: Moderate. Meals: BLD.

This wildly popular theme restaurant recently opened two locations in Disney World, one at the Marketplace and one just outside the gates to the Animal Kingdom. You don't need to buy an Animal Kingdom ticket to eat at the restaurant there, however. The restaurant combines a conservation theme and wild rainforest décor with unusual twists on classic food items, such as burgers (both beefy and meatless), pasta dishes, steaks, ribs, and much more. Breakfast is served at both locations as well.

FLAME TREE BARBECUE

This Safari Village stand offers fresh-from-the-smoker beef brisket, chicken breast, and pork shoulder along with St. Louis ribs, seasoned fries, and a barbecue combo platter. Its aromas will tempt you as you walk by – can you resist?

PIZZAFARI

Another restaurant in the centrally located Safari Village, this one has several distinct themed rooms: Home, Nocturnal, Upside Down, Camouflage, Four Seasons, and Bug Rooms. The food includes pepperoni or cheese pizzas, grilled chicken Caesar salads, and roasted vegetable calzones. Breakfast pizzas and Belgian waffles are available early.

RESTAURANTOSAURUS

A big counter-service restaurant, the Restaurantosaurus offers cheeseburgers, hot dogs, and McDonald's Chicken McNuggets with fries. There's also a daily all-you-can eat breakfast buffet here featuring Donald Duck and other Disney characters.

TUSKER HOUSE

This restaurant in the Harambe village in the Africa section of the park offers salads, rotisserie chicken, and sandwiches with tabbouleh, potato wedges, or mashed potatoes. One of the better quick-service restaurants in Disney World.

CHIP 'N' DALE'S COOKIE CABIN
Here at Camp Minnie-Mickey, you can snack on cookies and ice cream sandwiches.

DINO DINER
Dinoland USA's spot for breakfast breads and turkey legs as well as fresh fruit.

KUSAFIRI COFFEE SHOP & BAKERY
Assorted pastries, muffins, cookies, and cakes are served alongside espresso, cappuccino, hot chocolate, tea, and more here, at this counter at the corner of Tusker House.

TAMU TAMU REFRESHMENTS
Frozen yogurt, floats, and sundaes are available here.

DAWA BAR
Adjacent to Tusker House, this open-air bar offers beer, wine, mixed drinks, and contemporary African music.

MR. KAMAL'S BURGER GRILL
Cheeseburgers are served at this riverside stand between Africa and Asia.

ANANDAPUR ICE CREAM
Asia's spot for cold, creamy goodness.

15. OTHER DISNEY ATTRACTIONS

Surprisingly few people realize until they arrive at the Vacation Kingdom that there's more than just the big four theme parks to Walt Disney World. There's a shopping village, three water parks, 72 holes of miniature golf, three separate dining/shopping/entertainment complexes, dozens of exciting nightclubs and restaurants, a sports venue, and more.

DISNEY'S WIDE WORLD OF SPORTS

Opened in 1997, Disney's Wide World of Sports is a 200-acre state-of-thc-art complex designed to give both athletes and fans an unparalleled sports experience and features a diverse array of events and facilities.

GETTING AROUND

Buses travel between here and the Disney-MGM Studios parking lot, but there's no transportation to any other Disney areas. Also, since the schedule of the buses may not coincide with the event you wish to attend, so it's best to arrange your own transportaition here. To get here by car from:

- Disney World locations: Follow signs to SR 536/Florida's Turnpike. Get off the Osceola Parkway (SR 536) at Victory Way and take that straight to the parking lot.
- Kissimmee: Take US 192 to maingate and follow signs to WWoS.
- Orlando/International Drive: Take I-4 west to exit 25B and follow signs to WWoS.
- Points west on I-4: Take exit 24C onto World Drive and follow Osceola Parkway signs to Victory Way.

DISNEY'S WIDE WORLD OF SPORTS
VITAL STATISTICS

Disney's Wide World of Sports, P.O. Box 10000, Lake Buena Vista, FL 32830.

On the Internet: *www.disneyworldsports.com.*

Phone: *407/939-PLAY.*

Hours: *10am to 5pm daily, sometimes later to accommodate special events.*

Admission: *Standard admission is $8 for adults and $6.75 for children ages 3 to 9. Most professional events require separate admission media. Length-of-event passes are also available. To order advance tickets for specific events, call 407/839-3900.*

Parking: *Free.*

Time to See: *Varies.*

When to See: *Anytime.*

EVENTS

There's always a wide variety of events happening at the $100 million Wide World of Sports complex, for both spectators and participants of all sports.

The two-time defending World Series champion **Atlanta Braves** hold their spring training at the Wide World of Sports and play 16 home games each spring in the complex's 9,500-seat baseball field. Individual game tickets generally go on sale in early January.

The annual **NFL Quarterback Challenge** is held here as well, as the biggest names in the game attempt to pass their way into the winner's circle. There's also the **NFL Experience** simulated training camp, with passing accuracy tests, a punt-pass-kick competition, practice punt returns, catch passes, throw snap passes, and obstacle courses as well as a kids' area.

For tennis fans, the **ERA Real Estate Clay Court Championships** are held on the complex's Centre Court facility. The tournament runs the first week in May, tickets are available on December 1.

Other sporting events here include Harlem Globetrotters' basketball games, Disney's Holiday Basketball Classic women's NAIA tournament and the Summit Sports 3 vs. 3 Soccer Shootout.

Participatory events at the complex include AAU leagues, Pop Warner football, baseball, fastpitch and slowpitch softball, lacrosse spring training, track and field training, a marathon and half marathon, in-line hockey, and more.

FACILITIES

The 5,000-seat **Fieldhouse** offers 30,000 square feet of technologically advanced competition space with unprecedented flexibility, new age playing surfaces, and new "Florida Picturesque" construction. This venue hosts wrestling, marital arts, basketball, and in-line hockey.

The WWoS **Tennis Complex** features Centre Court, with 1,000 permanent seats and another 7,500 added for special events, plus an additional ten courts.

Out of the 8,500 seats at the **Baseball Stadium**, an amazing 80% of them are between first and third base, allowing for excellent views. The stadium boasts pretty much all the amenities of the major league parks. Impressive.

There are also four baseball fields with Tifway 419 Bermuda turf, bullpens, batting tunnels, pitching machines, and pitching mounds. One field is lit for night play. There are also four softball fields.

The **Foot Locker Track & Field Complex** surrounds a 400-meter track with ample seating. Four multi-purpose fields covered in Tifway 419 are available for soccer, football, lacrosse, archery, and field hockey. One is lit for night play. There has been talk of adding swimming pools and an ice rink to the complex, but no concrete plans have been made yet.

SHOPPING

The **D Sports** store is located at the entrance of the complex and offers sports merchandise for children and adults. Also, during Braves games and special events, **Disney's Clubhouse** offers baseball merchandise.

DINING

The **Official All-Star Café** has a location near the Fieldhouse. Admission is not required to eat here. They serve American fare at lunch and dinner in a sports-themed environment. Permanent concession stands are located in most of the major venues as well, and vendors wander the aisles during events.

DOWNTOWN DISNEY MARKETPLACE

The former Disney Village Marketplace and Pleasure Island were combined with the brand new West Side shopping/dining/entertainment complex to form the Downtown Disney entertainment complex, which offers a ton of options to keep yourself busy.

GETTING AROUND

The bus station is located in front of World of Disney. To get to the Marketplace:
- From the Disney Institute: Walk or take the bus.
- Old Key West Resort, Port Orleans, and Dixie Landings Resorts: Take the water taxi or the bus.
- The Hotel Plaza: It's easiest to walk or drive yourself, but you can take the bus.

DOWNTOWN DISNEY VITAL STATISTICS

Downtown Disney, PO Box 10000, Lake Buena Vista, FL 32830.
On the Internet: *www.downtowndisney.com*
Phone: *407/824-4321.*
Hours: *Marketplace is open 10:30am to 11pm. Pleasure Island shops are open from 10:30am to 2am, dining and entertainment hours are 7pm to 2am. West Side is open 9:30am to 11pm. Nightclubs' and restaurants' hours may vary.*
Admission: *Pleasure Island admission is approximately $19 after 7pm, although a ticket is not required to visit the shops before then. The Marketplace and West Side do not charge admission, although some clubs and attractions on the West Side do.*
Parking: *Free. Valet parking is available.*
Money: *ATMs are located in all three sections of Downtown Disney.*
Time to See: *At least two hours.*
When to See: *Anytime.*

- All Other WDW Resort Areas: Take the bus.
- Off-site hotels in Lake Buena Vista: Take S.R. 535 to Hotel Plaza Blvd. and go straight to the Marketplace.
- Off-site hotels via I-4: Take interchange 26B (EPCOT Center/Disney Village) into WDW, the exit for the Marketplace is the first one, turn right after getting off and follow the signs about a quarter of a mile. It'll be on your left.

PARKING

Parking is free and plentiful. Valet parking is available by the Empress Lilly and by Village Spirits.

ADMISSION

Entry is free.

MONEY

There is a branch of the Sun Bank located in the Marketplace, offering cash advances, traveler's check services, personal check cashing, arrange for a wire transfer of money from a guest's home bank to the Sun Bank, and exchange foreign currency. Disney Resort ID is accepted for purchases.

PHONES

Located alongside EUROSPAIN, outside the Lakeside Terrace restaurant, by the Gourmet Pantry, The City, the Empress Lilly, and Chef Mickey's Village Restaurant.

RESTROOMS

Found at EUROSPAIN, Guest Services, Lakeside Terrace, Minnie Mia's Italian Eatery, Empress Lilly, and Chef Mickey's Village Restaurant.

GUEST SERVICES

The building adjoining You and Me Kid offers information, brochures, magazines, gift certificates, gift wrapping, stroller and wheelchair rental, film, special event tickets, and two-hour photo processing.

PRACTICAL INFORMATION

Alcoholic beverages: Allowed, sold at the Gourmet Pantry, Village Spirits, and most eateries.

Baby strollers: Available for rental at Guest Services.

Cigarettes: Available at Village Spirits.

Information: A directory of Pleasure Island and the Marketplace is available at Guest Services and most shops.

Wheelchair guests: All areas of the Marketplace are wheelchair accessible. To get onto the dock, use the ramp by the Rainforest Cafe. Wheelchair rental is available at Guest Services.

SHOPPING

The original Disney Village Marketplace is now the Disney Downtown Marketplace, a pleasant collection of colorful cedar-sided buildings, garnished with gardens and twinkling lights, offers plenty of unique shops, restaurants, and other fun stuff.

DISNEY AT HOME

This shop offers imaginative and innovative housewares for bed and bath, with items that are fun, stylish, and functional.

DISNEY'S DAYS OF CHRISTMAS

Orlando has never had a white Christmas, though shoppers here may think differently. It's yuletide season year round here, as a 24-foot tree towers over the festivities here, while caroling bells chime in the background. The goods on sale at this charming shop include American and European tree ornaments, décor, nutcrackers, snow globes, collectibles, and character merchandise.

EUROSPAIN

This interesting shop features a variety of handcrafted gifts and decorative articles from prestigious European artisans and designers. Demonstrations are held daily.

TOYS FANTASTIC

Disney-themed toys and Mattel toys, especially Barbie and Hot Wheels toys, are featured here.

LEGO IMAGINATION CENTER

This new shop offers a huge selection of LEGO toys in a crazy atmosphere, with an interactive outdoor playground and Brickley, a 50-foot LEGO sea serpent in the lagoon.

POOH CORNER

Get your Pooh on here with apparel, plush toys, accessories, and gifts in a setting straight out of the Hundred Acre Wood.

RAINFOREST CAFÉ SHOP

This is the place for logo merchandise from the popular theme restaurant.

WORLD OF DISNEY

Walt Disney World's signature shop, the World of Disney is a character shop with 12 themed rooms based on Disney classics, a mountain of plush toys, and everything from jewelry and lingerie to infant wear and plush toys.

HARRINGTON BAY CLOTHIERS

Boys' and men's apparel of all kinds is sold here, including Polo, Ralph Lauren, Tommy Hilfiger, and Calvin Klein.

GOURMET PANTRY

Specialty housewares, accessories, cookbooks, and culinary gifts are offered here, in addition to groceries ranging from sundry to exotic, including Godiva chocolates, specialty sandwiches, salads, pastries, and gourmet coffees. Staples found here include orange juice, breads, cereals, yogurt, beer, and soft drinks. Delivery is available (see above). This shop opens at 9:30.

THE ART OF DISNEY
This unique gallery sells Disney animation art and collectibles including unique art pieces by renowned artists, including sculpture, pottery, crystal, animation cels, reproductions, and sericels.

RESORTWEAR UNLIMITED
Women can find the latest in lightweight, vivid fashions, plus sportswear and swimwear, all from famous labels like Liz Claiborne and Catalina. Jewelry, hats, handbags, and other accessories are also sold.

STUDIO M
This one-stop photo shop offers professionally taken pictures with Mickey Mouse, airbrushed t-shirts, and more.

SUMMER SANDS
Florida gifts, apparel, jewelry, sun care products, straw hats, and bags are sold here.

TEAM MICKEY'S ATHLETIC CLUB
Sporting apparel featuring your favorite Disney characters can be found here, along with ESPN logo swag, golf apparel and equipment, Nike apparel and shoes, and much more.

2 R'S: READING AND RITING
Here you can find bestsellers, children's books, Disney books, music, and videos, cards, and stationery, as well as cappuccino and espresso.

SERVICES & ENTERTAINMENT
CAPT'N JACK'S MARINA
Hit the waters of the 35-acre Buena Vista Lagoon in a pontoon boat, canopy boat, or water sprite. Or, if you prefer, two, three-, and four-hour fishing expeditions are available. Minimum age to rent a boat is 12, and more information is available by calling *407/WDW-PLAY*.

DOCK STAGE
Entertainment and special events at the water's edge.

OTHER FACILITIES
There's also a sand playground and train ride for the kids as well as three whimsical fountains.

SPECIAL EVENTS
Florida Earth Day - Endangered species presentations, demonstrations, and corporate displays mark the occasion. Held in April.
Disney Village Wine Festival - Held in February of each year, sixty wineries from Europe, California and the rest of the U.S. put their best grape forward.
Boat Show - Central Florida's largest in-water boat show features 200 boats in and around Buena Vista Lagoon. Held in October.
Halloween - Local youngsters dress up for a costume contest, and the atmosphere is spiced up by "halloween-ifying" the Captain's Tower with cobwebs, Halloween merchandise, and the presence of villains from Disney flicks.
Festival of Masters - Held at the beginning of each November, this is one of the biggest events of the year at the Marketplace, and the hype is decidedly worth it. This art show draws award-winning artists from around the country and is attended by locals and tourists with equal and ample enthusiasm, as one can see from the parking lot, packed to capacity.
The Glory and Pageantry of Christmas - Truly a sight to behold. This nativity pageant takes place in the Village Marketplace and is based on a French pageant from the 13th century. Three dozen actors, all dressed in period costumes, participate in this beautiful event. The production goes up every Thanksgiving and lasts until New Year's. It would be a shame to visit Walt Disney World during this time of year and miss this.

DINING
The popular **Cap'n Jack's Oyster Bar** overlooks the Lagoon and serves a variety of seafood. The **Ghirardelli Soda & Chocolate Shop** offers world famous San Francisco chocolates and ice cream. **The Gourmet Pantry** offers sandwiches, salads, and bakery goods. There's also a gigantic **McDonald's** here, open until 1am or later every night. The **Rainforest Café** has its second Disney location here, offering adventurous food and atmosphere. **Wolfgang Puck Express** offers a limited menu of pizza, salads, and snacks.

PLEASURE ISLAND

In 1989, Disney opened a nighttime entertainment complex to rival downtown Orlando's Church Street Station. According to legend, Pleasure Island is the former home of 19th century Pittsburgh ship merchant Merriweather Adam Pleasure. Merchant sailing was on a downturn during Pleasure's heyday, but the advent of private yachting more than made up for the loss in his business, Pleasure's Canvas and Sailmaking, Inc. Pleasure Island was a community developed to advance his business as well as yearning for adventure.

The legend goes on. In 1939, Pleasure put the Island into the hands of his children as he went to circumnavigate the globe. He was lost at sea. The place fell into disrepair and remained that way until Disney "discovered" it in 1986 and transformed it into a paradise of nightclubs, restaurants, and shops.

Pleasure Island is now a part of the Downtown Disney entertainment complex; see Downtown Disney for info on getting around, parking, etc.

ADMISSION

At press time, admission to Pleasure Island was approximately $18.86 per person, $54.95 for an annual pass, and was included in some admission media (Unlimited Magic, Park Hopper Plus passes). Note that you must be 18 to enter Pleasure Island after 7pm, and 21 to enter Mannequins and BET Soundstage Club.

NIGHTLIFE & ENTERTAINMENT
ROCK & ROLL BEACH CLUB

Originally planned as the XZFR (say zephyr) Rockin' Rollerdrome, a dance club with a futuristic theme and roller skating, this club was extensively revamped to create a beach party atmosphere and arguably the best dance club on the island. Supposedly, this was a wind tunnel in which Pleasure developed a flying machine. The first level holds the dance floor, which is a little bit diminutive, but there is plenty of seating. The second and third floors hold billiards tables and games.

There are often live bands here, and they are always top-notch. Oldies and current rock music is played here, loud. The bands play about 45 minutes every hour, and a disc jockey takes over during breaks to offer nonstop dancing. The Orbiter Lounge, on the first floor, offers alcoholic beverages, soft drinks, and snacks. Spinners, on the third floor, sells potato straws, pizza, burgers, chicken, and ice cream.

MANNEQUINS DANCE PALACE

The warehouse where Pleasure kept the materials for his business is no more. Now, it is the premier over-21 dance club on the island. The name of the club is taken from the mannequins who stand watch across the dance floor, whichi s a rotating turntable. There are several dressed as felines from the Andrew Lloyd Webber musical "Cats," others representing Yul Brenner and Deborah Kerr performing the musical number "Shall We Dance" in the movie version of The King and I.

Special effects are king here. There is a collection of 70 robotically controlled lighting instruments, plus machines that can cause it to shower confetti, bubbles, or even snowflakes inside the club. The music is mainstream contemporary, Top 40, and recorded. On Thursdays, a band called DV8 plays alternative rock, techno, house, and industrial music. Carts throughout the club offer seafood, chicken, steak, and potato chips. Bars scattered throughout sell specialty cocktails, beer, wine, and soft drinks. No one under 21 years of age admitted.

8 TRAX

This one club has undergone more metamorphosis than any of the others. It started life in 1989 as Videopolis East, a club for the 13-to-20 set, selling no alcohol and taking its name from the Videopolis attraction in Disneyland. For reasons including a too-complicated ticket system, underage drinking, Orlando gangs, and the whole image of Pleasure Island, Imagineers scrapped Videopolis East, replacing it with CAGE!. Now, it has been changed yet again, this time to 8 Trax, a dance club featuring classic pop and rock from the 1970's.

ADVENTURER'S CLUB

A plaque at the entrance presents the credo of the club, and of Merriweather Adam Pleasure: "Explore the unknown, discover the impossible." Inside, there are stuffed animal heads who turn to one another and begin talking (Audio-Animatronics, of course), eccentric characters, cast members who mingle with guests, and knick-knacks from wall to wall, all supposedly collected by Pleasure during his journeys.

This is the only truly Disney creation on the island, modeled after a British explorer's club. It's actually a sort of a comedy presentation, but since there is neither a posted schedule nor any announcement that there is a show, many people walk in, check it out, and leave, missing the best part. Sit at the bar, order a drink from one of the bartenders, all of whom happen to be named Nash, and wait. Once every thirty or forty minutes, all guests present are ushered into library for the comic show. Exotic food and drink are served up here, ranging from shrimp Trinidad to Lebanese steak tartare. Wine, beer, specialty drinks, and soft drinks are also offered.

BET SOUND STAGE CLUB

This new club offers urban contemporary entertainment, including R&B and hip-hop acts as well as live DJs. There's also a martini bar and a decent menu of Southern, Cajun, and Caribbean food. Note that you must be 21 to enter this club.

THE COMEDY WAREHOUSE

Once, energy for the activities on the Island was produced here. Now, energy is produced by a troupe of five decidedly off-center improvisational comedians and a musician who, five times nightly, partake in skits based on audience suggestions, including riotous spoofs of Walt Disney World. Also, the comics have been known to make phone calls in the middle of the show, usually to the phone by the last seat in the fifth row. Avoid this seat if you're at all inhibited.

Guests sit on stools packed like sardines in a tiered arena, so everyone has a good view. Each show is different and equally entertaining, and this is the most popular club on the Island. If you don't plan to see the first or last show, expect a 30 to 45 minute wait in line. This is the only club that you can not come to and go from as you please. Popcorn, soft drinks, cocktails, beer, and wine are served.

PLEASURE ISLAND JAZZ CO.

Current innovators and legendary voices perform at this relaxed club, which features excellent music and a stacked menu filled with sandwiches, finger foods, salads, and more.

NEW YEAR'S EVE STREET PARTY

Throughout each evening, live bands and/or dancers entertain on the West End Stage, on the end of Hill Street. At a designated time each night (11 PM on Sunday-Thursday, midnight Friday and Saturday), a countdown begins: 10... 9... 8... As you reach zero, everybody is encouraged to shout "HAPPY NEW YEAR" at the top of his or her lungs, dance around, and revel in fireworks, search lights, music, dance, and a rain of confetti. The Island Explosion Dancers cavort on rooftops and the street party rages.

Be sure you're outside at the designated time. It's New Year's Eve every evening here, and the party is a highlight of any visit to the Island. Guests are encouraged to get party hats, noisemakers, and even champagne to celebrate the occasion.

WILDHORSE SALOON

The spot on Pleasure Island for kickin' country music, Wildhorse offers the best in contemporary country seven nights a week. The resident

Wildhorse Dancers show off their moves and give line-dancing lessons, and there's a 1,500-foot dance floor for you to strut your stuff on, as well as a menu of barbecued ribs, chicken, and steaks. Memorabilia is available at the Wildhorse shop at the West Side.

FRONT PAGE

You can appear on the cover of various national magazines for a fee. All needed accessories are provided.

SUPERSTAR STUDIOS

Lip sync to your favorite songs and star in a music video or use a karaoke machine to record your voice on tape.

STREET GAMES

Hill Street is peppered with midway-style games and folks who are willing to bet that they can guess your age, height, and weight. Also, street vendors sell everything from fruit-flavored ices to champagne, from t-shirts to noisemakers.

PROPELLOR HEADS

Pleasure Island's arcade features a good selection of video games and is open from 11am until 2am.

SHOPPING

AVIGATOR'S

Winged alligators mug on the label created exclusively for Pleasure Island. The "avigator" and the logo of the Adventurer's Club can be found on mugs, shirts, and magnets. Also, expedition wear, lightweight clothes of natural fabrics, leather jackets, and accessories are in stock.

DTV

The official Disney shop on Pleasure Island, this shop offers a huge selection of baseball caps plus apparel, plush toys, gadgets, jewelry, and more.

ISLAND DEPOT

This shop offers beachwear from Mossimo, Stussy, No Fear, Quick-silver, and more. Swimming trunks, sunglasses, beaded necklaces, shoes, shorts, and button-down shirts are for sale here.

MUSIC LEGENDS SHOP

Here you can find the history of rock and roll documented with CDs, t-shirts, box sets, posters, and autographed memorabilia.

REEL FINDS

One-of-a-kind movie memorabilia is sold here.

SUSPENDED ANIMATION

Original and reproduction posters, prints, lithographs, cels, and other animation art.

DINING

Fulton's Crab House is a high-energy, traditional seafood restaurant on the Empress Lilly riverboat. The **Portobello Yacht Club** offers upscale Italian fare.

The **Neon Armadillo** has fajita bars offering chicken fajitas, chili, nachos, sausages, pickled eggs, and fresh pepperoni. The **Rock & Roll Beach Club's** *Spinners* on the third floor, sells potato straws, pizza, burgers, chicken, and ice cream.

Inside **Mannequins**, carts offer seafood, chicken, steak, and potato chips. The **Adventurers' Club** has some exotic food and drink, ranging from shrimp Trinidad to Lebanese steak tartare.

DOWNTOWN DISNEY WEST SIDE

The newest addition to Downtown Disney, this is a collection of stellar shops, restaurants, clubs, and two of Disney's most intriguing attractions – the interactive Disney Quest and the breathtaking Cirque du Soleil installation, La Nouba.

Attractions & Clubs

AMC PLEASURE ISLAND 24 THEATRES

Super-comfy stadium seating for over 5,000 and state-of-the-art sound mark this huge complex. *For showtimes, call 407/298-4488.*

DISNEY QUEST

This huge blue building on the edge of the West Side houses five stories of interactive entertainment, a "virtual" theme park loaded with techno-heavy adventures. Disney Quest is divided into four "zones," the Explore Zone, where guests are immersed in exotic and ancient locales, the Score Zone, a sort of "superhero competition city," the Create Zone, which allows guests to flex their creative muscle, and the Replay Zone, a lunar carnival with classic rides and games with a Y2K kinda twist.

The best experiences here are CyberSpace Mountain, where you can design and then ride your own roller coaster... in space. There's a Virtual Jungle Cruise, and the Aladdin Magic Carpet Ride sim formerly found in Innoventions. In Ride the Comix, you put on a VR helmet and battle supervillains with a laser sword. There's also attractiosn based on Hercules, ExtraTERRORestrial Alien Encounter from the Magic Kingdom, Toy Story, Mighty Ducks, and more.

This is the perfect rainy day activity, and can keep kids occupied for hours. The Cheesecake Factory runs two counter-service eateries here, and there's a gift shop as well. Tickets are $27 for adults and $21 for kids aged 3 to 9.

LA NOUBA

Only the second permanent installation of the Cirque du Soleil in the world (the other one is in Las Vegas), this spellbinding show features 60 performers and artists, exotic costumes, lighting, and original sets and music twice a day in the 1,671-seat theatre on the very western edge of the complex. The creative team behind all the other Cirque du Soleil shows is at work again here, and this is as breathtaking an experience as you're likely to find in Disney World. "La nouba" means party, and this particular party is rife with pre-millennial tension and a dark mood at times.

It is recommended that you arrive 30 minutes prior to showtime. Tickets can be ordered by calling 407/939-7600, and are $62 for adults and $38 for kids ages 3 to 9. It's steep but few people walk away disappointed.

HOUSE OF BLUES

One of Central Florida's top music venues, the House of Blues club offers top-name national entertainment across the spectrum of rock, blues, country, house, and more, several nights a week. For talent schedules and information, surf to www.hob.com. *For ticket information, call 407/934-2583.* Note that tickets are not required to visit the House of Blues restaurant.

Shopping
ALL STAR GEAR
This shop offers licensed merchandise from the Official All-Star Café at the Wide World of Sports.

CELEBRITY EYEWORKS
Designer sunglasses and prescription eyewear are available hear.

MOVIE PREMIERE SHOP

This shop offers memorabilia and merchandise from premiering movies, with toys, dolls, games, t-shirts, and other goodies.

GUITAR GALLERY BY GEORGE'S MUSIC

Guitars from Fender, Ibanez, and other manufacturers are available here, along with accessories, books, clothing, and learners' packages.

HOYPOLOI

One of my favorite shops here, this store is an impressive collection of ceramics, art glass, and sculpture in metal, wood, and stone. While pricey, some of the stuff here can't be found anywhere else.

MAGNETRON

Magnets. Tons of em. I mean TONS of em.

SOSA FAMILY CIGARS

Inside the humidor you'll find cigars from the Sosa family line and others, along with smoking accessories of all kinds.

STARABILIAS

This nostalgia-laden showroom offers autographed Hollywood memorabilia plus kitschy collectibles of all kinds.

VIRGIN MEGASTORE

An amazing store, with two floors of books, music, and movies, including huge selections of imported CDs and vinyl. With 20 video stations and 300 CD listening stations along with comfortable sofas and seats amid the bookshelves, Virgin is an incredibly user-friendly place to pick up music.

WILDHORSE STORE

Contemporary country apparel and gifts are sold at this store.

DINING

Bongo's Cuban Café showcases the cuisine of the island nation in this restaurant created by Gloria Estefan and her husband Emilio. The **House of Blues** offers surprisingly good Cajun, Creole, and American fare, plus live music nightly. **Planet Hollywood** offers up pizzas and American fare inside a huge spherical building. **Wolfgang Puck's Café** offers the creations of the popular California chef.

Lighter fare is available at **Disney's Candy Cauldron**, where mouthwatering candy is made right before your eyes, and **Forty Thirst Street,** a shop serving coffee drinks, juices, smoothies, and more. See Chapter 9 for more details on the larger of these restaurants.

Once upon a time, on a tropical resort village, not so long ago, life was great. Then, a huge and terrible typhoon roared across the ocean and smashed into the village with all of its might. An earthquake and volcanic eruption turned bad to worse. Then, the clouds cleared, the cobwebs were cleaned, and Typhoon Lagoon was created. Flumes cut paths into once-impenetrable rock and formerly elegant buildings were now rubble. But most amazing of all was the sight of the Miss Tilly, a shrimp boat out of Safen Sound, Florida, atop 85-foot-high Mount Mayday. Every few minutes, the impaled craft attempts to free itself by sending a 50-foot stream of water into the air.

And there is the legend of Typhoon Lagoon, the most spectacular blend of water and imagination ever, and measuring 56 acres, it's the world's largest water park. Mount Mayday, incidentally, is the world's largest manmade watershed mountain.

GETTING AROUND

The bus station is located at the main entrance.
• From All WDW Resort Areas: Take the bus.
• Off-site hotels in Lake Buena Vista: Take S.R. 535 to Hotel Plaza Blvd. and turn left at the Marketplace. The park will be on your left.
• Off-site hotels via I-4: Take interchange 26B (EPCOT Center/Disney Village) into WDW, the exit for the Marketplace is the first one, turn right after getting off and follow the signs about a quarter of a mile. It'll be on your right.

PRACTICAL INFORMATION

Age restriction: You must be 10 years of age to enter without an adult.

Alcoholic beverages: You may not bring alcohol into the park. However, you can purchase it at Leaning Palms and Typhoon Tilly's.

Changing Rooms: Located at Leaning Palms.

Dress Code: Swim attire with buckles, rivets, or exposed metal is not allowed on water attractions.

First Aid: Located at Leaning Palms.

Information: A park map is available at the entrance.

Lifeguards: Highly trained and qualified, on hand at all attractions.

Life jackets: Available for free at High and Dry Towels. A deposit is required, though.

Lockers: Located near Shark Reef. Lost and Found: Located at High and Dry Towels. Due to the nature of some rides, glasses, jewelry, and loose articles should be removed beforehand.

Lost Children: Report to High and Dry Towels.

Picnicking: Allowed, as are coolers, however, glass bottles and alcohol may not be brought into the park.

Resting: Hammocks and lounge chairs scattered throughout.

Showers: By Singapore Sal's. Towels: May be rented at High and Dry Towels. But it may be easier to bring your own.

Tube Rentals: Available at Castaway Creek Raft Rental for use in bobbing wave pool, all tube ride attractions, and castaway creek. Tubes are not allowed in the surf pool.

Volleyball: Nets are set up on the beach.

TYPHOON LAGOON VITAL STATISTICS

Walt Disney World, P.O. Box 10,040, Lake Buena Vista, FL 32830-0040.

On the Internet: www.disneyworld.com/

Tel.: 407/560-4100

Hours: Opens 10 AM daily, closes at 9 PM in the summer, at 5pm during the rest of the year. The park closes during January.

Admission: $26.95 adults, $21.50 for children ages 3 to 9.

Parking: Free.

Time To See: Four to six hours.

When to See: From least to most crowded, Sunday, Friday, Monday, Tuesday, Saturday, Wednesday, Tuesday.

ATTRACTIONS

TYPHOON LAGOON

The foremost attraction in Typhoon Lagoon is the one with the same name. This is a huge (2.75 million gallon) wave pool, pure and simple, and covers two acres. The waves here, released every ninety seconds, are either bobbing waves or the kind of waves adored by surfers and dreaded by landlubbers. It switches every hour. During the bobbing periods, tubing is allowed on the 2- to 3-foot waves. However, when the waves switch, ditch your tube and bear down for a 4-to 6-foot wave.

I can personally vouch for the size of these waves. Only bodysurfing is allowed at the Lagoon during these times, and this is how you do it.

Watch several waves from onshore to get an idea of how to handle them. Then, hop in and swim about three fourths of the way to the wall from whence the waves come. When the machine lets one rip you'll know by a buzzer, the crash of water, the screams of surfers, and the feeling that you get when your life flashes before your eyes. Now, swim towards the beach as fast as you can. The waves were created so that they will not slam you down on your face but either carry or bypass you.

Warning: the biggest danger in the Lagoon is collisions. So, to avoid getting nailed, swim out past the crowd. Also, the lagoon's waves are known for their ability to remove everything from your body except your suit. Take off the glasses and watches, empty your pockets before jumping in. If you are more keen on swimming than surfing, go to Blustery Bay or Whitecap Cove, on either side of the surf pool.

CASTAWAY CREEK

If the excitement of the surf lagoon and the body slides has left you sapped, you will adore Castaway Creek. Just wade into the water from any one of the entrances, find a vacant tube floating by, and plop in. You can ride all the way around the 2,100-foot circuit or get out at any entrance point. There's never a line, and cruising along the 3-foot deep, 15-foot wide waterway is extremely placid. In the relaxing orientation tour of Typhoon Lagoon, you will travel under six bridges, through the Water Works, a mess of dripping pipes that overlooks the river, into the dark Forgotten Grotto, and through a delightfully misty and dense rain forest. A round trip takes about 30 minutes.

KETCHAKIDDIE CREEK

This area is open only to those of the under-four-feet persuasion. There are watered-down (no pun intended) slides, boats, fountains, waterfalls, a rapids ride, raft rides, bubbling jets, and assorted floating toys. Children must be accompanied by an adult.

raft rides

Three flumes on the south side of Mount Mayday offer the chance to board a small inner tubes for a journey down a river. All three rides measure about ten miles an hour. Keelhaul Falls allows you to spiral down a 400-foot slide at a tame pace. Gangplank Falls puts you and up to three others on a six-foot-wide tube for a trip down a 300-foot slide. In Mayday Falls, the most exciting of the three, the beginning is quick, then you slow down in a catch pool, then speed up for the rest of the 460-foot voyage. You must be four feet tall to ride Keelhaul and Mayday Falls.

HUMUNGA KOWABUNGA

The biggest thrill in the area is to stand at the center of Mount

Mayday, look down on the action below, lay down in the rapidly flowing water streaming down the mountainside, wait for the attendant to raise the bar, and push off. You then drop like a rock, falling 51 feet down the 214-foot slide.

The thrill is intense and the sensation of speed is greater than in roller coasters, because you are making the 30 mph journey with no car, no train, only your swimsuit. You must be four feet tall to ride. Pregnant women and those with back or neck problems are advised against riding. A wild ride, the view is a little bit sobering and the sight of the drop is scary, but it's over before you can shout "I haven't written my will!" all too soon for many.

STORM SLIDES

These three wild adventures go by the names of Stern Burner, Jib Jammer, and Rudder Buster and put guests in a 20 mph downhill corkscrew. All three rides load from the same line and all take in pretty much the same route and the same sights. All are about 300 feet long and feature waterfalls, forests, caves, rocky crags, and other great scenery.

SHARK REEF

This is a chance to dive into the Living Seas. Here, you are equipped with fins, mask, snorkel, and wetsuit (you may not bring your own), then showered, and finally, instructed on your dive. You then plunge into the 72-degree salt-water pool, chock full of some 4,000 creatures, including nurse and bonnethead sharks, rays, and others, all clustered around the coral reef and the sunken tanker in the center of the pool.

Visit this attraction first thing in the morning, because the lines here build fast, and as an added bonus, when you dive early, often with very little in the way of fellow divers, attendants are more lenient when it comes to spending extra time in the pool and deviating from the path. Otherwise, the attendants rush you through the pool and make the often hour-long investment of time seem unworthy.

MOUNT MAYDAY SCENIC OVERLOOK

You can take a path to the top of the mountain, where the view is exceptionally breathtaking.

SINGAPORE SAL'S SALEABLE SALVAGE

This building houses all the souvenirs sold in Typhoon Lagoon, mainly character merchandise, suntan lotion, film, swimsuits, sunglasses, hats, thongs, chairs, souvenirs, and clothing for men, women, and children. The atmosphere here is funky, with items displaced in the typhoon all over.

DINING

Leaning Palms is the main snack bar, serving burgers, sandwiches, pizza, salads, and drinks. **Typhoon Tilly's** serves a more limited selection of menu items. **Lowtide Lou's Snacks** and **Let's Go Slurpin'** offer frozen drinks, ice cream, and snacks.

Before Typhoon Lagoon, there was River Country. Opened in 1976 at Fort Wilderness on the shores of Bay Lake, this was designed as the archetypical swimming hole, the kind of place where Huck Finn and Tom Sawyer would frequent. There are fewer slides and rides here, making for longer lines, but there's not as much in the way of crowds. Relaxation is stressed more than excitement here.

RIVER COUNTRY VITAL STATISTICS

Walt Disney World, P.O. Box 10,040, Lake Buena Vista, FL 32830-0040.

On the Internet: *www.disneyworld.com/*

Tel.: *407/824-2760.*

Hours: *Opens 10am daily, closes at 8pm in the summer, at 5pm during the rest of the year. The park closes from January to mid-February.*

Admission: *$15.95 for adults, $12.50 for kids ages 3 to 9.*

Parking: *$6 per car. Free for WDW Resort guests and annual passholders.*

Time To See: *Three to four hours.*

When to See: *anytime except summer weekends.*

GETTING AROUND

To get to Fort Wilderness attractions:
- Magic Kingdom, Contemporary Resort, Discovery Island: Take the green-flagged boat to the Fort Wilderness dock.
- TTC: Take the bus.
- All Other WDW Resort Areas: Take the bus to either the Magic Kingdom and transfer to the green-flagged boat or to the TTC and hop on a bus.
- Off-site hotels from Lake Buena Vista and I-4: Exit from I-4 at S.R. 535 North. Take it to Vista Blvd. (about 1 mile past the entrance to the

Grand Cypress Golf Club) and turn left. Take Vista Blvd. to Fort Wilderness Trail, about two miles.

PRACTICAL INFORMATION

Age restriction: You must be 10 years of age to enter without an adult.

Alcoholic beverages: You may not bring alcohol into the park. However, you can purchase it at Pop's Place and Waterin' Hole.

Dress Code: Swim attire with buckles, rivets, or exposed metal is not allowed on water attractions.

Information: A park map is available at the entrance.

Lifeguards: Highly trained and qualified, on hand at all attractions.

Lockers: Located near the entrance.

Picnicking: Allowed, as are coolers, however, glass bottles and alcoholic beverages can not be brought into the park.

Resting: There are hammocks and lounge chairs scattered throughout the beach.

Towels: Small towels can be rented, but it may be easier to bring your own.

ACTIVITIES

BAY COVE

This, a roped-off section of Bay Lake, is the main part of River Country. Swimming here is delightful, as is riding a tire swing or jumping off a ship's bow.

OL' SWIMMIN' HOLE

There is a kidney-shaped, 330,000-gallon heated swimming pool and the adjacent Ol' Wadin' Pool, perfect for the young'uns.

SLIPPERY SLIDE FALLS & WHOOP'N'HOLLER HOLLOW

These two waterslides feature similar rides down a hillside on your back, one flume 260 feet long, the other, about 100 feet less. Both spit you out into Bay Cove.

WHITE WATER RAPIDS

You board an innertube for a pleasant, tame journey down a winding stream about ten feet wide from Raft Rider Ridge to Bay Cove. It's not as exciting as the flumes, but some people consider it a better ride.

UPSTREAM PLUNGE

Here, you plunge down one of two slides into the Ol' Swimmin Hole. As you fly out of the chute, seven feet above the water, the sensation is as close to flight as man gets.

RIVER RELICS

This is the place where you can buy film, sundries, and souvenirs of River Country.

With the opening of the Animal Kingdom, Discovery Island closed its doors forever in early 1999. Disney has not decided on its plans for the island; discussions have included a kids' camp and a honeymoon resort.

DISNEY'S BLIZZARD BEACH

The new, 66-acre **Blizzard Beach**, scheduled to open in mid-1995, combines the chills of a Northern ski resort with the thrills of a high-tech water park next to the All-Star Resorts. The Imagineers behind the park put quite a bit of off-center humor into the park. The opportunity for such visual gags is presented by the very thought of a ski resort in Florida.

GETTING AROUND

The bus station is located at the main entrance.
- From All WDW Resort Areas: Take the bus.
- Off-site hotels in Lake Buena Vista: Take S.R. 535 to Hotel Plaza Blvd. and turn left at the Marketplace. Follow signs to the Disney-MGM and Blizzard Beach.
- Off-site hotels via I-4: Take interchange 25B (192 West/Magic Kingdom), take the exit for the Magic Kingdom, and follow signs to Disney-MGM and Blizzard Beach.

PRACTICAL INFORMATION

Age restriction: You must be 10 years of age to enter without an adult.

Alcoholic beverages: You may not bring alcohol into the park. However, you can purchase it at the restaurants.

Dress Code: Swim attire with buckles, rivets, or exposed metal is not allowed on water attractions.

Information: A park map is available at the entrance.

Lifeguards: Highly trained and qualified, on hand at all attractions.

Life jackets: Available for free. A deposit is required, though.

Lockers: Located near the entrance.

Picnicking: Allowed, as are coolers, however, glass bottles and alcohol may not be brought into the park.

Resting: Hammocks and lounge chairs scattered throughout.

Towels: May be rented , but it may be easier to bring your own.

Volleyball: Nets are set up on the beach.

BLIZZARD BEACH VITAL STATISTICS

Walt Disney World, P.O. Box 10,040, Lake Buena Vista, FL 32830-0040.

On the Internet: www.disneyworld.com/

Phone: 407/824-4321.

Hours: Opens 10am daily, closes at 9pm in the summer, at 5pm during the rest of the year. The park closes during January.

Admission: $26.95 adult, $21.50 for children ages 3 to 9.

Parking: Free.

Time To See: Four to six hours.

When to See: From least to most crowded – Sunday, Friday, Monday, Tuesday, Saturday, Wednesday, Tuesday.

ACTIVITIES

SUMMIT PLUMMET

120 feet straight down the side of Mt. Gushmore at speeds up to 60 miles an hour. Zoinks. Guests must be at least 4' tall to ride.

TEAMBOAT SPRINGS

Six-passenger whitewater rafts twist down a 1,200-foot series of waterfalls.

TOBOGGAN RACERS

This eight-lane waterslide sends guests racing over "moguls" as they zoom down the "slopes."

SNOW STORMERS

Three flumes wind down the mountain, following a switchback course through slalom gates.

RUNOFF RAPIDS

Two open slides and one enclosed "black hole" twist and turn down the mountain on this inner tube run.

CHAIR LIFT

Wooden-bench chair lifts carry guests from the base of Mt. Gushmore to its summit.

TIKE'S PEAK

This is the kiddie-sized version of Blizzard Beach, including a scaled-down version of Mt. Gushmore.

MELT-AWAY BAY

A one-acre pool at the base of Mt. Gushmore, Melt-Away Bay is constantly fed by "melting snow" waterfalls.

CROSS COUNTRY CREEK

This lazy creek circles the park, including a "bone-chilling" trek through an ice cave.

BLIZZARD BEACH SKI PATROL TRAINING CAMP

This area is specially designed to appeal to pre-teens, with a rope swing, T-bar, culvert slides, and a challenging ice-floe walk along slippery, floating icebergs.

BEACH HAUS

Souvenirs and supplies are sold here.

DINING

The **Lottawatta Lodge** is the main restaurant, with burgers, hot dogs, pizza, sandwiches, and more. **Avalunch** serves hot dogs, nachos, and ice cream. **The Warming Hut** offers turkey legs, hot dogs, and nachos. The **Polar Pub** offers full bar service as does **Frostbite Freddie's**.

DISNEY'S BOARDWALK

This combination hotel and entertainment/dining/shopping complex, located between Epcot and the Disney-MGM Studios, offers a quirky variety of goodies.

GETTING AROUND

To get to the Boardwalk:
- From Disney-MGM Studios: Take the motor launch.
- From Epcot Center and the Epcot Resorts: Walk.

• All Other WDW Resort Areas: Take the bus.
• Off-site hotels via I-4: Take interchange 26B (Epcot Center/Disney Village) into WDW, and follow signs for Disney's Boardwalk.

BOARDWALK VITAL STATISTICS

Walt Disney World, P.O. Box 10,150, Lake Buena Vista, FL 32830-0150.

On the Internet: *www.disneyworld.com/*
Phone: *407/939-5100.*
Hours: *10am to 11pm daily. Hours at restaurants differ.*
Admission: *Free.*
Parking: *Free.*
Time To See: *Two hours.*
When to See: *Anytime.*

NIGHTLIFE & ENTERTAINMENT

ATLANTIC DANCE

This hot new nightspot features live dance music, ranging from swing to blues and everything in between. They offer 25 signature martinis plus hand rolled cigars. The club is 21 and up, and costs $5 on weekends, $3 on weeknights.

ESPN CLUB

The ultimate sports bar. There's cutting edge interactive sports video entertainment and late-breaking sports info. Live broadcasts, sports notables, and an American menu are featured in a high-energy atmosphere.

JELLYROLLS

Dueling pianos and spontaneous interaction with performers make this nightclub a favorite. Guests must be 21 to enter.

MIDWAY GAMES

Wildwood Landing on the Boardwalk offers a variety of midway games of chance and skill.

Shops

DISNEY'S CHARACTER CARNIVAL

This shop at the heart of the Boardwalk features children's apparel and accessories plus a large selection of Disney character merchandise for all ages.

SCREEN DOOR GENERAL STORE

A replica of a Mid-Atlantic general store, this shop offers groceries, dry goods, snacks, and beverages.

THIMBLES AND THREADS

This shop presents resortwear, swimwear, and accessories for men and women.

WYLAND GALLERIES

This shops offers distinctive contemporary American artwork in the style of Wyland environmental art, featuring marine animals in a beautiful natural setting.

DINING

Spoodle's caters to the adventurous tongue with tapas and intriguing entrees. **Flying Fish Café** is an upscale seafood eatery. The **Big River Grille and Brewing Works** brews several different varieties of beer on site. The menu at the **ESPN Café** is family-friendly, lively, and cheap. See Chapter 9 for full details.

WALT DISNEY WORLD SPEEDWAY

Located near the parking lot of the Magic Kingdom, the Indy Racing League kicks off its season every January with the WDW Indy 200. This is also the venue for the Richard Petty Experience, where you can ride or drive an authentic stock car. Call 800/822-INDY for information on the race and 800/BE-PETTY for information on the Richard Petty Experience.

16. SEA WORLD
OF FLORIDA

Central Florida's other "World" is devoted to marine life, and is the most popular marine attraction in the world, with over 4 million visitors each year. **Sea World**, with more than 200 acres, has a completely different feel to it than WDW. The pathways are wider, the pace of things more leisurely, more Floridian. Oh, did I mention that there are no Audio-Animatronics here? Every animal is real.

When seen towards the end of your vacation, Sea World serves almost as a decompression chamber, to allow you to recover from the vacation. Most of the attractions are shows held in stadiums big enough to accommodate several thousand people at once, so waiting and lines are rare. Also, snacks and beverages are sold in the bleachers where the shows are performed. Smoking is prohibited in all stadiums, gift shops, and restaurants.

GETTING TO SEA WORLD

To get to Sea World from:
- Walt Disney World: Take I-4 east to exit 27A. The park will be on your right. Or, take EPCOT Center Drive, which will turn into International Drive. Take I-Drive to the Central Florida Parkway, and turn left.
- Kissimmee: Take I-4 east to exit 27A. The park will be on your right.
- Lake Buena Vista: Take I-4 east to exit 27A. The park will be on your right. Or, take S.R. 535 south to International Drive, turn left, and take I-Drive to the Central Florida Parkway, turn left.
- International Drive, Sand Lake Drive, Universal Studios area: Take International Drive south to Central Florida Parkway, turn right.
- Orange Blossom Trail: Take the Trail to the Central Florida Parkway, go west past I-Drive.

SEA WORLD VITAL STATISTICS

7007 Sea World Drive, Orlando, FL 32821.
On the Internet: *www.seaworld.com/*
Tel.: *Tel. 800/327-2424 or 407/351-3600.*
Hours: *Park open 9am daily and closes at 9 or 10pm during busy seasons and 6 or 7pm during off seasons.*
Admission: *$44 for adults, $35 for kids aged 3 to 9. Two day passes are $10 more per person. Also available are Orlando FlexTickets including admission to several different theme parks for one price.*
Parking: *$6.*
Time To See: *One full day.*
When to See: *Monday, Tuesday, or Wednesday.*
Don't Miss: *Wild Arctic, Journey to Atlantis, Shamu Adventure, Manatees: The Last Generation, and the Key West Dolphin Fest.*

• Downtown: Take I-4 to Exit 28 (Beeline Expressway). Take the first exit from the Beeline (International Drive). Turn left, go under the highway, and turn right at the Central Florida Parkway.

ADMISSION

ORLANDO FLEXTICKET

New this year is the Orlando FlexTicket, which provides unlimited admission to four or five area Orlando area attractions for seven to ten days. The 4-Park Orlando FlexTicket includes unlimited admission for seven consecutive days to Universal Studios Florida, Islands of Adventure, Sea World, and Wet 'N' Wild. Price on a 4-park pass is $160 for adults and $128 for kids 3 to 9. A 5-Park Orlando FlexTicket includes ten consecutive days' unlimited admission to the four parks listed above plus Busch Gardens in Tampa. This pass is $197 for adults and $158 for kids ages 3 to 9.

PRACTICAL INFORMATION

Alcoholic Beverages: Allowed, sold at Bimini Bay Cafe and many counter-service eateries.

Baby Services: Diaper changing facilities are located adjacent to most ladies' restrooms. Nursing facilities are next to Penguin Encounter.

Baby Strollers: Available for rental at the Information Center.

Banking: An ATM machine is located at the entrance.

Cameras: Available for loan at Shamu Emporium.

Dress Code: Shirts and shoes must be worn at all times.

First Aid: Registered nurses are on duty. In an emergency, ask the nearest Sea World employee to contact one.

Information: Visit the Information Center on the left side of the entrance plaza for maps and info.

Kennel: Free, self-service, south of main entrance.

Lockers: By the Information Center by the main entrance.

Lost and Found: Report to or claim at the Information Center by the main entrance.

Lost Parents: If you find yourself separated from your children, report to the Information Center by the main entrance.

Same Day Reentry: Get your hand stamped at the entrance.

Wheelchair Guests: Wheelchair rental is available at the Information Center. Wheelchair ramps and facilities are located throughout the park and at all show areas. Sea Lion and Otter viewing area has a special entrance. Viewing areas are inside the other attractions.

TIPS

Touring Sea World is less complicated than other theme parks, due in large part to the fact that the majority of attractions are shows playing at specific times or continuous exhibits, which means that you'll spend a minimum of time in line here. That being said, note that the few rides at the park – Wild Arctic, Kraken, and Journey to Atlantis – are crowdwd most of the day, so ride 'em early.

SHOWS

CLYDE AND SEAMORE TAKE PIRATE ISLAND

Rating: 8. Location: At Sea Lion and Otter Stadium. Duration of Show: 25 minutes.

This fun new incarnation of the park's sea lion and otter show features trainer Eric Lang and his first mate, Clyde the sea otter. Clyde and his cohorts team up for swashbuckling action on an awesome set. This show is quite enjoyable and well worth your time.

INTENSITY GAMES WATER SKI SHOW

Rating: 7 1/2. Location: Atlantis Bayside Stadium. Duration of Show: 20 minutes.

Inspired by ESPN2's X-Games, this show features a cast of 20 skiers and wakeboarders who zoom across the water to the sounds of Jock Rock type high-energy arena anthems.

HAWAIIAN RHYTHMS

Rating: 4. Location: Hawaiian Village Theater. Duration of Show: 25 minutes.

What exactly is the purpose of this show? No other attraction in Sea World has anything to do with Hawaii. Hawaiian Rhythms consists of a three-man band and three dancing women. Many in the crowd leave before the show ends.

THE SHAMU ADVENTURE
Rating: 10. Not to be missed. Location: Shamu Stadium. Duration of Show: 35 minutes.

Sea World's living, breathing answer to Mickey Mouse, Shamu, has his own show, narrated by animal expert Jack Hanna. The show explores the similarities between killer whales in the ocean and at Sea World and uses the huge ShamuVision high-definition video screen to transport guests to Alaska, Norway, the Crozet Islands, and more.

KEY WEST DOLPHIN FEST
Rating: 7. Excellent. Location: Key West Dolphin Stadium. Duration of Show: 25 minutes.

Part of the Key West-themed area of the park, this show incorporates tropical island music, playful interactions, and new animal behaviors, performed by charming bottlenose dolphins and false killer whales.

PETS ON STAGE
Rating: 6. Location: Sea World Stadium. Duration of Show: 20 minutes.

This entertaining show is performed by an array of domestic animals, many of whom were rescued from area shelters. The case includes 18 cats, 12 dogs, birds, rats, pigs, and even a horse performing vaudeville.

CIRQUE DE LA MER
Rating: 7. Location: Nautilus Theatre. Duration of Show: 20 minutes.

This show stars Peruvian comic Cesar Aedo and relates South American folklore to guests with musicians, athletes, acrobats, and dancers.

ANHEUSER-BUSCH BEER SCHOOL
Rating: 5. Location: Hospitality Center. Duration of Show: 30 minutes.

As Homer Simpson would say: Mmm. Beeeeeeeer. "Beer school" is where Sea World's corporate daddy leads through the beermaking process, right up to that most important step where you get to sip free samples of Anheuser Busch brews.

EXHIBITS & RIDES
JOURNEY TO ATLANTIS

Rating: 9. Not to be missed. Location: A landmark, on the outskirts of the park, facing International Drive. Duration of Ride: 6 minutes.

This "water coaster" puts guests right in the crossfire of an epic clash for the lost city of Atlantis, as the Sirens will do anything to keep tourists from invading their home, which has risen out of the harbor of a Greek fishing village. The 6-acre, 10-story Atlantis is glorious from the outside – with classic Mediterranean architecture and Greek temples poking out of rocky cliffs.

The ride itself teams guests with Hermes, who attempts to lead the travelers to safety, and includes some genuine thrills, impressive special effects including lasers, holograms, and LCD lights, two near-freefalls, and some roller coaster elements at the tail end of the ride – with more splashy wet goodness than you can shake a stick at – which is great if you're a hot, sweaty, cranky traveler, and not such a good thing if you're a travel writer with a week's worth of notes inside a now-soaked backpack. Not that I would know anything about that sort of thing.

This is one of the best water rides in the Orlando area, and is one of Sea World's top attraction, living up to all the hype surrounding it. I recommend this attraction as not to be missed. Note that if kids under 42" are not permitted to ride.

KRAKEN

Rating: Not open at press time. Location: Behind Journey to Atlantis. Duration of Ride: Almost 4 minutes.

When this ride opens in mid-2000 it will become Orlando's fastest, tallest, and longest roller coaster, weighing in at 65 mph, 151 feet, and 4,177 feet, respectively. It's a floorless coaster with open-sided seats riding on a pedestal suspended over the track. Themed after the massive sea serpent kept by Poseidon, this ride includes a 144-foot suicide drop, seven inversions, high G-forces, weightlessness, three underground plunges, and portions where riders look down and see nothing but water.

PENGUIN ENCOUNTER

Rating: 9 1/2. Location: Next to Sea Lion and Otter Stadium.

A moving sidewalk carries you past over 200 penguins, plus puffins and other Antarctic sea birds. The indoor, glassed-in "penguin pen" is so Antarcticly chilly that it actually snows. "It's ninety-five in the shade out here, and those penguins get a ski slope," summer visitors often lament.

TERRORS OF THE DEEP

Rating: 8 1/2. Location: Sea World Theater.

You travel down a moving sidewalk in a tunnel through an aquarium featuring the deadliest creatures to ever roam the oceans. That's right, through the aquarium. There's 500 tons of sea water above and around you along with creatures like the surgeon-fish, sharks, lionfish, puffer-fish, scorpion-fish, and more.

But "Terrors" is a bit of an exaggeration. It won't really scare anyone (just remember that six inch pane of acrylic all around you when staring down a shark), but it affords enough fright for the truly chicken-hearted.

TROPICAL REEF

Rating: 7 1/2. Location: Sea World Theater.

The Reef is a 160,000-gallon pool illuminated by neon coral bigger than a house. The exhibit's inhabitants include raccoon butterfly-fish, morey eels, lobsters, surgeon-fish, clownfish, Florida alligators, fanged baby sharks, and more. This exhibit is to conventional aquariums what Space Mountain is to conventional roller coasters. It's something special, one of the reasons people spend thirty bucks to get in.

PACIFIC POINT PRESERVE

Rating: 7 1/2. Location: Between the main entrance and Dolphin Stadium.

Here you can come nose-to-soggy-nose with a variety of animals including turtles, dolphins, stingrays, and seals. You can feed them, touch them, pet them, and learn about the species represented here.

SHAMU: CLOSE UP!

Rating: 8. Location: By Shamu Stadium.

A 1.7 million gallon killer whale habitat lets visitors get even closer to Shamu and his friends. The naturalistic habitat includes an integrated collection of pools which make up the largest, most sophisticated marine mammal habitat and research facility in the world.

Playtimes, training sessions, and the mammal nursery all delight visitors. Amid the hundreds of tons of rockwork are slideouts and a rubbing rock beach, where the whales can engage in their favorite pastimes, namely tummy rubbing and back scratching.

MANATEES: THE LAST GENERATION?

Rating: 6. Location: On the northern fringe of the park.

This new exhibit immerses guessts in the beautiful underwater world of the endangered Florida manatee.

KEY WEST AT SEA WORLD
Rating: 7. Location: On the northern edge of the park.

This 5-acre section of Sea World is devoted to the southernmost city in the United States, featuring a trio of naturalistic new animal habitats hosting several of the Keys' most popular species, including Atlantic bottlenose dolphins, stingrays, and endangered sea turtles.

SHAMU'S HAPPY HARBOR
Rating: 8 1/2. Location: By Shamu Stadium. Comments: Closes at dusk.

This is an all-new, 3-acre play area, kind of a souped-up Cap'n Kids'. The equipment includes four stories of cargo netting, steel drums that guests can smash away on, a water maze, radio-controlled cars, an air bounce, slides, crow's nests, ball crawls, and vinyl mountains.

Like at Cap'n Kid's, there are restrooms and an abundance of shaded seating. Boogie Bump Bay, a smaller area, is intended specifically for kids 3' 6" or less and features scaled-down versions of most of the equipment.

MISSION: BERMUDA TRIANGLE
Rating: 10. Absolutely not to be missed. Location: By Shamu Stadium.

In this ride, guests board flight simulators similar to those found in Body Wars and Star Tours for a trip to the bottom of the 440,000-square mile section of the Atlantic that has spelled the doom of hundreds of ships and planes over the years. The "divers" board one of three, 59-seat "subs" and head off on the adventure with a high-definition, undersea film, which with the flight simulation, is as close as many will ever come to the Triangle and live to tell about it.

This simulator is comparable to those in Epcot and the Studios, and this one has more realism. See it before 11 AM if you can.

WILD ARCTIC
Rating: 8 1/2, not to be missed. Location: East side of park, behind Shamu Stadium.

This multi-faceted adventure attraction serves to unravel the mystery of the Arctic, combining a thrilling flight over the frozen north with encounters with animals who reside there.

Combining a high-definition film with high-powered flight simulation, the adventure begins as jet helicopters Borealis and Snow Dog take off and race against an incoming storm. Breathtaking vistas are blended with suspense while dangerous Arctic hazards are experienced before guests are delivered safely to the research center.

There, guests enter Base Station Wild Arctic, built (according to legend) around a 150-year old British exploration ship. Guests view polar bears, walruses, beluga whales, and seals from bot habove and below water level as they forage for food, dive, swim, and interact with Base Station workers. It's a fascinating look at a habitat which remains an enigma to us.

SKY TOWER

Rating: 6 1/2. Location: A landmark. Comments: Costs $3 extra per ride, per person.

For a few bucks, you can buy a ticket, then ride an elevator up a 400-foot tower to a superb vantage point from which you can see not only all of Sea World, but most of International Drive, the airport, and even Walt Disney World. One of only three real rides at Sea World, waits for this 15-minute ride seldom exceed a quarter of an hour.

SHOPPING

offers jewelry and pearls in the oyster. **Gulliver's** has knickknacks, clothes, and dolphin-related gifts. **Coconut Bay** sells candles, frames, shoes from Teva and Skechers, figurines, jewelry, and suncatchers. Near the entrance of the park, **Shamu's Emporium** offers the park's best selection of souvenirs and character merchandise. The **Arctic Shop** has stuffed polar bears, seals, and other goodies based on the Wild Arctic attraction.

DINING IN SEA WORLD

In addition to the restaurants listed here, there's also the Aloha Polynesian Luau dinner show, covered in Chapter 19. Note that admission to the park is not required to check out the Luau. *Call 407/351-3600 for reservations and info.*

BIMINI BAY CAFE

Location: On the shores of the central lagoon in the park. Prices: Budget to moderate. Cuisine: American. Meals: LD.

The menu here, at Sea World's only full-service restaurant, includes Key West conch chowder, fried gator tail, seafood sandwiches, shrimp scampi, fried chicken, crab quiche, salads, sandwiches, and daily chef's specials.

BIMINI BAY KIOSK

The fare served at this stand, located outside Hawaiian Rhythms and Bimini Bay Cafe, offers buffalo wings, fish fingers, French fries, beer, soda, coffee, and mixed drinks (L,D,S).

BUCCANEER SMOKEHOUSE
Here, you can fill up on barbecue platters with cole slaw, a roll, and ribs or chicken, picnic-style. Guests dine on umbrella-covered outdoor tables by Atlantis Lagoon (L,D).

CAPTAIN PETE'S ISLAND EATS
This surprising little kiosk offers up conch fritters, smoothies, key line funnel cakes, and more, representing Key West cuisine to its fullest (S).

CHICKEN & BISCUIT
This huge restaurant flips you the bird, baked, fried, or barbecued. There are two- and three-piece meals with French fries and a biscuit, or for kids, a platter with either one drumstick or two wings, fries, and a cookie (L,D,S).

THE DELI
Located at the Anheuser-Busch Hospitality Center, this lunchtime locale offers hand carved turkey and roast beef sandwiches plus German sausage sandwiches, stacked clubs, salads, and desserts (LS).

MAMA STELLA'S
The fare in this restaurant is exactly what its appellation suggests: pizza, spaghetti, eggplant Parmesan, sausage sandwiches, antipasto, and other Italian fare (L,D,S).

MANGO JOE'S CAFÉ
This new counter-service restaurant offers sizzling beef and chicken fajitas, seafood and fajita salads, fried fish and other hot and cold sandwiches, and an impressive selection of desserts (LDS).

SPINNAKER CAFE
This nautical-themed restaurant offers sandwiches, soups, and salads, but what the Spinnaker is renowned for is desserts: there's cheesecake, strawberries and cream, Key Lime pie, and Black Forest chocolate cake (L,D).

TREASURE ISLE ICE CREAM SHOP
A variety of frozen treats and ice cream novelties are offered at this eatery by the main entrance (S).

WATERFRONT SANDWICH GRILL
This lagoon-view restaurant offers hamburgers and sandwich platters, including the California Light, a turkey breast with sprouts and

cheese. A children's platter with a turkey sandwich, fruit salad, and a cookie is available. Guests can sit at closely-spaced indoor tables or more spacious outdoor, dockside areas (L,D).

DISCOVERY COVE

In July 2000, Sea World will open up a second park called Discovery Cove, across the street from the existing park. A completely different kind of experience than any other theme park, the centerpiece of the experience is the opportunity for guests to swim with dolphins. Guests will also snorkel through colorful reefs filled with 10,000 fish, tropical rivers, shipwrecks, and grottos. There's a huge aviary where you can play with 300 different birds. Guests will be treated to the utmost in personal attention, as they check in at the concierge desk and are escorted by a guide on a personal tour.

Reservations are required for the experience, and daily attendance is limited to 1,000 guests. The price is steep – $179 per person – but is all inclusive, covering admission, lunch, lockers, use of masks, snorkels, and other equipment, and parking, plus a pass offering seven days' unlimited admission to Sea World. Packages without the dolphin-swim are $79 per person. For information or reservations, surf to www.discoverycove.com or call 877/4-DISCOVERY.

17. UNIVERSAL STUDIOS FLORIDA

Universal Studios is the inaugural theme park of the Universal Studios Escape complex, which includes Islands of Adventure, CityWalk, the Portofino Bay Hotel, and several other attractions and hotels still under construction or in the planning stages.

The $630 million Universal Studios Florida is the most recognizable part of the complex, and has been rated by some the #1 theme park in Orlando. It's a reasonable choice for the distinction: between breathtaking thrill rides, genre-bending multimedia, top-notch entertainment, and shockingly realistic street scenes, you'd be hard pressed to find anything at this park that isn't done well.

Many people ask whether they're better off choosing to visit Universal or Disney-MGM. Optimally, do both. There's not much overlap in terms of the type of experiences that each park offers, as they focus differently. Universal has far better thrill rides and is geared towards a more adult audience, while Disney-MGM has better backstage studio tours, more comprehensive behind-the-scenes exposure, and attractions more geared towards a younger, less sophisticated audience.

Pricewise, the parks are about the same – single day admission prices are almost identical, and both parks are included in other multi-park admission media. Obviously, Disney-MGM us more accessible to guests staying at WDW hotels and Universal is more convenient to the International Drive area.

GETTING TO UNIVERSAL

To get to Universal Studios from:
• Walt Disney World, Kissimmee, Lake Buena Vista. Take I-4 east to exit 30A (Universal Blvd.) and turn left, following signs to the parking deck.

• International Drive: Take Universal Blvd. Straight to the park entrance. Universal Boulevard runs parallel to I-Drive, one block to the east. Alternatively, take I-Drive to Kirkman Road and turn left, driving 1.1 miles to the park entrance.

UNIVERSAL VITAL STATISTICS

1000 Universal Studios Plaza, Orlando, FL 32819-7610.

On the Internet: *www.usf.com*

Tel.: *407/363-8000 or Tel. 888/U-ESCAPE*

Hours: *Park opens at 9am daily, 8am for Universal Escape Resort guests. Closing times vary.*

Admission: *$44 for adults, $35 for kids 3 to 9. Two-day passes are $80 and $65. Three-day passes are $100 and $80. The Orlando FlexTicket is also available (see chapter 16).*

Parking: *$6.*

Time To See: *At least a full day.*

When to see: *From least to most crowded, Sunday, Friday, Monday, Saturday, Wednesday, Tuesday, Thursday.*

Don't Miss: *Twister, Back to the Future...The Ride!, E.T. Adventure, Jaws, Kongfrontation, "Alfred Hitchcock: The Art of Making Movies," and Terminator 2: 3D.*

PRACTICAL INFORMATION

Alcoholic Beverages: Allowed, sold at most table-service joints.

Baby Services: Located at Guest Relations and First Aid. Changing tables are available in all restrooms.

Baby Strollers: Can be rented next to Southeastern Bank.

Banking: There are ATMs at the main entrance plaza, both inside and outside the turnstiles, plus one at Amity/San Franciso.

Cameras: Lights, Camera, Action! offers video cameras for rent, still cameras for loan, and film and tape for sale. Photos can be developed in one hour at The Darkroom.

Cigarettes: Available at most shops throughout the park.

First Aid: Located By Louie's Italian Restaurant.

Foreign Language Assistance: Foreign language maps and assistance are available at Guest Relations.

Guided Tours: A five-hour VIP tour with front-of-the-line access to approximately 8 attractions is available for $120 per person, on top of the admission fee. The non-private tour consists of you and up to 14 other peouple. For $1700, your group can enjoy a private eight-hour tour with priority entrance and preferred seating at any attraction you want to visit.

Hearing-impaired Guests: A Telecommunications Device for the Deaf (TDD) is available at Guest Relations.

Information: To get facts about attractions, shows, and dining, visit the Guest Relations office. Also, information booths are located at Amblin Ave. and 57th Street and elsewhere in the park. Also, the board in front of Mel's Diner lists which attractions have the longest and shortest waits.

Kennel: Pets are not allowed in Universal Studios. There is, however, an air-conditioned kennel next to the Toll Plaza. Reservations are not needed.

Lockers: Available for 50¢ per use, located next to the park exit and by the group entrance.

Lost Children: Report to Guest Relations.

Smoking, eating, and drinking: Not allowed in any attractions.

Wheelchair guests: Wheelchair rentals are available in limited quantities by the main entrance.

TOURING TIPS

There's a lot of marquee headliner attractions, which is good in a way because crowds are dispersed more rather than concentrated in two or three, but it also means that there's not really a lot of things you can just walk right on to. The attractions that should be tackled early in the day are Back to the Future and Terminator 2.

Note that fast food here is almost universally more expensive than that found at Disney – no pun intended. Better food bargains can be had if you get your hand stamped and leave the park in the middle of the day and eat at CityWalk or one of the surrounding area's many budget restaurants.

RIDE THE MOVIES

BACK TO THE FUTURE... THE RIDE!

Rating: 10!!!!! Arguably the single best theme park ride in Florida. Location: Expo Center, between the Animal Actor's Stage and the Amity side of the Lagoon. Duration of Ride: 4 1/2 minutes. Comments: Riders must be 3'10". As this is a very rough ride, it will sometimes induce motion sickness. Switching off and child swapping is available. This ride is not recommended for those with back or neck problems, heart conditions, or claustrophobia, also not recommended for pregnant women. Frightening? Yes. The effects are visual - very visual, and physical - very, very physical.

This ride can be summed up in one word: WOW! The Back to the Future trilogy was one of the most popular series in the past decade, and the ride almost serves as yet another sequel, except that it stars you as the intrepid time travelers. You will wander the halls of the Institute of Future Technology to reach a pre-show area where Doc Brown (Christopher Lloyd) informs you that he has completed a batch of faster, more efficient, eight-passenger Deloreans-turned-time machines.

He also glumly tells you that Biff Tannen (Thomas Wilson) has broken into the Institute and is plotting something not quite kosher. You have to hop into your time machine (which bears Florida license plate OUTATIME) and set off into a hemispherical, seven-story Omnimax theater with incredible flight-simulation effects. The liquid-nitrogen fog, the perfectly-timed hydraulic jolts, the 70mm film, and the multi-channel stereo surround sound all enhance the astonishing realism of the production.

On your journey, you chase Biff back past Leonardo da Vinci, the Wright Brothers, and over waterfalls, cliffs, and canyons, eventually into the mouth of a Tyrannosaurus Rex, over the lip of a volcano, and... well, let's just say that this is a quite intense ride from beginning to end. Kids over eight will usually love this ride, however, with younger kids, the fright potential is very high.

This ride is perpetually crowded, as it is THE ride of rides, and appropriately, the wait is THE wait of waits - up to two hours in peak seasons. By contrast, Back to the Future is usually all but empty as closing time approaches. But in an optimum situation, a guest would get to the park before opening and as soon as the gate drops, rush to The FUNtastic World of Hanna-Barbera and then E.T. Adventure, this way bypassing the first-ride rush that it experiences each morning, and then being able to experience it during a relative hiatus. The ride is unlike anything else in Orlando, so if you only had one ride to experience in Orlando, you should make Back to the Future that one ride.

TWISTER - RIDE IT OUT

Rating: 9 1/2. Genuinely scary, not to be missed. Location: New York, at 57th Street and Amblin. Duration of Show: Approximately 10 minutes. Frightening: Yes, even occasionally for jaded theme park travel writers.

Honestly, I don't remember the last theme park attraction that legitimately frightened me before this one. I don't know if there's been one. That's how realistic and incredible this ride is.

Based on the 1996 film starring Helen Hunt and Bill Paxton, this is one of the most technologically advanced theme park attractions anywhere. After a short preshow and a queue through realistically themed sets, guests are herded into the main auditorium, where you will witness an honest-to-god tornado. A five-story twister, 12 feet wide, the largest indoor tornado ever created. Excited yet?

The SFX, created by a combination of 18 seven-foot fans, 110 decibels of sound effects pumped through a 42,000-watt sound system with 54 speakers, hundreds of xenon strobe lights, are amazingly realistic, as Universal consulted with scientists and wind experts from engineering firm Cermak Peterka Peterson and Miami University of Ohio. Without giving away the surprises that make this attraction so terrifying, let me simply say that Universal truly has gone all out on this one. Not to be missed.

KONGFRONTATION

Rating: 6. An excellent ride adventure, well done. Location: New York, off 5th Avenue. Duration of Ride: 4 1/2 minutes. Comments: Riders must be 3'4". Children under 3 and expectant mothers are not allowed to ride. Frightening: Yes. Kong is extremely realistic, the ride is compellingly intense.

Another one of the premier attractions in Universal, Kongfrontation sets the tone immediately as you wander through a queue area designed after a subway terminal. As you wander through the area, notice the graffiti on the walls. Some of it was applied by artists prior to the attraction's opening. As for the majority of them, let's just say that some guests brought their own writing utensils. As you walk through the area, overhead television monitors tell of King Kong's rampage via news broadcast.

You finally reach the boarding area, where you are put on an aerial tram to Roosevelt Island. As you rise over the city, you can sense that something is wrong. Everywhere you look are fires, crushed buildings, broken water lines, and aerial trams-turned-scrap metal. Finally, you reach the Queensboro Bridge and there he is, all six tons of him. He grabs your tram and as he is about to smash it, a helicopter starts shooting at him and well, prepare to drop at 1.75 Gs. The tram somehow manages to get back to the ground intact, and a TV in the tram shows a news clip about your close call. The ride is very popular, but can be seen with a minimum wait in the first hour the park is open and after 6 PM.

E.T. ADVENTURE

Rating: 9. Charming, highly recommended. Location: Woody Woodpecker's KidZone. Duration of Ride: 5 minutes.

Many people consider E.T. to be Steven Spielberg's crowning achievement, even though it lost the Best Picture Oscar to Gandhi. Nevertheless, it serves as the basis for this spectacular ride adventure in which you board a bike or a gondola and set off through a redwood forest to E.T.'s home planet. Once there, you meet E.T's playmates, including mini-E.T.'s, dancing flowers, and other exotic flora and fauna. At the end of the ride, E.T. thanks you by name.

How does he do this? Well, let's rewind here for a second. As you enter the ride, you are given a special pass in exchange for your name when you are "cast." Then, you walk through a dim, dark forest. Right before you board, you give the card to an attendant. The cards have your name computer-coded on them, so the ride knows who's on the ride at any given time. Another little touch that makes this ride so special is the original music, composed by John Williams (Star Wars, Indiana Jones, Home Alone). To avoid crowds, which can really bottleneck at this attraction, ride it second thing of the day, right after Hanna-Barbera.

EARTHQUAKE: THE BIG ONE

Rating: 7. Almost too realistic. Location: San Francisco, on the Embarcadero. Duration of Show: 23 minutes, total. The ride itself is only a fraction of that. Frightening: Possibly. The visual effects are intense, and anyone who has lived through the horror of the real thing may want to skip this.

Earthquake first puts you in a queue area surrounded by photos of the aftermath of the 1906 San Francisco quake. You then enter a theater to watch clips from Earthquake, the movie, and to see some of the miniature buildings used in the production of the movie. After that, you go into a display in which six volunteers show how the stunts in movies like Earthquake are filmed, demonstrating with a child dumping foam rocks on the adults' heads. Finally, you board a real BART train for a trip from Oakland and San Francisco.

But no sooner do you set off than an 8.3 earthquake hits, triggering buckling concrete, falling tanker trucks, flash floods, and fires, much like what happens in Catastrophe Canyon in the Disney-MGM Studios, except far more intense.

Hint: The best view during the ride can be had in the second car from the front (on your left). Try to sit in the middle of the car, as the view from the front is somewhat obstructed.

THE FUNTASTIC WORLD OF HANNA BARBERA

Rating: 7. Funny, exciting, but not on a par with other simulators. Location: Production Central, at the corner of Plaza of the Stars and Nickelodeon Way. Duration of Ride: 4 1/2 minutes; 3 1/2 minute pre-show. Comments: May induce motion sickness. Those prone to motion sickness, those with back or neck problems, pregnant women, the elderly, and the very young are advised to sit in the front row of the auditorium, which does not move. Frightening: Yes. The physical effects are extremely intense, may be too much for some.

This is a flight simulation adventure that uses the technology of Body Wars and splices it with the lovable characters of eight-time Emmy Award and seven-time Oscar winners Bill Hanna and Joe Barbera. The storyline goes something like this: Dick Dastardly kidnaps Elroy Jetson, and Yogi and Boo Boo set off on a rocket to chase after Elroy, with pit stops in Bedrock and the future to pick up the Flintstones and Jetsons. Scooby Doo gets picked up along the way, and in the ensuing chase, the good guys win and the bad guys get their just desserts.

Funny, original, and altogether a decent experience, this attraction features long lines most of the day. See this as soon as you enter the park or right before leaving. Note that if you've already experienced Body Wars, Star Tours, or Back to the Future being placed in a cartoon will not impress you. This ride is more enjoyable if done first.

JAWS

Rating: 9. Well-done, well-acted, entertaining and suspenseful. Location: Amity, at the Lagoon. Duration of Ride: 5 minutes.

This new version of the Jaws ride is a thrilling adventure that pits a tour boat against the great white that terrorized the town of Amity again... and again... and again... and again. Only guess who's on the tour boat.

You leave from Amity Harbor for a guided tour, but no sooner do you make the first turn that you spot the wreckage of another boat. A dorsal fin pops up and chases you into a boathouse, where you can await backup safely. Right? Yeah, right. Jaws busts through the side of the boathouse and it's on the run again.

Your captain picks up a grenade launcher that conveniently happens to be located on the boat and fires it at Jaws. No good, this guy's tougher than the Terminator. Finally, the captain tries to maneuver the boat so the passengers can climb onto a dock. I don't want to give away the ending, but obviously, if Jaws won, there wouldn't be too much repeat business. But the way that the shark is defeated is rather novel. This ride is best seen before 11 a.m.

WOODY WOODPECKER'S NUTHOUSE COASTER

Rating: 5. Good for the little ones. Location: Woody Woodpecker's KidZone. Duration of Ride: 2 minutes.

This is a wacky, junior-sized kids' roller coaster straight out of the world of Woody Woodpecker. Climb into coaster cars shaped like crates of nuts – mixed nuts, salted nuts, and certifiably nuts. The 800 foot, 90-second ride is extremely big with the littlest ones.

LIVE & INTERACTIVE SHOWS
TERMINATOR 2: 3D

Rating: 10. Oh my GAWD. The standard by which all other 3D movies will forever be judged. Location: Hollywood Boulevard. Duration of Show: 20 minutes.

"I always said I'd be back," Arnold Schwarzenegger says. And back he is, reunited with the costars of T2, Edward Furlong, Linda Hamilton, and Robert Patrick, and the director of Terminator and True Lies, James Cameron, in this groundbreaking 3D film. Shot in 65 mm film, it utilizes amazing action shots, computer imaging, and three fifty-foot screens to wow the audience. It's the world's largest 3D theatre and the first to use the triple screen. Techniques similar to those used in Muppet Vision 3D and Honey, I Shrunk the Audience are used, and maxed out. Unbelievable. There just aren't words. Just see it. Again and again. Wow. It's that good.

"ALFRED HITCHCOCK: THE ART OF MAKING MOVIES"

Rating: 9. Amazing, not to be missed. Location: Production Central, 8th Avenue and Plaza of the Stars. Duration of Show: 40 minutes. Frightening: Some portions are extremely graphic and inappropriate for younger children. Universal rates this attraction PG-13.

This spectacular attraction is a fitting tribute to Alfred Hitchcock. You start off in a 3-D theater in which you will view a montage featuring his most famous films. The tribute's highlights are a scene from Dial M For Murder and the attack scene from The Birds, all done in three dimensions. It's frighteningly real.

You then go to a soundstage in which audience volunteers and professional actors combine their talents to reenact the most famous scenes, including Vertigo, Rear Window, Strangers on a Train, Saboteur, Spellbound, and the infamous Psycho shower scene (which was originally shot with 78 takes). After the visit to the soundstage, the tour deposits you in an interactive area where you can relive other famous scenes from Hitchcock's thrillers. Not to be missed.

THE GORY, GRUESOME, & GROTESQUE HORROR MAKE-UP SHOW

Rating: 7. Lively and fast-paced. Location: Hollywood, on Hollywood Boulevard. Duration of Show: 25 minutes. Frightening: Visually intense. Universal rates it PG-13.

This well-conceived, well-done show focuses in on the make-up effects that make films like Beetlejuice, The Fly, and The Exorcist so successful. The humor is tongue-in-cheek, and there's more than enough gore to satisfy anyone's craving for it. The best thing about this worthwhile show is the fact that it is pretty much a sleeper, thus receiving few of the gigantic herds that plague many of the other attractions.

THE ANIMAL ACTORS SHOW

Rating: 6. Warm and happy. Location: Expo Center, by the Hard Rock Cafe. Duration of Show: 20 minutes.

The actors who entertain you here aren't quite human. In fact, they're really a bunch of animals. Literally. Mr. Ed, Benji, Lassie, Jerry Lee, and 45 other animal actors put on a show here with their trainers. Part of the fun comes from the spontaneity of an animal not doing what a trainer tells it to do, an element of risk not found in shows starring humans.

DYNAMITE NIGHTS STUNT SPECTACULAR

Rating: 7. Dazzling, impressive. Location: On the Lagoon. Duration of Show: 20 minutes. Frightening: Explosions and other visually intense effects may put off a few.

In this stunt show, cigarette boats zoom across the Lagoon, one filled with drug smugglers and their loot, the other carrying the good guys. The ensuing chase and pyrotechnic display is comparable to the vehicle stunts in the Indiana Jones Epic Stunt Spectacular in the Disney-MGM Studios. This show is usually held at 7 PM. Hint: The most comfortable viewpoints when the weather is especially hot can be had in San Francisco's Lombard's Landing and Chez Alcatraz restaurants.

THE WILD, WILD, WILD WEST STUNT SHOW

Rating: 7. Exciting. Location: By Amity, on the far edge of the park. Duration of Show: 18 minutes. Frightening: Explosions and other violent acts are shown. Visually intense.

The other half of the Universal stunt show duo, the Wild West has Clod and Cole Hopper, a pair of fictitious cowboys, duking it out with bad guys, falling off buildings, running into buildings, blowing up buildings, etc. This show runs continuously and features clips from old Westerns and trade secrets. See it at your leisure.

A DAY IN THE PARK WITH BARNEY

Rating: 8 or –8, depending on your feelings towards the purple dinosaur. Location: Woody Woodpecker's KidZone. Duration of Show: 25 minutes.

This show, starring the (in)famous purple dinosaur and his friends, Baby Bob, BJ, and a new character, Mr. Pcekaboo, includes special effects and a sing-along. It's difficult for me to get too deep into a description of what exactly this attraction consists of, but let it suffice to say that you know what to expect, and if you don't, then you should probably skip this one anyway.

CURIOUS GEORGE GOES TO TOWN

Rating: 8. You're going to have a hard time getting the kids out of here. Location: A landmark, at the very edge of the park.

This interactive play area shows you the results of everybody's favorite mischief-making monkey (no, not Robert Downey, Jr.) as he runs amok, freeing all the animals in the zoo. Next thing you know, there's water flowing everywhere, as your kids can shoot pumps, sprays, water cannons, dump buckets, and otherwise create mayhem to the tune of 2,500 gallons per minute. There's also the Man in the Yellow Hat's ball factory, where kids can abuse 12,500 foam balls that you can shoot, blast, or dump. So much fun that even I couldn't drag myself away.

BEETLEJUICE'S GRAVEYARD REVUE

Rating: 6. Enjoyable. Location: At the border of New York and San Francisco. Duration of Show: 20 minutes.

Another new live show, this one follows in the footsteps of the Dead, with the dead. Beetlejuice has started up a band, whose members include Dracula, Frankenstein and his bride, and Wolfman. The 20-minute show is spooky and irreverent, the band straight from a Catskills gig. Dracula is reportedly the sixth New Kid on the Block, and he's the songwriter for the motley crew; the Bride of Frankenstein performs Carole King's *You Make Me Feel Like a Natural Woman*; the Phantom of the Opera sings *Great Balls of Fire*, showing off his past associations with Chuck Berry, Jerry Lee Lewis, and Little Richard; and Frankenstein preforms *When a Man Loves a Woman*.

THE BLUES BROTHERS

Rating: 7 1/2. If you're into Jake and Elwood, seeing this should be "a mission from God." Location: New York, Delancey Street. Duration of Show: 20 minutes.

Doppelgangers for Jake and Elwood Blues perform songs like "Think," "(Almost) Everything I need," "Soul Man," and many more several times daily on Delancey Street. They promote the show by driving across the New York area in the Bluesmobile.

TOURS
NICKELODEON STUDIO TOUR

Production Central, a landmark. Rating: 5 1/2. A letdown unless there is a taping. Duration of Tour: 25 minutes.

Here, you walk through Nickelodeon's hair, makeup, and dressing rooms, soundstages, wardrobe, and prop departments. This tour is unmemorable compared to the Disney-MGM Studio Tour, unless a show is in production when you visit. To find out whether a show will be in production at the time of your visit, call 363-8000 or inquire at Guest Relations. Hint: If your kids have ever lamented about wishing to appear on Double Dare so they could get a taste of toxic-sounding substances like gak or slime, this is the only spot in Orlando to can fulfill that wish! The kitchen at Nick Studios dishes out the stuff. Yum???

CHARACTERS

Here at Universal, you may run into characters as diverse as Marilyn Monroe and Popeye. Animated characters roaming the park include Yogi and Boo Boo Bear, Scooby Doo, the Flintstones, Rocky & Bullwinkle, and Fievel Mouskewitz. Celebrity lookalikes include Groucho, Harpo, and Chico Marx, W.C. Fields, Charlie Chaplin, Stan Laurel, Oliver Hardy, Ricky Ricardo, Beetlejuice, the Phantom of the Opera, and Wolfman Jack.

SHOPPING

Universal has twenty-six shops, many of them not warranting any particular interest, but there are some interesting marketplaces. The **Hanna-Barbera Shop** offers animation cels and memorabilia. The **Bates Motel Gift Shop** is a must for anyone with a Mother.

Safari Outfitters, Ltd. offers (among other things) a chance to pose for a picture in the fist of one King Kong for $5. At **E.T.'s Toy Closet**, you can pose with everyone's favorite alien and get souvenirs bearing his likeness. **Golden Gate Mercantile** offers souvenirs from Earthquake! and the city's sets. **Quint's Nautical Treasures** purveys New England- and nautical-theme gifts. **San Francisco Imports** offers Oriental items.

Set Streets

One of Universal's foremost assets is the presence of these open-access sets of locales as varied as Little Italy, the Upper East Side, the Theater District, Gramercy Park, Coney Island, Battery Park, and Central Park in New York; Ghirardelli Square, Fisherman's Wharf, the Embarcadero, and the SFRT Subway Station in San Francisco, Boston Bay, Amity Village, New England Street, and Amity Harbor in New England; Hollywood Boulevard, Beverly Hills, Rodeo Drive, Sunset Boulevard, and the Walk of Fame, all in Hollywood, and other assorted scenes like Angkor Wat, the Bates Motel, the Psycho House, and Doc Brown's Science Center.

DINING

Note that showing your AAA card is a good way to earn a 10% discount at restaurants here and at Islands of Adventure.

CLASSIC MONSTERS CAFÉ

Brainbug's "Nightmare," Alice Cooper's "Feed My Frankenstein," and other spooky songs set the tone for this cool restaurant, blasting from speakers outside the Café. Inside you'll find a rowdy monster-themed atmosphere and salads, pizzas, rotisserie chicken, pasta, and more being cooked up by the restaurant's "mad scientists."

MEL'S DRIVE-IN

Straight out of *American Graffiti*, this 50's throwback serves a family-style menu with entrees like burgers, hot dogs, chili, and chicken sandwiches. Rock music plays and a sock-hop atmosphere runs rampant (L,D,S).

FINNEGAN'S PUB

Service: Table-service. Meals: L,D. Cuisine: Irish. Prices: Budget to moderate. Location: New York, across from Kongfrontation.

Finnegan's Pub is one of the most convincing spots in Universal, portraying accurately a friendly, Big Apple Irish pub. The menu is comprised of simple Irish fare like Cornish pasti, Scotch eggs, sandwiches, corned beef, bangers and mash (sausage and mashed potatoes), Irish stew, fish and chips, beef casserole, Shepherd's pie, Yorkshire beef, and meat and chicken pies. Guiness Stout, Harp Lager, and Bass ale are available to wash down your meal. This bar and grill features a live and very good dinner show several times nightly, and piped-in Irish music at other times.

LOUIE'S ITALIAN RESTAURANT

Louie's is a good place to pick up pizza with a variety of toppings, linguine, spaghetti, tortellini, lasagne, and antipasto. For dessert, try the authentic Italian ices (L,D,S).

INTERNATIONAL FOOD BAZAAR

Service: Food court. Meals: L,D,S. Cuisine: International. Prices: Budget. Location: Expo Center, next to Back to the Future.

The International Food Bazaar is the only Expo Center location that has anything to do with a World's Fair expo. Five counters offer different cuisines.

The American counter serves fried chicken, barbecue pork sandwiches, hot dogs, and hamburgers. The Chinese counter sells lo mein, sweet and sour chicken, and stir-fried shrimp. The German stand sells bratwurst and knockwurst with potato salad or red cabbage. The Greek stand sells gyros, Greek salad, and spanakopita. Last, but not least is the Italian counter, serving jumbo shells, pizza, and salads. Desserts available include baklava, black bottom pie, Black Forest cake, Italian amaretto mousse, frozen yogurt, and ice cream.

ANIMAL CRACKERS

This snack stand sells decent smoked sausage hoagies, beef brochettes, hot dogs, and hamburgers (L,S).

BEVERLY HILLS BOULANGERIE

Located at the corner of Plaza of the Stars and Rodeo Drive, this is a great place to pick up sweets like eclairs, cookies, pies, croissants, and other pastries. Sandwiches are also served here. Domestic beer, and domestic and imported wines and champagnes are available to wash down that pastry (B,L,D,S).

CAFE LA BAMBA

There's an unlimited buffet featuring Mexican dishes like tacos, enchiladas, burritos, quesadillas, fajitas, beans, and rice. If you're not up to gorging yourself, an a la carte menu features Tex-Mex and ranchero burger platters with fries or chicken tostada salad. Beverages and desserts like flan, margarita mousse, and churros are also available (L,D,S).

BRODY'S ICE CREAM

Amity's own ice cream, sundaes, and floats (S).

BOARDWALK FUNNEL CAKE

Corn dogs and funnel cakes with delicious toppings are sold here (LS).

SCHWAB'S PHARMACY

Lana Turner was discovered here, according to Hollywood legend, but your likely discovery will be some of the best old-fashioned ice cream treats including sodas, shakes, malts, floats, cones, and sundaes (S).

BOARDWALK SNACKS

This snack area in Amity Village sells a variety of traditional board-walk eats, including corn dogs, hot dogs, potato knishes, and cotton candy (L,S).

LOMBARD'S LANDING

Location: On the waterfront in San Francisco/Amity. Prices: Moderate to expensive. Cuisine: American. Meals: LD.

Fisherman's Wharf hosts the "only restaurant in Florida with views of the Pacific and the Atlantic" – the casual, classy Lombard's Landing. Here, you can get casual meals like sandwiches, salads, Maryland crab cakes, New York strip steak, grilled chicken, fish and chips, and fettucine, alongside fancy dishes like grilled swordfish and stuffed veal.

CHEZ ALCATRAZ

This stand sells a variety of traditional and exotic seafood items, ranging from clam chowder, shrimp cocktail, crab cocktail, and a crab salad sandwich (LDS).

MIDWAY GRILL

Along the Amity waterfront, this stand sells sausage hoagies, Philly cheesesteaks, and ice cold beer.

SAN FRANCISCO PASTRY CO.

This is a relatively authentic street cafe except for the fact that you must stand in line to purchase your food. The menu is filled with so many goodies that you may have some trouble making up your mind. But it's hard to not enjoy the mousse, kiwi tarts, or cheesecake dished up up here (B,S).

18. ISLANDS OF ADVENTURE

In May 1999, Islands of Adventure became Universal's second Orlando theme park, and quite possibly the best theme park in the area. Great themes, technologically brilliant attractions, memorable characters, decent food, and some of the best thrill rides around make this park absolutely mindblowing.

With Steven Spielberg serving as creative consultant, this park features groundbreaking technology plus adventures based on characters like the Cat in the Hat, Popeye, Spider-Man, The Incredible Hulk, Jurassic Park dinosaurs, and more, Islands of Adventure contains some of the best rides in this or any other theme park in Orlando.

There are six themed lands here. Port of Entry prepares adventurers for the goodies beyond. Marvel Superhero Island is the home of amazing attractions based on Marvel comic adventures. Toon Lagoon offers several water rides themed after newspaper comic strips. Jurassic Park contains adventures based on the Spielberg film. The Lost Continent takes adventurers to a mystical time and place with medieval and mythical themed adventures and thrills. Seuss Landing is the only place in the world where your kids can meet the characters of Theodore Geisel's fabled books.

Islands of Adventure is located within walking distance of CityWalk and Universal Studios Florida.

GETTING TO ISLANDS OF ADVENTURE

To get to Universal Studios Escape from:
• Walt Disney World, Kissimmee, Lake Buena Vista. Take I-4 east to exit 30A (Universal Blvd.) and turn left, following signs to the parking deck.
• International Drive: Take Universal Blvd. Straight to the park entrance. Universal Boulevard runs parallel to I-Drive, one block to the east. Alternatively, take I-Drive to Kirkman Road and turn left, driving 1.1 miles to the park entrance.

ISLANDS OF ADVENTURE VITAL STATISTICS

1000 Universal Studios Plaza, Orlando, FL 32819-7610.

On the Internet: *www.uescape.com*

Phone: *407/363-8000 or Tel. 888/U-ESCAPE*

Hours: *Park opens at 9am daily, 8am for Universal Escape Resort guests. Closing times vary.*

    Admission: $44 for adults, $35 for kids 3 to 9. Two-day passes are $80 and $65. Three-day passes are $100 and $80. The Orlando FlexTicket is also available (see chapter 16).

    Parking: *$6.*

    Time to See: *Six to eight hours.*

    When to See: *Sundays, Tuesdays and Wednesdays are generally relatively quiet here.*

    Don't Miss: *Incredible Hulk Coaster, Dueling Dragons, Amazing Adventures of Spider-Man, Jurrasic Park River Adventure*

PRACTICAL INFORMATION

Alcoholic Beverages: Allowed, sold at many establishments.

Baby Services: Nursing facilities are available at Guest Services, on the right side of the entrance plaza.

Banking: ATMs are located at the right side of entrance plaza and at the Enchanted Oak Tavern in the Lost Continent area.

Cameras: De Foto's in the Port of Entry offers film and camera equipment.

Cigarettes: Available at many shops in the park.

First Aid: Across from Oasis Coolers in the Lost Continent.

Foreign Language: Maps and guides are available at guest services.

Guided Tours: A five-hour VIP tour with front-of-the-line access to approximately 8 attractions is available for $120 per person, on top of the admission fee. The non-private tour consists of you and up to 14 other peouple. For $1700, your group can enjoy a private eight-hour tour with priority entrance and preferred seating at any attraction you want to visit.

Information: A board between Port of Entry and Marvel Super Hero Island gives wait times for attractions,.

Lockers: In addition to full-day lockers at Port of Entry, there are additional lockers at the major thrill ride attractions, such as roller coasters. They're free for the first 30 to 60 minutes depending on location but after that add up quickly.

Lost Children: Report to Guest Services.

Smoking, eating, and drinking: Not allowed inside any attractions.

Wheelchair guests: Wheelchairs can be rented at Port of Entry along with strollers.

With the architecture and atmosphere of a seaside village, complete with a lighthouse whose beacon lures adventurers to the Islands. The 130-foot structure was inspired by the lighthouse in Alexandria, Egypt, one of the Seven Wonders of the World.

Essential services such as ATMs, lockers, stroller and wheelchair rental, and package pickup are available here, as well as some tasty dining and cool shops. There's also an information booth by the water at portside. Island Skipper Tour boats ferry passengers on a scenic route between here and Jurassic Park.

Shopping
ISLANDS OF ADVENTURE TRADING COMPANY
This big shop offers merchandise from every Island including apparel for men, women, and children, accessories, jewelry, gifts, toys, stationery, and themed collectibles.

ISLAND MARKET AND EXPORT
Gourmet foods and exports are sold here, as the store has a complete line of candies, tins, and gifts in a variety of specialty baskets and boxes.

SILK ROAD CLOTHIERS
North African styles of apparel are sold here along with accessories, jewelry, hats, blankets, watches, and scarves as well as bath and beauty products and executive gift sets.

DE FOTO'S EXPEDITION PHOTOGRAPHY
Cameras, camera supplies and accessories, film, post cards, albums, and other equipment are sold here.

PORT PROVISIONS
The last chance shop outside the entrance to the park, offers a limited selection of t-shirts, caps, and other last minute souvenirs.

MARVEL SUPERHERO ISLAND

Based on the adventures of characters like Spider-Man, the X-Men, and the Incredible Hulk, the attractions here are among the most technologically advanced in the world and rival any thrill ride in the world for sheer adrenaline.

The architecture is a sort of art-deco comic-book motif, with some buildings painted with chrome-illusion paint that changes colors depending on angle.

Attractions

THE AMAZING ADVENTURES OF SPIDER-MAN

Rating: 10. Sets a new standard for thrill rides. Location: The north side of the Island. Length of Ride: 8 minutes. Frightening: Not really. Intense but in a non-scary sort of way.

This absolutely incredible ride combines rapidly moving, highly mobile ride vehicles with 3-D action and pyrotechnics, vivid scene sets, and more. You wander along queue lines through the Daily Bugle and then chase off with Spider-Man as he tries to recover the Statue of Liberty, which has been stolen by Dr. Octopus and his anti-gravity ray. The ride, with effects including a 400-foot sensory drop, 25 three-dimensional projection screens and dozens of smaller ones, and pyrotechnic effects, takes riders on a rocky, rolling journey through comic book pages as Spider-Man fights Hobgoblin, Doc Ock, and many more, saves riders from a 400-foot plunge to the death, and even gets his revenge on his alter-ego's tyrannical boss, J. Jonah Jameson. If you only have one ride to experience in the Orlando area, ride this.

INCREDIBLE HULK COASTER

Rating: 9. One of the best roller coasters I've ever had the pleasure of riding. Location: "Oh, you mean the OTHER gigantic green roller coaster..." It's hard to miss. Duration of Ride: 2 minutes. Frightening: Quite possibly.

Big, mean, and green – it's only appropriate that the coaster is named for Bruce Banner's alter ego. After walking through Banner's lab, guests get into the coasters to participate in his gamma-ray accelerator tests. Riders are catapulted out of a 150-foot tunnel, going from zero to 40 mph with the same force as a F-16 fighter jet, and straight into a weightless, zero-g heartline roll. Riders are then plunged 105 feet to the ground, where they hit 60 mph as they skim the waves of the lagoon and then plunge below. The ride also includes seven inversions and two subterranean trenches. This ride is not to be missed if you're a coaster fan, and is best experienced early in the day. Note that there are lockers nearby where you can stow your stuff for free while you ride.

DOCTOR DOOM'S FEARFALL
Rating: 6. Cool view, cool effect, not worth a long wait in line. Location: Its two 200-foot steel towers are something of a landmark. Frightening: Yeah, but not as much as you'd think from an attraction with the word "fear" in its name.

These two 200-foot towers of steel are Dr. Doom's newest creation – a device designed to suck every last drop of fear out of them and channel the collected fear into a massive weapon. The 16-seat rings are shot skyward and sent towards the ground at breakneck speed. The rings then bounce up and down a bit like a bungee cord. The view from the top is cool, and the sensation of a fall is as well, but this ride isn't worth the long waits it often attracts.

Shopping
COMICS SHOP
This store offers accessories, trading cards, and countless volumes of contemporary and classic comic books.

MARVEL ALTERNAVERSE STORE
Superhero and supervillain costumes are sold here along with clothing, accessories, mugs, keychains, jewelry, collectibles, and artwork.

KINGPIN ARCADE AND NEWS
Exclusive Marvel Super Hero Island and Doctor Doom Freefall merchandise is sold here, and current arcade games as well.

SPIDER-MAN SHOP
For all your web slinging needs, swing into this shop.

Characters from Saturday morning cartoons and newspaper comics populate this Island. Exaggerated cartoon buildings dominate the landscape along with panels from featured comics.

Attractions
DUDLEY DO-RIGHT'S RIPSAW FALLS
Rating: 8. Fun and watery nostalgia. Location: A big wet landmark. Duration of ride: 8 minutes.

Dudley Do-Right must save Nell from the dastardly Snidely Whiplash in this log flume ride named for the city in 1960s cartoon Rocky and Bullwinkle. The 12-man rafts follow the hapless Do-Right's attempt to save the day, culminating in a drop where the level of incline steepens from 45 to 50 degrees halfway down, under the surface of the water into total darkness and up a roller coaster hill. A damn fun ride.

POPEYE AND BLUTO'S BILGE RAT BARGES
Rating: 8. An absolute hoot. Location: Along the edge of the water, on the southeast corner of Toon Lagoon. Duration of Ride: 10 minutes.

Popeye and his nemesis, the rotund Bluto, battle for the love of Olive Oyl and Swee' Pea in this whitewater rafting adventure. Longer, faster, and wetter than the raft ride at the Animal Kingdom, this offers big drops, water cannons, and a fully functional boat wash. Hope you brought your soap, because you're taking a bath. This ride is every bit as much fun as the other water ride in Toon Lagoon.

ME SHIP THE OLIVE
Rating: 5. A nice change of pace. Location: On the water's edge in Toon Lagoon.

Popeye's three-story boat is a family-friendly interactive playland featuring dozens of interactive activities. There's cargo nets, a crane where you can soak Bilge Rat Barge riders, music at the touch of a button, and much more.

Shopping
GASOLINE ALLEY
This shop offers travel-related souvenirs and a good selection of Florida-themed tourist items.

WOSSAMATTA U.
This seasonal shop sells Bullwinkle and Islands of Adventure clothing, accessories, watches, backpacks, totes, activity sets, rubber stamps, glassware, and collectibles.

TOON TOYS
Another seasonal shop, this one sells novelty gifts such as sipper straws, plush toys, costumes, activity sets, and stationery.

TOON EXTRA
This shop offers clothing, accessories, gifts, and souvenirs including personalized gifts and limited edition collectibles featuring Betty Boop, Popeye, Beetle Bailey, and more.

PHOTO FUNNIES
Here you can have your picture inserted into a comic strip.

Jurassic Park brings guests face to face with "living, breathing" dinosaurs who blink their eyes, flinch at your touch, and even spit. Here you will find some of the most technologically advanced animatronics figures anywhere.

JURASSIC PARK RIVER ADVENTURE
Rating: 8 1/2. Not to be missed. Location: On the north side of the island. Length of Ride: 10 minutes.

Climb aboard for a peaceful boat ride through the herbivore pens at Jurassic Park. Peaceful? Yeah right. Thanks to some unruly animals, your boat is diverted through the storehouses and loading docks of the island, through velociraptors and spitters who stalk the grounds, and then finally right at a huge tyrannosaurus rex. Never fear, your boat escapes the clutches of the meateater. Just don't ask me how ... okay, here's how: a 85-foot plunge down the fastest, longest, steepest water descent ever built. The T-Rex doesn't sound so bad now, does it?

TRICERATOPS ENCOUNTER
Rating: 7. Pleasant. Location: In the center of Jurassic Park.

Here, guests can pet a "living" dinosaur. This feed and control station contains a life-sized animatronic triceratops who guests can learn about the history of the creature from trainers who explain everything from his emotional state to feeding habits,. The creature's responses to touch include blinking his eyes and flinching his muscles.

PTERANADON FLYERS
Rating: 5. Skip if there's a line. Locaiton: Above Camp Jurassic. Length of Ride: 4 minutes.

Guests soar strapped into pteranadons who glide along an aerial track over the Jurassic Park compound. The line for this ride goes incredibly slowly, and the ride is intended mainly for small children and their parents.

JURASSIC PARK DISCOVERY CENTER

Rating: 6. Educational and entertaining. Location: By the bridge to The Lost Continent.

This massive building hosts laboratories where biochemists create the technologies that bring these dinosaurs to life, plus interactive opportunities to manipulate dinosaurs' DNA and create their own dinosaur, plus a T-Rex skeleton and a Raptor hatchery.

CAMP JURASSIC

Rating: 6. Location: Under the Pteranadon Flyers.

This interactive playground gives kids the opportunity to check out rainforests, lava pits, amber mines, decks, caves, and quarries.

Shopping
CAMP JURASSIC OUTPOST

This shop offers youth survival gear and accessories, open seasonally.

DINOSTORE

Located at the Discovery Center, this shop offers all things dinosaur, from the acacdemic to the frivolous.

JURASSIC OUTFITTERS

Jurassic Park River Adventure gear, outback equipment, and safari clothes are sold at this shop.

THE LOST CONTINENT

Mythology comes to life at this exotic corner of the park, with Middle Eastern, Greek, and medieval themed attractions and architecture along with more high-tech fun.

Attractions
DUELING DRAGONS

Rating: 9. Not to be missed. Location: Next to the Jurassic Park bridge.

As you walk through the elaborate queue area Merlin explains that a stroll in the forest is a dangerous proposition thanks to two dragons who breathe fire and ice and inhabit the forest. The idea is that you have to climb on a dragon's back and ride it to freedom.

This is a "dueling" roller coaster where the two coasters – Fire and Ice – fly fast and furious at each other, sometimes missing by a mere 12 inches. Three near misses and five inversions later, you're breathless and racing to get back in line for the other train.

With a top speed of 60 mph and 125 foot heights, this roller coaster isn't quite as adrenaline-heavy as the Hulk Coaster but is still an amazing white-knuckled experience.

POSEIDON'S FURY: ESCAPE FROM THE LOST CITY

Rating: 7 1/2. Intense SFX. Location: Inside the ruins of the temple across from the Enchanted Oak Tavern. Duration of Show: 15 minutes.

This multimedia presentation introduces "The Keeper," a man who has been guarding the secrets of Atlantis for thousands of years, as he leads guests through an amazing 42-foot vortex of water to witness an epic battle between Poseidon and his arch-enemy, the benevolent Zeus. Guests are trapped in the middle of a battle that combines 350,000 gallons of water with 200 flame effects including 25 foot fireballs. While the storyline is a bit weak and hard to follow, the special effects more than make up for it.

THE EIGHTH VOYAGE OF SINDBAD

Rating: 7. Location: Next to Poseidon's Fury. Duration of Show: 20 minutes.

This stunt show follows mythical sailing hero Sindbad as he striked out once again on his search for enormous riches. Along the way he encounters an evil sorceress who has taken a beautiful princess hostage, but the storyline is secondary to the stunts, battle scenes, and 50 pyrotechnic effects including a 10-foot circle of flames.

Shopping
THE DRAGON'S KEEP

Located at the exit from Dueling Dragons, this shop offers merchandise themed from that attraction and the Fire and Ice dragons. Books, magical tricks, games, toys, crystal balls, and pewter mugs are sold here.

A SHOP OF WONDERS

This shop offers silks, copper, brass, woven rugs, travel bags, leather, and cotton goods as well as jewelry.

TREASURES OF POSEIDON

Souvenirs from the deep are sold here along with goodies based on Poseidon's Fury.

OPEN AIR MARKET

Artisans throughout the Lost Continent hawk their wares – things like jewelry, wood carvings, leather sandals, silk garlands, coins, fortune telling, and more.

This area is geared towards children, who can meet the Cat in the Hat and other Dr. Seuss characters for the first time. The whimsical architecture of Theodore Geisel's books is recreated here. In keeping with the no-straight-lines theme, the palm trees found here were bent nearly in half by Hurricane Andrew.

Attractions

THE CAT IN THE HAT

Rating: 7. Dr. Seuss's memory is honored with a ride like this. Location: Just look for the big rooftop hat. Length of Ride: 5 minutes.

Couch potatoes of the world unite! Here you board a sofa and take a chaotic journey through Seuss's most famous book, with 130 ride effects and 30 animatronic characters along the 18 show scenes, including the Cat in the Hat, Thing 1 and Thing 2, and the poor goldfish entrusted the job of keeping the house in order.

ONE FISH TWO FISH RED FISH BLUE FISH

Rating: 5. Like Dumbo at the Magic Kingdom. Location: Next to Circus McGurkus Café Stoopendous. Duration of Ride: 3 minutes.

Much like Dumbo at the Magic Kingdom, guests board Seussian fish and fly, rising or descending up to 15 feet from the ground. The catch here is that there's a rhyme broadcast during the ride – if you don't follow the instructions in the rhyme, you get wet! If only getting your kids to follow directions was always this easy.

CARO-SEUSS-EL

Rating: 8. Heart warming. Location: A landmark, across from Cat in the Hat. Duration of Ride: 4 minutes.

This merry-go-round features 54 different mounts representing seven Seussian characters including cowfish from "McElligot's Pool," Elephant-birds from "Horton Hatches an Egg," AquaMop Tops and Twin Camels from "One Fish Two Fish Red Fish Blue Fish," Dog-a-lopes and Mulligatawnies from "If I Ran the Zoo," and Birthday Katroo from "Happy Birthday to You."

IF I RAN THE ZOO

Rating: 7. Really endearing. Location: Next to Port of Entry.

Eponomously based on the story of Gerald McGrew's quest to create a zoo of strange and unusual animals, this interactive playland features 19 interactive elements in the Hedges, Water, and New Zoo areas.

Shopping

CATS, HATS, AND THINGS

This shop offers clothing, gifts, and toys based on the Cat in the Hat attraction, including accessories, Cat Nap sleepwear, and Cat Bath merchandise.

DR. SEUSS' ALL THE BOOKS YOU CAN READ

This store hosts the full collection of Dr. Seuss books, videos, tapes, and educational software.

MULBERRY STREET STORE

Here you can purchase merchandise based on classic Seuss characters including the Lorax, Yertle, Sneeches, Horton, Sam I Am, and the Cat in the Hat. There's an extensive collection of stuffed animals, a Grinchmas area, and more.

PICTURE THIS

Put yourself in the middle of classic Dr. Seuss books in this keepsake photo shop.

SNOOKERS & SNOOKERS SWEET CANDY COOKERS

Candy and gifts in themed packaging are sold here.

DINING IN ISLANDS OF ADVENTURE

ARCTIC EXPRESS

This Port of Entry snack bar offers funnel cakes and homemade waffles with toppings, along with soft serve ice cream (S).

CONFISCO GRILLE AND BACKWATER BAR

Location: Port of Entry. Prices: Moderate. Cuisine: Steak and seafood. Meals: LD.

This full service restaurant near the park's entrance offers personal pizzas, pasta, fresh seafood, grilled meats, specialty burgers, fresh desserts, and full bar service. This is also the place to meet Islands of Adventure characters during the Confisco Character Lunch, which happens every weekday from noon to 2pm.

CROISSANT MOON BAKERY
Fresh baked pastries including the eponymous crescent rolls, desserts, specialty coffees, beer, wine, and soda are served here (BLDS).

SPICE ISLAND SAUSAGES
A variety of Italian sausages, chicken sausages, hot dogs, and corn dogs are sold here along with fresh cut French fries (LDS).

CAFÉ 4
Lunch for superheroes. You can pick up Italian fast food here, from minestrone soup to pizza slices to pasta and Caesar salads (LD).

CAPTAIN AMERICA DINER
Burgers, chicken sandwiches, apple pie, and other red-white-and-blue favorites are served here (LD).

BLONDIE'S: HOME OF THE DAGWOOD
Pick up massive Dagwood sandwiches, smoked turkey sandwiches, kosher hot dogs, veggie sandwiches, salads, and chicken noodle soup here (LD).

CATHY'S ICE CREAM
This Toon Lagoon ice cream shop specializes in hot fudge sundaes (S).

COMIC STRIP CAFÉ
Decorated in funny pages, this buffeteria offers American, Mexican, Italian, and Chinese fast food (LDS).

WIMPY'S
Popeye's sidekick offers burgers, hot dogs, and what else but spinach salad (LD).

THUNDER FALLS TERRACE
Rotisserie chicken and baby back ribs are offered at this restaurant with a stunning view of the Jurassic Park River Adventure (LD).

BURGER DIGS

Select from huge burgers, chicken sandwiches, gator bites, spiced fries, pina colada cole slaw, and more (LD).

PIZZA PREDATORIA

Jurassic Park's pizzeria also offers Caesar salad, Italian sausage sandwiches, and cold cut sandwiches (LD).

THE WATERING HOLE

This kiosk in Jurassic Park offers tropical frozen drinks and a full bar, plus plantain nachos, pretzels, sodas, beer, and wine (S).

MYTHOS RESTAURANT

Location: A landmark, on the water. Prices: Moderate. Cuisine: Greek and American. Meals: LD.

Set inside a dormant volcano, this stunningly beautiful restaurant in The Lost Continent is Islands of Adventure's signature eatery, offering steaks, wood fired pizzas, fresh seafood, and grilled meats, all with exotic preparation and an atmosphere that celebrates fantastic beasts of myth and legend (LD).

ENCHANTED OAK TAVERN

Sprawled on the shores of the Inland See, this restaurant serves hickory smoked barbecue chicken and ribs along with appropriate sides. The Alchemy Bar here serves 50 different beers (LD).

FIRE EATERS GRILL

This walk-up eatery offers gyros, chicken tenders, and sausages (LDS).

FROZEN DESSERT

Soft serve is served up here by Seuss Landing (S).

GREEN EGGS AND HAM CAFÉ

Would you, could you, on a trip? Would you, could you, cuz it's hip? Feast on the eponymous sandwich here along with other, more conventional meals (LDS).

CIRCUS McGURKUS CIRCUS STOOPENDOUS

This buffeteria in Seuss Island serves pizza, lasagna, fried chicken, calzones, spaghetti, and other family friendly specialties.

HOP ON POP ICE CREAM SHOP
Ice cream bars, waffle cone sundaes, banana splits, brownies, sundaes, and ice cream sodas are served up here.

MOOSE JUICE GOOSE JUICE
Orange and lemon lime slush is served here along with Rice Krispie Treats, cookies, and fruit cups.

19. ORLANDO'S OTHER THEME PARKS

Flip back to 1845 for a minute. Picture a soldier named Orlando Reeves, part of a party scouting for the Florida Indians in a Mosquito County settlement called Jernigan, after Georgian settler Aaron Jernigan. One night, Reeves was on duty, and some Indians disguised as pine tree logs infiltrated the camp. He fired his gun and woke the camp, saving their lives. Unfortunately, in the ensuing battle, Reeves was shot with an Indian arrow and died on the spot. Soon thereafter, the area was referred to as Orlando. The name just stuck. Later that year, Mosquito County became Orange County, and the city of Jernigan officially became Orlando in 1857.

Earlier in this century, the area immediately south of where Walt Disney World sits today, known as Kissimmee (Seminole for Heaven's Place), was a cow town (and still is, as is evidenced by its many farms and cattle auction houses). Its main drawing cards were the bars where cowboys could get a drink without dismounting. The whole community was a sleepy little place with virtually no tourist interest.

Enter Walt Disney. He came onto the scene and purchased the 28,000-acre tract of land known as the Reedy Creek Improvement District and changed the face of Florida. Orlando's population has more than doubled. In a true test of being on the scene, Orlando was awarded, in 1990, an expansion franchise of the NBA, the Orlando Magic. The team went platinum, selling out every home game in three seasons.

Orlando treats its new-found stardom the same way a working-class friend would treat winning $25 million in the lottery. The city is a little shy about it, more than a little surprised, but still friendly and approachable. It bears little resemblance to New York, Chicago, Washington, or even Tampa or Miami. The city is sparkling, almost everything less than 25 years old.

And since Disney, other attractions have sprung up. Most notably, Sea World and Universal Studios Florida. But other small, worthwhile spots exist, and this chapter delves into them.

THEME PARKS

BUSCH GARDENS TAMPA

Location: 3605 Bougainvillea Avenue, Tampa. Phone: Tel. 800/423-8368 or 813-987-5082. On the Internet: www.buschgardens.com. Hours: 10am to 6pm during off seasons, 9am to 7pm during peak seasons. Admission: $41 for adults, $35 for kids ages 3 to 9. Parking: $5. Time to See: One full day. When to See: Weekdays.

This attraction has always been one of Florida's most popular, with good reason. Busch Gardens is one part African safari-themed park, one part accredited zoo. With the introduction of the Animal Kingdom and the explosion of new theme park development in Orlando itself, Busch Gardens has kind of dropped off the radar for some Orlando guests. Regardless, those who are willing to make the 75-minute drive will be rewarded with things that you won't find anywhere else. As a theme park, Busch boasts three of the area's best roller coasters, three water rides, and lots more. As a zoo, it's received a myriad of awards including certificates for the first North American captive breedings of at least 13 species of animal, plus thirteen Gold Propagator certificates for breeding 50 of a species, both awarded by the American Association of Zoological Parks & Aquariums.

Zoological habitats are found in all areas of the park, but is concentrated in several sections: Myombe Reserve: The Great Ape Domain, the Bird Gardens, Nairobi, the Serengeti Plain, the Koala Habitat, the Clydesdale Hamlet, and the Elephant Habitat. All told, the collection houses 3,436 creatures representing 359 species. Special features include the Zoo Kitchen, with dieticians and veterinarians ensuring that park animals receive the proper nutrition; the Hospital, with operating rooms, x-rays, laboratories, recovery areas, and brooder rooms for birds; the Nairobi Field Station Animal Nursery, reminiscent of a turn-of-the-century African hospital, offering ample viewing space, skylighted playrooms, heated floors, and pens equipped with oxygen and 12 computerized isolettes (adapted human incubators) for newborns' health care.

Busch Gardens is divided into nine themed sections, the Bird Gardens, Crown Colony, Morocco, Nairobi, Serengeti Plain, Stanleyville, The Congo, Timbuktu, and Egypt.

To get to Busch Gardens from Orlando and Disney, take I-4 west to I-75 north. Take I-75 to exit 54, Fowler Avenue. Bear left on the exit ramp and take Fowler Ave. west to McKinley Avenue. Turn left on McKinley and follow it to the parking lot and main entrance to the park.

Bird Gardens

This area was one of the original attractions when the 300-acre park opened in 1959. The eponymous **Bird Gardens** still boasts lush foliage and nearly 2,000 exotic birds. Recently opened is the **Gwazi**, a dueling sit-down roller coaster that flings guests within inches of each other six times in 2 minutes with passing speeds of 100 mph. There's also **Land of the Dragons**, a children's play area, a show featuring birds of prey, and the **Anheuser-Busch Hospitality House**, similar to the one at Sea World.

The Congo

This is the thrill ride nerve center of Busch Gardens, with the **Kumba**, the largest and fastest roller coaster in the Southeast, including three first-of-a-kind elements, a diving loop, a camelback loop, and a vertical loop. Also featured here is the **Python**, a 1,200-foot roller coaster with a 360-degree double spiral that cars travel at speeds up to 50 miles an hour; the **Congo River Rapids**, in which 12 riders in a gigantic inner tube set off on a wild journey punctuated by geysers; leaky caves, white water, drops, rapids, and other wet wonders, made even more exciting by the fact that the ride is never the same twice.

The rafts drift in different patterns, so you could sit in the same seat twice and get soaking wet once and not feel a drop the second time around. Also, there's the Monstrous Mamba octopus ride, Ubanga-Banga Bumper Cars, and stations of the railroad and the sky ride. Also in the Congo is **Claw Island**, offering a rare look at yellow and white Bengal tigers in their natural habitat.

Crown Colony

This is a mock-up of a Colonial European outpost, this land features pre-Revolution African architecture and décor, as well as **Akbar's Adventure Tours**, a flight-simulator ride starring Martin Short as an African merchant who leads guests on a tour of Egypt's breathtaking sights. There's also **Edge of Africa**, a walking safari tour of the lion and hyena habitats along with hippo and crocodile enclosures and more, complete with trainers on hand to answer your questions.

Morocco

The **Jewel of Africa** is represented as a beautiful walled city featuring lots of shops that emote a bustling medina feel and restaurants, with a few entertainment venues. Foremost among these is the **Moroccan Palace Theatre**, which hosts the new "Hollywood Live on Ice," a dazzling display of skating prowess. The 1,200-seat theatre fills up about 20 minutes before midday shows, check an entertainment schedule for details.

The **Marrakesh Theater** hosts "American Jukebox," a song-and-dance revue featuring pop, rock 'n' roll, and country music from the 50's to the 90's.

Nairobi

The primary draw of this area of Busch Gardens is the brand-new **Myombe Reserve: The Great Ape Domain**, a stellar attraction paying tribute to man's closest relatives. Six lowland gorillas and eight common chimpanzees roam the simulated rain forest.

Also in the area is the **Nairobi Field Station**, with its baby birds and other animals frolicking around. Nocturnal Mountain is where the wild things are and where it is always after dark. The Nairobi Station of the Trans-Veldt Railroad is also located here. Hop on the train for views of the animals on the Serengeti Plain. Younger kids love the petting zoo and the elephant wash here.

Serengeti Plain

No big-name rides, no flashy shops here, only a wide-open, 80-acre tract of land, home to 800 African animals. Guests can observe animals from the railroad, sky ride, monorail, or from a promenade that winds through the park. The Serengeti Plain also has a successful breeding and survival program for animals, like the black rhino and Asian elephant.

Stanleyville

Feeling a little hot, sticky, icky, and sweaty? Visit Stanleyville, a bustling African village named for the distinguished explorer Sir Henry Morgan Stanley. Ride the **Stanley Falls Log Flume** through winding foliage and eventually over a 43-foot cliff. Still feeling a bit dry? Lose that arid feeling for good on the **Tanganyika Tidal Wave**, where you can get into a large raft for a climb up a 55-foot high track, surrounded by luxuriant scenery, and then you will reprove that what goes up must come down. Then, after the ride, you are given the opportunity to stand on a bridge right in the path of the impending splash. You may never dry out again.

The **Stanleyville Variety Show** includes serialists, jugglers, acrobats, and specialty acts. The show rotates so there are several different exhibitions over the course of the year. The Congo Comedy Corps will split sides in an audience-participation improv in the Zambezi Pavilion.

Timbuktu

Timbuktu is themed after an ancient desert trading center, and contains several major attractions: The **Scorpion**, a looping roller coaster almost as intense as The Python; The Phoenix, a ride in which centrifugal force puts you through a 360-degree loop in a boat; The Sandstorm, an aerial whip ride; and Carousel Caravan, a unique merry-go-round complete with camels and Arabian horses. One of the park's most intriguing shows, **Dolphins of the Deep**, has two bottle-nosed dolphins named Bud and Mitch, who with their sea lion friend and their trainers, make for a fast-paced show at Dolphin Theater.

Egypt

The Egypt pavilion includes the **Montu**, an inverted roller coaster that sends riders through four first-of-a-kind elements including a 60-foot vertical loop at a top speed of 60 mph and up to 3.85 G's. There's also a replica of **Tut's Tomb** and an interactive playground simlating an archaeological dig site.

CYPRESS GARDENS

Location: 2641 S. Lake Summit Drive, Winter Haven. Phone: 941-324-2111. On the Internet: www.cypressgardens.com. Hours: 9:30 AM to 5pm during the off season, 9:30 AM until 8 or 9pm during peak seasons. Admission: $31.95 adult, $14.95 for kids 3 to 9. Parking: Free. Time to see: Four to six hours. When to see: Anytime.

Cypress Gardens is a 223-acre, family-style theme park known worldwide for its ski revues, botanical gardens, and its old-fashioned Southern hospitality. The park is located in Winter Haven, 40 minutes from Walt Disney World. Take I-4 west to exit 23. Take U.S. 27 south to S.R. 540 and turn right. Wheelchairs, strollers, lockers, first aid, and a kennel are all available.

Cypress Gardens' attractions include **When Radios Were Radios**, a permanent exhibition of antique memorabilia commemorating the nostalgic years of radio with hundreds of different vintage radios from the 20's through 50's. **Feathered Follies** is an exotic revue with a colorful cast of performing birds combining entertainment with education.

Cypress Gardens cements its title as "Water Skiing Capital of the World" with its **Ski Xtreme** show, featuring traditional stunts like human pyramids, ramp jumps, ballet lines, and flag lines, along with audience participation and skiers who pick their own music and performance and rotate roles to create a dynamic, ever-changing show. The **Hot Nouveau Ice** skating show features world-renowned figure skaters, original music, sets, and costumes in a full production that showcases their amazing athleticism. The **Variete Internationale** show features award-winning professional dancers and Moscow Circus performers as well as clowns who steal the show.

Carousel Cove is a children's ride area with eight rides and a beautiful carousel. **Captain Robin's Flying Circus** features trapeze, web, spinning ladders, and tumbling acts, all blended with old-fashioned circus entertainment and trampoline performances. **Kodak's Island** in the Sky puts guests on a revolving platform for a 153-foot ascension, from which point you can see for miles around. **Cypress Junction** is an elaborate model railroad system with 1,100 feet of track and up to 20 trains traveling on it at once. **Cypress Roots** is a museum telling the story of the first Florida attraction, including a display of cameras from the 20's to the 70's, the waterskis used in original Cypress Gardens shows, and photos of celebrities who visited the park. Electric boats wind through a maze of landscaped canals with pleasant scenery.

Cypress Gardens also contains an accredited zoo and botanical garden. The original gardens feature 8,000 varieties of plants from 75 different countries. The zoo contains a free fly aviary, gator show, and the Critter Encounter petting zoo. The park also features several annual festivals including the **Spring Floral Festival**, with ten uniquely designed topiaries shaped as various animals (mid-March to mid-May), the **Chrysanthemum Festival** with the nation's largest collection of blooms (numbering over 2 million), and the **Garden of Lights Holiday Festival**, featuring extended hours so guests can enjoy the 5 million twinkling lights decorating the park.

GATORLAND

Location: 14501 S. Orange Blossom Trail, Orlando. Phone: 407/855-5496 or Tel. 800/393-JAWS. On the Internet: www.gatorland.com. Hours: 9am until dusk daily. Admission: $17 for adults, $8 for kids aged 3 to 12. Parking: Free. Time to See: Three hours. When to See: Anytime.

This is a zoo named for and starring the famed Florida carnivores. Alligators, crocodiles, and snakes are everywhere in this zoo, you even walk through a grotesquely large pair of gator jaws to enter the park. When inside, you can stroll along the boardwalk, watching for the reptiles sunbathing in swamps on either side. You've probably already seen Gatorland, provided that you've seen Indiana Jones and the Temple of Doom, Ernest Saves Christmas, Survival, Nickelodeon's Total Panic, Late Night with David Letterman, or National Geographic. **Gatorland** or its inhabitants have been involved in those projects and more.

There are three headliner shows here: the oldest being the famed **Gator Jumparoo**, in which reptiles leap out of the water for slabs of meat being dangled over the water. Who knew that gators could jump?!? Also, the **Snakes of Florida** show provides an entertaining and educational look at the 69 varieties of snakes native to Florida. Gator Wrestlin' "Cracker Style" disproves the myth that only Seminoles tangled with alligators, as men dressed as Florida Crackers (cowboys) go to battle.

A train ride carries guests around and affords photo opportunities, as do the Swamp Walk, Observation Tower, and Alligator Breeding Marsh walk. Pearl's Smokehouse sells gator ribs and gator nuggets, and several snack bars offer more traditional theme park fare. Also, for souvenirs, visit the gift shop at the main entrance. For those of you who aren't revolted by the thought of Gatorland Zoo selling alligator leather, there's a boutique at the main entrance as well.

To get to Gatorland from Walt Disney World or Kissimmee, take U.S. 192 east until you reach U.S. 17-92-441, the South Orange Blossom Trail. Turn left, the zoo will be on your right. The S.O.B.T. can also be accessed by the Beeline Expressway, Florida's Turnpike, the Central Florida Parkway, Sand Lake Drive, or I-4 (exit 33A).

KENNEDY SPACE CENTER/SPACEPORT USA

Location: NASA Parkway, Cape Canaveral. Phone: 407/452-2121. On the Internet: www.kennedyspacecenter.com. Hours: 9am to dusk daily. Admission: Free, but bus tours and IMAX films have separate admission. Parking: Free. Time to See: Six hours. When to See: Anytime.

The Kennedy Space Center's popular visitor center features a variety of exhibits, films, and tours, many of which are free. The remainder are priced so that a family of four could experience a full day of fun here for about the same as one admission to Disney.

The **International Space Station Center** showcases the actual facility where NASA is preparing the components for the International Space Station, the biggest, most complex structure ever put into orbit. There's an elevated observation room overlooking the processing bay, a full-scale mockup of the Habitation Module, and a theatre presentation where shuttle astronaut Bob Cabana explains the purpose and importance of the project.

KSC also hosts the world's only back-to-back IMAX theatres, featuring three separate presentations on 5 story tall screens. The three-dimensional *L5: First City in Space* presents a realistic picture of a future space city, through the use of NASA footage and data, through the point of view of a seven year old girl born on a giant orbiting space colony. *The Dream Is Alive* offers an insider's view of the space shuttle program, with 37 minutes of footage from 3 separate missions, narrated by Walter Cronkite. Finally, *Mission to Mir* looks at the effort between the United States and Russia to co-exist in space, with a look at life on the Russian space station Mir and even of the historic docking of space shuttle Atlantis with the Mir station.

The **LC 39 Observation Gantry** is located less than a mile from Launch Pads 39A and 39B, where the space shuttle is launched. The observation deck provides an air-conditioned, 360-degree view of the launch complex including the Vehicle Assembly Building, Launch Control Center, and the Crawlerway. There's a film featuring astronaut Marsha Ivins explaining the launch preparation process and an interactive area.

The **Apollo/Saturn V Center** includes the Firing Room Theatre, where footage from the original moon flight is shown, an actual 363-foot Saturn V rocket, the Lunar Surface Theatre, where you can experience the moon landing itself, and an exhibition gallery featuring hands-on displays representing NASA's vision of the future.

There's also a bus tour of the Space Center available. Tickets for the bus tour are $14 for adults, $10 for kids 3 to 11. Combine it with one IMAX film for $19 and $15, or with two IMAX films for $26 and $20, respectively. To get to Kennedy Space Center, take SR 528 (Beeline Expressway) east to SR 407 north, turning right on SR 405, following signs the whole way.

SILVER SPRINGS

Location: 5856 E. Silver Springs Blvd., Silver Springs, FL 32688. Phone: Tel. 800/234-7458 or Tel. 904/236-2121. On the Internet: www.silversprings.com. Hours: 9am to 5:30 PM daily. Admission: $30.95 adults, $21.95 for kids aged 3 to 10. Parking: Free. Time to See: Six hours. When to See: Anytime.

Silver Springs might be called Florida's oldest attraction, claiming to have drawn visitors for 10,000 years. Whether this bit is true or misinformation, Silver Springs makes a lovely place to spend a day, if you have the time. Like Sea World and Cypress Gardens, Silver Springs is a blessedly calm attraction that can serve to repose and recover from the frenetic pace of a normal WDW vacation.

There are five major attractions, the first of which is the **Jungle Cruise**. Unlike the Jungle Cruise at the Magic Kingdom, all the animals you will encounter on this boat jaunt are real. Six continents are represented by the animal population of this placid river voyage. The Glass Bottom Boats take you through waters of the largest artesian spring in the world, actually 14 springs so clear that sunlight can penetrate to depths of 83 feet. And now for something completely different, the **Jeep Safari** puts you in a convertible, tiger-striped Jeep Wrangler for an exciting venture through the jungles where the original Tarzan movies were filmed. On your safari, you may see deer, zebras, monkeys, macaws, and deer, with absolutely nothing coming between you and the animals, not even a cage, not even a pane of glass.

The **Lost River Voyage** takes you back thousands of years into a pristine Florida ecosystem, home to wild boar, deer, gators, osprey, wild turkeys, hawks, eagles, and 29 varieties of waterbirds. **Doolittle's Petting Zoo** would make its namesake proud. Younger kids also seem to enjoy this section of Silver Springs. Several different **Animal Shows** are performed daily as well. This year, Silver Springs will host over a dozen concerts, including the Charlie Daniels Band and Glen Campbell. Finally, a museum of nostalgic knick-knacks, antique cars, and phonographs, on display.

Silver Springs' boats are all covered, and free parking, kennels, camper parking, and handicap facilities are available. Picnic areas are available as well. Silver Springs is 72 miles north of Orlando. Take Florida's Turnpike north to I-75 north. From I-75, take exit 69, S.R. 40 east. The national landmark is one mile east of Ocala.

SPLENDID CHINA

Location: 3000 Splendid China Blvd., Kissimmee, FL 34747. Phone: Tel. 800/244-6226 or 407/396-7111. Hours: 9:30 AM to dusk daily. Admission: $29 for adults, $18 for kids 5 to 12. Parking: Free. Time to See: Four hours. When to See: Anytime.

From the folks that brought you the Cultural Revolution, the People's Republic of China brings you **Splendid China**, the Orlando area's newest attraction, with more than 60 of China's best-known scenic, historic, and cultural sites in both full scale and miniature.

The main attraction of the 76-acre park is a replica of the 4,200-mile **Great Wall**. The 2,600-foot miniature features over eight million one- and two-inch bricks to represent the original three-foot building blocks. It took 120 artisans two years to complete.

There is also a recreation of Beijing's **Forbidden City** and **Imperial Palace**. Constructed in 1420 A.D., the palace was so big that several emporors lived their whole lives without ever leaving it. The **Stone Forest**, a 65,000-acre park featuring primeval rock pillars in fantastic shapes, is recreated here as well. The 35-foot hand-carved replica of the **Leshan Grand Buddha Statue** is similar in every detail to the 24-story statue that was actually carved from the side of a mountain.

Other must-see exhibits include Longmen Grottoes, the Shanhaiguan Pass of the Great Wall, Potala Palace, Temple of Confucius, Summer Palace, the Terra Cotta Warriors, Shaolin Temple, the Temple of Heaven, and the mausoleums of Genghis Khan and Dr. Sun Yat Sen.

There are a dozen shops in Suzhou Gardens selling everything from t-shirts and similar souvenirs to shops offering porcelain, jewelry, silk embroidery, peronalized caligraphy, toys, teas, bonsai, wind chimes, and garden accessories. Live entertainment includes jugglers, dancers, artisans, acrobats, martial artists, Mongolian wrestlers, and other native performers.

For grumbling stomachs, there are five resaurants, serving Chinese and American food. The premier restaurant in the park, Suzhou Pearl, offers authentic gourmet Chinese cuisine in an elegant setting. Reservations are recommended.

Splendid China is easy to find. It's located about 2 miles west of the maingate to Walt Disney World off U.S. 192. Take exit 25B off I-4.

ADVENTURE ISLAND

Location: 10001 McKinley Drive., Tampa. Phone: 813-987-5660. On the Internet: www.adventureisland.com. Hours: Open 10am to 5pm with extended hours during summer and select holiday periods. Admission: $22.95 adults, $20.95 kids. Parking: $3.

Adventure Island is adjacent to Busch Gardens and is owned by the same parent company, Anheuser-Busch. The 22-acre park features a great number and variety of slides and attractions.

New for 1999 is Splash Attack, an playground with 50 interactive water elements in a massive treehosue environment, with cargo nets, bridges, and web crawl tunnels. Also new is the 700-foot Key West Rapids ride, sending guests down a 6-story plunge with twists, turns, pools, showers, gushers, and other surprises.

There's also Fabian's Funport, an all-new and expanded children's water play area, the Water Moccasin, three twisting tubes, the Caribbean Corkscrew, a high-speed adventure down twin braided translucent tubes, the Calypso Coaster, a 450-foot snaking chute, the Tampa Typhoon, a 7-story freefall slide, the adjacent Gulfscream, a speed slide that pales next to the Typhoon, the Everglides, toboggan slides, the Barratuba, an inner tube slide, Runaway Rapids, a 300-foot slide down a jungle mountain, Rambling Bayou, a lazy stream that carries you through the whole park, Endless Surf, where you can be battered by four-foot waves, and Paradise Lagoon, where you can unwind and overcome the hydrophobia that hit you when you went down the Typhoon.

Also at Adventure Island is an arcade, a gift shop, three volleyball nets, several stretches of beach, and two snack bars, the Surfside and Gulfscream Cafes. From Orlando, take I-4 west, exit to North I-75., take I-75 to exit 54 (Fowler Ave.), and follow signs to Busch Gardens. It's about an hour and a quarter drive.

BLIZZARD BEACH

See Chapter 15.

RIVER COUNTRY

See Chapter 15.

TYPHOON LAGOON

See Chapter 15.

WATER MANIA

Locaiton: 6073 W. Irlo Bronson Mem. Hwy., Kissimmee. Phone: Tel. 800/ 527-3092 or 407/396-2626. On the Internet: www.watermania-florida.com. Hours: 10am to 5pm, with extended hours during the summer. Open Wed. through Sat. only during off-seasons. Admission: $25.95 for adults, $18.95 for kids 3 to 9 and seniors over 55. Parking: $5.

Located on U.S. 192, just east of I-4, this 38-acre park has rides including the winding, 400-foot Anaconda raft ride, the Banana Peel, a two-person plunge down a water-filled chute, the Looney Flumes, three twisting slides, Whitecaps, a wave pool, Wipe Out, which pits you on a boogie board and one-on-one against simulated waves, The Screamer, with a 7-story drop, Cruisin' Creek, a placid, winding inner-tube ride, Riptide, a whitewater adventure, and last but not least, Aqua Xpress and the Rain Forest, aquatic playgrounds for the small folk.

If you prefer your fun without water, there's a miniature golf course, volleyball nets, a beach, and a wooded picnic area. A snack bar and gift shop arc also available. One disappointment about Water Mania, it lacks any of the natural beauty or lush landscaping that make Adventure Island, Typhoon Lagoon, River Country, and Buccaneer Bay so special. But on the other hand, Water Mania is often less crowded than headliner parks like Typhoon Lagoon and Wet'n Wild. Take exit 25A off I-4.

WET'N'WILD

Location: 6200 International Drive, Orlando. Phone: Tel. 800/992-wild OR 407/351-wild. On the Internet: www.wetnwild.com/orlando. Hours: Open 10am to 5pm, with extended hours during the summer and holidays, as late as 11pm during June and July. Admission: $26.95 for adults, $21.95 for kids 3 to 9, $13.48 for seniors over 55. Parking: $5.

The 25-acre park has the best assortment of water rides in the area. For family togetherness, ride the Bubba Tub, a 6-story, triple-dip slide in a tube big enough for the whole family; the Black Hole, an ominous-looking spaceship concealing a two-person raft adventure down a 500-foot, pitch-black tube for 30 seconds of simulated space reentry; Der

Stuka, a 6-story, 250-foot speedslide; the Blue Niagra, a twisting, 300-foot slide that starts six stories over the park; the Mach 5, a set of five twisting flumes totalling 2,500 feet; the Hydra Maniac, a translucent tube slide with a 360-degree loop; Raging Rapids, a whitewater tubing adventure; Lazy River, a gently flowing stream; Surf Lagoon, a 17,000 square foot pool with four-foot waves; the Knee Ski, in which you ride a cable-towed kneeboard around a half-mile course at speeds up to 15 mph; Bubble Up, a wet vinyl mountain for kids to climb and slide down into three feet of water; The Wild One, in which you ride tubes towed by a motorboat (additional charge); the Kid's Park, containing miniature versions of all the big rides, for children 48" and under; and the Bomb Bay, *Orlando Magazine's* choice for the greatest thrill ride in the city, with a 30 mph, 76-foot freefall through bomb bay doors.

During the summer, nighttimes are special in Wet'n Wild. The Beach Club features live entertainment, karaoke, and dancing to videos. This event draws a large crowd of locals, mainly in their teen years. The Orlando FlexTicket is another admission option, combining seven to ten days worth of admission to Sea World, Universal Studios Florida, Islands of Escape, Wet 'N' Wild, and Busch Gardens; see Chapter 16 for details. Snack bars and a gift shop are located on the premises.

To get to Wet'n Wild, take exit 30A (Kirkman Road south) to International Drive and turn right. Or, take exit 29, turn east on Sand Lake Drive, go one block, and turn left onto I-Drive.

WILD WATERS

5656 E. Silver Springs Blvd., Silver Springs. Tel. 363-0900, 904/206-2121, 800/243-0297 (FL). Hours: Open April to September. Spring and fall, 10 AM to 5 PM. Summer, 10 AM to 7 PM. Admission: $16.95 adult, $13.95 child 3-11, children under 3 admitted free.

Wild Waters, located adjacent to Silver Springs, has a wave pool, eight flumes, Water Bonanza child's play area, 9-hole miniature golf course, volleyball, snack bar, and gift shop. Take I-4 to Florida's Turnpike north. Take the Turnpike north to I-75 north. I-75 north to exit 69, U.S. 40 east.

AMUSEMENTS & DIVERSIONS

GREEN MEADOWS PETTING FARM

Location: 1368 S. Poinciana Blvd., Kissimmee. Phone: 407/846-0770. On the Internet: www.greenmeadowsfarm.com. Hours: 9:30 AM to 5:30 PM. Admission: $15.

Are your kids at that age when they think the coolest thing in the world would be living on a farm? Then take them to the Green Meadows Children's Farm, located in rural Kissimmee. For the price of admission, you receive a two-hour guided tour of the farm, with more than 200 animals. Everyone gets to milk the farm's cow, and the kids get pony rides. Picnic areas, souvenirs, snacks, and beverages are all available. From I-4, take exit 25A (U.S. 192 east). Take it three miles and turn right on Poinciana Blvd. Take Poinciana 5 miles, on your right. Before you decide to visit Green Meadows, realize that the ride is in a tractor-drawn hay wagon. If you are allergic, you might want to reconsider.

JUNGLELAND ZOO
Location: 4580 W. Irlo Bronson Mem. Hwy., Kissimmee. Phone: 407/396-1012. On the Internet: www.junglelandzoo.com. Hours: 9am to 6pm daily. Admission: $12 for adults, $7 for kids 3 to 11.

Alligators and unusual animals from around the world make this one of Central Florida's largest exhibits. Featured are animals indigenous to Florida, exotic cats, primates, birds, and much more.

KISSIMMEE RODEO
Location: 958 S. Hoagland Blvd., Kissimmee. Phone: 407/933-0020. On the Internet: www.ksarodeo.com. Hours: 8pm Fridays. Admission: $10, $5 for kids under 12.

Every Friday, cowboys and cowgirls from the area compete in events including calf roping, bareback riding, steer wrestling, team roping, barrel racing, and bull riding.

MEDIEVAL TIMES LIVING MUSEUM
Location: 4510 W. Irlo Bronson Mem. Hwy., Kissimmee. Phone: 407/396-1518. On the Internet: http://medievaltimes.com. Hours: 4pm to 8pm daily. Admission: $8, $6 for kids 3 to 12.

Described as a "step back in time," Medieval Life is the only permanent medieval village in the United States. Wander the cobblestone streets of "Raymondsburg," lined with thatched-roof buildings and observe faithfully-clothed artisans potters, blacksmiths, millers, carpenters, glassblowers working their trade with the materials and techniques of their ancestors. You can explore homes furnished with cooking utensils and housewares of the period, and even taste medieval fare in the kitchen. Sadomasochists in the crowd will appreciate a visit to the jail and dungeon, where torture devices and explanations of their uses await. The village square hosts a "birds of prey and hunting dog" demonstration.

MOVIE RIDER

Locations: 8815 International Drive, Orlando, (407/352-0050), 5390 W. Irlo Bronson Mem. Hwy., Kissimmee (407/396-4185). Hours: 10:30am to 11pm weekdays, 11am to midnight on weekends. Admission: $8.95, kids under 12 $6.95.

These two 20-minute simulator rides give guests the opportunity to sit in a race car, fly into a volcano, tour a haunted house, or engage in other unsavory activities.

MYSTERY FUN HOUSE

Location: 5767 Major Blvd.., Orlando. Phone: 407/351-3355. Hours: 10am to 10pm weekdays, 10am to 11pm on weekends. Admission: Fun House tickets are $11, Laser Tag tickets are $10, Mini Golf tickets are $5, Combination tickets are $20.

This attraction, located near Universal Studios, combines the eleven-room Mystery Fun House itself, with a mirror maze, pyramid tomb, and more; with Starbase Omega laser tag and indoor miniature golf to make a formidable rainy day choice. There's also an arcade, gift shop, and Pizza Hut Express.

To get here, take I-4 to exit 30B, Kirkman Road North. Turn right on Major Blvd., and the Fun House will be on your right. To get here from International Drive, simply turn left on Kirkman Road and follow I-4 directions.

RIPLEY'S BELIEVE IT OR NOT!

Location: 8210 International Drive, Orlando. Phone: 407/363-4418. On the Internet: www.ripleysorlando.com. Hours: 9am to 1am daily. Admission: $12.95 adults, $8.95 for kids 4 to 12.

Robert Ripley is famous for the cartoons, books, television specials, and museums that bear his name. The intrepid Ripley spent his whole life crisscrossing the globe searching for oddities to satisfy his neverending appetite for the unusual. The fruits of his labors are on display here at this new landmark museum on International Drive, just north of Mercado Mediterranean Village.

The building that houses the eclectic 8,900-square foot museum is as off-center as the exhibits — literally. The building was constructed on a slant, so it appears as if it is sinking into one of Florida's infamous sinkholes.

Items on display include a replica of Leonardo Da Vinci's Mona Lisa constructed of inch-square pieces of toast; a two-thirds scale model of a 1907 Rolls Royce made of over a million matchsticks; a Van Gogh self-portrait made of postcards; shrunken heads; clothing made of human hair; masks representing cultures from all over the globe, a dinosaur exhibit; a 10-foot square portion of the Berlin Wall; a vast miniatures collection including a grain of rice with a tropical sunset painted on it; n Egyptian mummy; and many more. It takes approximately an hour and a half to tour the museum at your own pace. There is a gift shop.

SKULL KINGDOM

Location: 5933 American Way, Orlando. Phone: 407/354-1564. On the Internet: www.skullkingdom.com. Hours: Vary by season. Open every night from 6 to 11:30 PM, with Saturday and Sunday afternoons year round in weekdays during the summer. Admission: $9.95.

This spookfest is well done and actually surprisingly frightening – dark rooms, well-placed special effects, live actors, and a macabre sense of humor make this 20-minute elaborate haunted house exhibit a fun way to give yourself insomnia.

TITANIC: SHIP OF DREAMS

Location: Mercado, 8445 International Drive. Phone: 407/248-1166. On the Internet: www.titanicshipofdreams.com. Hours: 10am to 11pm daily. Admission: $14.95 for adults, $9.95 for kids 6 to 11.

You'll feel like the king of the world when you visit its first permanent Titanic attraction. Located at the Mercado shopping center, this museum features the only full-scale re-creations of the Titanic's staterooms and facilities, including her world-famous Grand Staircase. You'll also find over 200 priceless artifacts, Leonardo DiCaprio's costume from the film Titanic, and live interactive interpretations by storytellers in period costume. For those of you who made $300 million for James Cameron's schmaltzy movie, it's a must see. If your t-shirt says "THE BOAT SANK, GET OVER IT," you may want to skip this one.

TRAINLAND OF ORLANDO

Location: 8255 International Drive, Orlando. Phone: 407/363-9002. Hours: 10am to 10pm. Admission: $6 adults, $4 kids.

This museum, located at International Station, features the largest indoor toy train layout operating in America. There's also a full-sized steam train that you can ride, a display of toy trains dating from the turn of the century to the present. For memorabilia and souvenirs, there's a gift shop.

Orlando has a wealth of nightlife, from splashy dinner shows to concert venues to chic dance clubs, there's something for everybody here. As you'll see from the descriptions, you'll want to bring your kids to some of these places and, for others, leave them with a babysitter so you can party on your own!

ALOHA POLYNESIAN LUAU

Location: Sea World, Orlando. Phone: Tel. 800/327-2424 or407/351-3600. On the Internet: www.seaworld.com. Admission: $35.95 for adults, $25.95 for kids 8 to 12, and $15.95 for kids 3 to 7.

Authentic Polynesian food is served here along the side of Sea World's big lagoon, including mahi mahi in pina colada sauce, sweet and sour chicken, smoked pork loin, sides, dessert, coffee, and tea. There's also a cash bar all night long.

ARABIAN NIGHTS

Location: 6225 W. Irlo Bronson Mem. Hwy., Kissimmee. Phone: Tel. 800/553-6116 or 407/239-9223. On the Internet: www.arabian-nights.com. Admission: $36.95 for adults, $23.95 for kids 3 to 11.

Arabian Nights is a dinner show about the exploits of a princess who searches for her true love, guided through time and space by a magical genie. Over 100 spectacular horses (eight different breeds) and performers dazzle audiences in 25 acts. The four-course meal consists of prime rib, garden salad, vegetable soup, dinner rolls, baked potato, dessert, and Miller Genuine Draft beer, wine, and soft drinks.

BACKSTAGE

Location: Clarion Plaza Hotel, 9700 International Drive, Orlando. Phone: 407/352-9700.

The Backstage Lounge, a $400,000 "danceterium," features a Happy Hour from 3 PM to 8:30 PM daily, a live band Wednesdays through Sundays, and DJ's and VJ's nightly.

BARBARELLA DANCE CLUB

Location: 68 Orange Ave., Orlando. Phone: 407/839-0457. Admission: $5.

This downtown nightclub features live bands and DJs Thursdays through Mondays, ranging from 80's, industrial, and goth to techno, jungle, and house music.

BLAZING PIANOS

Location: Mercado, 8445 International Drive, Orlando. Phone: 407/363-5104.

This hot new nightspot features three fire-engine red Yamaha pianos (hence the name) and rock'n'roll pianists who urge you to sing along. The desserts and appetizers are incredible and the atmosphere is wild fun.

BOB CARR PERFORMING ARTS CENTRE

Location: 401 W. Livingston Street, Orlando. Phone: 407/423-9999. On the Internet: www.orlandocentroplex.com.

The Carr Centre, located in the downtown area, features orchestral, choir, dance, and acting touring companies throughout the year. Full-scale Broadway musicals hit the Carr Centre every so often as part of the Orlando Broadway Series, which has in recent months included stops from Cats, Les Miserables, Joseph and the Amazing Technicolor Dreamcoat, and more.

CAPONE'S DINNER & SHOW

Location: 4740 W. Irlo Bronson Mem. Hwy., Kissimmee. Phone: Tel. 800/220-8428 or 407/397-2378. On the Internet: www.alcapones.com/ Admission: $32 adults, $17 kids 3 to 12.

Capone's Dinner and Show, a 1992 addition to the U.S. 192 landscape, features a 15-item unlimited Italian buffet, unlimited Budweiser, Bud Lite, Sangria, soda, or "Al's Rum Runners" to the accompaniment of a show taking place in 1931 Chicago's gangland that resembles a Guys and Dolls set.

CHURCH STREET STATION

Location: 124 West Church Street, Orlando. Phone: 407/422-2432. On the Internet: www.churchstreetstation.com. Admission: $17.95 for adults, $11.95 for kids age 4 to 12.

Long before Pleasure Island, there was Church Street Station, a more adult nighttime entertainment complex. Where the dilapidated Orlando Hotel once stood, there is now a spectacular experience waiting to happen. In fact, the restoration of Church Street Station was a catalyst in the revitalization of downtown Orlando.

In the daytime, Church Street Station is open, but features little in the way of entertainment or excitement. After the sun sets, though, the place explodes. There are five clubs here offering a variety of musical entertainment.

Church Street Station Showrooms

Rosie O'Grady's Good Time Emporium started it all. The club, built on the remains of the circa-1904 Orlando Hotel, calls itself "75 years behind the times and darn proud of it." It's the home of Rosie's Banjo Man, who performs in the afternoons, and in the evenings, Rosie's Good Time Jazz Band with the torchy "Last of the Red Hot Mamas". The club is a throwback to the era of strummin' banjos, Dixieland bands, Can-Can girls, Charleston dancers, and singing bartenders and waiters. Those with an eye for detail will notice the antiques lining the walls and ceiling, including the chandeliers (from Boston's First National Bank, circa 1904).

The Cheyenne **Saloon and Opera House** celebrated its tenth anniversary in June 1992. The club, which took 2 1/2 years to construct, is something of an antique museum, with hundred-year-old chandeliers from the Philadelphia Mint, pool tables from 1885 San Francisco, antique gun collections from the Stagecoach Museum in Shakopee, Minnesota, wooden Indians, pictures depicting the Wild West, buffalo and moose heads, even a stuffed brown bear from Kodiak Island, Alaska. The dining room seats, interestingly, are pews from an old Catholic church. The featured music is C&W, Grand Ole Opry style. James and the Cheyenne Stampede Band perform nightly, and big-name talent is not foreign to the Cheyenne.

Apple Annie's Courtyard features house band "Triple Action" and other folk and bluegrass artists in a Victorian garden atmosphere. Many of the items of furniture in the club came from churches and cathedrals across the east and south.

The **Orchid Garden Ballroom** is light bulbs, lattice, and tuxedoed waiters and barkeeps. The Ballroom's decor is dominated by Marilyn Monroe, at least one of a Belgian artist's exact reproductions of her stance over the subway grating in *The Seven Year Itch*. Dancing is done here to rock and roll from Chuck Berry and Elvis Presley to the Eric Clapton and U2. Blackjack is big here as well, despite the fact that card gambling is illegal in Florida. Gamblers rent scrip and compete for the title of Nightly Blackjack Champ.

In a mood to dance the night away? **Phineas Phogg's Balloon Works** can accommodate that desire with high-energy dance music. "Phogg's" is one of the more popular clubs with both locals and tourists. And in addition to a disco, it's also a ballooning museum of sorts. There's pictures and artifacts from some of the world's most historic balloon flights, including those made by Colonel Joe Kittiger of Rosie O'Grady's Flying Circus. You must be 21 to enter.

Commander Ragtime's Midway

On the third floor of Church Street Station Exchange is Commander

Ragtime's, an arcade with NAMCO pinball and video games, surrounded by turn-of-the-century London circus memorabilia. And suspended from the ceiling is 1,400 feet of model railroad track on which six electric trains zoom through the Midway. A sports bar in the Midway features pool tables, electronic dart games, and a big-screen television for watching major sporting events. Bar fare is served, including peanuts, hot dogs, wings, sausage, and milkshakes.

Carriage Rides

There are several hitching posts outside Church Street Station, and from this location, horse-drawn carriages depart for scenic tours of the downtown area and Lake Eola. The trip lasts about 30 minutes and the cost is $20 for a couple, $25 for a group of three or four. Call 855-2900 for information.

Historic Railroad Depot

If you walk around Church Street Station, you will come upon the railroad depot for which the entertainment complex is named. The station has its own steam engine, the "Old Duke," which was "borne" in 1912 at Baldwin Steam Engine and Iron Works in Baldwin, Ohio. The engine, found in Pensacola, was restored and may be seen here. Pushcart vendors also occupy the depot, and there are several shops, including Sunshine Sportswear, Totally Unique T-Shirts, and the Remedy Store.

Church Street Station Shopping

The **Bumby Gift Emporium** features T-shirts and glassware from Rosie's, Apple's Lili's, Phogg's, Ragtime's, Cheyenne, and the Orchid Garden. Videotape tours, albums by house artists, garters, jackets, belt buckles, playing cards, ashtrays, charms, and more. The **Church Street Station Exchange** has over fifty shops in a Victorian setting. For more information on this shopping center, see the section on "Shopping Centers" later in this chapter.

Street Parties

For locals, Church Street Station's eight annual street parties make an excellent excuse for buying a membership card. In January, there's the Boola Bowl, a post-Citrus Bowl party; in March, there's a St. Patrick's Day party; in April, the Island Fest kickoff summer, Bahamas style; in May, the Golden Oldies party features rock legends; the Oktoberfest in September features oom-pah-pah and beer; the Italianfest and Halloween Party in October make for unique fun; and the New Year's Eve party is a very sought-after ticket.

Church Street Station Memberships

Four different membership cards are available. The single membership is $24.95 and will get you in until the end of the year. A double membership lets you and a guest in for $39.95. A VIP pass lets you and three guests in for $69.95. A corporate membership lets in any four people for $99.95. To get to Church Street Station, take I-4 east to the Anderson Street exit. Follow the blue signs to the complex. Pay parking is available at the Sun Bank building, the Church Street Garage, and the Church Street Market garage. Metered parking is available under I-4.

WEEKLY SPECIALS AT CHURCH STREET STATION

Sunday: Ladies Night at Phogg's: 50¢ beer and frozen drinks for ladies. 7 PM to 2 AM.

Monday: Red Hot Monday at Rosie's: $1.50 beer, cocktails, and deli sandwiches. Live entertainment, free peanuts and popcorn. 4 to 7 PM.

Wednesday: Nickel Beer Night at Phogg's: Draft beer for 5_. 6:30 PM to 7:30 PM.

Thursday: Longneck Night at Cheyenne: 95¢ Longneck beer and wine coolers, $1.50 BBQ sandwiches, live C & W music. 4:30 to 7:30 PM.

Friday: S.O.B. Party at Crackers: Shrimp, Oyster and Beer for a buck. 4 to 7 PM. Blues Attic at Phogg's: Live blues and drink specials. 4 to 9 PM.

CITYWALK

Location: Universal Studios Escape, 1000 Universal Studios Plaza, Orlando. Phone: 407/363-8200. On the Internet: www.uescape.com. Admission: A Party Pass offering unlimited admission to all clubs plus one movie is $18. Admission to clubs can be purchased individually.

Universal's answer to Pleasure Island, this entertainment complex is certainly impressive, and honestly is my favorite out of the three Orlando nighttime entertainment complexes, by far.

Set on a slab of lakeside property between Islands of Adventure and the Studios, this 30-acre complex features **Jimmy Buffett's Margaritaville,** a restaurant and bar for Parrotheads everywhere, **Bob Marley – A Tribute to Freedom**, featuring live reggae in a re-creation of Marley's Kingston home, **Motown Café,** featuring R&B artists, the **Hary Rock Café and Hard Rock Live,** a live music venue featuring cutting edge artists from all genres of popular music, from house to country to rock. **NBA City** features a basketball theme. **NASCAR Café** offers American fare along racing memorabilia. **CityJazz** is a world-class performance center and jazz museum. **the groove** is one of the best venues in Orlando for underground dance music. **Latin Quarter** features a dance studio teaching tango, salsa, and samba along with live entertainment. There are also *lots* of shops and a state-of-the-art 20-screen **Universal Cineplex.**

CLUB AT FIRESTONE

Location: 578 N. Orange Ave., Orlando. Phone: 407/426-0005. Admission: Varies.

This club has been hurting somewhat ever since Orlando cracked down on raves and after hours venues, but this is still a lively, trendy club offering nationally and internationally known DJs. There are reggae nights, gay nights, and more every week.

CLUB LAVELA

Location: Lee Road Shopping Center, Orlando.

The new Orlando location for the popular Panama City Beach club featured on MTV features the same crazy assortment of theme rooms, bikini contests, drink specials, and all around good old-fashioned mayhem.

CRAZY HORSE SALOON

Location: 7056 S. Kirkman Road., Orlando. Phone: 407/363-0071.

The Crazy Horse Saloon features country and western music provided by the house's Rosebud Creek Band and others. Live entertainment is featured six nights a week, and dancing lessons are given on Tuesdays, Thursdays, and Fridays.

THE CRICKETERS ARMS

Location: Mercado, 8445 International Drive, Orlando. Phone: 407/354-0686.

The Cricketers Arms, calling itself "the oldest and newest English pub," offers 15 imported British stouts, lagers, and bitters served in 20 oz. mugs. Domestic beer, wines, ports, and sherries are also available, as are breakfast and an English lunch and dinner menu. Live entertainment is featured Tuesday, Wednesday, and Saturday nights, and a satellite dish will show English soccer and other sports on a big screen television.

CYBERZONE

Location: 843 Lee Road, Orlando. Phone: 407/599-2928.

Due to its status in unincorporated Orange County, this club is exempt from the city's 2am closing time for nightclubs, and often is going strong with house, trance, jungle, and breakbeat until the sun comes up.

HOOP-DEE-DOO REVUE

Location: Fort Wilderness Resort, Disney World. Phone: 407/934-7639. Admission: $38 for adults, $19.50 for kids 3 to 11.

The Hoop-Dee-Doo Revue is the absolute favorite among WDW veterans as far as fun and food are concerned, and performances often book up weeks in advance. At Pioneer Hall three times a night, the immensely popular show is full of song, dance, and slapstick comedy.

The food is nothing to sneeze at either, with all-you-can-eat fried chicken, barbecued ribs, corn on the cob, baked beans, and strawberry shortcake with unlimited beer, wine, and soda. Reservations are required and can be made up to 30 days in advance.

HOUSE OF BLUES

Location: Downtown Disney West Side. Phone: 407/934-2583.

One of Central Florida's top music venues, the House of Blues club offers top-name national entertainment across the spectum of rock, blues, country, house, and more, several nights a week. For talent schedules and information, surf to *www.hob.com. For ticket information call 407/934-2583.* Note that tickets are not required to visit the House of Blues restaurant.

HOWL AT THE MOON SALOON

Location: Church Street Market, 55 Church Street, Orlando. Phone: 407/ 841-4695.

This downtown bar offers the 21-and-up crowd a chance to watch dueling pianists and sing along to rock and roll favorites. Piano players begin at 6 p.m. Fridays and Saturdays, 8 p.m. the rest of the week.

ICON

Location: 20 East Central Blvd., Orlando. Phone: 407/649-6496. Admission: Varies.

This downtown club is another place to hear slammin' house music and club anthems, with a young, hip, good-looking crowd.

KING HENRY'S FEAST

Location: 8984 International Drive, Orlando. Phone: Tel. 800/883-8181 or 407/351-5151. Admission: $36.95 for adults, $22.95 for kids 3 to 11.

King Henry's Feast presents dueling knights, magicians, sword and fire swallowers, aerial ballerinas, and a court jester along with banquet fare including cream of potato and leek soup, tossed salad, rolls, roasted chicken, sliced pork, new potatoes, vegetable medley, and ice cream cake roll along with unlimited beer, wine, soda, coffee, and tea.

KNOCK KNOCK

Location: 50 E. Central Blvd., Orlando. Phone: 407/999-7739. Admission: Varies.

This chilled-out, relaxed, hip bar offers an eclectic assortment of DJs playing a variety of music, including a Saturday night residency by the legendary Q-Burn's Abstract Message.

LA NOUBA

Location: Downtown Disney West Side. Phone: 407/939-7600. Admission: $62 for adults, $38 for kids ages 3 to 9.

Only the second permanent installation of the Cirque du Soleil in the world (the other one is in Las Vegas), this spellbinding show features 60 performers and artists, exotic costumes, lighting, and original sets and music twice a day in the 1,671-seat theatre on the very western edge of the complex. The creative team behind all the other Cirque du Soleil shows is at work again here, and this is as breathtaking an experience as you're likely to find in Disney World. "La nouba" means party, and this particular party is rife with pre-millennial tension and a dark mood at times.

It is recommended that you arrive 30 minutes prior to showtime. Tickets should be ordered in advance by calling 407/939-7600, and are $62 for adults and $38 for kids ages 3 to 9. It's steep but few people walk away disappointed.

THE LAUGHING KOOKABURRA

Location: Wyndham Palace, 1900 Hotel Plaza Blvd., Disney World. Phone: 407/872-3722.

There's a live band, no cover charge, and 99 different brands of beer at this "good time grown-up bar" located in the heart of Walt Disney World. Happy hour is from 4 p.m. to 8 p.m., featuring free hors d'oeuvres.

MARK TWO DINNER THEATER

Location: 3376 Edgewater Drive, Orlando. Phone: Tel. 800/726-6275 or 407/843-6275. On the Internet: www.themarktwo.com. Admission: Varies, call for showtimes and prices.

Mark Two is one of the only "true" dinner theaters in Orlando, using Actor's Equity Association (AEA) performers in Broadway musicals and comedies. The cost of a show includes performance and a buffet featuring prime rib or beef sirloin tips.

For tickets or more information, call or write the Mark Two. To get there from points south, take I-4 east to exit 44, Par Avenue. Turn left and take it to Edgewater.

MEDIEVAL TIMES DINNER & TOURNAMENT

Location: 4510 W. Irlo Bronson Mem. Hwy., Kissimmee. Phone: Tel. 800/ 229-8300 or 407/396-1518. Admission: $37.95 adults, $22.95.

Does the name of this attraction sound familiar? It should, if you live in the vicinity of Lyndhurst, NJ; Buena Park, CA; Chicago; or Dallas. Medieval Times dinner shows are located in those four cities as well.

But what's the hype is all about?. Just the single most exciting dinner show in the state, that's all. The year is 1093 AD, the place is the court of His Grace, Count Don Raimundo II. Six brave knights compete in swordplay, falconry, sorcery, romance, and even a real joust. Which of the six knights do you root for? Well, your seat bears the same emblem on the shield of one of the knights. Find that one and keep an eye on him, because he's yours.

The menu includes appetizers, vegetable soup, whole roast chicken, spare ribs, herb-basted potato, pastries, coffee, beer, wine cocktail, and soft drinks.

MULVANEY'S IRISH PUB

Locations and phone: Dansk Plaza, 7220 International Drive, Orlando (407/352-7031), 27 W. Church Street, Orlando (407/872-3296).

Mulvaney's, styled after a real Irish pub, features live entertainment, traditional Irish fare (including Irish breakfast, served all day), and six imported beers on tap.

POLYNESIAN LUAU

Location: Polynesian Resort, Disney World. Phone: 407/WDW-DINE. Admission: $38 for adults, $19.50 for kids 3 to 12.

The Polynesian Luau, held twice each evening in Luau Cove, features authentic Polynesian dancing and specialty acts, many of which are performed by artists who have studied at the Polynesian Cultural Center in Honolulu. The meal includes Luau Barbecued Ribs, seafood moana, spit-roasted Hawaiian chicken, grilled Mahi-Mahi in herb butter, Oriental vegetables, fruit salad, fried rice, and flaming volcano ice cream dessert. Also included are unlimited soft drinks, beer, Mai Tais, melon coladas, and pina coladas. Like the Hoop-Dee-Doo Revue, this show requires reservations and accepts them up to 30 days in advance.

SAK COMEDY LAB

Location: 45 E. Church Street, Orlando. Phone: 407/648-0001. Admission: $8 to $13.

Improvisational comedy is performed at this theater, down the street from Church Street Station.

SLEUTHS MYSTERY DINNER SHOW

Location: 7508 Universal Blvd., Orlando. Phone: Tel. 800/393-1985 or 407/363-1985. Admission: $36.95 adults, $22.95 for kids 3 to 11.

Be forewarned. Every night at Sleuths, somebody dies. But don't worry, because this is International Drive's only murder mystery dinner theater. Four shows alternate through the week, but in all of them, the audience mingles with the actors, and it's up them to solve the crime. The successful sleuth who cracks the case receives a prize. The dinner includes hors d'oeuvres, crackers and cheese, rolls, honey glazed Cornish game hen, vegetable medley, mashed potatoes and gravy, herb stuffing, fruit garnish, "mystery" dessert, and unlimited beer, wine, and soft drinks.

From Kissimmee, Lake Buena Vista, and WDW, take I-4 east to exit 30A (Republic Drive). Go past International Drive and Wet'n Wild. It's four doors past the cinema, on the right. From Sea World and the International Drive area, take I-Drive north to Republic and turn right.

SULLIVAN'S

Location: 108 S. Orange Blossom Trail, Orlando. Phone: 407/843-2934.

This popular bar offers live country and western music, along with free country line dancing lessons nightly, a nonalcoholic all ages night on Tuesdays, penny longnecks on Wednesdays, and more weekly specials. Take exit 33B off I-4.

TERROR ON CHURCH STREET

Location: 135 S. Orange Ave., Orlando. Phone: 407/422-2434. Admission: $12 adults, $8 for children under 17.

This attraction is based on Pasaje del Terror, a 1987 production performed by a troupe of Argentinian actors. Magician Ignaicio Brieva came to Orlando and created the first American installment of the international attraction in two floors of an old Woolworth's. The attraction combines the use of live actors, theatrical sets, cinematic special effects, microchip technology, and 23 individual soundtracks in order to scare the living bejeezus out of you. Specially designed lights, sound effects, and the element of surprise plot against you, along with ever-changing scripts, actor improvisation, and audience participation, it's never the same experience twice.

WILD BILL'S WILD WEST DINNER SHOW AT FORT LIBERTY

Location: 5260 W. Irlo Bronson Mem. Hwy., Kissimmee. Phone: Tel. 800/883-8181 or 407/351-5151. Admission: $36.95 for adults, $22.95 for children 3 to 11.

One of the mainstays in the come-and-go world of Orlando dinner shows, Wild Bill's, formerly "Fort Liberty," is one of the best non-Disney dinner shows. Themed after an 1876 citadel called Fort Liberty, the 12-character show features Bob Hope-style entertainment for the soldiers of E Troop. Your hosts for the evening, the lovely Miss Kitty and Wild Bill, guide you through specialty acts including the Comanche Dance Group, who perform the Hoop Dance and Eagle Dance; Texas Jack Fulbright, an eighth-generation cowboy who performs tricks including gun spinning and roping; and Cetan Mani, who combines archery and knife throwing with humor. Audience participation is also a big part of the show.

The 22-acre, $29 million attraction can seat 600 people, and the menu includes fried chicken, barbecued pork ribs, corn on the cob, vegetable soup, baked potato, biscuits, salad, apple pie a la mode, and unlimited beer, wine, and Coca-Cola. Full bar service is available.

INDEX

THINGS CHANGE!

*Phone numbers, prices, addresses, quality of food, etc, all change.
If you come across any new information, we'd appreciate hearing
from you. No item is too small! Drop us an email note at:
Jopenroad@aol.com, or write us at:*

Disneyworld With Kids
*Open Road Publishing, P.O. Box 284
Cold Spring Harbor, NY 11724*

TRAVEL NOTES

TRAVEL NOTES

TRAVEL NOTES

OPEN ROAD PUBLISHING

U.S.A.
America's Cheap Sleeps, $16.95
America's Grand Hotels, $14.95
America's Most Charming Towns &
    Villages, $16.95
Arizona Guide, $16.95
Boston Guide, $13.95
California Wine Country Guide, $12.95
Colorado Guide, $16.95
Disneyworld With Kids, $14.95
Florida Guide, $16.95
Hawaii Guide, $18.95
Las Vegas Guide, $14.95
National Parks With Kids, $14.95
New Mexico Guide, $16.95
San Francisco Guide, $16.95
Southern California Guide, $18.95
Spa Guide U.S.A., $14.95
Texas Guide, $16.95
Utah Guide, $16.95
Vermont Guide, $16.95

MIDDLE EAST/AFRICA
Egypt Guide, $17.95
Israel Guide, $17.95
Jerusalem Guide, $13.95
Kenya Guide, $18.95

UNIQUE TRAVEL
Celebrity Weddings & Honeymoon
    Getaways, $16.95
The World's Most Intimate Cruises, $16.95

SMART HANDBOOKS
The Smart Home Buyer's
    Handbook, $16.95
The Smart Runner's Handbook, $9.95

LATIN AMERICA & CARIBBEAN
Bahamas Guide, $13.95
Belize Guide, $16.95
Bermuda Guide, $14.95
Caribbean Guide, $19.95
Caribbean With Kids, $14.95
Central America Guide, $17.95
Chile Guide, $18.95
Costa Rica Guide, $17.95
Ecuador & Galapagos Islands Guide, $17.95
Guatemala Guide, $18.95
Honduras & Bay Islands Guide, $16.95

EUROPE
Austria Guide, $15.95
Czech & Slovak Republics Guide, $18.95
France Guide, $16.95
Greek Islands Guide, $16.95
Holland Guide, $16.95
Ireland Guide, $17.95
Italy Guide, $19.95
London Guide, $14.95
Moscow Guide, $16.95
Paris Guide, $13.95
Portugal Guide, $16.95
Prague Guide, $14.95
Rome & Southern Italy Guide, $14.95
Scotland Guide, $17.95
Spain Guide, $18.95
Turkey Guide, $18.95

ASIA
China Guide, $21.95
Japan Guide, $19.95
Philippines Guide, $17.95
Tahiti & French Polynesia Guide, $18.95
Tokyo Guide, $13.95
Thailand Guide, $18.95
Vietnam Guide, $14.95

To order any Open Road book, send us a check or money order for the price of the book(s) plus $3.00 shipping and handling for domestic orders, to: **Open Road Publishing**, *PO Box 284, Cold Spring Harbor, NY 11724*